APPLE ASSEMBLY LANGUAGE

a course of study based on LazerWare software

OTHER BOOKS OF INTEREST
FROM COMPUTER SCIENCE PRESS

Wayne Amsbury
Structured Basic and Beyond

Lubomir Bic
MICOS: A Microprogrammable Computer Simulator

Peter Calingaert
Assemblers, Compilers, and Program Translation

William Findlay and David Watt
Pascal: An Introduction to Methodical Programming, Second Edition

Ellis Horowitz
Fundamentals of Programming Languages, Second Edition

Ellis Horowitz, Editor
Programming Languages: A Grand Tour

Vern McDermott and Diana Fisher
Learning Basic Step by Step, Student Text

Vern McDermott and Diana Fisher
Learning Basic Step by Step, Teacher's Guide

James J. McGregor and Alan H. Watt
Simple Pascal

Ronald H. Perrott and Donald C.S. Allison
PASCAL for FORTRAN Programmers

Gerald N. Pitts and Barry L. Bateman
Essentials of COBOL Programming: A Structured Approach

APPLE ASSEMBLY LANGUAGE

a course of study based on LazerWare software

W. DOUGLAS MAURER
The George Washington University

COMPUTER SCIENCE PRESS

Computer Science Press, Inc.
1803 Research Boulevard
Rockville, Maryland 20850

3 4 5 6   88 87 86

"Apple" is a registered trademark of Apple Computer, Inc.

Library of Congress Cataloging in Publication Data

Maurer, Ward Douglas, 1938-
    APPLE assembly language with Lazer systems software.

    1. Apple II (Computer)—Programming. 2. Apple III
(Computer)—Programming. 3. Assembler language
(Computer program language) I. Title. II. Title:
A.P.P.L.E. assembly language with lazer systems software.
QA76.8.A662M38 1984   001.64'24   82-18190
ISBN 0-914894-82-X

PREFACE

This is a book for a second course in computer programming, after the student has had a course in BASIC (or possibly PASCAL, FORTRAN, or PL/I). It can be used at the university level, in community colleges, in secondary schools, or for self-study. The author uses it at The George Washington University, in the Department of Electrical Engineering and Computer Science.

BASIC, and other *algebraic languages* such as FORTRAN and PASCAL, are to a great degree machine-independent. You can write a BASIC program for one computer and expect to run it, with at most only minor changes, on another computer. In this book, however, one studies *assembly language* and *machine language,* which are totally different for all the different families of computers. A program written in assembly language for one computer must be completely rewritten in order to run on a computer of a different family.

Given this situation, the first decision to be made is which computer to use. In this book it is assumed that you are using the APPLE, one of the most popular computers in the world. (By "APPLE" we shall always mean either an APPLE II + , an APPLE IIc, an APPLE IIe, or an APPLE III running in emulator mode.) The APPLE is a computer *system,* containing a computer called the 6502.* It is the assembly and machine language of the 6502, then, that is taught in this book.

In order to practice using these languages, you need an *assembler.* This is a program which processes assembly language somewhat as the various BASIC systems on the APPLE process the BASIC language. In this book, we will assume that you have the LISA 1.5, LISA 2.5 48K, or LISA 2.5 64K assembler.† LISA assemblers have been cited by various surveys as the best assemblers for the APPLE, and both the APPLE and the LISA assemblers are available in a large number of computer stores. If you have another version of LISA or another assembler for the APPLE, you can use it with this book as long as you use its manual from the beginning, and as long as you note those parts of this book which are specific to the LISA versions given above. You can even use this book with the ATARI 800 or the VIC-20, although the assembler, the debugging process, and the basic system subroutines would all be different.

---

*The 6502, because of the hardware technology it uses, is known as a *microprocessor.* It is made by MOS Technology, Inc., of Norristown, Pennsylvania; the APPLE is made by Apple Computer Corporation of Cupertino, California.
†It is made by LazerWare. Note that LISA assemblers have *nothing* to do with the LISA computer, manufactured by APPLE Computer Corporation.

Using LISA normally requires that you have at least 48K of memory and a disk unit. The disk unit, which again costs a few hundred dollars, is very useful with BASIC as well as with the assembler. Without a disk unit, you have to use cassette tape units, which are not nearly as fast or reliable, when connected to a computer. The additional memory, if you do not have as much as 48K, costs even less and is useful, although not essential, with BASIC; it permits larger programs and larger arrays to be processed by the APPLE.

Machine language is fundamental to all computers. Every computer processes only one language *directly*, and that is its machine language. There are only two ways for a computer to process any language other than its machine language. One is by translating programs from another language into its machine language, and then running the resulting machine language programs. This process is done by a program which is usually known as a *compiler*. Compilers exist for BASIC, FORTRAN, PASCAL, and many other languages. The other way is by having a program which translates one *statement* of the other language; then executes that statement; then translates the next statement and executes that one; and so on indefinitely. Such a program is called an *interpreter*. Most of the BASIC systems on the APPLE are interpreters (although there are also BASIC compilers for the APPLE).

Machine language is composed entirely of numbers in the binary system, which is also taught in this book. The analog of GOSUB in BASIC, for example, is the binary number 00100000 in the machine language of the 6502. Likewise, the binary number 0000100010101100 might correspond to the variable J in some particular program.

Because machine language is so cumbersome to work with, *assembly language* was developed. Assembly language is very much like machine language except that it uses names instead of numbers. Thus, the variable J in BASIC can still be called J in assembly language. The analog of GOSUB in the assembly language of the 6502 is JSR, which stands for "Jump to a Sub-Routine," just as GOSUB stands for "Go to a SUBroutine."

The close correspondence between assembly language and machine language makes it unnecessary to write a large program directly in machine language. Many large and successful programs, however, have been written, and continue to be written, in assembly language. Among these is the APPLE's monitor program— the fundamental program that drives the APPLE and allows it to accept and run machine language programs.

In further study of computer science, it is absolutely necessary to know the workings of both assembly language and machine language. This is true even if most of the programs that you actually write during your further study might be written in some other language, such as PASCAL or C. We feel that it is important for the student to be fluent in one assembly language, rather than having an overview of several of them.

Some computer scientists downplay the importance of assembly language. It is true that, in the past, many large programs have been written in assembly language which perhaps should not have been, due to excessive debugging costs. But the most successful programs continue, over the years, to be written in assembly language; these include the APPLE monitor, the CP/M system, and VISICALC. Generally, programs that require economy of speed or memory, such as operating systems and interpreters, are written in assembly language in order to achieve the required performance.

Also, some computer scientists teach machine language first, and then assembly language. In this book we teach assembly language first, because we expect the student to have access to an assembler. Machine language knowledge is necessary in debugging, but we do *not* expect students to program in it directly (as they might, for example, in a course on programming for hardware logic design).

In this book you will use the knowledge of BASIC* which you presumably already have. If you do not know BASIC but have learned FORTRAN, PASCAL, or PL/I, you may consult Table 1 in the Appendix, which explains the BASIC statements used in this book in terms of statements in those other languages. This book relies heavily on comparisons between BASIC and assembly language; if you know BASIC, but not very well, you should continue to review it as you read this book.

Machine language and assembly language have many more types of statements than BASIC does. The 6502 has 56 statement types, and this is actually quite low—some computers have over three times as many. The purpose of using BASIC to help explain assembly language and machine language is to get the student through this complexity as efficiently as possible.

The book is divided into 100 sections, with three exercises per section. For a fourteen-week, one-semester course, seven sections per week are recommended; for a ten-week, one-quarter course, you can take eight sections per week and stop at section 76 (the rest of the book consists of advanced topics). The string-handling in section 82, the sorting and searching in sections 83-86, and the floating point processing in sections 97-99, can be done earlier if desired. We should note that a great amount of effort has been expended in presenting the material in such an order that no concepts are used before they are explained.

Because of the large number of statement types necessary for doing even simple problems, we do *not* recommend that the student start almost immediately running programs on the computer. Instead, the learning process is based on written exercises, in a constant stream, three per section, involving all the basic concepts one must know in order to be an assembly language programmer.

Section 42 through 50 cover the processes of writing complete programs, desk checking, walkthroughs, editing, assembling, and several debugging techniques, including stepping, tracing, breakpoint debugging, and assembly-level patching.

---

*Not necessarily APPLE BASIC, of course.

All of this is done with specific reference to the APPLE, its monitor program, and LISA. After section 50, and after every tenth section thereafter, there is a suggested problem for computer solution. It cannot be urged too strongly that those who are using the book for self-study actually write these programs, or programs like them, on an APPLE. Book-knowledge of assembly language and machine language programming is not enough!

No hardware knowledge is required to understand this book, and very little hardware-oriented material is presented. A separate course on microcomputer hardware, interfacing, and software for logic design is recommended after the student has had the introductory material on assembly language and machine language presented here. On the other hand, assembly language and machine language knowledge is necessary in such areas as the construction of assemblers and compilers, where a knowledge of hardware is normally not required.

There is an extensive collection of tables in the Appendix, describing the 6502, LISA, and the APPLE monitor. All the features of LISA described in the Appendix are available in all versions of LISA. All the 6502 instructions are covered, but a few features of LISA and a number of features of the APPLE monitor have been omitted. After you are no more than halfway through this book, you should be ready to read the APPLE literature on your own.

Discussions of multiplication and division (including subroutines to multiply and divide) and of floating point are given, even though the 6502 has no multiply or divide instructions or floating point instructions of any kind. Similarly, quite a number of sections are devoted to 16-bit operations, even though the 6502 is an 8-bit machine. We remark that it is far easier to "pick up" the machine language of a 16-bit machine, after having learned on an 8-bit machine, than vice versa, since you can often do in one instruction on a 16-bit machine what takes several instructions, if not an entire subroutine, on an 8-bit machine.

This book could not have been written without the prior existence of two excellent books on the 6502. These are *Programming the 6502* (Berkeley, Sybex, 1978), by my friend and former student Rodnay Zaks; and *6502 Assembly Language Programming* (Berkeley, Osborne/McGraw-Hill, 1980), a 600-page book, with over 150 references, by Lance Leventhal. Mention should also be made of Adam Osborne's encyclopedic *An Introduction to Microcomputers,* which should be on every computer scientist's bookshelf; and the *APPLE II Reference Manual* and *LISA* (the manual), both of which are recommended as reference material supplementary to this book.

Many people helped in the preparation of this book. Ned Rhodes, Jose Sanchez, Bill Schultheis, and Richard Untied read the book from cover to cover and suggested numerous improvements and corrections. In addition, the author has class-tested this book in four successive semesters; every problem has been assigned, and every student has been exhorted to look for errors and report them.

The following students were especially helpful in this regard:

Tom Arden	Richard Gonyea	Young-Sil Muntean
Manjit Bakshi	Ann Gready	Claude Nogay
Bernard Benson	Phillip Grove	Jeffrey Peiffer
Gary Bowe	Daniel Houghton	Sarabjeet Singh
Janet Bruss	Hinda Kada	Lena Steele
Vinodh Coomaraswamy	Margarita Perez Kirk	Piraphong Suppipat
Susan Eisen	Rafi Krigman	Abdulaziz Tamamy
Nabil Esphahani	Lam Hon Wo	Farhad Verahrami
Maria Gear	Mary Lou Miller	Kathy Whitefield

Special thanks are due to Barbara Friedman and all the people at Computer Science Press, including Art Friedman, Sandy Kahl, Elizabeth Mergner, Beth Schwinn, Carol Wallace, and Rachel Witty for their unwavering support and encouragement. Finally, I would like to thank Professor Ray Pickholtz, of The George Washington University, for being a staunch friend and supporter.

W. D. Maurer
Washington, 1982

CONTENTS

LIST OF FIGURES

**TO MY FATHER
HARRY MAURER
WHO LOVES HIS FELLOW MAN**

1. CODES

In this book you will be learning to program in *machine language* and in *assembly language*. This is considerably harder than programming in BASIC or in FORTRAN, but you will be rewarded by being able to write programs which are several dozen times faster than typical BASIC programs. Also, you will gain an understanding of how a computer really works, from the programmer's viewpoint.* This will be invaluable to you in further study of computer science.

Almost all of what we have to learn, in machine language and assembly language programming, is based on the idea of a *code*.

There is an old children's game based on codes, which allows you to send secret messages. Suppose that your mother is making you take piano lessons, and you would rather be somewhere else. So your secret message is

PIANO LESSONS STINK

Now "count forward" in the alphabet from each of these letters by, let us say, three positions:

PIANO LESSONS STINK
QJBOP MFTTPOT TUJOL
RKCPQ NGUUQPU UVKPM
SLDQR OHVVRQV VWLQN

(where, in each column, we have counted forward: P, Q, R, S; I, J, K, L; and so forth). You write a note to a friend of yours that says

SLDQR OHVVRQV VWLQN

and then, if your mother finds it, or your piano teacher finds it, they have no way of knowing what you were saying (unless *they* played the game themselves when they were children).

---

*Not, however, from the hardware designer's viewpoint. Computer hardware and logic design is not taught in this book. See Leventhal's *6502 Assembly Language Programming* for an excellent discussion of the hardware of the 6502.

Of course, your friend might write a note back to you, saying

HVSHFLDOOB VFDOHV

In order to tell what your friend was saying, you have to count *backwards* through the alphabet, like this:

HVSHFLDOOB VFDOHV
GURGEKCNNA UECNGU
FTQFDJBMMZ TDBMFT
ESPECIALLY SCALES

Note the Y in ESPECIALLY; when we are counting forward, and we get to Z, we go back to A again. Similarly, when we are counting backward, and we get to A, we go back to Z again.

Another kind of code is a *number code*, where 1 stands for A because A is the first letter in the alphabet. If the note you passed to your friend was

16 9 1 14 15   12 5 19 19 15 14 19   19 20 9 14 11

this would be PIANO LESSONS STINK, again, because P is the 16th letter in the alphabet; I is the 9th letter in the alphabet; and so on. This code, though, would probably be much too easy for your mother to figure out; but it is the kind of code most often used in machine language and assembly language.

Codes are fundamental in our study of machine language, because *all* information in computers is kept in coded form. In your study of FORTRAN or BASIC you learned that a variable such as K can have a value such as 19, which is kept in the computer. In this book, we learn that what is kept in the computer is not really 19 at all, but rather a *code* for 19. On the 6502, the code is 00010011; this represents the number 19.

In the same way, alphabetic information is kept in computers in coded form. If we wanted to keep the sentence PIANO LESSONS STINK in the computer, then each letter of this sentence would be represented by a code.* On the 6502, the code for the letter P, for example, is 11010000. Whenever we put information into the computer, it will be converted into codes; whenever we take information from the computer and display it, these codes will be decoded. All this is done by code conversion programs, which we will learn, in time, how to write. Often we will write programs that we can understand more easily if we pretend that information is kept in the computer directly, rather than in coded form, but it is always necessary to understand that this is not actually the case.

---

*The blank space is also represented by a code. We will learn more about codes for characters in section 24.

The codes in the computer, such as 00010011 and 11010000, are *binary numbers*. In the next two sections, we will learn the elementary properties of binary numbers which we will need.

EXERCISES

1. Decode the following messages according to the first code described above:

   (a) ZKDW LV WKH DQVZHU WR SUREOHP ILYH?
   *(b) ILIWHHQ LQFKHV.
   (c) GDQQB LV FXWH!

2. Decode the following messages according to the second code described above:

   *(a) 13 5 5 20 13 5 2 5 8 9 14 4 20 8 5 6 5 14 3 5.
    (b) 7 5 20 12 15 19 20, 25 15 21 3 18 5 5 16!
   *(c) 23 9 12 12 25 15 21 7 15 15 21 20 23 9 20 8 13 5?

3. The following message was encoded in *both* ways (the first and then the second). Decode it.

   12 4 16 12 17 15 18 25 8 26 12 23 11 22 24 22 12 8.

2. BINARY NUMBERS

In order to understand the 6502, you have to understand binary numbers and the binary system. Sometimes people learn this as part of learning BASIC, or in mathematics in high school, but we will assume that you have never seen binary numbers before and start at the beginning.

Binary numbers are numbers made up of only zeroes and ones. Figure 1 shows the first 16 binary numbers (together with zero).

We may regard binary numbers as a code, very much like a secret code. Thus 111, for example, is a code for 7; 1001 is a code for 9.

In a computer, all numbers are given by such codes. If the number 9 is kept in a computer, it is kept in the form 1001 (or sometimes 00001001, or the like).

Ordinary numbers such as 7 and 9 are called *decimal numbers*. The *decimal system* is the system, which we all know, of giving values to numbers with more than one digit. Thus

$$3456 = 3000 + 400 + 50 + 6 = (3 * 1000) + (4 * 100) + (5 * 10) + 6$$
$$= (3 * 10^3) + (4 * 10^2) + (5 * 10^1) + (6 * 10^0)$$

with the exponents in order: 10^3, 10^2, 10^1, 10^0 (remember that $10^1 = 10$ and $10^0 = 1$).

The *binary system* is the same as the decimal system, except that 10 is replaced by 2. Thus, in the binary system we have

$$1001 = (1 * 2^3) + (0 * 2^2) + (0 * 2^1) + (1 * 2^0)$$
$$= (1 * 8) + (0 * 4) + (0 * 2) + (1 * 1) = 8+1 = 9.$$

Finding the code, such as 1001, for a number like 9 is called *converting* the number from decimal to binary. In order to do this, we first find the largest power of 2 which is no larger than the number we want to convert. For example, consider the number 1600. Look at Figure 2; the largest power of 2 which is not greater than 1600 is 1024.

Now we consider each power of 2 in turn, from that number down to 1. In each case, we subtract the power of 2 unless the result would be negative. Each

4

NUMBER (DECIMAL)	BINARY NUMBER
0	0
1	1
2	10
3	11
4	100
5	101
6	110
7	111
8	1000
9	1001
10	1010
11	1011
12	1100
13	1101
14	1110
15	1111
16	10000

Figure 1. The First 16 Binary Numbers.

x	2^x
0	1
1	2
2	4
3	8
4	16
5	32
6	64
7	128
8	256
9	512
10	1024
11	2048
12	4096
13	8192
14	16384
15	32768
16	65536

Figure 2. Powers of 2.

time we subtract a power of 2, we put 1 in the binary number; each time we do *not* subtract, we put 0 in the binary number. (See Figure 3.) When we are done, we read off the answer from top to bottom; in this case it is 11001000000. Another example is also given in Figure 3, in which 1331, converted to binary, is 10100110011.

Finding the number, such as 9, having a binary code like 1001 is also called *converting*, from binary to decimal. This is easier than converting the other way. We write out the digits of the number, as in Figure 4, and above each digit we write a power of 2 (from Figure 2), starting at the right. Now we *add* the powers of 2 that correspond to places in the binary number where a 1 appears. In each case in Figure 4, we can see that the same number which we converted from decimal to binary in Figure 3 is converted back to decimal.

A binary digit is called a *bit*. Thus the binary number 11001000000 contains eleven bits. (The phrase "BInary digiT" is contracted to "BIT.")

EXERCISES

1. Convert the following decimal numbers to binary:

   *(a) 100
    (b) 39
   *(c) 128

	1600			1331	
	$-\underline{1024}$	1		$-\underline{1024}$	1
	576			307	
	$-\underline{512}$	1	(512)		0
	64			307	
(256)		0		$-\underline{256}$	1
	64			51	
(128)		0	(128)		0
	64			51	
	$-\underline{64}$	1	(64)		0
	0			51	
(32)		0		$-\underline{32}$	1
	0			19	
(16)		0		$-\underline{16}$	1
	0			3	
(8)		0	(8)		0
	0			3	
(4)		0	(4)		0
	0			3	
(2)		0	(2)	$-\underline{2}$	1
	0			1	
(1)		0	(1)	$-\underline{1}$	1
				0	

ANSWER = 11001000000   ANSWER = 10100110011

Figure 3. Conversion from Decimal to Binary.

1024	512	256	128	64	32	16	8	4	2	1	
1	1	0	0	1	0	0	0	0	0	0	
1024 +	512			+ 64							= 1600
1024	512	256	128	64	32	16	8	4	2	1	
1	0	1	0	0	1	1	0	0	1	1	
1024		+ 256			+ 32 +	16			+ 2 +	1	= 1331

Figure 4. Conversion from Binary to Decimal.

2. Convert the following binary numbers to decimal:

  (a) 1000110
  *(b) 10001100
  (c) 111111

3. The following message was coded according to the second scheme of sec-

tion 1, and then by converting each decimal number to binary. Decode it.

1001   1 1101   1100 101 1 10010 1110 1001 1110 111
1 10 1111 10101 10100   11 1111 1101 10000 10101 10100 101 10010 10011.

3. ADDING AND SUBTRACTING IN BINARY

Since numbers are represented in computers in binary form, they are added and subtracted in this form. We will now learn how to add and subtract binary numbers. In the binary system, the rules for adding and subtracting numbers of more than one digit are exactly the same as they are in the decimal system, with 2 substituted for 10.

Consider how we add two numbers, such as

$$
\begin{array}{r}
6543 \\
+2481 \\
\hline
9024
\end{array}
$$

We go from right to left, as follows:

(1) 3 and 1 is 4.
(2) 4 and 8 is 12; *bring down* the 2 and *carry* the 1.
(3) 1 and 5 and 4 is 10; bring down the 0 and carry the 1.
(4) 1 and 6 and 2 is 9.

In the same way, we can add in binary:

$$
\begin{array}{r}
1010 \\
+110 \\
\hline
10000
\end{array}
$$

Again we go from right to left:

(1) 0 and 0 is 0.
(2) 1 and 1 is 10 (remember that 2, in binary, is 10); bring down the 0 and carry the 1.
(3) 1 and 0 and 1 is 10; bring down the 0 and carry the 1.
(4) 1 and 1 is 10; since we are at the end, bring down the 10, just as we would do with decimal numbers.

8

Referring to Figure 1, we can see that the answer is right. We are really adding $10 + 6 = 16$. If we convert all three numbers to binary, 10 is 1010; 6 is 110; and 16 is 10000.

(Sometimes decimal numbers can be confused with binary numbers. When we add $10 + 6 = 16$, we mean 10 as a decimal number, not 10 as a binary number. If we want to avoid confusion, we write the *base*—10 or 2—as a subscript, and the decimal or binary number in parentheses. Thus $(10)_2$ means 10 as a binary number; $(10)_{10}$ means 10 as a decimal number.)

Subtraction also follows the same rules in binary as in decimal. Consider

$$\begin{array}{r} 3528 \\ -1574 \\ \hline 1954 \end{array}$$

Here we go as follows, from right to left:

(1) 8 minus 4 is 4.
(2) 12 minus 7 is 5; *borrow* the 1.
(3) 14 minus 5 (not 15 minus 5, because 1 has been borrowed) is 9; borrow another 1.
(4) 2 minus 1 (not 3 minus 1) is 1.

Subtracting in binary goes the same way:

$$\begin{array}{r} 1100 \\ -110 \\ \hline 110 \end{array}$$

Proceeding from right to left:

(1) 0 minus 0 is 0.
(2) 10 minus 1 is 1 (that is, 2 minus 1 is 1); borrow the 1.
(3) 10 (not 11, since we borrowed the 1) minus 1 is 1.

Figure 1 again shows us that the answer is right; we have subtracted $12 - 6 = 6$. All these additions and subtractions are illustrated in Figure 5. The number 6 could also have been expressed as 0110, rather than 110, and we could have subtracted as follows:

$$\begin{array}{r} 1100 \\ -0110 \\ \hline 0110 \end{array}$$

The extra zero at the beginning of 0110 is called a *leading zero*. Leading zeroes make no difference in the value of a binary number, but they are often

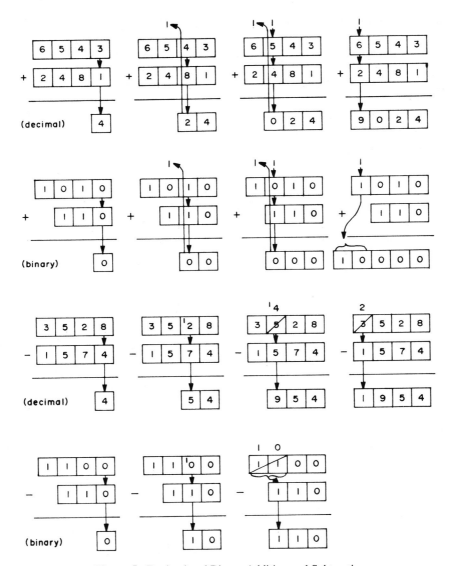

Figure 5. Decimal and Binary Addition and Subtraction.

used, particularly when we want all our binary numbers to have the same number of bits.

By looking at Figure 1, we can see that putting an extra zero at the *end* of a binary number is equivalent to multiplying that number by 2. Thus, for example, 110 in binary represents 6, while 1100 in binary represents 12, or 6 * 2. This, of course, is like multiplying decimal numbers by 10; thus adding a zero to 6 gives 60, or 6 * 10. A related fact is that all *even* numbers, in binary, end with a zero, while all odd numbers end with a 1.

EXERCISES

1. Perform the following additions in binary:

   (a) 100010   *(b) 1101   (c) 110110
       +10101   +1011   +1010

2. Perform the following subtractions in binary:

   *(a) 110111   (b) 100110   *(c) 100101
        -100100   -1011   -111

3. Add the following column of binary numbers; then convert each number to decimal, add the decimal numbers, and verify that the sum of one column is the conversion of the sum of the other column:

$$
\begin{array}{r}
11101 \\
1011 \\
110 \\
101 \\
1000 \\
11 \\
\underline{11001}
\end{array}
$$

(The following shortcut may be useful. Suppose that the sum of one column of bits is 6. In binary, this is 110, and you would bring down the 0 and carry 11. But it is simpler to carry 3—that is, half of 6—as a decimal number, and add to it the bits in the next column. The number brought down is 0, because 6 is even, and would be 1 if the sum were odd. Only in the leftmost column is it necessary for the sum to be brought down in binary.)

4. THE HEXADECIMAL SYSTEM

We have mentioned that 2 is the *base* of the binary system, which means that there are two digits—0 and 1—and the system is based on the powers of 2. Similarly, 10 is the base of the decimal system. There are also other systems, with bases other than 2 and 10. The most often used of these is the *hexadecimal system*, which has the base 16.*

There are sixteen digits in the hexadecimal system—0, 1, 2, 3, 4, 5, 6, 7, 8, 9, A, B, C, D, E, and F. Numbers in the hexadecimal system have values like those in the decimal system, with 16 substituted for 10. Thus in the decimal system we have

$$3456 = \begin{array}{l} 3 * 10^3 \\ +4 * 10^2 \\ +5 * 10^1 \\ +6 * 10^0 \end{array}$$

(see section 2), whereas in the hexadecimal system we have

$$3456 = \begin{array}{l} 3 * 16^3 \\ +4 * 16^2 \\ +5 * 16^1 \\ +6 * 16^0 \end{array} = \begin{array}{l} 3 * 4096 \\ +4 * 256 \\ +5 * 16 \\ +6 * 1 \end{array} = \begin{array}{r} 12288 \\ + 1024 \\ + 80 \\ + 6 \\ \hline 13398 \end{array}$$

(The first four powers of 16 are all we have to know: $16^1 = 16$, $16^2 = 256$, $16^3 = 4096$, and $16^4 = 65536$.)

This is the way in which a hexadecimal number is converted into decimal. To convert a decimal number into hexadecimal, we first convert the decimal

---

*The proper name for a system with base 16 is the ''sexadecimal'' system; but the hexadecimal system was first introduced to the computing world in 1963 by IBM, and IBM settled on a more decorous name for the system.

number into binary (as in Figure 3) and then convert this binary number into hexadecimal as follows:

(1) Divide the binary number into groups of four bits, starting from the right.
(2) Convert each of these groups into a single hexadecimal digit. (See Figure 6.)

Conversion from hexadecimal to binary works the same way in reverse (again see Figure 6):

(1) Express each hexadecimal digit as a group of four bits.
(2) Run all these bits together to produce the given binary number.

We can see from Figure 6 that converting between binary and hexadecimal is easier than the other conversions we have done. Let us see why this method works. Consider the binary number 1000101011010010; we can write

$$
\begin{aligned}
(1000101011010010)_2 &= 1 * 2^{15} + 0 * 2^{14} + 0 * 2^{13} + 0 * 2^{12} \\
&\quad + 1 * 2^{11} + 0 * 2^{10} + 1 * 2^9 + 0 * 2^8 \\
&\quad + 1 * 2^7 + 1 * 2^6 + 0 * 2^5 + 1 * 2^4 \\
&\quad + 0 * 2^3 + 0 * 2^2 + 1 * 2^1 + 0 * 2^0 \\
&= 2^{12} * (1 * 2^3 + 0 * 2^2 + 0 * 2^1 + 0 * 2^0) \\
&\quad + 2^8 * (1 * 2^3 + 0 * 2^2 + 1 * 2^1 + 0 * 2^0) \\
&\quad + 2^4 * (1 * 2^3 + 1 * 2^2 + 0 * 2^1 + 1 * 2^0) \\
&\quad + 2^0 * (0 * 2^3 + 0 * 2^2 + 1 * 2^1 + 0 * 2^0) \\
&= 2^{12} * 8 + 2^8 * 10 + 2^4 * 13 + 2^0 * 2 \\
&= (2^4)^3 * 8 + (2^4)^2 * 10 + (2^4)^1 * 13 + (2^4)^0 * 2 \\
&= 16^3 * 8 + 16^2 * 10 + 16^1 * 13 + 16^0 * 2 \\
&= (8AD2)_{16} \text{ (that is, 8AD2 in hexadecimal).}
\end{aligned}
$$

As we can see, the conversion technique depends on the fact that 16 is a power of 2.

The hexadecimal system is very widely used in machine language programming. This is because we often work with very large binary numbers, which can be confusing. If we write a binary number such as 1011011101001000, it is easy to make mistakes because of the large number of zeroes and ones. Since we can convert a binary number to hexadecimal so easily, and vice versa, it is better to keep all binary numbers in hexadecimal form, unless, for some reason, we need to examine the individual bits. For example, C8, in hexadecimal, with the leftmost bit changed, becomes 48, because C8 is 11001000 in binary; changing the leftmost bit of this results in 01001000; and this, converted back to hexadecimal, is 48.

Binary	1000101011010010	Binary	Hexadecimal
		0000	0
	1000 1010 1101 0010	0001	1
		0010	2
	8 A D 2	0011	3
		0100	4
Hexadecimal	8AD2	0101	5
		0110	6
		0111	7
		1000	8
Hexadecimal	8AD2	1001	9
		1010	A
	8 A D 2	1011	B
		1100	C
	1000 1010 1101 0010	1101	D
		1110	E
Binary	1000101011010010	1111	F

Figure 6. Conversion Between Binary and Hexadecimal.

EXERCISES

1. Convert the following decimal numbers into hexadecimal:

   *(a) 100
   (b) 781
   *(c) 4096

2. Convert the following hexadecimal numbers into decimal:

   (a) 9A
   *(b) 123
   (c) ACE

*3. Convert the following string of binary digits into a string of hexadecimal digits:

   1010111110101011110010101011010011011010101101

5. ADDING AND SUBTRACTING IN HEXADECIMAL

Not only the binary and the decimal systems, but *all* similar number systems, have similar addition and subtraction rules. In the hexadecimal system, we need only to substitute 16 for 10; other than that, the processes are the same as they are in the decimal system. For example, let us add, in hexadecimal,

$$
\begin{array}{r}
B785 \\
+\ 2C84 \\
\hline
E409
\end{array}
$$

The addition here goes as follows, from right to left:

(1) 5 and 4 is 9 (just as in the decimal system).
(2) 8 and 8 is 10 (this corresponds to decimal 8 and 8 = 16); bring down the 0 and carry the 1.
(3) 7 and C is 13 (this corresponds to 7 + 12 = 19, in decimal); 13 and 1 (from the carry) is 14; bring down the 4, carry the 1.
(4) B and 2 is D, and one more from the carry is E. (This corresponds to 11 + 2 + 1 = 14 in decimal.)

As another example, let us subtract, in hexadecimal,

$$
\begin{array}{r}
834E \\
-\ 2E5A \\
\hline
54F4
\end{array}
$$

This time the procedure, from right to left, is:

(1) E minus A is 4 (this is 14 − 10 = 4 in decimal).
(2) 4 minus 5 becomes 14 minus 5, which is F (not 9; be very careful); borrow the 1. (In decimal, 14 − 5 becomes 20 − 5, or 15, which is F in hexadecimal.)
(3) 3 minus E becomes 13 minus E, which becomes 12 minus E because we borrowed 1. This is 4 (corresponding to 18 − 14 = 4), and we borrow 1 again.

(4) 8 minus 2, or 7 minus 2 because of the borrow, is 5, just as in the
    decimal system.

When adding hexadecimal numbers, remember not to carry unless the sum is
greater than F. Thus $25 + 25 = 50$ (decimal), but $25 + 25$ (hexadecimal) is 4A,
and *not* 5A (remember that $5 + 5 = A$, *without* carry, in hexadecimal).

Conversion between decimal and hexadecimal forms may also be done with
tables. Table 2 in the Appendix helps you to convert a hexadecimal number of
up to four digits into decimal, or a decimal number of up to five digits into hexadecimal.

Certain hexadecimal numbers, such as B5, DEF7, and the like, can look like
variable names, and care must be taken not to confuse the two. As we shall see,
the LISA system assumes that a hexadecimal quantity such as B5 is written as
$B5 to distinguish it from a variable called B5. Some systems, such as the
APPLE monitor program, assume that *all* quantities are given in hexadecimal,
so that the $ is unnecessary (and incorrect, in fact). Others, such as most BASIC
systems, do not use hexadecimal numbers, and B5, for example, always stands,
in BASIC, for the name of a variable, and not a hexadecimal constant.

Binary and hexadecimal numbers can also be multiplied and divided; we will
take this up in section 38. Also, *fractions*, such as 1/2, may be expressed in
either binary or hexadecimal form; this subject is examined in section 97.

EXERCISES

1. Perform the following additions in hexadecimal:

    (a)   137   *(b)   B159   (c)   FADE
          +652   +2551   +BEAD

2. Perform the following subtractions in hexadecimal:

    *(a)   519   (b)   C650   *(c)   FEED
           -304   -1881   -FACE

3. Add the following column of hexadecimal numbers; then convert each
    number to decimal, add the decimal numbers, and verify that the sum of
    one column is the conversion of the sum of the other column:

                              36B
                              C2
                              4F
                              980
                              D
                              E7
                              15A

6. REGISTERS, CELLS, AND BYTES

Think of the 6502—or any computer—as having a large collection of boxes in which you can store numbers. Each box on the 6502 contains eight bits; that is, it can contain any binary number from 00000000 through 11111111 (one and only one number at any given time).

There are two kinds of boxes. One kind is called a *register*. There are many registers on the 6502, but we will start by looking at three basic registers, called A, X, and Y. The other kind of box is called a *cell*, and all the cells of the 6502, taken together, are known as its *main memory*. The maximum number of cells (without the use of special techniques) is 65536, or 2^{16}, although there are some 6502 systems which have a smaller number of cells.

In the hexadecimal system, each register, or cell, can contain any *two-digit* hexadecimal number, from 00 to FF. In the decimal system, $(FF)_{16}$ is 255, so that a register or a cell can contain any decimal number from 0 through 255.

Note that $255 = 256 - 1 = 2^8 - 1$. The number 2^8, in binary, is 100000000, or 1 followed by eight zeroes. If we subtract 1 from this number, in binary, we get 11111111.

This illustrates a general principle about binary numbers: *If we have n available bits* (here n is 8), *then these bits can hold* (a binary code for) *any number from 0 through $2^n - 1$* (here $2^8 - 1$). This principle will be used frequently in what follows.

The cells in the main memory have cell numbers, called *addresses*, and these addresses start from zero. Thus we have cell number 0, cell number 1, and so on; or, we can refer to the cell with address 0, the cell with address 1, and so on.* The largest possible address is 65535, or $2^{16} - 1$, since the maximum number of cells is 65536 (including the cell with address zero). By our general principle, *any address*—that is, any number from 0 through $2^{16} - 1$—*may be contained in 16 bits*; that is, in *two* of our 65536 cells, or, if necessary, in two registers (such as A and X).

Let us consider an example of this. In section 2, Figure 3, we saw that the

---

*The cell with address 59 is *the fifty-ninth cell* in the computer (not counting cell 0), in the same way, for example, that the house with address 59 Elm Street is (theoretically) *the fifty-ninth house* on Elm Street.

decimal number 1600 corresponds to the binary number 11001000000. Let us write this as a 16-bit number, with some leading zeroes:

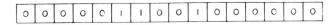

Now we can split up this number between the A register and the X register, as follows:

A - REGISTER   X - REGISTER

In decimal, the A register now contains 6, and the X register contains 64. Between them, they contain the 16-bit decimal number 1600. A formula for obtaining this decimal number, in this case, is 256 * A + X; in this case, 256 * 6 + 64 = 1536 + 64 = 1600.

Besides addresses, or cell numbers, certain cells, in any program, also have *names*. These are the names of variables, much like variables in BASIC. If you have a cell called K, you can keep the value of K in that cell. This value may change; for example, we might have a BASIC program such as

```
FOR K = 1 TO 100
(further statements)
NEXT K
```

where K takes every value from 1 through 100. We can keep all these values in the cell called K; when K is 55, for example, then 55 is the number in this cell.

Many other computers have registers which contain more than eight bits; they may contain 24 bits, 36 bits, and so on. However, a register size of eight bits is very common, and it has a special name, which seems to have originated at IBM: it is called a *byte*. "One byte" and "eight bits" mean the same thing; thus an address, from what we have seen above, may be kept in two bytes. On computers having *cells* which are eight bits long, such as the 6502, the words "byte" and "cell" are often taken as synonymous; for example, we speak of 65,536 *bytes* of memory, or 64K bytes for short. Here K means "times 1,024," and one *kilobyte* (or Kbyte) is 1,024 bytes, or 2^{10} bytes.*

Besides main memory, there is *auxiliary memory*. A diskette, for example, contains over 100,000 bytes of memory. You cannot use this memory directly, however; you must copy the information on it into main memory first. This pro-

---

*There is also *one megabyte*, or Mbyte, which is 2^{20} or 1,048,596 bytes. Although 6502-based systems cannot have as much as a megabyte, others can (such as those based on the 8088 or the 68000). On computers having cells which are *more* than eight bits long, each cell is often called a *word*, and we speak of 16-bit words, 36-bit words, and so on.

cess, known as *reading* the diskette, will be considered further in sections 91 and 92.

Always be careful not to confuse an address with the number in the cell with that address. For example, the cell with address 6 can contain any number from 0 through 255; it does not have to contain the number 6. (To say that it has the address 6 means only that it is *the sixth cell,* of all the cells in the computer, and nothing more.)

EXERCISES

1. Which of the following numbers can be kept in the A register?

   (a) 200
   *(b) 300
   (c) 400

2. Suppose that each of the following numbers were to be kept in two registers, the A register and the X register. What quantity would be kept in the A register, and what quantity in the X register? (All these numbers are decimal.)

   *(a) 256
   (b) 1000
   *(c) 10000

*3. An older computer called the PDP-8 had 12-bit registers. What is the largest decimal number that can be kept in such a register?

7. MULTIBYTE QUANTITIES AND TWOS' COMPLEMENT

It might seem that there is a problem with cells of this kind, since we can only keep numbers from 0 to 255 in them. We cannot keep *large* numbers (greater than 255); we cannot keep *negative* numbers (less than zero). If we want to keep large numbers and negative numbers in computers, we must use special techniques, which we will now learn.

We can keep large numbers by using more than one cell for each number. If we use two cells, as we did with addresses, then we can keep numbers from 0 through $2^{16} - 1$, or 65535. If one cell contains p, and the other contains q, then the two cells together contain $256p + q$; this is similar to the formula $256A + X$ given in the preceding section. If we use more than two cells, say n cells, we can keep any number from 0 through $2^{8n} - 1$. For example, if n is 4, then $2^{8n} - 1$ is $2^{32} - 1$, which is over 4,000,000,000.

We can keep negative numbers in one of two ways. The first is to set aside the leftmost bit as a code for the sign; 0 means "positive" and 1 means "negative." In a cell containing eight bits, 10000011 would represent -3; the first 1 means "negative," and the rest of the cell, 0000011, represents 3 (with five leading zeroes). This is called the *signed magnitude representation*. It is *not*, ordinarily, used on the 6502; it was used, mainly, in the computers of the early 1960s.

The other way to represent negative numbers is similar to the three-digit counter found on many audio tape players. When the tape rewinds, this counts backwards; when it gets down to 000, it proceeds to 999, then 998, and so on. In the same way, if we continue to subtract 1 from an 8-bit binary number, and it reaches 00000000, it proceeds to 11111111, then 11111110, and so on. Thus 11111111 is a representation of -1; 11111110 is a representation of -2; and so on. The numbers from -5 to 5 are given in this way, in decimal, binary, and hexadecimal, in Figure 7.

We can find the representation of $-x$ by subtracting x from binary 100000000. Thus, for example, 45 (decimal) is 101101 in binary, and, if we subtract this from 100000000, we get 11010011. It is easier, in fact, to subtract

DECIMAL	BINARY	HEXADECIMAL
−5	11111011	FB
−4	11111100	FC
−3	11111101	FD
−2	11111110	FE
−1	11111111	FF
0	00000000	00
1	00000001	01
2	00000010	02
3	00000011	03
4	00000100	04
5	00000101	05

Figure 7. Twos' Complement Integers.

x from binary 11111111, and then add 1 to the answer (this works because 11111111 + 1 = 100000000 in binary). Thus we can calculate either

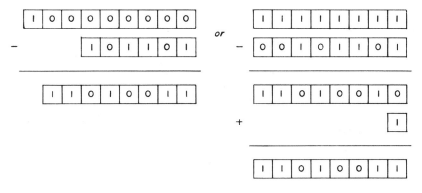

The second calculation is easier because *there is never any borrow* when you subtract from all 1's. Every subtraction is either 1 − 0 = 1 or 1 − 1 = 0. In fact, you do not even have to subtract; just change every 0 to a 1 and every 1 to a 0. This is called *complementing* the number, or taking the *ones' complement*. (The *complement* of 0 is 1; the complement of 1 is 0.) When you add 1 as above, you get the *twos' complement*.*

---

*This term is a misnomer, which survives for historical reasons. You do *not* get the twos' complement of *x* by subtracting *x* from 22222222, or the like; you simply add one to the ones' complement of *x*.

The *twos' complement representation* is the technique of representing a *positive* number x as the bit 0 followed by the binary number x, and a *negative* number $-x$ as the bit 1 followed by the twos' complement of x, or $2^{d-1} - x$, in a register containing d bits. If $d = 8$, the largest number in this representation is 01111111 (decimal 127) and the smallest is 10000000 (decimal -128); in general, the range is from -2^{d-1} to $2^{d-1} - 1$, and numbers in this range are called *signed numbers*. A positive signed number x is represented, in binary, as x; a negative signed number $-x$ is represented as $2^{d-1} + (2^{d-1} - x)$, or $2^d - x$. The twos' complement of a *negative* number is again its ones' complement *plus* one (not minus one); thus the ones' complement of 11010011 is 00101100, and this plus one is 00101101.

The twos' complement representation is used on almost all computers today, mainly because, as we shall prove in section 88, it allows the operations of signed and unsigned addition to become the same. For example:

UNSIGNED	BINARY	SIGNED
3	0 0 0 0 0 0 1 1	3
+ 2 5 1	+ 1 1 1 1 1 0 1 1	+ (- 5)
2 5 4	1 1 1 1 1 1 1 0	- 2

Note that if 11111011 is unsigned, it cannot be -5, so it must be 251; if it is signed, it cannot be 251 (remember that the signed numbers range from -128 to 127), so it must be -5. We often use a binary number like 11111011 to represent two different numbers (251 and -5, here); and as we have seen, there is never any confusion. We have to remember what kind of data our binary numbers represent, because there is *no way* to test a register, or a cell, to see whether it is supposed to contain a signed integer, an unsigned integer, or some other kind of data.*

Fractions, and other real numbers, may also be represented in the 6502. We will take up this subject in section 98.

---

*It is true that in certain very high level languages, such as LISP and SNOBOL, tests like these appear to be possible; but all such languages use a trick, which we shall discuss in section 100.

EXERCISES

1. Express the following decimal numbers in binary, as they would be contained in the A register, using the twos' complement representation:

    (a) −23
    *(b) 54
    (c) −1

2. Express the following binary numbers, as they would be contained in the A register in twos' complement notation, as signed decimal numbers. (Remember that a signed number is not necessarily negative.)

    *(a) 11101000
    (b) 01110111
    *(c) 10000011

3. Suppose that the binary numbers of the preceding exercise are considered as *unsigned* numbers. Under these conditions, express them as decimal numbers.

8. LOADING AND STORING

Suppose now that we have the BASIC statement L = K. This sets the new value of L equal to the value of K. If K was 55, then the new value of L is 55. In the 6502, we must *move* the number 55 from the cell called K to a cell called L. (For now we will assume that $0 \leqslant K \leqslant 255$ and $0 \leqslant L \leqslant 255$, for unsigned quantities K and L; or $-128 \leqslant K \leqslant 127$ and $-128 \leqslant L \leqslant 127$, for signed quantities K and L. We will remove this restriction in section 12.)

Moving a number from K to L is done in two steps:

(1) Move the number K into a register. This is called *loading* the register. (You load a register with a number just like you might load your car with a package.)

(2) Move the number from the register into L. This is called *storing* the register. (You store a number from a register just like you might store a package which you took out of your car.)

On the 6502, there are six *instructions* that load and store registers. (An instruction on the 6502—sometimes called a *statement*—is like a statement in BASIC.) These are:

LDA *v*	Load the A register with *v*
LDX *v*	Load the X register with *v*
LDY *v*	Load the Y register with *v*
STA *v*	Store the A register in *v*
STX *v*	Store the X register in *v*
STY *v*	Store the Y register in *v*

Here LD stands for "load"; ST stands for "store"; and *v* can be any cell in the main memory.

This gives us three ways to do the BASIC statement L = K on the 6502. If we want to use the A register, we can write, as part of an assembly language program,

```
LDA   K
STA   L
```

If we want to use the X register or the Y register, we could write

```
LDX K     or     LDY K
STX L            STY L
```

We can also load a *constant*.* Suppose that instead of L = K we wanted to do the BASIC statement L = 100. In that case, using the A register, we could write

```
LDA   #!100
STA   L
```

Note the "number sign" (#) which *we must use* for a constant ("the number 100," in this case). The special character ! here means that 100 is a *decimal* number. We could also use % for binary numbers, or $ for hexadecimal numbers; thus either

```
LDA #%01100100   or   LDA #$64
STA L                 STA L
```

would set L equal to the decimal number 100. We could also use the X register or the Y register, and write

```
LDX #!100    or    LDY #!100
STX L              STY L
```

In BASIC, we know that, if we set L = K, this does not change K; the new value of L is the same as that of K. In the same way, on the 6502, when we load a register with K, this does not change K, and, when we store a register into L, this does not change the register. In particular, consider the instructions

```
LDA   P
STA   Q
STA   R
```

We load the A register with P; then we store it into Q; then we store it again into R. This is the same as writing

```
Q = P
R = P
```

in BASIC, since P is still in the A register when we store R.

---

*Such a constant must fit into a register; that is, we must have $0 \leq k \leq 255$ for an unsigned constant k, or $-128 \leq k \leq 127$ for a signed constant k.

As another example, suppose we want to take the number in K and put it in L, and also take the number in L and put it in K. (If we had K = 3 and L = 8, this would set K = 8 and L = 3.) This is called *interchanging* K and L. We can do it on the 6502 by writing

```
LDA   K
LDX   L
STA   L
STX   K
```

There are four instructions here. First we load the A register with K and load the X register with L. Now the A register (which contains the value of K) is stored in L; while the X register (which contains the value of L) is stored in K.

Always remember that a register can contain one and only one number at any given time. For example, if you write LDA K followed immediately by LDA L then the value of K, in the A register, would be lost.

EXERCISES

1. Give sequences of instructions on the 6502 corresponding to each of the following BASIC statements. (Remember that, just as in any programming language, all variable names are written "on the line"; we never write B_5 or B_3, for example, but rather B5 or B3.)

    *(a) B5 = B3
     (b) D9 = 57
    *(c) Z = 0

2. Give one or more BASIC statements to correspond to each of the following sequences of instructions on the 6502. (Remember that hexadecimal constants are not allowed in BASIC.)

    (a)
    ```
    LDA   C1
    STA   C2
    ```

    *(b)
    ```
    LDX   #!50
    STX   W
    STX   W2
    ```

    (c)
    ```
    LDY   #$5D
    STY   K
    ```

*3. Give a sequence of instructions on the 6502 which performs a "triple interchange" of P, Q, and R. That is, it sets Q to the old value of P; R to the old value of Q; and P to the old value of R. (Note that a triple interchange is *not* the same as three ordinary interchanges.) Use the A and Y registers only, not the X register (that is, do not use LDX or STX).

9. INCREMENTING AND DECREMENTING

On any computer, we can add and subtract. On the 6502, there are tricks to adding and subtracting. We will not learn these tricks until sections 15 and 17. However, there are two special cases which are easy: adding 1 (which is known as *incrementing*) and subtracting 1 (which is known as *decrementing*).

There are six instructions on the 6502 which increment and decrement:

INC *v*	Increment *v*
DEC *v*	Decrement *v*
INX	Increment the X register
DEX	Decrement the X register
INY	Increment the Y register
DEY	Decrement the Y register

Here *v* can be any cell in the main memory, as before. Note that *we cannot increment, or decrement, the A register.*

We can use these instructions to do BASIC statements such as K = L + 1. This would be done in three steps:

(1) Load a register with L.
(2) Increment the register (add 1 to it).
(3) Store the register in K.

If we wanted to use the X register, this could be done by

```
LDX   L
INX
STX   K
```

In the same way, we could set U = V − 1, using the Y register, by

```
LDY   V
DEY
STY   U
```

28

On the other hand, if we just wanted to set K = K + 1 (that is, add 1 to K), we would write only one instruction:

```
INC    K
```

Note that

```
INC    L
LDA    L
STA    K
```

is *not* a good way to set K = L + 1. It does set K = L + 1, but it also changes L. (When we set K = L + 1, we want to make sure that K, and only K, is changed.) The change to L is called a *side effect*. (If you take aspirin for a headache, and the aspirin cures the headache but also gives you an upset stomach, this is also called a side effect.)

Increment and decrement instructions are often used to add 2 or subtract 2. Thus we can set K = L + 2 by

```
LDX    L
INX
INX
STX    K
```

or K = K − 2 by

```
DEC    K
DEC    K
```

We could also add or subtract 3, 4, and so on, in this way, but we usually do this with add or subtract instructions (to be taken up in sections 15 and 17).

Always remember that INC K and DEC K *do not change* what is in the A register. In particular, INC K followed by STA L will *not* set L equal to K + 1.

Incrementing 255 produces zero, and decrementing zero produces 255. Thus, for example, if the X register contains zero (or 00000000 in binary), and we do a DEX, it will now contain binary 11111111 (255 as an unsigned number, or −1 as a signed number), as we saw in section 7. Similarly, if the Y register contains binary 11111111, and we do an INY, it will now contain zero.

An instruction such as INC K is often referred to as a *use* of INC. Similarly, LDA L is a use of LDA, and STX M is a use of STX. For example, the sequence of instructions

```
LDA    #!0
STA    K1
LDA    #!1
STA    K2
STA    K3
```

contains two uses of LDA and three uses of STA.

EXERCISES

1. Give sequences of instructions on the 6502 corresponding to each of the
    following BASIC statements:

    (a) F6 = F4 + 1
    *(b) F4 = F4 + 1
    (c) W = W − 1

2. Give one or more BASIC statements to correspond to each of the following
    sequences of 6502 instructions:

    *(a)
                                    LDX   K4
                                    DEX
                                    STX   K3

    (b)
                                    DEC   C
                                    DEC   C

    *(c)
                                    LDY   S
                                    STY   J
                                    INY
                                    STY   C

3. Give two 6502 instructions which are equivalent to the three instructions

                                    LDX   #$30
                                    DEX
                                    STX   B

10. MACHINE LANGUAGE AND ASSEMBLY LANGUAGE

There is another kind of code which is kept in cells of the 6502. This is the code for *instructions*. Every instruction has an *instruction code,* which we will always express in hexadecimal, and which may take up one, two, or three cells in main memory. For example, LDA #$64 has the instruction code

A9 64

(that is, A9, or 10101001 in binary, in the first cell, and 64, or 01100100 in binary, in the second cell).

The instruction code for STA L would depend on the address of L (that is, the address of the cell containing L). We may remember that every cell has a cell number, or address, and that this address is given by 16 bits, or two bytes. It is therefore also given by *four* hexadecimal digits. Suppose that the cell containing L has the address 08C4. Then STA L has the instruction code

8D C4 08

The first byte (or the first two hexadecimal digits) of an instruction code is called the *operation code* (or ''opcode''). This is a code for the particular operation; thus A9 is a code for ''load the A register with a constant,'' while 8D is a code for ''store the A register into a variable with a 16-bit address.''

Whenever a constant is involved in an instruction (such as LDA #$64), there are *two bytes* in the instruction code, and the second byte is the constant (hexadecimal 64, in this case). Such instructions are sometimes called *immediate data instructions.*

Whenever a variable with a 16-bit address is involved in an instruction, there are *three bytes* in the instruction code, and the second and third bytes give this address. Note that *these two bytes are always reversed.* The address 08C4 became C4 08 in the instruction code for STA L. This is done for reasons of simplifying the hardware design of the 6502.

These codes, then, are kept in cells in main memory; and *these* cells, of course, also have addresses. Suppose that the A9 of A9 64 (as above) is kept in the cell with address 0807. Then the next byte, 64, is kept in *the next cell*—in this case, the cell with address 0808.

If LDA #$64 is followed immediately by STA L—that is, if we are setting L = 100—then the three bytes of STA L are kept in the three following cells, which have addresses 0809, 080A (remember that addresses are hexadecimal numbers), and 080B. This may be tabulated as follows:

ADDRESS	CONTENTS	INSTRUCTION
0807	A9	LDA #$64
0808	64	
0809	8D	STA L
080A	C4	
080B	08	

The first two columns here are called the *machine language* form of the instructions. The third column is called the *assembly language* form. The machine language form is often compressed, as follows:

MACHINE LANGUAGE	ASSEMBLY LANGUAGE
0807 A9 64	LDA #$64
0809 8D C4 08	STA L

The three-letter codes for the instructions, like LDA, are called *mnemonics*.* Thus "load the A register with a constant" has the operation code A9 and the mnemonic LDA. "Mnemonic" means "memory aid" (yours, not the computer's); LDA is easier to remember than A9.

On the 6502, *several instructions with different operation codes may have the same mnemonic.* Thus "load the A register with a variable having a 16-bit address" has the operation code AD, rather than A9, but its mnemonic is still LDA.

Some instructions, like INX, *consist of only a mnemonic.* These instructions, in machine language, consist of only an operation code (E8, for INX); that is, there is only this *one byte* in the instruction code.

The word "contents" at the top of the second column, above, is widely used to stand for what is *contained* in a cell *c*. Of course, this is the value of the variable *c*, in the usual sense.

We have studied twelve instructions on the 6502 so far: LDA, LDX, LDY, STA, STX, STY, INC, INX, INY, DEC, DEX, and DEY. There are many more; and they are all given in three tables in the Appendix. Table 3 explains

---

*Pronounced "ne MON iks." Note carefully that LDA K is not a mnemonic; it is a use of the mnemonic LDA. The variable K is known here as the *operand* of LDA.

each instruction; Table 4 lists all assembly language instructions in alphabetical order, with corresponding machine language forms; and Table 5 lists all machine language instructions in numerical order, with corresponding assembly language forms. In addition, we will study the instructions intensively, singly and in groups, in the sections which follow.

The idea of keeping instructions, as well as data, in memory in coded form is the basic idea of the computer, discovered at approximately the same time by the inventors of the computer—Aiken, Atanasoff, Eckert and Mauchly, and Goldstine and von Neumann. It is known as the *stored program concept.*

EXERCISES

*1. Assuming that the cell containing M has the address 08DA, give the machine language form, starting at the address 080B, of the assembly language instructions

        LDA   # ! 0
        STA   M

(It cannot be said too often that *precision and careful attention to detail are important,* in both machine language and assembly language. Here and in all further exercises in this book, note that the contents of any cell are always given. in *machine* language, as *two* hexadecimal digits.)

2. Assuming that the cell containing N has the address 08DB, give the assembly language form of the machine language instructions

        0810   A9 FF
        0812   8D DB 08

*3. Under the assumptions of both of the preceding exercises, give BASIC statements corresponding to the machine language instructions

        0815   A9 03
        0817   8D DA 08
        081A   8D DB 08

11. THE ASSEMBLER AND PSEUDO-OPERATIONS

The next question is how we can find out what the address of a variable is in a given program, and how we can assign it a value. The answer is that this is done by a program, called an *assembler*.

The assembler translates assembly language into machine language. That is, you write your program in assembly language, and then the assembler produces the machine language form of that program. Only when this is done, and the instruction codes are all in memory, can we *run*, or *execute*, the program.

Throughout this book we shall assume that we have some version of the LISA assembler. Like all assemblers, this has its own conventions, some of which are unique. For example, the use of the special characters ! % $ to denote decimal, binary, and hexadecimal numbers is peculiar to LISA.

Whenever we use an assembler, we write the instructions, or *operations*, of our program, and we also write certain *pseudo-operations*. These look like instructions, but they are not; they tell the assembler various things it needs to know. The most important of these pseudo-operations, in LISA, are ORG (or "origin"), END, and DFS (or Define Storage). An example of the use of these is given in Figure 8.

The pseudo-operation ORG tells LISA where to start. If you write ORG *n* then LISA starts at the address *n* (which is usually given as a hexadecimal number), and goes on from there. Thus in Figure 8, ORG $0807 tells LISA to start at address 0807, which means that the next instruction (LDA L) is translated into a machine language form (AD C5 08) in cells 0807 (see the left-hand column), 0808 and 0809. The next cell after 0809 is 080A (not 0810—be careful!) so the next instruction after that (STA K) is translated into machine language form (8D C4 08) in cells 080A (again see the left-hand column), 080B, and 080C. As we noted in the preceding section, AD is the operation code for "load the A register with a variable having a 16-bit address," and this is different from the operation code for "load the A register with a constant," which is A9.

The pseudo-operation END must be given, once and only once, at the end of the program (as in Figure 8).

The pseudo-operation DFS is used once with each variable in the program, to tell LISA how much storage, or main memory, is used by that variable. If v is any variable, then v DFS n specifies v as taking up n bytes, or cells, in the memory. (In LISA 2.5, v DFS n, 0 will set all these bytes initially to zero.) Thus, in Figure 8, we have ORG $08C4 and K DFS !1, which means that K takes up one cell, and specifically (see the left-hand column) the cell with address 08C4 (since ORG $08C4 requests LISA to start at cell 08C4, as noted above). Then we have L DFS !1, which means that L takes up one cell—the next cell, which therefore (see the left-hand column again) has address 08C5.

MACHINE LANGUAGE		ASSEMBLY LANGUAGE	
			ORG $0807
0807	AD C5 08		LDA L
080A	8D C4 08		STA K
			ORG $08C4
08C4		K	DFS !1
08C5		L	DFS !1
			END

Figure 8. Machine Language and Assembly Language.

This program has a *program section*, consisting of the operations in the program (LDA and STA, here), and a *data section*, consisting of the data (K and L, here). Each section begins with an ORG statement. From now until section 45, where we study more general programs, we shall assume that *every program has a program section and a data section*, as above. The addresses of the ORGs must be between 0800 and 17FF (hexadecimal); this is the area which the LISA system sets aside for your programs. Either the program section or the data section may come first.

Make sure that the program and data sections do not overlap. If the program section extends from cell 0800 to cell 0834 (for example), the data section can start at cell 0840, but it cannot start at cell 0820 (since only one number can be in any cell at any given time).

Note the blanks before and after ORG, LDA, STA, and so on. There may be one blank, or more than one; but these blanks must appear, and they must *not* appear where they are not specified. (You cannot write LD A instead of LDA, for example.)

In assembly language, we can always specify a variable by giving its address. In the example above, the address of K is 08C4; so instead of STA K we could write STA $08C4 with the same result. In particular, we can write LDA !5 or LDA $5 and this will load, into the A register, *the contents of the cell whose address is 5*. This is quite different from LDA #!5 (or LDA #$5), which loads the A register with the *number* 5. Leaving out the "number sign" # is a common beginners' error; remember that, if you do this, the LISA system *will not mark it as an error*, since it has a legitimate meaning.

All the pseudo-operations of LISA are explained in Table 6 in the Appendix. We will discuss these in detail in the sections which follow. Table 7 in the Appendix discusses all the special characters (# ! $ % and the like) which are used by LISA. We may note that ! is required for all decimal numbers in LISA 1.5 (and we will use ! for all decimal numbers in this book); but, *in LISA 2.5*, the ! is *optional and may be omitted.**

EXERCISES

1. Give the machine language form of the following assembly language program:

```
        ORG   $0900
    M   DFS   ! 1
    N   DFS   ! 1
        ORG   $0910
        LDA   # ! 10
        STA   M
        STA   N
        END
```

*2. Give the assembly language form, using ORG, END, and DFS, and a variable called C, of the following machine language program:

```
    08D0    A9 50
    08D2    8D FA 08
```

3. Give the assembly language form, using ORG, END, and DFS, and variables called P1, P2, and P3, of the following machine language program:

```
    08DD    A9 00
    08DF    8D 09 09
    08E2    8D 0A 09
    08E5    8D 0B 09
```

(Note that the cell or cells used by a variable are used *only* by that variable, and by no other variable.)

---

*There is an exception to this: if you really want to operate on cells with decimal addresses (that is, LDA !10 to load the cell with address 000A, or decimal 10) the ! is required. This should never make a difference in your programs, however, since addresses should always be given in hexadecimal.

12. TWO-BYTE NUMBERS AND ADDRESS EXPRESSIONS

The DFS pseudo-operation can be used to specify a two-byte, or 16-bit, number called J; we write J DFS !2 for this.

The two bytes of such a number are often called the *left half* and the *right half*, or the *upper half* and the *lower half*. Thus if the value of J is 08C4, then 08 is the left half, or the upper half; C4 is the right half, or the lower half.

An ordinary 8-bit (positive) number may be expressed as a 16-bit number by putting zero in front of it. Thus 03 and 0003 are the same number; so 3, as a 16-bit number, consists of zero in the left half and 3 in the right half.

A *negative* number, expressed in 8 bits, in twos' complement form, can be expressed in 16 bits, also in twos' complement form, by putting *all ones* (binary 11111111, or hexadecimal FF, or decimal -1) in front of it. We recall from section 7 that the negative number $-x$ is given as $2^d - x$, in a d-bit register or cell. If $d = 16$, this becomes $2^{16} - x$, or hexadecimal $10000 - x$. Thus, for example, -8, which is hexadecimal F8 (or $100 - 8$) in 8 bits, becomes hexadecimal FFF8 (or $10000 - 8$) in 16 bits. The lower half is F8, and the upper half is FF.

If we were to write, in assembly language (for example)

```
        ORG     $0950
  J     DFS     !2
```

then the two halves of J would be kept in the cells with addresses 0950 and 0951, in hexadecimal. The *address of J* would be 0950. In general, *the address of a quantity which takes up more than one byte is the address of its first byte.**

It is quite common to keep all two-byte quantities, on the 6502, *with the bytes reversed*, just as we did for addresses (see section 9). In the case above, the left half would be in the cell whose address is 0951; we can abbreviate this

---

*There is a bug in LISA 1.5 (corrected in LISA 2.5) which sometimes makes it appear (in the *listing only*, not in the resulting machine language program) that this is not the case.

and say that the left half is *at the address* 0951. (From now on all addresses will be given in hexadecimal.) In the same way, the right half is at the address 0950.

Suppose now that we have a two-byte number J and another two-byte number N, and we wish to set N = J. On the 6502, this must be done *one byte at a time*. That is, we must:

(1) Load the lower half of J and store it in the lower half of N.
(2) Load the upper half of J and store it in the upper half of N. (We can do (2) first and then (1), if we like.)

This may be done, using the X register, as follows:

```
LDX     J
STX     N
LDX     J+!1
STX     N+!1
```

The expression J+!1 is an *address expression*. If J is a variable with address 0950, then J+!1 is a variable with address 0951.

An address expression may contain constants and variables. Any variable which it contains is taken to stand for the address of that variable. In this case, J stands for 0950, and adding 1 to this produces 0951.

The address given by an address expression appears in the machine language form of the program. For example, we have the following program in both machine language and assembly language form:

MACHINE LANGUAGE				ASSEMBLY LANGUAGE	
				ORG	$0900
0900	AE	50	09	LDX	J
0903	8E	52	09	STX	N
0906	AE	51	09	LDX	J+!1
0909	8E	53	09	STX	N+!1
				ORG	$0950
0950			J	DFS	!2
0952			N	DFS	!2
				END	

Here AE is the operation code for "load the X register with a variable having a 16-bit address." The address of J is 0950, and this appears as 50 09 (with reversed bytes, as before). The address of J+!1 is 0951, and so this appears as 51 09.

Address expressions can be confusing. It might look as if LDX J+!1 is putting the value of J, plus one, in the X register. We have seen that this is not the case; more importantly, *this cannot be done in only one instruction*. If we wanted to load X with the value of J, plus one, we would have to use two instructions:

```
        LDX    J
        INX
```

EXERCISES

*1. Give the machine language form of the following assembly language program:

```
            ORG    $0980
    N1      DFS    ! 2
    N2      DFS    ! 1
            ORG    $09C0
            LDA    # ! 0
            STA    N2
            STA    N1
            STA    N1 + ! 1
            END
```

2. Give the assembly language form, using ORG, END, DFS, and a two-byte variable called AD, of the following machine language program:

```
    0888    A9  01
    088A    8D  F1  08
    088D    A9  00
    088F    8D  F0  08
```

*3. Give machine language statements, starting at address 0840, and making reference to a two-byte variable J at addresses 0858 and 0859 (with bytes reversed as usual), corresponding to the BASIC statement J = 100. Store the *upper half* of J first. Use the A register.

13. SUBSCRIPTED VARIABLES AND INDEX REGISTERS

The DFS pseudo-operation can also be used to specify an *array* (declared with the DIM statement in BASIC).

Suppose that T is an array of one-byte integers, ranging from T(0) through T(10). There are eleven of these integers (T(1) through T(10), and also T(0)) and each one is a variable which requires one cell in main memory. We can specify all these variables by writing

```
T       DFS     !11
```

The addresses of these eleven variables are given in Figure 9, if we assume that the address of T(0) is 0858. The *address of T*, in this situation, is the address of T(0); that is, it is 0858. (This illustrates our general rule that the address of a quantity taking up more than one byte is always the address of its *first* byte.)

Looking at Figure 9, we can see that there is a general formula for the address of T(k), for any value of k from 0 to 10: it is 0858 + k. In general, *the address of T(k) is k plus the address of T(0)*.

This formula may be used to specify an array element with a *constant subscript*. In section 8, if we wanted to do the BASIC statement L = T(6) instead of L = K, we could write

```
LDA     T+!6
STA     L
```

We have used another address expression here. If T has address 0858, then T+!6 means the variable with address 0858+6, or 085E. We can see from Figure 9 that this is indeed T(6). (Again we must note that this does *not* load the A register with the value of T, plus 6. To do this we would have to do LDA T and then add 6, using an add instruction. These are considered in section 15.)

VARIABLE	ADDRESS	
T(0)	0858	(=0858 + 0)
T(1)	0859	(=0858 + 1)
T(2)	085A	(=0858 + 2)
T(3)	085B	(=0858 + 3)
T(4)	085C	(=0858 + 4)
T(5)	085D	(=0858 + 5)
T(6)	085E	(=0858 + 6)
T(7)	085F	(=0858 + 7)
T(8)	0860	(=0858 + 8)
T(9)	0861	(=0858 + 9)
T(10)	0862	(=0858 + 10)*

Figure 9. Addresses of Elements of an Array.

Our formula may also be used when the subscript is *variable*. Suppose that the BASIC statement is L = T(J) rather than L = T(6). We may now proceed as follows:

(1) Load the *index*—that is, the subscript, in this case J—into an *index register*. On the 6502, the index registers are the X and Y registers.
(2) Load T(J) into the A register with an *indexed instruction*. On the 6502, an indexed instruction contains v, X or v, Y (where v is an array name), rather than just v (where v is a variable name).
(3) Store L, just as before.

Using the Y register, this would be

```
LDY   J
LDA   T, Y
STA   L
```

The instruction LDA T,Y loads the A register with the quantity whose address is $0858 + k$, where k is in the Y register. We have seen that this is the address of T(J) in this case. In general, LDA T, Y *adds the address of T to the* (unsigned) *contents of Y* and gets an address called the *effective address;* and then the number in the cell with *that* address is loaded into the A register. Using the X register, which is the other index register (hence the name "X register"), we could set T(J) = L by writing

```
LDX   J
LDA   L
STA   T, X
```

*This is, of course, the *hexadecimal* address 0858 plus the *decimal* number 10.

The instructions LDX v, Y and LDY v, X (but *not* LDX v, X or LDY v, Y) may also be used, where v is any array name. However, STX and STY *may not* be used with the forms v, X or v, Y (except in a special case which we will take up in section 74).

The instructions which we have studied so far may be divided into five classes, with examples as follows:

LDA	Q, X	Indexing by register X
LDA	Q, Y	Indexing by register Y
LDA	Q	No indexing
LDA	#n	Constant
INX		No address or constant

These five are examples of *addressing modes*. There are many further addressing modes on the 6502, which are explained in Table 8 in the Appendix. Not every addressing mode can be used with every instruction; Table 4 in the Appendix shows which addressing modes can be used with which instructions.

The mnemonic code and the addressing mode, taken together, determine the machine language operation code. Thus, for example, if T is at address 0890, then we have the following correspondences between assembly language and machine language:

STA	T	8D 90 08
STA	T, X	9D 90 08
STA	T, Y	99 90 08

Note that the address, in the machine language form, does not change—only the operation code. (Also see Table 4 in the Appendix.)

The fact that the X and Y registers can contain only numbers from 0 to 255 (because each of them is eight bits long) means that *most arrays on the 6502 cannot have more than 256 bytes apiece.* Any array longer than that is a *long array*; processing of long arrays will be deferred to section 77.

EXERCISES

1. Give an assembly language form of each of the following BASIC statements (omit ORG, END, and DFS). Remember to treat constant subscripts and variable subscripts in different ways, as indicated in this section. (A constant subscript can, theoretically, be treated as a special case of a variable subscript; but you will use an extra instruction this way each time, and it is not recommended.)

   (a) I = T(K)
*(b) T(6) = J
   (c) T(N) = T(7)

2. Give a BASIC statement which corresponds to each of the following sequences of assembly language statements:

   *(a)
LDX	J
LDA	T, X
STA	U, X

    (b)
LDA	T + ! 1
STA	N

   *(c)
LDX	M
DEC	U, X

3. Give a *machine language* program corresponding to the BASIC statement T(5) = 16, assuming that T is as in Figure 9 and the program starts at address 08A8. Use the A register; use as few instructions as possible.

14. THE NUMBER SYSTEM WITH BASE 256

We have learned to work with the binary number system (base 2) and the hexa-decimal system (base 16), as well as the decimal system (base 10). The *octal* system (base 8) is also in use, but it is not needed for our purposes. There is one other number system of concern to us, having the base 256.

Of course, we do not propose to write 256 different characters for the digits of this system; no computer keyboard has that many characters. Instead, we consider *two hexadecimal digits*, taken together, as if they were a single digit in the system with base 256.

Adding and subtracting numbers of more than one digit is the same in this system as in the decimal system, with 256 in place of 10. We have seen that this is a property of all number systems with bases. Let us first consider addition. In section 5 we added two four-digit numbers in hexadecimal:

$$
\begin{array}{r}
B785 \\
+\ 2C84 \\
\hline
E409
\end{array}
$$

Let us add these same two numbers, as *two-digit* numbers in the system with base 256:

$$
\begin{array}{r}
(B7)\ (85) \\
+\ (2C)\ (84) \\
\hline
(E4)\ (09)
\end{array}
$$

The digit (85) plus the digit (84) is the two-digit number (01) (09); so we bring down the (09) and carry the 1. The digit (B7) plus the digit (2C), *plus one*, is now the digit (E4).

In section 5, we also subtracted two four-digit hexadecimal numbers:

$$
\begin{array}{r}
834E \\
-\ 2E5A \\
\hline
54F4
\end{array}
$$

Subtracting these as two-digit numbers in the system with base 256, we obtain:

$$
\begin{array}{r}
(83)\ (4E) \\
-\ \underline{(2E)\ (5A)} \\
(54)\ (F4)
\end{array}
$$

In the first subtraction, we have to borrow 1. The two-digit number (01) (4E), minus the digit (5A), is the digit (F4). In the second subtraction, the digit (83) minus the digit (2E), *minus one*, is the digit (54).

The system with base 256 is important because *each digit corresponds to a byte*. Suppose that we have two 16-bit numbers, or two-byte numbers, to *add*, as follows:

$$
\begin{array}{r}
ab \\
+\ \underline{cd} \\
ef
\end{array}
$$

where *a, b, c, d, e,* and *f* are digits in the system with base 256. Then we proceed as follows:

(1) Add *b* and *d* to get *f*, and note the carry.
(2) Add *a* and *c* and the carry, if any, to get *e*.

Subtraction is done similarly. If we are subtracting

$$
\begin{array}{r}
ab \\
-\ \underline{cd} \\
ef
\end{array}
$$

then the procedure is:

(1) Subtract *d* from *b* to get *f*, and note whether we have to borrow 1.
(2) Subtract *c* from *a*, and then subtract one more if we borrowed 1, to get *e*.

EXERCISES

1. Perform the following two-digit operations in the number system with base 256:

*(a) (5A) (C3)   (b) (A2) (38)
      +(3A) (2F)   −(45) (1E)

(Remember that, for example, (5A) (C3) and 5AC3 are quite different; one is a two-digit number, and one is a four-digit number.)

*2. Suppose that we have two 24-bit (or three-byte) numbers to add, as follows:

$$
\begin{array}{r}
\text{abc} \\
+\underline{\text{def}} \\
\text{ghi}
\end{array}
$$

What is the procedure to add these numbers?

3. Suppose that we have two 32-bit (or four-byte) numbers to subtract, as follows:

$$
\begin{array}{r}
\text{abcd} \\
-\underline{\text{efgh}} \\
\text{ijkl}
\end{array}
$$

What is the procedure to subtract these numbers?

15. ADDITION ON THE 6502

We will now learn how to add both 8-bit and 16-bit numbers on the 6502. On this computer, 8-bit addition must be treated as a special case of 16-bit addition.

We saw that the X and Y registers are called *index registers* (hence the name "X register"). The A register is called an *accumulator* (hence the name "A register"). It is where a sum accumulates, or builds up. On the 6502, *adding can be done only in the A register* (except for the special case of adding 1, which we treated in section 9).

Most computers have an "add Q" instruction which adds Q to the accumulator. If we want to set $L = J+K$, for example, the procedure is:

(1) *Load* J (put J in the accumulator).
(2) *Add* K (so that $J+K$ is now in the accumulator).
(3) *Store* L (so that the new value of L is $J+K$).

Now suppose that J, K, and L are 16-bit numbers, stored in two bytes each, with the bytes reversed as before. Following the procedure of the last section, we would add them as follows:

(1) *Load* J (the lower half).
(2) *Add* K (the lower half, and note the carry).
(3) *Store* L (the lower half).
(4) *Load* J +!1 (the upper half).
(5) *Add* K+!1 *and add one more if there was carry before* (this is known as *add with carry*, for short).
(6) *Store* L+!1 (the upper half).

On the 6502, the carry is kept in a *one-bit* register called the *carry status flag*. Like the A, X, and Y registers, the carry status flag can be loaded with a constant—either zero or one. Loading a zero is called *clearing*, and there is an instruction, CLC (Clear Carry), which loads zero into the carry flag. (In the same way, LDA #!0 is often referred to as clearing the A register; if this is followed by STA Q then Q is said to be cleared.*) Loading 1 (into a one-bit register) is called *setting* the register, and there is an instruction, SEC (Set Carry), which loads 1 into the carry flag.

The "add with carry" instruction on the 6502 is ADC. It adds to the A register; it also adds the number in the carry flag (either zero or one). If the result is less than 256, it *clears* the carry flag; otherwise, it *sets* the carry flag. In particular, the instruction ADC K+!1 performs step (5) above; it adds the upper half of K, and also adds the carry if the carry flag is 1.

The ADC instruction is *the only add instruction on the 6502* (except, as we have noted, for the special case of adding 1). In order to add *without* carry (such as in step (2) above), we first clear the carry, using CLC. Then we "add with carry"; but the carry flag is zero, so the ADC adds zero, which does nothing.

The entire 16-bit addition program is therefore:

```
LDA    J
CLC
ADC    K
STA    L
LDA    J+!1
ADC    K+!1
STA    L+!1
```

The *ordinary* (8-bit) addition, L = J+K, is then just the first four instructions above:

```
LDA    J
CLC
ADC    K
STA    L
```

Suppose now that we want to add *three* unsigned 8-bit numbers, say I, J, and K. We load I, clear the carry, and add J. Now the carry should be clear, so we don't have to clear it again before we add K. (If the carry is not clear, then I+J ≥ 256, so that the answer will be wrong anyway.) Thus the program to set L = I+J+K is

```
LDA    I
CLC
ADC    J
ADC    K
STA    L
```

---

*In the study of hardware, *clearing* is often referred to as *resetting*.

Just as we can load a constant, we can add a constant. If we want to set L = J+20, we can do this by

```
LDA    J
CLC
ADC    #!20
STA    L
```

An instruction like ADC is often spoken of as producing a *nine-bit result*, in the eight bits of the A register *preceded* by the carry flag. Thus C0+C0 = 180 (hexadecimal), and adding C0 and C0, with ADC, will produce 1 in the carry flag and 80 (hexadecimal) in the A register. In general, if the result of adding is k, and if $k \geq 256$, then ADC will leave $k-256$ in the A register (and the carry flag set to 1).

EXERCISES

1. Give an assembly language form of each of the following BASIC statements (omit ORG, END, and DFS):

   *(a) J = K5+K6
    (b) S = T(1)+T(2)+T(3)
   *(c) T(J) = U(J)+5

   (Note: In this and all similar exercises, assume that all variables in the given BASIC statements are 8-bit quantities, unless otherwise specified.)

2. Give a BASIC statement which corresponds to each of the following sequences of assembly language statements:

   (a)
   ```
   LDA    K
   LDX    J
   CLC
   ADC    T,X
   STA    T,X
   ```

   *(b)
   ```
   LDA    N1
   CLC
   ADC    #$20
   STA    W
   ```

   (c)
   ```
   LDA    #!20
   LDY    S
   CLC
   ADC    P4,Y
   ADC    P5
   STA    B
   ```

*3. Write an assembly language program (omitting ORG, END, and DFS) to
     add two 24-bit quantities V1 and V2, to produce the 24-bit quantity V3.
     Assume that the three bytes of V1 are kept in memory with the rightmost
     first, and similarly for V2 and V3.

16. THE RELATION BETWEEN CARRYING AND BORROWING

The carry status flag is also used as a *borrow* status flag, for subtraction. In order to understand how borrowing works on the 6502, we have to know the relation between carry and borrow.

When do we want to borrow, when subtracting the digit b from the digit a? We want to borrow when b is larger than a (or $a < b$), so that, if we subtracted b from a, the answer would be negative.

Now suppose that, instead of treating $a - b$ as a subtraction, we treat it as an addition of the negative of b, that is, $a + (-b)$. Like any addition, this addition may produce carry. When does it do so?

Remember that the negative number $-b$ is $256 - b$ in twos' complement form. When we add, $a + (-b)$, we are really adding $a + 256 - b$. This produces carry when the answer is too large to fit into a byte. That is, the answer is greater than 255; or, to put it another way, it is greater than or equal to 256. So the condition under which we have carry is

$$a + 256 - b \geq 256$$

Cancelling 256 from both sides, we get

$$a - b \geq 0$$

or, in other words,

$$a \geq b$$

We now note a peculiar fact: this is exactly the condition in which there is *no* borrow, when we subtract b from a. This is the basic relation between carry and borrow: *borrow is the complement of carry*. If the addition $a + (-b)$ produces carry, the *subtraction, $a - b$,* does *not* produce borrow; and vice versa.

The main reason that we need to know this is in order to understand the instruction SBC (Subtract With Carry). Like ADC, SBC operates on the A register; and, on the 6502, *subtraction, like addition, can only be done in the A register* (except for the special case of subtracting 1).

Just as ADC Q adds Q to the A register, SBC Q subtracts Q from the A register. It does this by adding −Q to the A register; this is done to simplify the hardware of the 6502. The carry from this addition is placed in the carry status flag.

The instruction ADC Q adds an extra 1 if the carry flag was set (equal to 1). The instruction SBC Q subtracts an extra 1 if the carry flag was *clear* (equal to 0), because this is when borrow *does* take place.

We could also say that ADC Q adds *the number* (0 or 1) *in the carry status flag*. In the same way, SBC Q subtracts the *complement* of the number in the carry status flag.

Note, by the way, that the increment and decrement instructions (INC, DEC, INX, DEX, INY, DEY) *do not affect the carry status flag*. Thus, even if the X register contains 255, adding 1 to this, with INX, does not set the carry, although adding 1 to the A register, with CLC and ADC #!1, would set the carry if the A register contained 255.

Likewise, *loading and storing do not affect the carry status flag*. Thus, for example, in any of the instruction sequences of the preceding section, we could interchange the first two instructions, putting CLC before LDA, because the LDA does not change the carry flag (and thus leaves it clear).

Let us now consider some examples of addition and subtraction, with attendant carry flag settings:

(1) A = 3, carry = 0, ADC #!5. The result in the A register is 8 (=3 + 5); the carry flag remains zero (the result is less than 256).

(2) A = 5, carry = 1, ADC #!10. The result is 16 (= 5 + 10, plus 1 for the carry). The carry flag is set to zero.

(3) A = 200, carry = 0, ADC #!200. The result is 144 (that is, 200 + 200 − 256). The carry flag is set to one, because 200 + 200 is greater than 255.

(4) A = 255, carry = 1, ADC #!0. The result is zero (255 + 0, plus 1 for the carry, minus 256). The carry flag remains one because the original result (255 + 0 + 1) is larger than 255.

(5) A = 9, carry = 1, SBC #!3. The result in the A register is 6 (= 9 − 3); the carry flag remains 1 (there is no borrow status—the result is not less than zero).

(6) A = 10, carry = 1, SBC #!20. The result is 246 (= 10 − 20 + 256); the carry flag is set to zero (borrow status; 10 − 20 is less than zero).

(7) A = 15, carry = 0, SBC #!5. The result is 9 (15 − 5, minus one more for the borrow status, since the carry is zero). The carry flag is set to 1.

(8) A = 30, carry = 0, SBC #!30. The result is 255 (30 − 30, minus one more for the borrow, plus 256); the carry remains zero.

We may note that SBC, when it borrows, always borrows 256; that is, it subtracts $(256 + p) - q$ if the given subtraction of $p - q$ would produce a negative result. Likewise, if the result of addition is greater than 255, then ADC "brings down" a quantity equal to that result minus 256.

EXERCISES

1. In each of the following three cases, does the given subtraction produce borrow? Why or why not?

   *(a) $4 - 3$
   *(b) $4 - 4$
   *(c) $4 - 5$

2. In each of the three cases above, express the subtraction as an addition of the negative of the second quantity, expressed in a single byte in twos' complement form. Does this addition produce carry? Why or why not?

3. *(a) Suppose that the A register contains 5, and the carry flag is clear. What result is left in the A register after the instruction SBC #!3 is performed? Will the carry flag be cleared or set?
   (b) Answer both questions in part (a) above if the carry flag was set, rather than clear, before SBC #!3 was performed.

17. SUBTRACTION ON THE 6502

As with addition, we will consider subtraction for both 8-bit and 16-bit numbers. Suppose we want to set $L = J - K$, where these are all 8-bit quantities. The procedure is:

(1) *Load* J (put J in the accumulator).
(2) *Subtract* K (so that $J - K$ is now in the accumulator).
(3) *Store* L (so that the new value of L is $J - K$).

If J, K, and L are 16-bit numbers, stored in two bytes each with the bytes reversed, then we would do the same subtraction as follows, using the procedure of section 14:

(1) *Load* J (the lower half).
(2) *Subtract* K (the lower half, and compute the carry, as indicated in the preceding section, to show the borrow status).
(3) *Store* L (the lower half).
(4) *Load* J+!1 (the upper half).
(5) *Subtract* K+!1 *and subtract one more if there was borrow before* (in other words, subtract K+!1 with carry).
(6) *Store* L+!1 (the upper half).

The instruction SBC K+!1 performs step (5) above. It subtracts the upper half of K from the A register, and subtracts one more if the carry was *clear* (indicating a borrow status). If the answer is negative, SBC *clears* the carry; otherwise, SBC sets the carry.

The SBC instruction is *the only subtract instruction on the 6502* (except for the special case of subtracting 1). In order to subtract *without* borrow (such as in step (2) above), we must first *set* the carry, using SEC. (Always remember to *clear* the carry before addition without carry, and *set* the carry before subtraction without carry.) The entire 16-bit subtraction program is therefore:

```
LDA   J
SEC
SBC   K
STA   L
```

54

```
LDA    J+!1
SBC    K+!1
STA    L+!1
```

The ordinary 8-bit subtraction, L = J−K, is then just the first four instructions above:

```
LDA    J
SEC
SBC    K
STA    L
```

We may also subtract constants; if we want to set L = J−20, we can do this by

```
LDA    J
SEC
SBC    #!20
STA    L
```

To set L = −J, we would set L = 0−J, which is the same thing:

```
LDA    #!0
SEC
SBC    J
STA    L
```

Note that SEC, like CLC, can be placed first in any sequence like these, since LDA does not change the carry flag (and therefore leaves it set, in this case).

Just as we can calculate I+J+K without clearing the carry after adding J, so we can calculate I−J−K without *setting* the carry after *subtracting* J. If I−J is non-negative, the carry will be set anyway. In fact, if I−J is positive, we can calculate I−J+K in a strange way: by loading I, *clearing* the carry (!), subtracting J, and then adding K *without* clearing the carry. This actually subtracts J+1 and then adds K+1, so that the answer comes out right. In the same way, if I+J is less than 255, we can calculate I + J − K by loading I, *setting* the carry, adding J, and subtracting K without setting the carry (actually, I+(J+1) − (K+1) is calculated).

EXERCISES

1. Give an assembly language form of each of the following BASIC statements (omit ORG, END, and DFS):

   (a) T = P3 − P4
   *(b) S9 = P+9−R(L)
   (c) U = −V(8)

2. Give a BASIC statement which corresponds to each of the following
    sequences of assembly language statements:

*(a)

```
LDX   J
LDA   T, X
SEC
SBC   T+!3
STA   H
```

(b)

```
LDA   N
SEC
SBC   M+!5
STA   L
DEC   L
```

*(c)

```
LDA   #$A0
LDX   I
CLC
ADC   T, X
SEC
SBC   U, X
STA   U, X
```

3. Write an assembly language program (omitting ORG, END, and DFS) to
    subtract two 32-bit quantities XA and XB, to produce the 32-bit quantity
    XC. Assume that the four bytes of XA are kept in memory with the right-
    most first, and similarly for XB and XC.

18. TRANSFER INSTRUCTIONS AND COMMENTS

We have learned that numbers cannot be moved directly from one cell to another on the 6502. We can move a number from a cell to a register (loading), or from a register to a cell (storing). We can also move a number from one register to another. On the 6502, this is done by means of a *transfer instruction*.

The most important transfer instructions on the 6502 are:

TAX	Transfer from A to X
TAY	Transfer from A to Y
TXA	Transfer from X to A
TYA	Transfer from Y to A

Note that we cannot transfer directly from X to Y, or from Y to X.

Transfer instructions are often used when we are loading two registers with the same constant. Instead of writing

```
LDA    # ! 1
LDY    # ! 1
```

(for example), we can write

```
LDA    # ! 1
TAY
```

We saw in section 10 that an instruction consisting of only a mnemonic, such as TAY, has a one-byte instruction code, whereas LDA #!1 and LDY #!1 have two-byte instruction codes. Hence we are saving space by using only three bytes instead of four.

Sometimes we must move data from one register to another because of differences in what the registers do. To set L = T(J+K), for example, we write

```
LDA    J
CLC
ADC    K
TAX
LDA    T , X
STA    L
```

Note that we must calculate J+K in the A register (clearing the carry, as noted in section 15), and then the result must go into an index register (X in this case) in order to be used in the indexed instruction (LDA T,X).

We may note that TXA cannot be replaced by

LDA   X

To see why, consider the machine language form. When we write LDA Q we put the address of Q in the second and third bytes of its machine language form; but there is no address of X, because only cells have addresses, and X is not a cell, but rather a register. (The instruction LDA X is accepted by the APPLE assembler, but this refers to a *variable* called X, not to the X register.)

When we transfer data from one register to another, this does not change what is in the first register; the same number will be in both registers after the transfer. Transfer instructions are like load and store instructions in this respect.

Any assembly language instruction may be accompanied by a *comment*, which starts with a blank followed by a semicolon. Thus the program above could have been written as

```
LDA   J    ;  PUT J IN THE A REGISTER
CLC        ;  ADD K, PRODUCING J+K IN
ADC   K    ;    THE A REGISTER (CLC FIRST)
TAX        ;  PUT J+K IN THE X REGISTER
LDA   T,X  ;  SO WE CAN GET T(J+K) AND
STA   L    ;    STORE IT IN L
```

(The blank *after* the semicolon is not required.) An entire line may also *start* with a semicolon, in which case it is a comment.

Comments in assembly language are like comments in BASIC; they are there for you to tell yourself (or to tell the person who will maintain the program) what you were doing. Assembly language is harder to understand than BASIC, however, and for this reason it is recommended that *every statement be accompanied by a comment, as above.*

EXERCISES

1. Give an assembly language form of each of the following BASIC statements (omit ORG, END, and DFS):

   *(a) P1(I+J) = 5
   (b) K = T4(I−M)
   *(c) J = N(N(J))

2. Give a BASIC statement which corresponds to each of the following sequences of assembly language statements:

    (a)
    ```
    LDA    J
    TAX
    STA    T, X
    ```

    *(b)
    ```
    LDY    V
    INY
    TYA
    CLC
    ADC    U
    STA    W
    ```

    (c)
    ```
    LDA    T+!3
    CLC
    ADC    T+!4
    TAX
    LDA    T, X
    STA    R
    ```

3. Two programs are *equivalent* if they do the same calculation. For example, the following two programs are equivalent:

    ```
    LDA    M          LDA    M
    SEC               CLC
    SBC    #!8        ADC    #$F8
    STA    N          STA    N
    ```

    since they both set N = M−8 (−8 being hexadecimal F8). In each case below, construct a program which is equivalent, in this sense, to the given program, but shorter (fewer instruction code bytes; this is often called *improving* the program):

    *(a)
    ```
    LDA    C
    LDY    C
    STA    U, Y
    ```

    (b)
    ```
    LDX    #!5
    LDA    T, X
    TAX
    ```

    *(c)
    ```
    LDX    V
    INX
    STX    V
    ```

19. BRANCHING AND LABELS

A *branch instruction* on the 6502 is an instruction which goes to, or *branches to*, some place in the program if some condition is true. It is like IF *b* THEN *n* in BASIC, for some condition *b* and some line number *n*. This statement goes to line number *n* if *b* is true; otherwise, it goes to the next line number in sequence.

There are two branch instructions on the 6502 which have to do with the carry status flag. They are:

BCC L	Branch to L if carry is clear
BCS L	Branch to L if carry is set

Here BCC means "branch on carry clear" and BCS means "branch on carry set."

In assembly language, unlike BASIC, *there are no line numbers*. There are *statement labels*, which act something like line numbers, but with two important differences. First, *not every statement has a label*. In BASIC, every statement, or group of statements, has a line number, but in assembly language the only statements which have labels are normally those that need labels—that is, those with branches (or the like) that go to them.

The other difference is that *labels are not numbers*. They can be letters, such as L; but they can also be more general than that. The rules, in LISA, for labels are:

(1) A label must start with an (upper case) letter.
(2) A label can contain just one letter, or any number of characters up to (and no more than) six (LISA 1.5) or eight (LISA 2.5).*
(3) The other characters in a label may include letters, digits, and certain special characters (as discussed further below).

---

*In LISA 1.5, longer labels are *not* marked as errors, but only their first six characters are used. This feature of LISA is not recommended because it can lead to confusion; thus MULTIPLICAND and MULTIPLIER are considered to be *the same label* (MULTIP).

Thus you have a wide range of labels to use. Here are some:

I	HEAT	DOG	HAND	LOVE	C6502
J	LENGTH	CAT	FOOT	HATE	C6502A
W	START	HIPPO	NOSE	ENVY	A2B3C4
Z	NEXT	RHINO	EAR	PRIDE	DARN
B2	LAST	BOSTON	CARTER	GOGOGO	HECK
H4	DONE	MIAMI	REAGAN	STOPPP	GOSH

LISA 1.5 allows quite a few special characters in labels, but this author does not recommend their use. Such labels as U=V or I*J or even X'$#. " can be used with LISA 1.5, but long programs are usually confusing enough enough already without such complications. (LISA 2.5 allows the special characters . and _ only.)

The same rules apply to *variable names* and *array names* in assembly language programs. A variable name or an array name is just a label. Remember not to use labels with too many characters (like BALTIMORE) or labels that start with digits (like 4SCORE).

Every label starts at the beginning of the line, or, as we say, in *column 1*. If an instruction does not have a label, it starts with at least one space (column 1 must be blank).

The instructions BCC and BCS can be used to check for error conditions. If we wish to go to ERROR if I+J $\geq$ 256, we can do

```
LDA   I       ;   LOAD I
CLC           ;   CLEAR THE CARRY
ADC   J       ;   CALCULATE I+J, BUT IF THIS
BCS   ERROR   ;   IS > 255, INDICATE ERROR
```

This kind of checking for carry is useful when you are adding an unsigned 8-bit quantity R to a 16-bit quantity Q. Of course, we could consider R as a two-byte quantity with its upper half zero; then, when we added the upper halves, we would load the upper half of Q, *add zero* (with carry), and store in the upper half of Q again. However, this is the same as adding 1 to Q if the carry is set, and that takes two instructions instead of three. If our 16-bit quantity is kept in Q and Q + !1, with bytes reversed as usual, the complete sequence will thus be

```
     LDA   Q     ;   ADD THE LOWER HALF OF Q
     CLC         ;     (CLEARING THE CARRY FIRST)
     ADC   R     ;   TO THE 8-BIT NUMBER R
     STA   Q     ;   AND STORE IT BACK
     BCC   Z4    ;   IF CARRY WAS SET, THEN ADD
     INC   Q+!1  ;   1 TO THE UPPER HALF OF Q
Z4   (next instruction)
```

In the same way, if we were subtracting R from Q, we could load the upper half of Q, *subtract* zero (with SBC), and store in Q; but this is the same as subtracting 1 from Q if the carry is *clear* (indicating a borrow status), and again we save one instruction. The complete sequence here is

```
      LDA   Q       ;   SUBTRACT THE 8-BIT NUMBER
      SEC           ;   R (SETTING THE CARRY FIRST)
      SBC   R       ;   FROM THE LOWER HALF OF Q
      STA   Q       ;   AND STORE IT BACK
      BCS   Z7      ;   IF CARRY WAS CLEAR, SUBTRACT
      DEC   Q+!1    ;   1 FROM THE UPPER HALF OF Q
  Z7  (next instruction)
```

EXERCISES

1. Which of the following labels can be used in LISA? For each label that cannot, or should not, be so used, explain why not.

    (a) V
    *(b) CHECKRANGE5
    (c) 6502C
    *(d) CMPUTR
    (e) JPLUSK

2. Give an assembly language form of each of the following BASIC statements, branching to ERROR if any stage of the computation produces an answer greater than 255:

    *(a) M = T1 + T2 + T3
    (b) C = D(I + J)
    *(c) T(K + L) = R + 4

3. What BASIC statement corresponds to the following sequence of assembly language instructions? (Assume that the label TWENTY corresponds to line number 20 in BASIC.)

```
      LDA   J
      SEC
      SBC   K
      BCC   TWENTY
```

20. COMPARING, ZERO STATUS, AND JUMPS

There are many more branch instructions than BCC and BCS. Two of them, BEQ ("branch on equal") and BNE ("branch on not equal"), are often used when we want to *compare* two numbers, as we might do in BASIC by

        IF P = Q THEN 200
        IF P <> Q THEN 200

(remember that $<>$ in BASIC means $\neq$). In order to do this, we use a *compare instruction*, of which there are three on the 6502:

CMP	v	Compare the A register with v
CPX	v	Compare the X register with v
CPY	v	Compare the Y register with v

Thus either of the BASIC statements above would be done as follows:

(1) Load P into a register.
(2) Compare that register with Q.
(3) Branch on equal (or branch on not equal).

If the label L200 corresponds to line number 200, this would be

        LDA P   LDX P   LDY P
        CMP Q   *or*   CPX Q   *or*   CPY Q
        BEQ L200   BEQ L200   BEQ L200

for the first statement above.

Each compare instruction does a subtraction, in this case P minus Q.* However, the result of the subtraction does *not* go back into the register, as is the case with SBC. It is used for comparison purposes only. If P = Q, then P − Q = 0; and this is what a compare instruction tests (among other things).

---

*The subtraction is always done *without* borrow, whether the carry is clear or set. Thus we never need to do an SEC before a compare instruction, as we normally do before SBC.

If the result of the subtraction is zero, then the compare instruction sets a flag, called the *zero status flag*. This is another one-bit flag, like the carry status flag. If the result of the subtraction is not zero, then the compare instruction *clears* the zero status flag.

The instructions BEQ and BNE then test the zero status flag that has just been set or cleared. Specifically, we have:

> BEQ L   Branch to L on equal (zero status flag set)
>
> BNE L   Branch to L on not equal (zero status flag clear)

Note that the zero flag is equal to *zero* (that is, clear) if the result of the compare is *unequal* to zero.

We can compare to a *constant*; thus, if the condition is P = 3 instead of P = Q, we could write

```
LDA  P              LDX  P              LDY  P
CMP  #!3     or     CPX  #!3     or     CPY  #!3
BEQ  L200           BEQ  L200           BEQ  L200
```

We can also compare the A register (but not X or Y) to a subscripted variable, using an index. Thus

```
LDX    J        ; SET UP THE INDEX J
LDA    T,X      ; LOAD T(J) AND COMPARE
CMP    U,X      ;  IT WITH U(J), AND GO
BNE    DIFFER   ;  TO DIFFER IF UNEQUAL
```

goes to DIFFER if T(J) $\neq$ U(J). Note the semicolons in this example which are not followed by blanks; as we have noted, this is allowed by LISA.

The branch instructions on the 6502 are *conditional*; they branch only when some condition holds. There are also *jump* instructions, which are like branch instructions except that they are *unconditional*; they *always* go to a certain place. The main jump instruction is JMP α (Jump to α), which always goes to the label α; it is like GO TO α in BASIC or FORTRAN.*

A very common error made by beginners is to write an instruction which branches to ALPHA (say), *followed immediately by the label* ALPHA. A sequence like

> BCC   ALPHA
>
> ALPHA   (next instruction)

is always wrong. (Think about it a minute. If the carry is *clear*, you branch to ALPHA. Otherwise, you don't branch; so you do the next instruction after the

---

*We may note that the distinction between the terms "branch" and "jump" is peculiar to the 6502; other computers may use these terms in different ways.

BCC, which is ALPHA. In other words, you go to ALPHA whether the carry is clear or not!) Whenever you have a conditional branch in your program, make sure to put something, immediately following it, which expresses what your program does if it does *not* branch; that is, if the condition is false.

EXERCISES

1. Give an assembly language form of each of the following BASIC statements (using the label TWENTY to stand for line number 20):

   *(a) IF B+C=D THEN 20
    (b) IF T(J) +1<>R THEN 20
   *(c) IF C−T(6) =3 THEN 20

2. Give a BASIC statement which corresponds to each of the following sequences of assembly language statements (using the line number 20 to stand for the label TWENTY):

   (a)
   ```
           LDA     W
           SEC
           SBC     W1
           CMP     # ! 4
           BNE     TWENTY
   ```

   *(b)
   ```
           LDY     R
           DEY
           CPY     S
           BEQ     TWENTY
   ```

   (c)
   ```
           LDA     J
           CLC
           ADC     K
           TAX
           LDA     L
           CMP     T, X
           BNE     TWENTY
   ```

*3. What is wrong with the following assembly language code to compare W with T(J)?

   ```
           LDY     J
           LDX     W
           CPX     T, Y
           BEQ     TWENTY
   ```

21. LOOPS

The zero status flag is very often used in *loops* on the 6502. In BASIC, a loop is usually done with a FOR statement, such as

```
FOR J = 1 TO N
(statements in the loop)
NEXT J
```

In machine language and assembly language, there are no FOR statements, or their equivalent; we have to use other statements instead. We can use other statements even in BASIC; for example, we could write the above loop as

```
10    J = 1
20    (statements in the loop)
30    J = J+1
40    IF J <= N THEN 20
```

We can do something like this* on the 6502, but the test at line 40 ($J <= N$) is not as easy, on the 6502, as a test for an equal or an unequal condition. Note that

```
10    J = 1
20    (statements in the loop)
30    J = J+1
40    IF J <> N THEN 20
```

would not be correct, in this case; the loop would be done only $N - 1$ times, not N times. The last time through the loop, J would be equal to $N - 1$; then J is set to N at statement 30, which means that statement 40 does not go back to the start of the loop.

---

*If you have not had loops like this in your study of BASIC, go through the loop above and make sure you understand why it does the same thing as the FOR loop above it.

There are several ways to fix this problem. One is to test against N+1, rather than N:

```
10    J = 1
20    (statements in the loop)
30    J = J+1
40    IF J <> N+1 THEN 20
```

On the 6502, this is also a bit harder, unless N is a constant. Another way of fixing the problem is to move J = J+1 up to the beginning:

```
10    J = 0
20    J = J+1
30    (statements in the loop)
40    IF J <> N THEN 20
```

Note that this time we have to start with $J = 0$ instead of $J = 1$, because $J = J+1$ adds 1 to 0, the first time through the loop.

This is how loops on the 6502 are quite often done. Let us keep the value of J in the X register, rather than in a cell in memory called J (this is called *register assignment*; we are assigning the variable J to the X register). If the statements in the loop consist of the single statement $T(J) = 0$, we can now write

```
         LDX    #!0    ;   SET J = 0
         TXA           ;   SET A-REGISTER TO ZERO
LOOP     INX           ;   SET J = J+1
         STA    T,X    ;   SET T(J) = 0
         CPX    N      ;   COMPARE J WITH N
         BNE    LOOP   ;   IF UNEQUAL, GO BACK
```

As we noted in the preceding section, the CPX will set the zero status flag if $J - N = 0$ (that is, $J = N$), and will clear this flag if $J \neq N$. The BNE will then branch if the flag is clear—in other words, if $J \neq N$, which is what we want.

Register assignment is a very useful assembly language programming technique. Note, in particular, that the A register is also assigned, in this loop; it is given the constant value of zero. In this way, we do not have to reload it with zero every time we set a new $T(J)$ equal to zero, and this saves us some time. Of course, the loop above must be accompanied by a data section containing N DFS !1 and T DFS n (for some n), at least.

Always remember, when working with expressions such as Q,X or Q,Y in instructions on the 6502, that it is not permitted to write Q,J or Q,N or the like— the array name (such as Q) can only be followed by the name of the index register (X or Y). Also, *do not treat a constant subscript as if it were a variable subscript.* To load the A register with T(6), do an LDA T + !6 (and do *not* do an LDX #!6 and then an LDA T,X—this will work but it takes extra time, an extra instruction, and a register that might be used for something else). Note that if you try to treat a *variable* subscript as a *constant* subscript—if you write LDA T + N or the like—this will be wrong, not just inefficient. (LDA T + N adds the *address* of N to T, not its value.)

EXERCISES

1. Write a FOR loop* in BASIC which corresponds to each of the following assembly language programs. In each case, denote the contents of the X register by J in the BASIC program.

    (a)
    ```
              LDX    # ! 0
    LOOP      INX
              LDA    T, X
              STA    U, X
              CPX    L
              BNE    LOOP
    ```

    *(b)
    ```
              LDX    # ! 0
              LDA    W
    TR54      INX
              CMP    V, X
              BEQ    EIGHTY
              CPX    # ! 100
              BNE    TR54
    ```

    (Use the line number 80 to stand for the label EIGHTY.)

    (c)
    ```
              LDX    M
              DEX
              LDA    # ! 0
              CLC
    ADD       INX
              ADC    T, X
              CPX    N
              BNE    ADD
    ```

    (Denote the contents of the A register by S, and put the statement S = 0 immediately preceding the FOR loop.)

2. Write an assembly language program which corresponds to each of the following FOR loops in BASIC.

    *(a)
    ```
         FOR J = 1 TO M
         T(J) = J
         NEXT J
    ```

---

*Make sure that each of your loops has a FOR statement in it.

(Remember that STX T,X is not a 6502 instruction.)

(b)
```
K = 0
FOR M = 1 TO 50
IF T(M) = W THEN K = K+1
NEXT M
```

(Keep W in the A register throughout the loop. Test whether T(M) = W, and, if they are *not* equal, branch ahead to LOOP2.* If they *are* equal, you will do the next instruction.)

*(c)
```
FOR I = 1 TO K+1
T(I) = T(I) −1
NEXT I
```

(Use a new variable, KP1, whose value is K+1. Make sure that your program does *not* change the value of K; that would be an unwanted side effect.)

3. Write an assembly language program which stores zero in T(2), T(4), T(6), and so on up through T(100).

---

*The instruction IF T(M) = W THEN K = K +1 is not available in some varieties of BASIC. It is equivalent to a sequence such as

```
10 IF T(M) <> W THEN 30
20 K = K+1
30 (next instruction)
```

22. MORE ON LOOPS AND ZERO STATUS

The real power of the zero status flàg is that it is set and cleared by many instructions other than compare instructions. These include:

> Load—LDA, LDX, LDY
> Increment—INC, INX, INY
> Decrement—DEC, DEX, DEY
> Add—ADC
> Subtract—SBC
> Transfer—TAX, TAY, TXA, TYA

and many others that we will see later.

In each case the 6502 tests the *result* of the operation. If this is zero, the zero flag is set. Otherwise, the zero flag is cleared.

Thus we can go to NON if Q is not zero by

```
LDA Q          LDX Q          LDY Q
        or             or
BNE NON        BNE NON        BNE NON
```

Whichever register (A, X, or Y) we load, the zero flag will be set if the result is zero and cleared if it is nonzero. Thus the BNE will branch if, and only if, Q is nonzero.

If we want to set $Q = R - S$ and then go to NON if Q is not zero, we can write

```
LDA   R     ;   LOAD R
SEC         ;   REMEMBER TO SET THE CARRY
SBC   S     ;     BEFORE SUBTRACTING S
STA   Q     ;   STORE (DOES NOT CHANGE FLAGS)
BNE   NON   ;   IF NONZERO, GO TO NON
```

Be careful here: the zero status flag is *not* set by the STA instruction (or by STX or STY). These instructions *do not affect* the zero status flag at all.* The flag is

---

*See Table 3, in the Appendix, to check which instructions set the zero status flag. (They are those containing a Z in the "Flags" column.)

set by the SBC instruction; if the result of subtraction is zero (that is, $Q = 0$), the flag is set. Otherwise, the flag is cleared (and we go to NON).

A very common use of BNE is after a *decrement* instruction at the end of a loop. In fact, the most common kind of loop on the 6502 proceeds as follows:

(1) Load a register (usually X or Y) with the number of times the loop is to be done.
(2) Do a single calculation of the loop.
(3) Decrement the register (usually DEX or DEY).
(4) If the result is nonzero, go back to step 2.

Instead of X or Y, we could also use a cell in memory. If this is called COUNT, then we decrement it in step 3, using DEC COUNT, and store its initial value in step 1. We would not normally use the A register for this purpose, since there is no way to decrement that register (other than SEC followed by SBC #!1).

Of course, this kind of a loop is done "from back to front." Since the index register starts at N (where N is the count), we do the N-th calculation first. For example, suppose we are setting T(1) through T(N) to zero; again keeping the value of J in the X register, as in the preceding section, we can write

```
        LDX    N       ;   SET J  = N
        LDA    #!0     ;   SET A-REGISTER TO ZERO
LOOP    STA    T,X     ;   SET T(J)  = 0
        DEX            ;   SET J  = J-1
        BNE    LOOP    ;   IF J NOT ZERO,  GO BACK
```

This will set T(N) equal to zero, then T(N−1), and so on. Note that T(0) is *not* set equal to zero. The last time through the loop, X will be 1, and T(1) is set to zero; then X is decreased by 1; and then, since X is now zero, we do not go back to LOOP, but go on instead to the next instruction (this is sometimes called "falling through"). As before, N DFS !1 and T DFS *n* must appear in the data section of this program.

It is generally true, on any computer, that *checking to see if a variable is zero is faster than checking to see whether it is equal to any nonzero quantity.* In the loop above, we are testing for zero, and the loop itself contains only three instructions—STA, DEX, and BNE. In the assembly language loop of the preceding section we were testing for equal to N, and there were *four* instructions in the loop—INX, STA, CPX, and BNE. Three instructions, *done N times,* are a lot faster than four instructions, done N times, especially when N is large.

This general rule should affect your appreciation of other programming languages. In BASIC or FORTRAN, for example, if you have a variable which is either zero or one and you want to check whether it is equal to 1, check instead whether it is *unequal* to zero. When your program is translated into machine language by a compiler (if a compiler is used), the resulting machine language program should be made slightly faster in this way.

Note, when ending a loop with DEX and BNE, not to put any instructions between DEX and BNE that might affect the zero status flag. Thus, in the sequence DEX-LDY-BNE, the BNE will branch if Y (not X) is zero. In general, it reduces confusion if BEQ or BNE is *immediately* preceded (if at all possible) by the instruction that sets or clears the zero status flag for it.

EXERCISES

*1. Write an assembly language program, without any compare instructions (CMP, CPX, or CPY), which corresponds to the following BASIC program:

```
10 K = 0
20 FOR J = 1 TO N
30 IF T(J) <> 0 THEN 50
40 K = K+1
50 NEXT J
```

Do the assembly language loop from back to front; that is, look at T(N) first, then T(N−1), and so on. Keep K in the Y register, and store it only at the end.

2. Each of the assembly language programs in exercise 1 of the preceding section performs a loop in which the index increases (using INX or INY). Modify the first two of these loops in such a way that the index decreases (using DEX or DEY).

*3. How can the following sequence of instructions be improved (see exercise 3, section 18), and why?
```
DEY
CPY    #!0
BNE    BACK
```

23. OFFSETS

As soon as we start to consider loops in assembly language, we come across problems which arise from the fact that, *in most arrays* T, *the element* T(0) *is left out, since it is never used.* In such an array, the symbol T, in assembly language, stands for the cell that contains T(1).

Figure 10 gives the addresses of ten variables T(1) through T(10), starting at the address 0859. Note that these addresses are the same as they were in Figure 9. However, in Figure 9, the address of T was 0858; here, the address of T is 0859.

In section 13, in order to refer to the element T(6), we used the address expression T+!6 in the instruction. This gave the address $0858+6 = 085E$ (hexadecimal). For an array like that of Figure 10, we would have to use T+!6−!1 (or T+!5). This would give the address $0859+6-1$ (or $0859+5$), which is again 085E.

VARIABLE	ADDRESS	
T(1)	0859	$(= 0859 - 1 + 1)$
T(2)	085A	$(= 0859 - 1 + 2)$
T(3)	085B	$(= 0859 - 1 + 3)$
T(4)	085C	$(= 0859 - 1 + 4)$
T(5)	085D	$(= 0859 - 1 + 5)$
T(6)	085E	$(= 0859 - 1 + 6)$
T(7)	085F	$(= 0859 - 1 + 7)$
T(8)	0860	$(= 0859 - 1 + 8)$
T(9)	0861	$(= 0859 - 1 + 9)$
T(10)	0862	$(= 0859 - 1 + 10)$

Figure 10. Addresses of Elements of an Array T Starting from T(1).

Also in section 13, we used the instruction LDA T,Y to refer to T(J), where J is in register Y. Here we would use LDA T−!1,Y to do the same thing. The address T−!1 is $0859-1$, or 0858, and then the contents of the Y register (that is, J) are added to 0858, just as they were in section 13.

73

The quantity $-!1$ in both of these examples is the *offset*. Whenever an array starts with some T(k) for $k \neq 0$ (here k is 1), then k is the offset and must be subtracted from T in situations like these. The address of T (that is, the address of T(k)), minus k, gives the address where T(0) *would* be kept if there were a T(0) in the array.

Another important use of offsets is in the case where *a subscript contains a constant added to, or subtracted from, a variable or more general expression.* Consider, for example, T($J + 6$). We can load this into the A register by

```
LDA   J      ;   LOAD J AND REMEMBER
CLC          ;     TO CLEAR THE CARRY
ADC   #!6    ;   BEFORE ADDING 6
TAX          ;   PUT J+6 IN THE X REGISTER
LDA   T,X    ;     TO GET T(J+6)
```

but it is simpler to write

```
LDX   J        ;   SET UP INDEX J
LDA   T+!6,X   ;   GET T(J+6)
```

The expression $T+!6$ stands for the address of T, plus 6; and to this the computer adds J (which is in register X). This is exactly the same as adding $J+6$ to the address of T, as is done in the first example above. Likewise, T($J-1$) could be stored from the A register, in an array T starting from T(0), by

```
LDX   J      ;   LOAD J INTO THE X REGISTER
DEX          ;   SUBTRACT 1, PRODUCING J-1
STA   T,X    ;   STORE A IN T(J-1)
```

but it can be done in one fewer instruction by

```
LDX   J        ;   LOAD J INTO THE X REGISTER
STA   T-!1,X   ;   STORE A IN T(J-1)
```

Here, instead of adding $J-1$ to the address of T, we add J to a quantity equal to the address of T minus one, which is the same thing.

As an example of offsets in a loop, we can rewrite the program of section 21 to set T(1) through T(N) to zero, where the array T now starts with T(1), as in Figure 10:

```
        LDX   #!0      ;   SET J = 0
        TXA            ;   SET A-REGISTER TO ZERO
LOOP    INX            ;   SET J = J+1
        STA   T-!1,X   ;   SET T(J) = 0
        CPX   N        ;   COMPARE J WITH N
        BNE   LOOP     ;   IF UNEQUAL, GO BACK
```

Note that the program of section 21 did *not* set T(0), even though the array T, in that program, was assumed to contain an element T(0). If we wanted to set T(0) (thus setting a total of N+1 bytes to zero) in that program, we could merely change the initialization:

```
        LDX   #$FF    ;  SET J = −1  ($FF = −1)
        LDA   #!0     ;  SET A-REGISTER TO ZERO
LOOP    INX           ;  SET J = J+1
        STA   T,X     ;  SET T(J) = 0
        CPX   N       ;  COMPARE J WITH N
        BNE   LOOP    ;  IF UNEQUAL, GO BACK
```

Starting a loop by setting $X = -1$ and then immediately doing an INX (which sets it to zero) is a quite common device, which you will often find uses for. In LISA 2.5 (though not in LISA 1.5) you can replace #$FF by #!−1 (or by #−1) in the LDX instruction. (Note that *hexadecimal* numbers are generally taken to be unsigned.)

As another example, we can replace STA T,X by STA T−!1,X in the second program of section 22, and the resulting program would set *all* N *bytes of the array* T to zero (rather than skipping T(0)). This is useful even when we are not thinking of our array T as being like an array in BASIC.

EXERCISES

*1. Do Exercise 1 of the preceding section under the assumption that the array T starts at T(1) (that is, there is no T(0)).

2. Give a BASIC statement which corresponds to each of the following sequences of assembly language statements. Assume in each case that the array T starts at T(0).

(a)
```
        LDX   K
        LDA   T+!3,X
        STA   T+!4
```

*(b)
```
        LDA   I
        SEC
        SBC   J
        TAY
        LDA   T−!2,Y
        STA   S
```

(c)   LDX   M
                                             LDA   T+!3,X
                                             TAX
                                             LDA   T+!2,X
                                             STA   T,X

3.   Show how each of the following sequences of assembly language statements
     can be improved (see exercise 3, section 18).

     *(a)   LDX   D
                                             INX
                                             LDA   T,X

     (b)   LDY   E
                                             DEY
                                             LDA   T,Y

     *(c)   LDA   N
                                             CLC
                                             ADC   #!10
                                             TAX
                                             LDA   T,X

24. CHARACTER CODES

We have learned that the sequence of eight zeroes and ones (sometimes called a *bit pattern*) in a cell in memory can represent either (a) an unsigned number, (b) a signed number, (c) part of a 16-bit number (in two bytes), or (d) part of an instruction code (in one, two, or three bytes). It can also be a code for a *character*. There are many kinds of characters, including:

(1) *letters* (A, B, C, and so on through Z);
(2) *digits* (0, 1, 2, and so on through 9);
(3) the *blank* (thus "A Z" is A, blank, Z);
(4) *special characters* (. , + − * / = ; : $ and so on).

The character codes for these characters, on the APPLE, are shown in Tables 9 and 10 in the Appendix. The special characters are shown in Table 10, and the others in Table 9.

Each character has several *modes*. Four of these modes apply to the screen of the APPLE:

(1) *normal mode* (light characters on a dark background);
(2) *inverse mode* (dark characters on a light background);
(3) *blinking mode* (going back and forth between normal mode and inverse mode—this is sometimes called *flashing mode*);
(4) *lower case* (*a, b, c,* etc., rather than A, B, C, etc.; this is standard on the APPLE IIe, but requires some optional extra hardware on the APPLE II +).*

Two of the modes (normal and control) apply to characters which are typed on the APPLE keyboard. A character in control mode, or a *control character*, is typed by pressing the CTRL ("control") key and, *while that key is being held down,* pressing another key. Thus we speak of "control-X" or "ctrl-X," for example, for which we press X while holding the CTRL key down.

---

*On the APPLE IIe, there is also *inverse lower case*, which can replace the blinking mode if the user so desires.

Control-H is equivalent to the *backspace* (←), which allows us to back up and correct errors. Control-M is equivalent to the *carriage return*, given at the end of a line; after the carriage return, the next line starts in column 1 (see section 19). Of course, on a screen, there is no carriage to return, as there is on many typewriters; but the term continues to be used, for historical reasons. Both the backspace and the carriage return have their own keys, but most of the control characters do not. (See Table 9 for other control characters with alternative meanings.)

Any instruction that acts on a constant may also act on a *constant character*, enclosed in double quotes. Thus

CMP   # " + "

compares the A register with hexadecimal AB, the character code for "plus" (in normal mode, that is, as this character would normally be typed in, or displayed). This is, of course, the same as

CMP #$AB   *or*   CMP #%10101011   *or*   CMP #!171

Address expressions may involve constant characters. For example, suppose that the A register contains a hexadecimal digit from 10 through 15. By subtracting 10 and adding "A" we obtain the character code for the corresponding hexadecimal character, A through F. If the carry flag is clear, then

ADC   # " A " − ! 10

does this in one instruction. For any character c, we may use " c as a shorthand form for # " c " (but " c cannot be part of any address expressions as above).

An English word, phrase, sentence, or paragraph is treated by the computer as a sequence of characters, often called a *string* of characters. Each of these characters is represented by its code. Each code is kept in one cell, and these cells are kept in an array. For example, ENTER THE FIRST NUMBER may be stored in the cells with addresses 0A40 through 0A55 as pictured in Figure 11. (Note particularly the blank characters.)

Note that the character code for a digit is *not* the same as the digit itself; thus the code for 5 is not 5, but 181 (decimal), or B5 (hexadecimal). However, the codes for the digits are in sequence; the code for n is always n more than the code for zero. Also note that a constant character in quotes is a *single* character; we cannot, for example, write # "CR" to denote the code for a carriage return, although we can write #$8D for this (see Table 9 in the Appendix).

The APPLE character codes are a form of ASCII, which stands for American Standard Code for Information Interchange. Various forms of ASCII are used on all microcomputers. LISA also supports a second form of ASCII, in which the character codes for the letters and digits all have *leftmost bit zero*, instead of

ADDRESS	CONTENTS	
	HEXADECIMAL	CHARACTER CODE
0A40	C5	E
0A41	CE	N
0A42	D4	T
0A43	C5	E
0A44	D2	R
0A45	A0	blank
0A46	D4	T
0A47	C8	H
0A48	C5	E
0A49	A0	blank
0A4A	C6	F
0A4B	C9	I
0A4C	D2	R
0A4D	D3	S
0A4E	D4	T
0A4F	A0	blank
0A50	CE	N
0A51	D5	U
0A52	CD	M
0A53	C2	B
0A54	C5	E
0A55	D2	R

Figure 11. Addresses of Characters of a String in Memory.

leftmost bit 1.* Thus the normal character code for 5 is hexadecimal B5, or binary 10110101, and is represented by "5" (*double quotes*). In the alternate form, the character code for 5 is binary 00110101 (with the leftmost bit changed from 1 to 0, and the rest of the code the same), or hexadecimal 35, and is represented by '5' (*single quotes*).

The character code is a perfectly good secret code, like those of section 1. Thus PIANO LESSONS STINK would be coded, for example, as

D0 C9 C1 CE CF A0 CC C5 D3 D3 CF CE D3 A0 D3 D4 C9 CE CB

EXERCISES

1. Using the character code as a secret code, decode the following messages:

   (a) D3 C5 C5 A0 CD C5 A0 C1 D4 A0 D3 C9 D8
   *(b) D6 C5 CC CD C1 A0 C4 D9 C5 D3 A0 C8 C5 D2 A0 C8 C1 C9 D2
   (c) D9 CF D5 D2 A0 C6 CC D9 A0 C9 D3 A0 CF D0 C5 CE

---

*This form is used, for example, on the Commodore 64.

2. Using the character code as a secret code, put each of the following messages into code:

   *(a) NUMBER TOO BIG
    (b) LABEL TOO LONG
   *(c) ILLEGAL CODE

3. Write an assembly language program that sets the X register to -1 if Q contains the character code for a hyphen (minus sign), and sets the X register to zero otherwise. Use double quotes.

25. INPUT-OUTPUT, SUBROUTINES, AND "EQU"

On the APPLE we perform input-output by means of subroutines. A subroutine is called by the instruction JSR, which stands for Jump to Subroutine. Thus JSR S calls the subroutine S. (In section 60, we will see how JSR actually works; in sections 69 and 70, we will learn how input-output subroutines are actually written.)

We will very often use certain basic APPLE system subroutines, such as COUT (Character Out), which puts a character from the A register onto the screen; RDKEY (Read Key), which waits until you type a character and then reads this character into the A register (and also puts it on the screen); and GETLNZ (a variant of GETLN, Get Line) which reads, using RDKEY, an entire line of characters (up to a carriage return) and puts them in an array, starting at address $0200, called the *standard input buffer* or INBUF.*

Normally, we use COUT by loading the A register with a character and then calling it. Thus we can display N characters from an array T, using a loop, as follows:

```
          LDY    #!0      ;  SET INDEX OF FIRST CHARACTER
WLOOP     LDA    T,Y      ;  LOAD THIS CHARACTER
          JSR    COUT     ;  PUT IT OUT
          INY             ;  MOVE TO NEXT CHARACTER
          CPY    N        ;  HAVE WE DONE N CHARACTERS
          BNE    WLOOP    ;  -- IF NOT, LOOP BACK
```

Whenever we use COUT, we have to tell LISA where it is. As it happens, COUT has the hexadecimal address FDED. Therefore, somewhere in our program, we write

```
          COUT   EQU    $FDED
```

The pseudo-operation EQU (meaning "equals") is used to set a symbol equal to a value. Thus COUT is set to the value $FDED, which means that JSR COUT is the same as JSR $FDED (in this program).

---

*A *buffer*, in general, is any array used for input-output purposes.

Similarly, we can use RDKEY by calling it and then storing the A register, or using this register in any other way. Thus the instructions

```
JSR    RDKEY    ;   READ ONE CHARACTER
CMP    #"Y"     ;   IS IT A "Y" (FOR "YES")
BNE    ANSRNO   ;   IF NOT, GO TO ANSWER-NO
```

will wait for a character to be typed, and then branch to ANSRNO if that character is not a Y. Note that after JSR RDKEY we do *not* need a JSR COUT to display this character, since RDKEY does this for us.

We can use GETLNZ by calling it, after which the characters which we typed will be in locations $0200, $0201, $0202, and so on. Thus the following program reads an input line and prints out a copy of it:

```
           JSR    GETLNZ    ;   GET ONE LINE OF INPUT
           LDX    #$FF      ;   START AT INDEX = −1
           JMP    ECHO2     ;   GET FIRST CHARACTER
ECHO1      JSR    COUT      ;   OUTPUT THIS CHARACTER
ECHO2      INX              ;   MOVE TO NEXT CHARACTER
           LDA    INBUF,X   ;   LOAD CURRENT CHARACTER
           CMP    #$8D      ;   IS IT A CARRIAGE RETURN
           BNE    ECHO1     ;   IF NOT, KEEP LOOKING
           STX    LENGTH    ;   STORE NO. OF CHARACTERS
INBUF      EQU    $0200     ;   STANDARD INPUT BUFFER
GETLNZ     EQU    $FD67     ;   LOCATION OF GETLNZ
COUT       EQU    $FDED     ;   LOCATION OF COUT
```

Note that, whenever we use GETLNZ, we have to tell LISA where it is and also where INBUF is; and this is done by EQU statements, just as with COUT. As it happens, GETLNZ has hexadecimal address FD67; similarly, RDKEY has address FD0C. All these special addresses are given in Table 11 in the Appendix, where COUT, GETLNZ, RDKEY, and many other APPLE subroutines are more fully described.

EQU is also useful for giving names to other kinds of constants. In the preceding program, we could have written

```
CRET      EQU    $8D
MINUS1    EQU    $FF
```

and then used CMP #CRET instead of CMP #$8D (or LDX #MINUS1 instead of LDX #$FF).

Usually we read an entire line, rather than one character at a time, because this gives us a chance to correct mistakes. If you use RDKEY, the computer will immediately act on whatever key you strike, whether it was wrong or not. Also, *RDKEY and GETLNZ use the X and Y registers for their own purposes.* This means that, for example, the following program has a bug in it:

```
         LDY    N         ;   TRY TO PROCESS N CHARACTERS
RLOOP    JSR    RDKEY     ;   READ ONE CHARACTER
         (further statements to process this character)
         DEY              ;   DECREASE Y AND LOOP BACK
         BNE    RLOOP     ;   THIS DOES NOT WORK AS USUAL
```

because it assumes that the Y register will count downwards: N, N − 1, N − 2, and
so on. This will not happen because RDKEY uses the Y register for its own
purposes, and so the DEY is *not* decreasing N by 1, but rather is decreasing some
other quantity by 1, for example, the first time through the loop. Therefore, in a
RDKEY loop, *keep the loop count in a cell in memory.* We do not have this problem
with COUT, because COUT *saves and restores* the X and Y registers, a technique
discussed further in section 57.

EXERCISES

1. Describe, in words, what each of the following instruction sequences
    does. (Do not simply give comments; the point is to describe what an
    entire sequence does, not what each individual instruction does.)

*(a)
```
              LDA    # ! 1 0
              STA    LCOUNT
       LOOP   JSR    RDKEY
              LDX    LCOUNT
              STA    REV − ! 1, X
              DEC    LCOUNT
              BNE    LOOP
```

(b)
```
              JSR    RDKEY
              CMP    # "  "
              BNE    P7
              LDA    # "$"
       P7     JSR    COUT
```

*(c)
```
              JSR    RDKEY
              CLC
              ADC    # ! 1
              CMP    # "Z" +! 1
              BNE    J4
              LDA    # "A"
       J4     JSR    COUT
```

2. (a) The system subroutine CROUT (at address FD8E) outputs a carriage
    return. Give a sequence of instructions which is equivalent to JSR
    CROUT, using COUT.

(b) The system subroutine GETLNZ outputs a carriage return and then calls the system subroutine GETLN (at address FD6A). Thus we may use GETLN to get characters which are not necessarily displayed at the left-hand end of the screen. (Note that GETLN and GETLNZ have exactly the same effect on the character codes of the input line; in both cases, the codes go into the standard input buffer, starting at hexadecimal address 200. The difference between GETLN and GETLNZ is *only* in how these characters are displayed on the screen.) Give a sequence of instructions which is equivalent to JSR GETLNZ, using GETLN.

*3. Suppose that, in the program in this section which calls GETLNZ, we wrote LDA #$8D and CMP INBUF,X instead of LDA INBUF,X and CMP #$8D. What further improvement in this program would now be possible? (Hint: Look at what is in the A register in the loop.)

26. CONSTANT DECLARATIONS

There is a pseudo-operation BYT in LISA, which is very much like DFS !1 except that it not only sets aside one byte (hence the name, BYT) but *gives that byte a value*. Compare the following:

```
J1    DFS   !1      ;   VARIABLE J1
J2    BYT   !6      ;   VARIABLE J2, WITH VALUE 6
J3    BYT   $20     ;   VARIABLE J3, WITH VALUE 32
J4    BYT   "Q"     ;   VARIABLE J4, WITH VALUE "Q"
K1    DFS   !2      ;   TWO-BYTE VARIABLE K1
K2    BYT   $CD     ;   TWO-BYTE VARIABLE K2, WITH
      BYT   $AB     ;      VALUE $ABCD (BYTES REVERSED)
L     BYT   $10-!1  ;      VARIABLE L, WITH VALUE $F
```

The value given is eight bits long. If you specify more than eight bits, BYT will use the rightmost eight bits that you specify; thus:

```
M     BYT   $1A3D   ;   VALUE OF M IS $3D
M1    BYT   $256    ;   VALUE OF M1 IS $56
M2    BYT   !256    ;   VALUE OF M2 IS ZERO
```

Suppose now that we want to specify a constant *string* of characters, such as the word ERROR, corresponding to the label ERR. We could write

```
ERR   BYT   "E"
      BYT   "R"
      BYT   "R"
      BYT   "O"
      BYT   "R"
```

but there is another pseudo-operation, ASC (which stands for "ASCII data"), that allows us to do this more simply:

```
ERR   ASC   "ERROR"
```

We can now display ENTER THE FIRST NUMBER on the screen with

85

```
            LDY   #!0        ;   START AT FIRST CHARACTER
    PMSG1   LDA   MSG1,Y     ;   LOAD CURRENT CHARACTER
            JSR   COUT       ;   DISPLAY THIS CHARACTER
            INY              ;   MOVE TO NEXT CHARACTER
            CPY   #!22       ;   ARE ALL 22 CHARACTERS DONE
            BNE   PMSG1      ;   - - IF NOT, LOOP BACK
```

where MSG1 is defined in the data section, as follows:

```
    MSG1    ASC   "ENTER THE FIRST NUMBER"
```

One problem here is having to count the characters (22 characters in this case); it is easy to make a mistake. Instead, we can insert a carriage return ($8D) after the message, as follows:

```
    MSG1    ASC   "ENTER THE FIRST NUMBER"
            BYT   $8D        ;   CARRIAGE RETURN
```

and then rewrite the instructions to check for a carriage return:

```
            LDY   #!0        ;   START AT FIRST CHARACTER
    PMSG1   LDA   MSG1,Y     ;   LOAD CURRENT CHARACTER
            CMP   #$8D       ;   IS IT A CARRIAGE RETURN
            BEQ   DONE       ;   IF SO, WE ARE DONE
            JSR   COUT       ;   IF NOT, DISPLAY IT
            INY              ;   MOVE TO NEXT CHARACTER
            JMP   PMSG1      ;   AND LOOP BACK
    DONE    (next instruction)
```

We can make this easier to understand by writing BYT CRET instead of BYT $8D and CMP #CRET instead of CMP #$8D (provided that we have defined CRET EQU $8D as in the preceding section). The instructions above can also be used to display the standard input buffer (see the preceding section) because this always contains a carriage return character following the characters typed in.

BYT and ASC, in addition to DFS, are called *constant declarations*. Further examples of constant declarations are given in sections 63 and 73. In general, assembly language programming *requires* a constant declaration for *every* variable. Note that there are very often alternatives to BYT. For example, we can replace LDA J2, where J2 BYT !6 is given, by simply LDA #!6 which saves two bytes, one for J2 BYT !6 and one because LDA #!6 is a two-byte instruction whereas LDA J2 is a three-byte instruction.

The double-quote character may itself be contained in a string declared with ASC, but you write it *twice* for every time it appears in the computer. Thus, the constant declaration

                    ASC   "I'M NOT ""HOT, "" I'M ""COOL"""

produces the string I'M NOT "HOT, " I'M "COOL" in the computer.

Single quotes may be used in ASC, and produce strings in the computer in which *every* byte has its leftmost bit set to zero (see section 24). A single-quote character may appear in such a string; but, as with double quotes above, it must appear twice. Thus

                    ASC   'I''M NOT "HOT, " I''M "COOL"'

produces the string I'M NOT "HOT, " I'M "COOL" but with every byte of this string having its leftmost bit set to zero.

A *semicolon* may also appear in a string. (This implies that a semicolon appearing between quotes does not start a comment.)

EXERCISES

1. Give BYT statements which define:

    (a) A variable called K whose value is 99.
    *(b) A variable called KPRIME whose value is the APPLE character code for a plus sign.
    (c) A variable called U with the two-byte hexadecimal value $DAFF, with bytes reversed.

*2. What is the final hexadecimal value of K as calculated by the following program? (Hint: Use Table 9 in the Appendix.)

```
            ORG    $0800
            LDA    K1
            CLC
            ADC    K2
            ADC    K3
            STA    K
            ORG    $0900
    K       DFS    !1
    K1      BYT    "C"
    K2      BYT    $22
    K3      BYT    %10101
            END
```

3. Rewrite the first program of this section, which prints ENTER THE FIRST NUMBER, using DEY rather than INY. Use a program section starting at $0800 and a data section starting at $08A0, and assume that COUT EQU $FDED has already been specified. (Hint: The usage of ASC in this program must be changed. Why, and how?)

27. THE PROGRAM COUNTER AND RELATIVE ADDRESSING

Besides the A, X, and Y registers, the 6502 has certain *internal registers*—"internal" meaning that we cannot load them, store them, or use them for any other purpose since they are used only by the hardware. Among these are an 8-bit *instruction register* (IR), which holds the current operation code byte, and a 16-bit *program counter* (PC) register, which holds the address of the current instruction byte.

The computer always proceeds as follows (this is called its *instruction cycle*):

(1) Load IR with the number in the cell whose address is contained in PC, and add 1 to the contents of PC. (This step is sometimes called *instruction fetch*.)

(2) Execute the instruction whose operation code is in IR. In particular, just *before* execution:

   (a) If this instruction is two bytes long, some internal register (other than IR and PC) will be loaded with the number in the cell whose address is contained in PC, and then the computer adds 1 to the contents of PC, just as in step 1 above.

   (b) If this instruction is three bytes long, *two* internal registers will be loaded with the numbers in the two cells with addresses n and $n+1$, where n is contained in PC; and then PC is incremented by 2.*

(3) Return to step 1.

The important point to note is that, in step 2, when we do the current instruction, the PC register always contains the address of the *next instruction in sequence;* but by step 3, PC must contain the address of the *next instruction to be done* (which is different, if the computer branches at this point). This is necessary to know in order to construct the addresses in branch instructions.

---

*If the instruction is JMP, these two internal registers are then moved to the two bytes of PC; because, when we go back to step 1, we want to do the instruction *to which* we just jumped.

There are two kinds of instructions on the 6502 that go to a label—the *jumps* JMP and JSR, and the *branches* (BCC, BEQ, and the like). This is not merely an arbitrary choice of words; it affects the machine language form of these instructions.

A *jump* uses an address like a load, a store, and so on. Thus the instruction JSR COUT has machine language form 20 ED FD if the address of COUT is FDED. Here 20 is the operation code for JSR, and then the address, FDED, follows (with bytes reversed as usual). This instruction loads the PC register with FDED.

A *branch* to a label L, however, uses a special address called a *relative address*. Whereas an ordinary address is an *unsigned 16-bit* quantity, a relative address is a *signed 8-bit* quantity. This is *added* to the program counter in step 2 above, if the branch is taken.

Every branch instruction is two bytes long, one for the operation code and one for the 8-bit relative address. If the branch instruction is at the address CA (current address), then PC contains CA + 2 at step 2, as we have noted. If RA is the relative address, then CA + 2 + RA is the *branch address* BA—the address of L, where the branch instruction branches to L.

As an example of this, consider the following instructions:

MACHINE LANGUAGE		ASSEMBLY LANGUAGE		
0840	AD __ __	LOOP	LDA	N
0843	F0 05		BEQ	CON
0845	20 __ __		JSR	F
0848	90 F6		BCC	LOOP
084A	8D __ __	CON	STA	Q

The 16-bit addresses of N, F, and Q are immaterial. The main point to observe here is the calculation of the relative addresses 05 and F6. Let us consider BEQ CON first. Our equation is CA+2+RA = BA. Here CA, the current address, is 0843; BA, the branch address, is 084A. Thus 0843+2+RA = 084A, from which it follows that RA is 5 (or 05, in two hexadecimal digits).

Now let us consider BCC LOOP. Again the equation is CA+2+RA = BA; this time CA, the current address, is 0848, and BA, the branch address, is 0840. Thus 0848+2+RA = 0840, so that RA is −10 (decimal), or F6 (hexadecimal, in twos' complement notation).

In writing assembly language programs, it helps to remember that branch instructions have only two bytes, while jump instructions have three. For example, if we have

```
BCC    ALPHA    ;  IF CARRY CLEAR, GO TO ALPHA
JMP    BETA     ;  GO TO BETA
```

in our program, we can save one byte if we replace it by

```
          BCC   ALPHA    ;   IF CARRY CLEAR, GO TO ALPHA
          BCS   BETA     ;   IF CARRY SET, GO TO BETA
```

Note that the BCS will always branch.

More importantly, we cannot branch more than 129 bytes forward, or 126 bytes backward, because the relative address is a signed 8-bit quantity.* If we have to branch farther than that, we can replace

```
          BEQ   ALPHA    ;   IF EQUAL, GO TO ALPHA
```

(for example) by†

```
          BNE   BETA     ;   IF UNEQUAL, DON'T GO TO ALPHA
          JMP   ALPHA    ;   OTHERWISE, GO TO ALPHA
    BETA  (next instruction)
```

EXERCISES

*1. Translate the following program into machine language, making sure to calculate all proper relative addresses:

```
          INBUF    EQU    $0200
          FZERO    EQU    $0860
          ERRORZ   EQU    $0888
                   ORG    $0840
                   LDX    #!255
          CHECKZ   LDA    INBUF,X
                   BNE    FZERO
                   DEX
                   BNE    CHECKZ
                   STA    ERRORZ
                   END
```

2. At the time that STA (in the above program) is being executed, what number is in the program counter? (Hint: It is *not* 084A. Why not?)

*3. Give an assembly language version of the following machine language program. Assume that the BNE instruction goes to the label FZERO, and

---

*Note that this limits our ability to replace JMP by a conditional branch as in the preceding paragraph.
†Some programmers make the mistake of following a conditional branch by JMP *all the time*. Remember that you can replace BEQ-JMP by BNE, BNE-JMP by BEQ, and so on, unless the conditional branch would have to branch "too far" as indicated here.

define FZERO by using EQU, as was done in Exercise 1 above. Assume also that INBUF is as in Exercise 1.

```
08E0    A2  FF
08E2    E8
08E3    DD  00  02
08E6    F0  FA
08E8    D0  06
```

28. SIGN STATUS AND GENERAL COMPARISONS

Every 6502 instruction which sets the zero status flag also sets another flag, the *sign status flag*, to the sign of the result* (1 if the result is negative, 0 otherwise). Two instructions, BPL (Branch on Plus) and BMI (Branch on Minus), act on the sign status flag like BEQ and BNE do on the zero status flag:

> BPL L   Go to L if sign status flag = 0
> BMI L   Go to L if sign status flag = 1

Thus we can go to QNEG if Q is negative by

```
LDA  Q          LDX  Q          LDY  Q
         or              or
BMI  QNEG       BMI  QNEG       BMI  QNEG
```

Or we can add two signed numbers P and Q, and immediately go to SUMPOS if the sum is *non-negative* (that is, positive *or zero*):

```
LDA    P       ;   LOAD P AND ADD Q
CLC            ;     (CLEARING THE CARRY FIRST)
ADC    Q       ;   ADDING Q SETS THE SIGN FLAG
BPL    SUMPOS  ;   IF NON-NEGATIVE, TO SUMPOS
```

The main use of the zero status flag, however, does not apply here. We saw in section 20 that, if $P = Q$, then $P-Q = 0$, so that we can test for $P = Q$ by a compare instruction (which subtracts) and then a test of the zero status flag. Now it is also true that if $P < Q$ then $P-Q < 0$. But *we cannot use a compare instruction, followed by a test of the sign status flag, to test for $P < Q$* (or any other inequality test). This is true regardless of whether P and Q are signed or unsigned.

It is important to understand the reason for this. Let us consider unsigned data

---

*An exception to this rule is given in section 55.

first. If P is 3 and Q is 5, then P—Q is —2, which is indeed negative. But now suppose that P is 100 and Q is 229. Then P—Q is —129, which *should* be negative; but, as a pattern of *eight bits*, it is not. In fact, 129 has the bit pattern 10000001 (decimal 128+1); so it has a *negative sign*, and tests as negative. The twos' complement of this is 01111111; this would represent —129, but it has a positive sign.

The same problem comes up if P and Q are signed. Suppose that P is —29 and Q is 100. Then P—Q is again —129, and again this does not have a negative sign in an eight-bit representation.

For *unsigned* numbers, the solution to this problem is to use the carry flag. We recall that P < Q if there is borrow when we subtract Q from P (or compare P with Q), and the carry flag is set to zero. Hence we can branch on carry clear to L, and this will go to L if P < Q:

```
LDA P          LDX P          LDY P
CMP Q    or    CPX Q    or    CPY Q
BCC L          BCC L          BCC L
```

Similarly, we can go to L if P ≥ Q by branching on carry set:

```
LDA P          LDX P          LDY P
CMP Q    or    CPX Q    or    CPY Q
BCS L          BCS L          BCS L
```

To test for P ≤ Q, we use a trick. The condition P ≤ Q is the same as the condition Q ≥ P, so we can test for this:

```
LDA Q          LDX Q          LDY Q
CMP P    or    CPX P    or    CPY P
BCS L          BCS L          BCS L
```

In the same way, we can test for P > Q by testing for Q < P:

```
LDA Q          LDX Q          LDY Q
CMP P    or    CPX P    or    CPY P
BCC L          BCC L          BCC L
```

The above sequences are very useful, but sometimes hard to remember; refer to them as you would to a table. Comparison of *signed* numbers will be taken up in sections 54 and 56.

If you are using sequences like these several times in a single program, be careful not to use the same label (such as L, here) more than once. *All labels in an* *assembly language program must be distinct,* just as all line numbers in a BASIC program are distinct.*

So far, we have studied four registers, namely A, X, Y, and the program counter, and three status flags, namely the zero, carry, and sign flags. There are many more registers and flags on the 6502, and these are described in Table 12 in the Appendix. (Also refer to the second column in Table 3 for the status flags set by each instruction: Z for the zero flag, C for carry, S for the sign flag, and V for another flag which we shall meet in section 56.) The remaining registers and flags will be studied in greater detail as we proceed through the book.

The LISA assembler allows you to write BLT (Branch on Less Than) instead of BCC, and BGE (Branch on Greater or Equal) instead of BCS. This may help you to understand your own programs better, so you do not have to think back, every time, as to why you are branching on carry clear or on carry set.

EXERCISES

1. Give a BASIC statement which corresponds to each of the following sequences of assembly language statements. Use the line number 50 to correspond to the label FIFTY; assume that the array T starts at T(0), while the array U starts at U(1).

    (a)
    ```
              LDA   Q1
              CLC
              ADC   Q2
              CMP   #!10
              BCC   FIFTY
    ```

    *(b)
    ```
              LDY   J
              LDA   U-!1,Y
              LDY   K
              CMP   U-!1,Y
              BCS   FIFTY
    ```

    (c)
    ```
              LDA   W
              LDX   K
              CMP   T+!5,X
              BCC   FIFTY
    ```

2. Give an assembly language form of each of the following BASIC statements (omit ORG, END, and DFS). Use the label FIFTY to correspond to

---

Local labels in LISA 2.5 (see the LISA 2.5 manual) are an exception to this general rule.

the line number 50; assume that the array T starts at T(0), while the array U starts at U(1).

*(a) IF A2>=T(K+1) THEN 50
  (b) IF U(5)<=U(6) THEN 50
*(c) IF U(U(J))>2 THEN 50

3. What is wrong with the following method of going to ONE if the signed quantity J is positive, to TWO if J is zero, and to THREE if J is negative?

```
LDA   J
BPL   ONE
BEQ   TWO
JMP   THREE
```

29. TWO-BYTE COMPARISONS

When we add two numbers of two bytes apiece, we add them from right to left. When we *compare* these same two quantities, however, we compare them from left to right. Suppose that we are comparing 19 with 25; we cannot start on the right, because 9 is greater than 5 but 19 is less than 25. We say that the 9 and the 5 are less *significant* than the 1 and the 2.

In any two-byte quantity *ab*, *a* is the *most significant byte* (MSB) and *b* is the *least significant byte* (LSB). Similarly, for quantities of two hexadecimal (or decimal) digits, we have the *most significant digit* and the *least significant digit*.

The following program branches to ALPHA if P < Q, assuming that P and Q are 16-bit quantities kept with bytes reversed:

```
        LDA    P+!1     ;   COMPARE MSB'S FIRST
        CMP    Q+!1     ;   IF UNEQUAL, THEN P IS LESS
        BNE    DECIDE   ;      THAN Q IF CARRY IS CLEAR
        LDA    P        ;   OTHERWISE, COMPARE LSB'S
        CMP    Q        ;   AND AGAIN P IS LESS THAN Q
DECIDE  BCC    ALPHA    ;      IF CARRY IS CLEAR
```

We saw in the last section that P < Q if the carry is clear after comparing P and Q. Suppose now that the most significant bytes, at P+!1 and Q+!1, are unequal. In that case the least significant bytes do not matter; we go to DECIDE, and we compare only the most significant bytes. (The carry flag is not changed by the BNE.)

If the most significant bytes are equal, then we look at the other two bytes (if our two-byte quantities are *ab* and *ac*, then *ab* < *ac* is equivalent to *b* < *c*). Note that the same BCC instruction is used to compare the MSBs or the LSBs, depending on whether the MSBs are equal.

To go to ALPHA if P ≥ Q, we simply replace BCC by BCS:

```
        LDA    P+!1     ;   COMPARE MSB'S FIRST
        CMP    Q+!1     ;   IF UNEQUAL, THEN P IS NOT LESS
        BNE    DECIDE   ;      THAN Q IF CARRY IS SET
        LDA    P        ;   OTHERWISE, COMPARE LSB'S
        CMP    Q        ;   AND AGAIN P IS NOT LESS THAN Q
DECIDE  BCS    ALPHA    ;      IF CARRY IS SET
```

To go to ALPHA if P ≤ Q, we go to ALPHA if Q ≥ P, as before:

```
          LDA    Q+!1    ;  COMPARE MSB'S FIRST
          CMP    P+!1    ;  IF UNEQUAL, THEN Q IS NOT LESS
          BNE    DECIDE  ;     THAN P IF CARRY IS SET
          LDA    Q       ;  OTHERWISE, COMPARE LSB'S
          CMP    P       ;  AND AGAIN Q IS NOT LESS THAN P
DECIDE    BCS    ALPHA   ;     IF CARRY IS SET
```

Finally, to go to ALPHA if P > Q, we go to ALPHA if Q < P:

```
          LDA    Q+!1    ;  COMPARE MSB'S FIRST
          CMP    P+!1    ;  IF UNEQUAL, THEN Q IS LESS
          BNE    DECIDE  ;     THAN P IF CARRY IS CLEAR
          LDA    Q       ;  OTHERWISE, COMPARE LSB'S
          CMP    P       ;  AND AGAIN Q IS LESS THAN P
DECIDE    BCC    ALPHA   ;     IF CARRY IS CLEAR
```

Like the 8-bit compare, the 16-bit compare does not require the A register. We can substitute LDX (or LDY) for LDA, and CPX (or CPY) for CMP, throughout these programs, if desired. As with L in the preceding section, we may note that the label DECIDE, in these sequences, has to be replaced, in an actual case, by some unique label if more than one such sequence is to be used in the same program.

Another term that is often used for the most significant byte, in a two-byte quantity, is the *high-order byte*. The least significant byte is then the *low-order byte*. (We saw in section 12 that these can also be called the left half and the right half, or the upper half and the lower half.)

EXERCISES

*1. Write an assembly language program to branch to LESS if P+Q < R, where P, Q, and R are 16-bit quantities with bytes reversed. Omit ORG, END, and DFS. (Hint: You will need a temporary place to keep the lower half of P+Q until it is used in the comparison. Keep it in the X register.)

2. Write an assembly language program to branch to LESS if P < Q, where P and Q are 24-bit quantities with bytes reversed. (Do not use a loop.)

*3. Write an assembly language program to branch to LESS if P < Q, where P and Q are N-byte quantities (N is a signed integer variable). Use a loop. (Start with LDX N and LDA P−!1,X. Be careful of the case in which P = Q.)

30. TWO-BYTE INCREMENT, DECREMENT, AND COMPLEMENT

A number of further operations on two-byte quantities make use of instructions which we have already learned. For example, consider adding 1 to a two-byte quantity. It should be clear that just adding 1 to the lower half (or to both halves) will not work. If we study the examples

$$
\begin{array}{ccc}
26 & 83 & 49 \\
\underline{+1} & \underline{+1} & \underline{+1} \\
27 & 84 & 50
\end{array}
$$

of adding 1 to a two-*digit* quantity, we see that 1 is added to the second digit, while the first digit stays the same unless the second digit becomes zero. In that case, 1 is added to the first digit. So the assembly language program to add 1 to a two-byte quantity V, with bytes reversed, becomes

```
        INC   V      ;  ADD 1 TO LOWER HALF
        BNE   P17    ;  HAS INC SET THE ZERO FLAG
        INC   V+!1   ;  IF SO, ADD 1 TO UPPER HALF
P17     (next instruction)
```

Now suppose we wish to subtract 1 from a two-byte quantity. If we study the examples

$$
\begin{array}{ccc}
27 & 84 & 50 \\
\underline{-1} & \underline{-1} & \underline{-1} \\
26 & 83 & 49
\end{array}
$$

of subtracting 1 from a two-digit quantity, we see that 1 is subtracted from the second digit, and also from the first digit if the second digit *was originally* zero. We cannot use DEC V followed by BNE, because this tests whether V *becomes* zero. Therefore the assembly language program to subtract 1 from V, as described above, is

```
        LDA  V        ;  LOOK AT LOWER HALF
        BNE  P17      ;  IS IT ZERO
        DEC  V+!1     ;  IF SO, DECREMENT UPPER HALF
P17     DEC  V        ;  ALWAYS DECREMENT LOWER HALF
```

Here LDA, of course, could be replaced by LDX or LDY.

The easiest way to form the twos' complement of a two-byte quantity is to subtract it from zero, using the two-byte subtraction method of section 17. Thus to set V2 = −V1, where V1 and V2 are two-byte quantities like V above, we could write

```
        LDA  #!0      ;  SUBTRACT LOWER HALF OF V1
        SEC           ;  (SETTING THE CARRY AS USUAL)
        SBC  V1       ;  FROM LOWER HALF OF A 16-BIT
        STA  V2       ;  ZERO CONSTANT (BOTH BYTES 0)
        LDA  #!0      ;  NOW SUBTRACT THE UPPER HALF
        SBC  V1+!1    ;  FROM ZERO, WITH THE BORROW
        STA  V2+!1    ;  FROM THE PREVIOUS SUBTRACTION
```

Note that the twos' complement of a two-byte quantity is *not* formed by taking the twos' complement of each byte. In fact, if *cd* is the twos' complement of *ab*, then *d* is the twos' complement of *b*, but, unless $d = b = 0$, *c* is the *ones'* complement of *a*.

We may note the curious fact that the BNE, in either of the first two sequences above, always branches *five bytes ahead*—two for the BNE instruction itself, and three for the following INC or DEC. A BNE instruction which branches five bytes ahead may always be written as

```
        BNE    *+!5
```

The character ∗ or something like it (sometimes $ or .) may be found in all assembly languages. It stands for "the location of the current instruction"; thus, for example, JMP ∗+!17 and ALPHA JMP ALPHA+!17 are equivalent. It may theoretically be used for *all* branches in a program; but it is dangerous when used in this way, for one good reason. If you change your program, by putting new instructions in or taking old ones out, several of the constants may change. (For example, if you make such a change between ALPHA and BETA, and you are using ALPHA+!17 to refer to BETA, then the number of bytes between ALPHA and BETA will almost certainly change, from 17 to some other number *n*, and ALPHA+!17 must be changed to ALPHA+!*n*.) It is very easy to forget to change one of these constants, and this produces a bug in your program that is almost impossible to find. This is because the incorrect program might branch to a byte that is not an operation code; it might be an immediate data byte, or one of the bytes of an address, but, whatever it is, *the computer will assume that it is an operation code*, producing totally unpredictable results. (This is called "going out of alignment"; see also sections 45 and 55.)

In general, all of the instructions to which your program can branch, or jump, ought to have labels. The only reasonable exception to this is in an instruction like BNE * + !5 above, where a standard and very short sequence of instructions is being used.* In any case, remember that the constant 5 is a number of *bytes*, and not, as it would be on some other computers, a number of instructions. (The machine language form of BNE *+!5 is always D0 03; the relative address is 3 here, since the two bytes of the BNE itself are not counted, as we learned in section 27.)

EXERCISES

1. Give a BASIC statement which corresponds to the following sequence of assembly language statements, assuming that P and Q are 16-bit quantities:

P	DFS	!2
Q	DFS	!2
	LDA	P
	CLC	
	ADC	Q
	TAX	
	LDA	P+!1
	ADC	Q+!1
	TAY	
	INX	
	BNE	L4
	INY	
L4	STX	Q
	STY	Q+!1

*2. Write an assembly language program to add 1 to a three-byte quantity P, kept with bytes reversed.

3. Write an assembly language program to subtract 1 from a three-byte quantity P, kept with bytes reversed.

---

*Even this usage can be avoided in LISA 2.5, by writing BNE >1 where ^1 (not >1) is a local label. (See the LISA 2.5 manual for a description of local labels.)

31. MULTIPLYING AND DIVIDING BY TWO

In the decimal number system, putting a zero on the end of a number is the same as multiplying it by 10. We saw in section 3 that putting a zero on the end of a *binary* number multiplies it by 2; thus 11011, in binary, times 2 is 110110.

In a register, this multiplication by 2 means that each zero-bit or one-bit is *shifted to the left*:

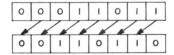

with a *zero-bit* always inserted at the right. There is an instruction which does this to the A register: ASL (for Arithmetic Shift Left).

The instruction ASL will also multiply a signed number by 2, even if it is negative. This is because ASL performs the unsigned calculation $A = 2*A$, or $A = A+A$; but we saw in section 7 that the operations of signed addition and unsigned addition are the same, if the twos' complement representation is used. Therefore ASL also performs the *signed* calculation $A = A+A$, which is the same as $A = 2*A$, just as before.

The inverse operation to multiplying by 2 is *dividing* by 2. This is done, naturally, by shifting to the *right*, as follows:

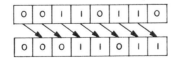

with a zero-bit always inserted at the *left*. The instruction which does this to the A register is called LSR (for Logical Shift Right).

Unlike ASL, LSR does *not* work properly on negative numbers. In fact, the result of an LSR shift is always *positive or zero,* since LSR shifts in a zero-bit at the

the left. An *arithmetic shift,* in general, is any shift that always multiplies or divides properly. A *logical shift,* by contrast, is any shift that always introduces a zero-bit. (ASL is a logical shift as well as being an arithmetic shift.)

Both ASL and LSR can shift directly in memory, as well as shifting the A register. Thus ASL Q multiplies Q by 2; LSR Q divides the (unsigned) quantity Q by 2. One can even shift an indexed quantity as long as the register X (and *not* Y) is used. Thus ASL T,X multiplies T(J) by 2 if the array T starts from T(0) and J is in the X register. Under the same conditions, LSR T,X divides the unsigned quantity T(J) by 2. (On the other hand, the X and Y registers *cannot* be shifted directly on the 6502.)

Both ASL and LSR are sometimes used to multiply or divide by 4, 8, and other powers of 2, simply by repeating them. Thus ASL Q followed by another ASL Q multiplies Q by 4, for example, since $(Q*2)*2 = Q*4$. (Do not make the common mistake of trying to multiply by 3, rather than 4, by shifting twice.) Note that ASL Q and LSR Q, like INC Q and DEC Q, do *not* change the A register.

The bit which is shifted *out* (to the left, for ASL, or to the right, for LSR) is *not* lost completely. Instead, *it is put in the carry status flag.* For LSR, this gives us a way to go to ODD, for example, if the A register is odd:

```
LSR              ;   SHIFT RIGHTMOST BIT INTO CARRY
BCS     ODD      ;   IF IT WAS 1, THEN A WAS ODD
```

since an odd number, in the binary system, ends with a one-bit, while an even number ends with a zero-bit (see the end of section 3). For ASL, it is the normal carry from the multiplication by 2 which goes into the carry status flag. If z is the quantity being shifted, then, if $2*z < 256$, the carry flag will be set to zero. This fact can often be used to advantage; thus, in the sequence

```
LDA     Q        ;   PUT Q IN A-REGISTER
ASL              ;   PUT 2*Q IN A-REGISTER
ADC     Q        ;   2*Q + Q = 3*Q
STA     V        ;   SET V = 3*Q
```

we do not need to do a CLC before the ADC, since the carry flag is zero (otherwise the answer is wrong anyway because 3*Q cannot fit into a single byte if 2*Q does not).*

Another use of the carry flag after LSR is in "rounding up." LSR "rounds down"; thus, for example, 21 divided by 2, using LSR, is 10 (the next integer *less* than 21/2 or 10½). If we wanted to "round up," producing 11 in this case (the

---

*If we are multiplying a *signed* quantity Q by 3, we need the CLC, because now the carry flag will be set to 1 by the ASL whenever Q is negative.

next integer *greater* than the answer), we would use ADC #!0 after the
LSR. This adds 0 if the A register was originally an even number (and thus the
answer is exact); and it adds 1 if the A register was originally odd.

The zero and sign status flags are also set in the normal way by ASL and
LSR; that is, they are set to the zero status and the sign status of the *result* of the
shift. (See Exercise 1, section 35, for an application of this.)

On some computers, there are shift instructions which will shift by more than
one bit. The absence of such instructions is only a minor inconvenience on the
6502, however, since a one bit shift may always be repeated as many times as
necessary.

EXERCISES

1. Give a BASIC statement which corresponds to each of the following
    sequences of assembly language statements:

    *(a)
    ```
    LDA   Q
    ASL
    ASL
    ADC   R
    STA   P
    ```

    (b)
    ```
    LDA   G
    SEC
    SBC   H
    LSR
    STA   F
    ```

    *(c)
    ```
    LDA   B1
    ASL
    ASL
    ASL
    STA   B2
    ```

2. What does the sequence, LSR followed by ASL, do to the contents of the
    A register?

*3. What is wrong with the following program to set S = T(2*M)? (Assume
    that the array T starts at T(0).)
    ```
    LDX M
    ASL X
    LDA T, X
    STA S
    ```

32. ARRAYS OF TWO-BYTE QUANTITIES

There are two ways of keeping an array of 16-bit, or two-byte, quantities. One way is simply by keeping two arrays. For example, if we want to keep T(0) through T(99) as two-byte quantities, we can keep two arrays, each 100 bytes long, called UPPERT and LOWERT (and defined by UPPERT DFS !100 and LOWERT DFS !100). To branch to LESS if T(J) < T(K), for example, we might write (using a 16-bit comparison process from section 29):

```
          LDX    J          ;  SET UP INDEX J
          LDY    K          ;  SET UP INDEX K
          LDA    UPPERT,X   ;  COMPARE UPPER HALF OF
          CMP    UPPERT,Y   ;   T(J) TO UPPER HALF
          BNE    DECIDE     ;   OF T(K). IF EQUAL,
          LDA    LOWERT,X   ;   THEN COMPARE LOWER
          CMP    LOWERT,Y   ;   HALF OF T(J) TO
DECIDE    BCC    LESS       ;   LOWER HALF OF T(K)
```

The arrays LOWERT and UPPERT are sometimes called *parallel arrays*.

The other way is to keep *one* array T (defined, in this case, by T DFS !200), as in Figure 12. Notice, however, that, if we do this, we cannot use the X and Y registers in quite the same way as in the program above. To see why, suppose that 3 is in the X register. Now turn back for a moment to Figure 9. Here the address of T(3) was equal to the address of T(0) plus 3; but, in Figure 12, we have to add *six, not three,* to the address of T(0). In general, in a *serial array* like that of Figure 12, we put *twice* the index, rather than the index itself, into the index register.

To do this, we load the index into the A register first; then multiply it by 2, using ASL (as in the previous section); and then move it to X (or Y). This lets us use LDA T,X to load the A register with the lower half of T(J), for example. If we wanted the upper half, whose address is one more than this, we could write LDA T+!1,X (using another offset as in section 23). To branch to LESS if T(J) < T(K) under these conditions, we might write (using the same 16-bit comparison as before):

VARIABLE				ADDRESS
T(0)	(lower)	0858	=	0858 + 2*0
T(0)	(upper)	0859	=	0858 + 2*0 + 1
T(1)	(lower)	085A	=	0858 + 2*1
T(1)	(upper)	085B	=	0858 + 2*1 + 1
T(2)	(lower)	085C	=	0858 + 2*2
T(2)	(upper)	085D	=	0858 + 2*2 + 1
T(3)	(lower)	085E	=	0858 + 2*3
T(3)	(upper)	085F	=	0858 + 2*3 + 1
T(4)	(lower)	0860	=	0858 + 2*4
T(4)	(upper)	0861	=	0858 + 2*4 + 1
T(5)	(lower)	0862	=	0858 + 2*5
T(5)	(upper)	0863	=	0858 + 2*5 + 1
. . . .				
T(99) (lower)		091E	=	0858 + 2*99
T(99) (upper)		091F	=	0858 + 2*99 + 1

Figure 12. Addresses of Elements of an Array of Two-Byte Quantities.

```
            LDA   J       ;  SET UP INDEX J (MUST
            ASL           ;    BE MULTIPLIED BY 2
            TAX           ;    AND PUT IN X)
            LDA   K       ;  SET UP INDEX K (MUST
            ASL           ;    BE MULTIPLIED BY 2
            TAY           ;    AND PUT IN Y)
            LDA   T+!1,X  ;  COMPARE UPPER HALF OF
            CMP   T+!1,Y  ;    T(J) TO UPPER HALF
            BNE   DECIDE  ;    OF T(K).  IF EQUAL,
            LDA   T,X     ;  THEN COMPARE LOWER
            CMP   T,Y     ;    HALF OF T(J) TO
DECIDE      BCC   LESS    ;    LOWER HALF OF T(K)
```

If a serial array T, such as this one, starts with T(1) rather than T(0), another kind of offset is needed. Note that in this case the first *two* bytes of the array, rather than the first one, are omitted, so that T−!2 rather than T−!1 is used in the instructions which reference T(J). In fact, the last six instructions above become

```
            LDA   T−!1,X  ;  COMPARE UPPER HALF OF
            CMP   T−!1,Y  ;    T(J) TO UPPER HALF
            BNE   DECIDE  ;    OF T(K).  IF EQUAL,
            LDA   T−!2,X  ;  THEN COMPARE LOWER
            CMP   T−!2,Y  ;    HALF OF T(J) TO
DECIDE      BCC   LESS    ;    LOWER HALF OF T(K)
```

under these conditions. (Here T−!1 is actually T+!1−!2.)

Constant indices in serial arrays of two-byte quantities must also be multiplied by 2. Thus T(3), if the serial array T starts at T(0), is kept, not at T+!3, but at T+!6 and T+!7. Similarly, if an index in such an array contains a constant that is added or subtracted, this constant must be multiplied by 2. Thus the following program sets W equal to T(N+3) under these conditions:

```
LDA   N        ;   SET UP INDEX N  (MUST
ASL            ;     BE MULTIPLIED BY 2
TAX            ;     AND PLACED IN X)
LDA   T+!6,X   ;   ADDRESS HERE IS  (T+6)
STA   W        ;     +(2*N), WHICH IS EQUAL
LDA   T+!7,X   ;   TO T+2*(N+3) -- THIS
STA   W+!1     ;   SETS W = T(N+3)
```

where we must be careful, as before, not to use T+!3 in the program.

In the examples of this section, we used both X and Y, in many cases, because this was necessary. In general, however, you should try to use as *few* registers as you can (without sacrificing space or time). This is because, as your programs get larger, you will be able to make good use of any registers that you have carefully stayed away from.

EXERCISES

1. Write an assembly language program to correspond to each of the following BASIC statements, under the assumption that the serial array T, of 16-bit quantities, starts at T(0), and that B is a 16-bit quantity:

    *(a) B=T(5)
     (b) T(K) =B
    *(c) B=B+T(K-3)

2. Write an assembly language program to correspond to each of the BASIC statements of Exercise 1 above, under the assumption that T is kept in two parallel arrays, LOWERT and UPPERT, starting from LOWERT(1) and UPPERT(1), and that B is a 16-bit quantity.

*3. Write an assembly language program to branch to LESS if T(J) < T(K), under the assumption that T is a serial array of 24-bit quantities, starting from T(0), with bytes in *normal order* (that is, *not* with bytes reversed). Do not use a loop. (Hint: This time, it is not correct to multiply the indices J and K by 2, using ASL. Why not?)

33. MULTIPLYING BY TEN

There is no instruction on the 6502 that multiplies two arbitrary numbers. This must be done by means of subroutines (see sections 39 and 40). However, we can multiply the A register by 10 in five instructions, as follows:

```
ASL              ;   SET A TO 2*A
STA     TEMP     ;   SAVE 2*A IN TEMP
ASL              ;   NOW MULTIPLY THE
ASL              ;     ORIGINAL A BY 8
ADC     TEMP     ;   8*A + 2*A = 10*A
```

This sequence saves 2*A in a *temporary location*, here called TEMP, and then uses it later. In general, a temporary location is a place that is used in short calculations like this one, and whose value is not needed after the short calculation is finished. Note that we do not need CLC before ADC (if our numbers are unsigned), for the same reason as at the end of section 31.

Suppose now that we have an integer N between 0 and 255, expressed in character code form somewhere in an array B of characters. We would like to calculate N and put it in the Y register. The character codes for the digits of N are in sequence, starting with B(J), where J is in the X register, and terminated by a non-digit. (For example, if N is two digits long, then B(J) and B(J+1) are the two digits, in character code form, while B(J+2) is not the character code for a digit. Note that we do not know, in advance, whether N has one, two, or three digits.) We may proceed as follows:

1. Set N to zero.
2. If B(J) is not the character code for a digit, stop.
3. Convert B(J) into its corresponding digit D. (For example, if B(J) = "7" or hexadecimal B7, then D = 7. See Table 9 in the Appendix.)
4. Set N = 10*N+D. (For example, if N is 15 and D is 4, then N becomes 154, because 10*N+D = 10*15+4 = 150+4 = 154.)
5. Increase J by 1 (so we can look at the next character in the array B) and go back to step 2.

The following program does this. Note that steps 2 and 3 above are combined. We test whether B(J) > "9" (actually, B(J) ≥ "9" +1). If so, we are done (step 2). If not, then *the carry must be clear* (otherwise we branched on carry set). We want to subtract "0"—the character code for zero—to convert B(J) into D (step 3; in hexadecimal, this subtraction is B7 − B0 = 07.) Therefore we subtract "0" *minus one, but with borrow* (since we know the carry flag is clear, indicating a borrow status); and this subtracts "0" without doing an SEC first, thus saving one instruction. If B(J) was less than "0" then this subtraction will produce borrow, leaving the carry flag clear, and we branch to DONE again. If B(J) is *neither* less than "0" *nor* greater than "9" then it must be the character code for a digit, and we proceed to step 4 above. (For another application of the basic idea of this program, see section 62.)

```
          ORG   $0860        ;  START OF PROGRAM SECTION
          LDY   #!0          ;  KEEP N IN REGISTER Y
CONV      LDA   B,X          ;  GET NEXT CHARACTER
          CMP   #"9"+!1      ;  IS IT GREATER THAN "9"
          BCS   DONE         ;  YES, END OF NUMBER
          SBC   #"0"-!1      ;  CONVERT FROM CHARACTER CODE
          BCC   DONE         ;    TO DIGIT D (IF THIS IS
          STA   D            ;    LESS THAN ZERO, END OF NUMBER)
          TYA                ;  MOVE N (FROM Y) TO A
          ASL                ;  **** FIVE INSTRUCTIONS ****
          STA   TEMP         ;  **** FROM START OF      ****
          ASL                ;  **** THIS SECTION       ****
          ASL                ;  **** (MULTIPLY A        ****
          ADC   TEMP         ;  **** BY 10)             ****
          ADC   D            ;  A=10*N+D  (NO CLC NEEDED)
          TAY                ;  N=10*N+D
          INX                ;  BUMP THE CHARACTER INDEX
          JMP   CONV         ;  AND GET NEXT CHARACTER
DONE      (next instruction)
          ORG   $0920        ;  START OF DATA SECTION
D         DFS   !1           ;  CURRENT DIGIT
TEMP      DFS   !1           ;  TEMPORARY STORAGE FOR 2*Y
B         DFS   !256         ;  ARRAY OF CHARACTERS
```

When we are done with the character B(J), we pass to the next character, B(J+1), by setting J = J+1, or (since J is kept in the X register) by incrementing X. This is popularly known as "bumping" X (or J). We may note, in the above program, the register assignment (see section 21) of N to the register Y.

Multiplication by integer constants other than 10 is similar, and, in particular, never involves CLC, because, if the answer fits into one byte, the carry flag will always be clear throughout the multiplication.

EXERCISES

1. Give a BASIC statement which is equivalent to each of the following sequences of assembly language statements. Your BASIC statement should contain *no plus signs*.

*(a)

```
          LDA    T
          CLC
          ADC    T
          ADC    T
          STA    T
          ASL    T
```

(b)

```
          LDA    V
          STA    U
          ASL
          ASL
          ADC    U
          ASL
          ADC    U
          STA    U
```

*(c)

```
          LDA    G
          ASL
          ADC    G
          ASL
          ASL
          ADC    G
          STA    F
```

2. Does the sequence of instructions

```
          LSR
          STA    TEMP
          LSR
          LSR
          CLC
          ADC    TEMP
```

divide the A register by 10? If not, what does it set the A register to?

*3. Consider the following sequence of instructions:

```
     LDA    B,X          ;    GET  NEXT  CHARACTER
     CMP    #"9"+!1      ;    IS  IT  GREATER  THAN  "9"
     BCS    DONE         ;    YES,  END  OF  NUMBER
     SBC    #"0"-!1      ;    SUBTRACT  "0"  WITH  CARRY
     BCC    DONE         ;    IF  LESS  THAN  0,  END  OF  NUMBER
```

as described in the text for checking whether the next character is numeric
(between ''0'' and ''9'', inclusive) and converting it from a character
code to an integer. Is there a similar sequence of five instructions in which
SBC comes before CMP? If so, what are the constants involved? If not,
why not?

34. ROTATION AND 16-BIT SHIFTING

Suppose now that we have a two-byte (16-bit) unsigned number which we want to multiply by 2. Can we simply shift both bytes to the left? There is one problem with this, as illustrated below:

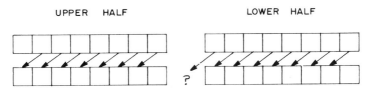

As we can see, all 16 bits are shifted properly except for the one in the middle, which should go from the lower half into the upper half.

Let us shift the lower half first. Then this bit, the leftmost bit of the lower half, goes into the carry status flag, as noted in section 31. What we need now is an instruction which shifts the upper half to the left, but which *also* shifts the carry flag into the *rightmost* bit of the upper half. Such an instruction is ROL (Rotate Left).

Like ASL, ROL shifts the leftmost bit of the given register or cell in memory (call it z) into the carry flag. We can think of z, together with the carry flag, as a nine-bit cycle, and ROL moves the bits around the cycle (hence the name "rotate"), thus:

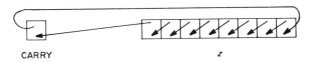

CARRY z

We can apply ROL to the A register or to memory, possibly indexed by the X register, just as we can with ASL. For a 16-bit quantity M with the lower half in M and the upper half in M+!1, as usual, we would write

```
ASL   M     ;   16-BIT SHIFT
ROL   M+!1  ;    TO THE LEFT
```

to shift it left by 1. (This is often called a *double shift*.)

A similar problem arises in shifting a 16-bit number to the right:

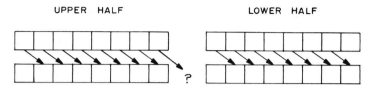

UPPER HALF   LOWER HALF

As before, there is one bit which is not shifted properly. If we shift the *upper* half first, then this bit goes from the right-hand end of the upper half into the carry flag. Now we need an instruction which shifts the lower half to the right, and which also shifts the carry flag into the *leftmost* bit of the lower half. This instruction is ROR (Rotate Right), which has the same rotation properties as ROL, as seen below for ROR z:

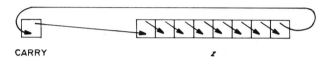

CARRY z

As with ROL, we can apply ROR to the A register, or to memory, possibly indexed by the X register. For the 16-bit quantity M as above, we would write

```
        LSR    M+!1   ;   16-BIT SHIFT
        ROR    M      ;   TO THE RIGHT
```

to shift it right by 1. (As before, this is a double shift.)

The ROR instruction can be used to divide a *signed* quantity by 2, after the original sign bit is put into the carry flag by ASL. Thus to divide the A register by 2, as a signed quantity, we might write

```
        TAX    ;   SAVE A IN X
        ASL    ;   LEFTMOST BIT TO CARRY FLAG
        TXA    ;   RESTORE A FROM X
        ROR    ;   SIGNED RIGHT SHIFT
```

The ROR will shift to the right, but the leftmost bit of the A register, under these conditions, will be the same as it was before. If it was 0, it will still be 0; if it was 1, it will still be 1. This is necessary in dividing by 2, because, if z is positive, then $z/2$ is positive, while if z is negative, then $z/2$ is negative. A shift like this is often called a *sign-extending shift,* since the sign bit is both preserved and extended to the right.*

---

*Any sign-extending shift is an arithmetic shift, since it divides properly. On some computers, there is a single instruction which performs a sign-extending shift.

Like ASL and LSR, ROL and ROR set the zero and sign status flags, and in the usual way, as discussed at the end of section 31. Note that the final program above saves the A register in X, and then restores it (that is, brings it back into A). This is a quite useful technique whenever the X (or Y) register is free.

EXERCISES

1.   (a) Write an assembly language program to set N = 10∗N + D, where N and D are both two-byte quantities with bytes reversed. (Hint: Use the process you have already learned for multiplication by 10; but use 16-bit, rather than 8-bit, shifting and addition.)

    ∗(b) Write an assembly language program to shift a 24-bit quantity P, with bytes reversed, to the left by 1.

     (c) Write an assembly language program to shift an N-byte quantity P (where N is variable), with bytes reversed, to the right by 1. Use a loop.

∗2.   In adding a column of two-digit numbers, such as

$$
\begin{array}{r}
12 \\
14 \\
39 \\
+27 \\
\hline
92
\end{array}
$$

by hand, we normally add all the right-hand digits first (2+4+9+7, in this case) and then all the left-hand digits. On the computer, however, when adding several two-byte quantities, we normally add each quantity to a partial sum; and, in any event, we *cannot* add all the right-hand bytes first, and then all the left-hand bytes. Why not? (Hint: What happens to the carry?)

3.   In shifting a two-byte quantity M to the left by *two* positions, we would normally use sequence (a) below, and we *cannot* use sequence (b) below:

```
(a) ASL  M          (b) ASL  M
    ROL  M+!1           ASL  M
    ASL  M              ROL  M+!1
    ROL  M+!1           ROL  M+!1
```

Explain why sequence (b) is wrong.

35. BIT PROCESSING AND PARITY

Just as we can go through all the bytes in an array, using a loop, so we can go through all the *bits in one byte*, also using a loop. We can do this either from left to right or from right to left.

The commonest way is to use a shift, and then test the carry flag. Each time we shift, a new bit from the byte is shifted into the carry flag to be tested. We do this eight times.

As an example, suppose we want to count the number of one-bits in the A register (that is, the number of bits that are equal to 1). We can do this from left to right by

```
        LDX   #!8      ;   LOOP COUNT IS 8
        LDY   #!0      ;   BIT COUNT IS ZERO
CB      ASL            ;   SHIFT A BIT INTO THE CARRY
        BCC   CB1      ;   IS IT ZERO
        INY            ;   IF NOT, INCREASE THE BIT COUNT
CB1     DEX            ;   DECREASE THE LOOP COUNT
        BNE   CB       ;   IF NOT ZERO, GO BACK
```

Or we can do it from right to left; all we have to do is to substitute LSR for ASL in the program above.

The *parity* of a byte is *one* (or *odd*) if the byte has an odd number of one-bits. Otherwise, the parity is *zero* (or *even*). We saw in section 3 that an odd binary number ends with 1, while an even binary number ends with zero. It therefore follows that the parity (zero or one) is the rightmost bit of the count, as we have calculated it above. Thus we can test the parity of the A register by the program above, followed by the instructions

```
        TYA            ;   LOAD A WITH BIT COUNT
        LSR            ;   CHECK ITS RIGHTMOST BIT
        BCS   ODDP     ;   IF EQUAL TO 1, ODD PARITY
```

or the like. We shall take up the major use of parity in section 90.

As another example, suppose we wanted to convert the byte Q into output form—that is, a string of eight bytes, each of which is either (the character code for) zero or one, that is, "0" or "1". If we output each byte using COUT,

113

as we form it, the bytes must come out from left to right, which means that a left shift is to be used. We might do this by

```
        LDA     Q           ;   KEEP Q IN A TEMPORARY
        STA     TEMP        ;     CELL TO BE SHIFTED
        LDX     #!8         ;   LOOP COUNT IS 8
OCONV   ASL     TEMP        ;   GET THE NEXT BIT
        LDA     #"0"        ;   ASSUME IT IS ZERO
        BCC     OCONV1      ;   IS IT REALLY ZERO
        LDA     #"1"        ;   IF NOT, SET IT TO 1
OCONV1  JSR     COUT        ;   DISPLAY "0" OR "1"
        DEX                 ;   DECREMENT THE LOOP COUNT
        BNE     OCONV       ;   IF NOT ZERO, GO BACK
```

We can also use bit processing to *construct* a byte out of eight bits. This is done by putting each bit into the carry flag and then shifting it into the byte, using a rotate (ROL or ROR). For example, suppose we had an eight-*byte* array called BITS, and each byte is either "0" or "1". (Note that the rightmost bit of each byte is 0 or 1, depending on whether the byte is "0" or "1".) We can convert these bytes into the single byte Q which they represent, by the following program:

```
        LDX     #!0         ;   START LOOP COUNT AT ZERO
CBYTE   LDA     BITS,X      ;   LOOK AT CURRENT CHARACTER
        LSR                 ;   RIGHTMOST BIT TO CARRY
        ROL     Q           ;   ROTATE THIS BIT INTO Q
        INX                 ;   INCREASE THE LOOP COUNT
        CPX     #!8         ;   COMPARE IT WITH MAXIMUM
        BNE     CBYTE       ;   IF UNEQUAL, GO BACK
```

Bit processing is especially helpful in general multiplication and general division, which we shall take up in sections 38−40.

The second program of this section uses a trick which very often saves an instruction. We have to load the A register with either "0" or "1", depending on the carry flag. If we *test* the carry flag first, we need four instructions:

```
        BCS     OCONV1      ;   IS THE CARRY CLEAR OR SET
        LDA     #"0"        ;   CLEAR, SO LOAD "0"
        JMP     OCONV2      ;   AND JUMP AHEAD
OCONV1  LDA     #"1"        ;   SET, SO LOAD "1"
OCONV2  (next  instruction)
```

We could save one byte by changing JMP to BCC, since the carry must be clear (that trick was mentioned near the end of section 27); but the second program of this section does this even better, avoiding the jump entirely: *load* "0" first; *then* test the carry; and, finally, load "1" if the carry is set. Note that COUT must be defined in this program (by COUT EQU $FDED) as usual.

EXERCISES

*1. Consider the following suggested improvement to the first program of this section:

```
        LDY    # ! 0    ;   INITIALIZE THE COUNT
        ASL             ;   LEFTMOST BIT OF A TO CARRY
CB      BCC    CB1      ;   IS THIS BIT A ONE
        INY             ;   IF SO, INCREASE THE COUNT
CB1     ASL             ;   MOVE TO NEXT BIT
        BNE    CB       ;   IF NO MORE BITS, DONE
```

This takes advantage of the fact that ASL sets the *zero* status flag. If the rightmost k bits in the A register are zero, then the last k times through the loop are saved, because the BNE does not branch. However, there is a bug in the above program. Find it. (Hint: Try $C0, $80, and zero as initial contents of the A register.)

2. In the second program of this section, we have used the three instructions

```
        LDA    # " 0 "
        BCC    OCONV1
        LDA    # " 1 "
```

in place of four instructions, as discussed in the text. This may be further improved; we may replace the three instructions above by *two* instructions, of which the first loads the A register with a constant, and the second is ROL. What is the constant (in binary), and why does this work?

*3. Rewrite the third program of this section by decreasing the X register (using DEX) rather than increasing it (using INX). Note that LDA BITS,X must be changed to LDA BITS−!1,X if this is done. Why? Also, what fundamental change must be made, in this case, in the method of constructing the byte?

36. TABLE LOOKUP AND PROGRAM TIMING

There is another way to do the parity calculation of the preceding section, which is many times faster:

```
TAX
LDA     PARITY, X
BNE     ODDP
```

where PARITY is an array of 256 bytes, such that PARITY(J) = 0 if J has even parity, and PARITY(J) = 1 otherwise, for *every possible* byte J; that is, for every J from 0 through 255.

Such an array is often called a *table* (in this case, a *256-position* table), and programs like the one above are said to use *table lookup*. Another example of table lookup is in *dividing* an integer Q by 10, producing an integer result (thus, for example, 85 divided by 10 is *not* 8½, but rather 8, with a remainder of 5). If we have a 256-position table DIV10, such that DIV10(J) = J/10 (in this sense) for every possible byte J, then we can divide Q by 10 in two instructions:

```
LDX     Q
LDA     DIV10, X
```

The important disadvantage of table lookup is the amount of *space* (that is, the great number of cells in the memory) that it often uses. Especially in a small computer, 256 cells are quite a lot. Some tables, however, are not that large. For example, we could also multiply by 10, using a table MULT10, where MULT10(J) = 10*J, and here J ranges from zero to 25, because 26*10 (= 260) is too large to fit into one byte. Thus the table, in this case, is only a 26-position table.

Since the table lookup programs above save so much time, it is interesting to calculate exactly how much time they save. On the 6502, the amount of time taken by each instruction is given in *cycles*. These cycle times appear in

Table 4 in the Appendix.* (On the APPLE, one cycle is approximately one *microsecond,* or one millionth of a second, so that there are approximately 1,000,000 cycles per second, or *one megahertz.* The actual figure is 1,023,000 cycles per second.[†] Other 6502-based systems sometimes operate at 2,000,000 cycles per second, or *two megahertz.*

From Table 4, we can see that:

(1) TAX takes 2 cycles;
(2) LDA PARITY,X takes 4 cycles (ignore the zero-page addresses of the form Z or Z,X or Z,Y in Table 4 for the moment—these will be taken up in section 74);
(3) BNE ODDP takes 2 cycles (unless it actually branches).

This is a total of 8 cycles, to which we add one more if the BNE branches. (We actually add *two* more, if the BNE branches to an address having a different high-order byte from that of the address of the BNE itself. Similarly, one extra cycle must be added for indexed instructions if adding the 8-bit index to the 16-bit address changes the high-order byte of that address. In all our further discussion, however, we shall ignore these effects, since, if absolutely necessary, they can always be avoided.)

Now let us compare this with the parity program in section 35 (the first program of that section with three extra instructions—TYA, LSR, and BCS ODDP—as indicated):

(1) First we consider the instructions that are in the loop. There are five of them (ASL, BCC, INY, DEX, BNE). If neither the BCC nor the BNE branches, each one of these takes 2 cycles, for a total of 10 cycles.
(2) The BNE actually branches every time except the last. So we have 11 cycles.
(3) If the BCC branches, it takes one more cycle but the INY is not done, so the total is actually one cycle less, or 10 cycles. Thus, each time through the loop takes either 10 or 11 cycles.
(4) Since the loop is done eight times, we have a total of from 10*8 to 11*8, or 80 to 88 cycles.

---

*Table 4 can also be used to find the number of *bytes* in any instruction. For example, LDA Q is given in machine language form, in Table 4, as AD *cd ab*; so there are three bytes (AD, *cd,* and *ab*).

[†]It may be argued that 1,022,700 cycles per second is a more accurate figure; however, this is subject to a certain amount of drift. The figure of 1,023,000, which we use throughout, is specified in the APPLE reference manual.

(5) From this we have to subtract 1, since the BNE does not branch the last time through the loop. This leaves a total of anywhere from 79 to 87 cycles.

(6) Finally, we add 10 more cycles, two for each of the five instructions (LDX, LDY, TYA, LSR, BCS) that are *outside* the loop. The final total is thus 89 to 97 cycles, plus one more if the BCS branches. Note that a load instruction (LDA, LDX, or LDY) takes only two cycles if a *constant* is being loaded.   /

The very high speed of computers is one of the great secrets of their power. Note that the above loop, even though it is done eight times, still takes less than 100 microseconds, which means that it can be done over ten thousand times every second! Sometimes we say that such a program takes less than one tenth of a *millisecond* (one millisecond being $1/1,000$ of a second).

Always remember, when calculating the timing of a program, to take into account *the number of times a loop is executed*. If the statements in a loop take a total of n cycles, and the loop is executed k times, then this makes nk cycles (actually $nk - 1$, almost always, because the last instruction in the loop is usually a conditional branch, which takes one *fewer* cycle the last time through the loop, as we saw above). In addition, there will always be certain instructions which are not in any loop, and which are done only once; and we have to add the amount of time that these take, to obtain the total.

EXERCISES

1. It is a bit tedious to write out the constant definitions for a long table. Thus, for example, 26 uses of BYT are required for the 26-position table for multiplication by 10 (BYT !0, BYT !10, BYT !20, and so on). Instead of doing this, we can write a program to store these 26 numbers in the table MULT10. This can then be done once, before the table is ever used. Write such an assembly language program. (Use DEX.)

*2. Determine the amount of time (expressed in cycles) taken by the assembly language program of section 21. Express this as a formula involving the value of N. Show your work. Also determine the total number of bytes in the instruction codes for this program.

3. Determine the amount of time, expressed in cycles, taken by the second assembly language program of section 22. Express this as a formula involving the value of N. Show your work. Also determine the total number of bytes in the instruction codes for this program. Note that this program does the same thing as that of section 21. Is it an improvement?

37. SPACE-TIME TRADEOFFS

We have now had many examples of a program that takes less time, but more space, than another program that does the same thing. This situation is called a *space-time tradeoff*. Sometimes space is more important than time; other times it is less important. How do we decide, in any given case? There are many criteria we should consider:

(1) *How much space, and how much time, is involved.* If one program takes twice the space of another, but only one-tenth as much time, then time may be more important. If it takes twice the time, but only one-tenth the space, then space may be more important.

(2) *How often the program is done.* If it is inside a loop, or a subroutine, then any time which is saved is multiplied by the number of times the loop is done, or the subroutine is called. This effect is multiplied further if the loop, or the subroutine, is itself inside a loop, or inside a subroutine.

(3) *How much total space is available.* There are APPLE computers with fewer than the total 65,536 bytes; there are microcomputer systems with a very small number of bytes. In such a situation, space becomes critical; you should probably save space whenever you can.

(4) *Whether your program is interacting with other devices which may have their own timing requirements.* Such programs are called *real-time programs*; sometimes (although not always) they must be written with speed, first and foremost, in mind.

(5) *Whether you are paying for computer time.* On a large computer, you often pay by the second. It is thus very important to save time. On a microcomputer, time is usually so cheap as to be almost free. Therefore, *normally you will want to save space, rather than saving time, when working with a microcomputer.*

As another example of space-time tradeoff, consider the following alternative way of dividing Q by 10:

```
LDA   Q       ;   SET A = Q AND COUNT (NO. OF TIMES
LDX   #$FF    ;     THAT 10 IS SUBTRACTED) = −1
SEC           ;   SET CARRY FOR SUBTRACTION
```

```
DTEN   INX              ;   INCREASE THE COUNT AND SUBTRACT
       SBC    #!10      ;      10 - - IF CARRY SET (RESULT
       BCS    DTEN      ;      STILL POSITIVE), REPEAT
       TXA              ;   COUNT (A/10) TO A-REGISTER
```

This program takes 12 bytes of memory, as opposed to 262 (256 + 6) for the program given in the preceding section to divide Q by 10. It takes anywhere from 16 to 191 cycles (average, 103½ cycles), as opposed to 8 cycles. So it is almost 13 times slower, but over 21 times shorter, than the other division program.

Actually, all of these figures are imprecise. The TXA in the above program is often not used; instead, X is stored directly, using STX. More importantly, the average of 103½ cycles, given above, assumes that we are dividing randomly chosen numbers. It usually happens, in a program, that small numbers are divided much more often than larger ones. This pattern of usage of the program would speed it up considerably. Imprecision of this kind occurs much more often than not; for this reason, *timing calculations are rather uncommon in practical programming,* although they are of great theoretical interest.

Sometimes, of course, what appears to be a tradeoff is not a tradeoff at all; one program is *both* shorter and faster than another equivalent program. For example, the program at the end of section 22 is both shorter and faster than the equivalent program at the end of section 21.

There is a third quantity which trades off with both space and time, namely *programmer time.* A program which takes a long time to write and a long time to debug can be very costly, even if it takes less computer time and less space in memory than an alternative. For this reason it is very common to write simple, easily understood, but relatively slow programs (the slang expression for these is "quick and dirty" programs). If a program will be run only once, or only a few times, or will be modified every few times it is run, the quick and dirty method is almost always the best.

EXERCISES

*1.   Suppose that there is a BASIC program which runs one hundred times faster on one computer than it does on another. Are there any conditions under which the second computer is actually preferable to the first, for running this program?

 2.   Compare the program

```
              TAX
              LDA    MULT10,X
```

(where MULT10 is as specified in section 36) with the first program of section 33, which does the same thing. How much slower, and how much shorter, is one of these programs, compared to the other? Show your work. Remember to count *both* data bytes and program (instruction code) bytes in both cases.

*3.   Compare the two programs at the beginning of section 32. Is there a space-time tradeoff here? Why or why not? (You do not need to be specific about the number of bytes and cycles.)

38. BINARY MULTIPLICATION AND DIVISION

Suppose now that we have the BASIC statement K = I*J. How do we do this in assembly language? On some computers there are instructions, like our ADC and SBC, which multiply and divide. On such a computer we would use three instructions: load I, multiply by J, and store in K. The 6502, however, does not have multiplication or division instructions; we have to use subroutines instead. These subroutines, unlike RDKEY and COUT, are not provided in the APPLE monitor, so we have to provide our own. We will learn how to write and use such subroutines; in order to do so, we must first see how binary numbers are multiplied and divided.

We saw in section 3 that the rules for adding and subtracting numbers of more than one digit are the same in the binary number system as they are in the decimal system, with 2 substituted for 10. The same is true of multiplication and division. For example, here is 173 times 199, in both decimal and binary:

$$
\begin{array}{r}
173 \\
\times 199 \\
\hline
1557 \\
1557 \\
173 \\
\hline
34427
\end{array}
\qquad
\begin{array}{r}
10101101 \\
\times 11000111 \\
\hline
10101101 \\
10101101 \\
10101101 \\
00000000 \\
00000000 \\
00000000 \\
10101101 \\
10101101 \\
\hline
1000011001111011
\end{array}
$$

The binary multiplication is longer, but it is also, theoretically, easier. Note that in the decimal multiplication we have to multiply 173 by 9, getting 1557. We never have to do anything like this in binary multiplication; we always multiply by either 1 or 0, which is easy.

Multiplying two 8-bit quantities produces a 16-bit quantity. We can write a program to multiply the A register by the X register, for example; but the answer will not fit into one register. We can put the answer in the A and X registers together, with the upper half in A and the lower half in X.

Sometimes the answer will be an 8-bit quantity. In the case above, this would be the X register, and the A register would be zero. We could also write a simpler multiplication program which assumes that (and does not work unless) the answer is an 8-bit quantity.

Similarly, here is 34427 divided by 173, in both decimal and binary:

```
          199                              11000111
     ┌─────────              ┌──────────────────────────
 173 │ 34427        10101101 │ 1000011001111011
       173                     10101101
      ────                     ────────
      1712                     10111111
      1557                     10101101
      ────                     ────────
      1557                     100101110
      1557                     10101101
      ────                     ─────────
         0                     100000011
                               10101101
                               ─────────
                               10101101
                               10101101
                               ────────
                                      0
```

The division, like the multiplication, is longer but theoretically easier. In the decimal division we have to multiply 173 by 9, just as in the decimal multiplication. In the binary division, we are always subtracting the same quantity, in this case 10101101.

Division is the inverse of multiplication; so we start with a 16-bit quantity and divide by an 8-bit quantity. In a program, we might start with a quantity in the A and X registers together, with the upper half in A and the lower half in X, and divide this by the quantity in the Y register.

The result of this division might not fit into one 8-bit register. (In particular, dividing by 1 produces the original 16-bit number.) But it is customary for the answer to be 8 bits long in this case; if the actual answer is longer than this, the division program goes to an error exit. (The same thing happens if we try to divide by zero, which is an undefined operation.)

A simple and clever test may be used for both overflow and division by zero. If we are dividing $256*A+X$ by Y (note that the 16-bit quantity with upper half in A and lower half in X has value $256*A+X$), with the result $Q \geqslant 256$ (the overflow case), then $256*A+X \geqslant Q*Y \geqslant 256*Y$, or $A+(X/256) \geqslant Y$; since A and Y are integers and $X < 256$ (so that $X/256 < 1$), this implies $A \geqslant Y$. But if Y is zero, then also $A \geqslant Y$—so that the single test that $A < Y$ is sufficient to insure that there will be *neither* overflow nor division by zero.

There is an 8-bit *remainder,* as well as an 8-bit quotient. At the end of the division program, we may leave the quotient in the X register, and the remainder in the A register.

The rules for multiplying and dividing *hexadecimal* numbers are the same as those for binary numbers, with 16 substituted for 2. The interested reader may work out some examples of this; but we will not need to concern ourselves with it. Indeed, it may be argued that the easiest way to multiply or divide hexadecimal numbers is to convert them to binary, multiply or divide them that way, and then convert the results back to hexadecimal.

EXERCISES

1. Do the following multiplications in binary, multiplying two *four-bit* numbers:

    (a) 9 × 9
    *(b) 3 × 10 (Note: Do 3 × 10—*not* 10 × 3)
    (c) 15 × 15

2. Do the following divisions in binary:

    *(a) $111 \overline{\smash{\big)}\, 1000110}$

    *(b) $1010 \overline{\smash{\big)}\, 1000000}$

    *(c) $1101 \overline{\smash{\big)}\, 11001000}$

3. In each of the divisions of Exercise 2 above, what are the decimal numbers that are being divided, and what are the quotient and remainder as decimal numbers?

39. A MULTIPLICATION SUBROUTINE

Figure 13 shows a subroutine to multiply two 8-bit quantities. You can include this subroutine as part of your program and call it with JSR MULT (just as you would call JSR COUT to display a character, for example).

Before you call MULT, you put the quantities to be multiplied in the A- and X-registers; MULT will multiply what it finds in A and X and produce a 16-bit answer, which it leaves in A and X (left half in A, right half in X). After the JSR MULT you may, for example, store A and X in the two bytes of a 16-bit variable. Of course, if you know that your answer will fit into eight bits, then it will be left in the X register, and zero will be left in the A register. All quantities to be multiplied are considered as *unsigned* numbers. (In section 88, we will see how to multiply signed quantities.)

For example, to set M3 = M1*M2, where M1, M2, and M3 are all 8-bit unsigned quantities, we could write

```
LDA   M1      ;   SET UP QUANTITIES TO
LDX   M2      ;     BE MULTIPLIED
JSR   MULT    ;   NOW MULTIPLY THEM
STX   M3      ;   AND PUT THE RESULT IN M3
```

If M3 were a 16-bit quantity, kept with bytes reversed, we would put STA M3+!1 on the end of this sequence, to store the left half (STX M3 already stores the right half).

We say that MULT is *entered* with I and J in the A and X registers, and that MULT *exits* with I*J, as a 16-bit quantity, in the A and X registers. This is a very common technique used with assembly language subroutines: if they act on data, this data is often entered in the registers, and, if they produce a result, the result is often left in the registers. You can thus call a subroutine many times, loading different quantities into the registers each time, and storing the result in a different place each time. (In the same way, COUT is entered with the character to be output in the A register; RDKEY exits with the input character in the A register.)

This multiplication program, and the division program of the next section, are presented as examples of how efficiently programs can be written in assembly language. They are *not* presented as examples of how efficient *your own* pro-

```
                 ; MULTIPLICATION SUBROUTINE  - - K = I*J (UNSIGNED)
                 ; K IS 16 BITS LONG  - - I AND J ARE 8 BITS LONG
                 ; ENTER WITH I AND J IN REGISTERS A AND X
    LINE         ; EXITS WITH K IN REGISTERS A AND X
   NUMBER        ; (LEFT HALF OF K IN A, RIGHT HALF OF K IN X)
      1   MULT      STX   MDATA1   ; STORE I AND J, WITH I
      2             LSR            ;   ALREADY SHIFTED RIGHT AND
      3             STA   MDATA2   ;   RIGHTMOST BIT IN CARRY
      4             LDX   #!8      ; LOOP COUNT
      5             LDA   #!0      ; SUM STARTS OUT AT ZERO
      6   MULT1     BCC   MULT2    ; IS THIS BINARY DIGIT ZERO
      7             CLC            ; NO, CLEAR CARRY AND
      8             ADC   MDATA1   ;   ADD J
      9   MULT2     ROR            ; INDENT THE SUM (DOUBLE SHIFT)
     10             ROR   MDATA2   ; NEXT BINARY DIGIT TO CARRY
     11             DEX            ; REPEAT THIS 8 TIMES FOR
     12             BNE   MULT1    ;   8 BITS IN I AND J
     13             LDX   MDATA2   ; RIGHT HALF OF ANSWER SHIFTED
     14             RTS            ;   INTO MDATA2. LOAD IT AND EXIT
     15   MDATA1    DFS   !1       ; DATA (I)
     16   MDATA2    DFS   !1       ; DATA (J)
```

Figure 13. A Multiplication Program.

grams ought to be at this stage. Each of them was the result of a long process of refinement—far more than one ought to spend on any but the most commonly used subroutines.

We will now explain how MULT works. We start MULT by giving some general comments, each of which is on a line that *starts* with a semicolon (see section 18). These tell what the subroutine does, what it is entered with, and what it exits with, in a precise way. Be sure to do this for *any* subroutine you write.

We are adding eight quantities, as in the preceding section. This is done in a loop with a counter in the X register, originally set to 8 (line 4). It is decremented at the end of the loop (line 11) and tested for zero (line 12).

The addition takes place in a double register, with the upper half in A and the lower half in MDATA2. The left-hand $7+k$ bits of this register are used when we are adding the kth quantity (when $9-k$ is in the X register). The rest of MDATA2, with one intervening bit (which is always zero), holds the quantity which was originally in the A register. We are multiplying by this quantity and looking at the bits of it from right to left. Every time one of these is a one-bit, we add the original contents of X. Otherwise, we do not need to add. This is because $X*1 = X$ and $X*0 = 0$.

Using MDATA2 for two different purposes works because both quantities are being shifted to the right, with one being shifted in, and the other being shifted out. At the end, the second quantity is shifted entirely out and the 16-bit register (that is, A and MDATA2) holds the answer. Then we load X with MDATA2 (line 13), so that A and X hold the answer, as we specified.

The program starts by setting the original values of MDATA1 (line 1) and MDATA2 and the carry flag (lines 2 and 3). Note that, when we get to MULT1, the carry flag already contains the rightmost bit of the A register; this bit will be tested at MULT1. Also we set the sum to zero (line 5) so that we can add eight quantities to it.

At MULT1, we test the current bit of the A register. If this is 1, we add J to the sum, clearing the carry first (lines 7 and 8). This addition may or may not produce carry. At MULT2, we shift the partial sum to the right so that the next term can be added. Normally this would be done by LSR and ROR (see section 34); but we replace the LSR by another ROR *so as to shift in the carry from the addition*, as noted above. (If the branch at MULT1 was taken, the carry will be clear, so that zero is shifted in.) This double shift (lines 9 and 10), at the same time, puts the next bit of MDATA2 (counting from right to left) into the carry flag, to be tested the next time through the loop (at line 6).

This is a subroutine, and thus has a *return instruction*, RTS (Return from Subroutine). This is like RETURN in BASIC or FORTRAN. (In section 60, we will see how RTS actually works.) Note that RTS is followed *immediately* by the data; we will *not use a data section* with a *subroutine* in assembly language.

EXERCISES

1. Give a BASIC statement which corresponds to each of the following sequences of assembly language statements (assuming that MULT is as specified in Figure 13):

    *(a)
    ```
    LDA   P
    CLC
    ADC   Q
    LDX   R
    DEX
    JSR   MULT
    STX   S
    ```

    (b)
    ```
    LDA   #!10
    LDX   N
    JSR   MULT
    TXA
    CLC
    ADC   D
    STA   N
    ```

*(c)
```
              LDX   J
              TXA
              JSR   MULT
              TXA
              JSR   MULT
              STX   K
```

2. Give an assembly language form of each of the following BASIC state-
    ments (omit ORG, END, and DFS). Assume that the array T starts at T(1),
    and that all variables correspond to 8-bit quantities.

    (a) Q = R * S - 1
    *(b) T (J) = K * (J - 5)
    (c) W = T (I * J)

3. (a) How many bytes are used by the program of Figure 13? Show your
        work by adding up the number of bytes in each instruction (use Table 4
        in the Appendix)* and one for each data byte.
    *(b) How many cycles (maximum and minimum) are used by the *loop* of
        the program of Figure 13? Show your work by adding up the number
        of cycles in each of the two cases (when the BCC branches, and when
        it does not), multiplying by the number of times the loop is done, and
        subtracting 1 since the BNE takes one fewer cycle when it does not
        branch. Use Table 4 in the Appendix. Remember that the ADC is done
        only when the BCC does *not* branch.
    *(c) Obtain the total number of cycles (maximum and minimum) used by
        the program of Figure 13 by adding the cycle times of the instructions
        outside the loop to the result of part (b) above. Show your work as in
        part (b).

---

*When using Table 4, remember not to use the Z options. For example, under STX, you will find
both STX Q, which is given as a three-byte instruction (8E *cd ab*), and STX Z, which is given as a
two-byte instruction (86 *ef*). Do not use the STX Z, or any other instruction with a Z in it, in Table 4,
until you have come to section 74, where you will learn what the Z options are for.

40. A DIVISION SUBROUTINE

Figure 14 shows a subroutine to divide a 16-bit quantity by an 8-bit quantity; both quantities are unsigned. To use this subroutine, first put the 8-bit quantity in the Y register and the 16-bit quantity in the A and X registers, with the upper half in A and the lower half in X. (If you are dividing one 8-bit quantity by another, put the first 8-bit quantity in X and put zero in A, as usual.) Now call DIV (JSR DIV); this will divide the first quantity by the second, producing an answer (the *quotient*), which it leaves in the X-register, and a *remainder*, which it leaves in the A register. After the JSR DIV you will normally store X and ignore what is in the A register, since, when we divide, we normally don't care about the remainder. However, the remainder, often called MOD(I, J) (where we are dividing I by J), is there if you need it for some reason.

For example, to set M3 = M1/M2, where M1, M2, and M3 are all eight-bit unsigned quantities, we could write

```
LDA    #!0    ;   SET UP
LDX    M1     ;     QUANTITIES TO
LDY    M2     ;       BE DIVIDED
JSR    DIV    ;   NOW DIVIDE THEM
STX    M3     ;   AND PUT THE QUOTIENT IN M3
```

If M1 were a 16-bit quantity, kept with bytes reversed, we would replace LDA #!0 by LDA M1+!1 (LDX M1 remains the same).

This division program *exits with the carry set to indicate an error*. There are two sources of error: we might be trying to divide by zero; or the answer, after division, might be too large to fit into one byte. In either of these cases, the carry will be *set* when DIV exits; otherwise, the carry will be *clear*. Thus JSR DIV may be followed immediately by BCS ERROR (or the like) to test this. DIV also exits with the quotient in X and the remainder in A, and is entered with the dividend in A and X and the divisor in Y, using the terminology of the preceding section.

We will now explain how DIV works. First, as before, we give comments (starting with semicolons) that explain what DIV does, and its entry and exit conditions. We start by storing the divisor (line 2) and the right half of the dividend

```
         ; DIVISION SUBROUTINE  -- K = I/J (UNSIGNED)
         ; I IS 16 BITS LONG  -- J AND K ARE 8 BITS LONG
         ; ENTER WITH J IN Y, AND I IN A AND X
         ; (LEFT HALF IN A, RIGHT HALF IN X)
         ; EXITS WITH K IN X, AND REMAINDER IN A
 LINE    ; EXITS WITH CARRY = 0  -- NORMAL, 1 -- ERROR
NUMBER   ; (DIVISION BY ZERO, OR ANSWER TOO LARGE)
   1   DIV    STX    DDATA2   ; RIGHT HALF OF DIVIDEND
   2          STY    DDATA1   ; DIVISOR
   3          LDX    #!8      ; LOOP COUNT
   4          CMP    DDATA1   ; IS ANSWER TOO BIG, OR DIV BY 0
   5          BCS    DIV4     ;   -- YES, EXIT WITH CARRY SET
   6   DIV1   ROL    DDATA2   ; SHIFT DOUBLE REGISTER (INDENT
   7          ROL             ;   AND SHIFT IN AN ANSWER BIT)
   8          BCC    DIV2     ; IS 17-BIT RESULT OF THE SHIFT
   9          SBC    DDATA1   ;   -- YES, ALWAYS SUBTRACT
  10          SEC             ; BUT ANSWER BIT IS A 1
  11          BCS    DIV3     ;   (THIS ALWAYS BRANCHES)
  12   DIV2   CMP    DDATA1   ; WILL SUBTRACTION PRODUCE A
  13          BCC    DIV3     ; NEGATIVE RESULT (ANS BIT 0)
  14          SBC    DDATA1   ;   -- NO, SUBTRACT (ANS BIT 1)
  15   DIV3   DEX             ; IF NOT DONE, REPEAT WITH NEW
  16          BNE    DIV1     ;   ANSWER BIT IN CARRY FLAG
  17          ROL    DDATA2   ; SHIFT IN LAST ANSWER BIT AND
  18          LDX    DDATA2   ; LOAD X WITH ANSWER (CARRY 0)
  19   DIV4   RTS             ; QUIT (CARRY 1 = ERROR)
  20   DDATA1 DFS    !1       ; DIVISOR
  21   DDATA2 DFS    !1       ; RIGHT HALF OF DIVIDEND; ANSWER
```

Figure 14. A Division Program.

(line 1), and setting up the loop count (line 3) just as we did in MULT. (The loop in this program ends, just as in MULT, with DEX and BNE, which are at lines 15 and 16, in this case.) Now we test to see whether the upper half of our 16-bit quantity is less than Y. If not, we have one of our two error cases: either Y = 0, or the answer will be too large (as explained in section 38). We return from the subroutine (line 19) with the carry set (because we branched on carry set). Otherwise, we continue, and, as we shall see, the carry will be clear at the end.

The subtraction takes place in a double register, with the upper half in A and the lower half in DDATA2. The left-hand $17-k$ bits of this register are used when we are subtracting for the kth time, to produce the kth bit of the answer (when $9-k$ is in the X register). The rest of DDATA2, with one intervening bit (which is always zero), holds the answer, which is being shifted into DDATA2 from the right. Using DDATA2 for two different purposes in this way works because both quantities are being shifted to the left.

The first time we get to DIV1, the carry will be clear (otherwise we would have branched to DIV4). So we rotate in the intervening zero bit. The double shift here operates on the double register mentioned above.

If the double shift produces carry, we have a 17-bit number, with the carry flag being the highest order bit. In this case we *always* subtract (line 9), and, since we do, the next answer bit is always 1. So we branch (line 11) to the end of the loop with the carry set to 1 (line 10). Note that the BCS always branches in this case.

If the double shift does not produce carry, we have to test to see whether subtraction is to be performed (line 12). If not, then we branch to the end of the loop (line 13) with the carry set to 0. If so, then the carry is set (otherwise we would take the branch) and so we can subtract without an SEC; *this subtraction itself leaves the carry set to 1* (because otherwise the answer would be negative).

The crucial point is that there are three ways to get to DIV3 (through the branch at line 11, through the branch at line 13, and through line 14); and, in each case, *the next bit of the answer is in the carry flag*.

Now we terminate the loop in the usual way. If we go back to DIV1, then the first ROL will rotate the next bit of the answer into DDATA2. (This ROL and the next one thus replace the usual sequence for a double shift, namely ASL and ROL.) If we do not go back, the last bit of the answer is rotated (line 17) into DDATA2. This also rotates the intervening zero-bit into the carry flag (so that the carry is clear on normal exit); and the answer is loaded into X (line 18). The remainder is now in the A register since it is nothing more than the result of the last subtraction.

EXERCISES

1. Give a BASIC statement which corresponds to each of the following sequences of assembly language statements (assuming that MULT is as specified in Figure 13, and DIV is as specified in Figure 14:

*(a)
```
        LDA     #!0
        LDX     Q
        LDY     R
        DEX
        INY
        JSR     DIV
        STX     S
```

(b)
```
        LDA     #!100
        LDX     #!0
        LDY     J
        JSR     DIV
        STA     C
```

*(c)
```
                    LDA    I
                    SEC
                    SBC    J
                    LDX    #!10
                    JSR    MULT
                    LDY    K
                    JSR    DIV
                    STX    L
```

2. Give an assembly language form of each of the following BASIC state-
    ments (omit ORG, END, and DFS), assuming that all variables correspond
    to 8-bit quantities:

    *(a) I = (J+K)/L
     (b) D = MOD(N,10)+C
    *(c) W = (L/M)/N

3. Do Exercise 3 (all three parts) of the preceding section for the program of
    Figure 14. In part (b), there are three cases to consider: when the first BCC
    does not branch; when the first BCC branches but the second does not; and
    when both BCCs branch. Be sure that in each of these three cases you count
    only the instructions that are actually executed in that case.

41. INPUT AND OUTPUT CONVERSION

We have learned how to perform character input (with RDKEY), character output (with COUT), line input (with GETLNZ), and line output (with a loop involving a call to COUT). In most programs, however—with the exception of those dealing with input and output as character strings only—we must also call subroutines which perform *conversion* of integers and other types of data.*

Every integer has an *internal form* and an *external form*. For example, consider the integer 209. It has the following forms:

	External Form	Internal Form
Hexadecimal	B2 B0 B9	D1
Binary	10110010 10110000 10111001	11010001
Character code	"209"	"Q"

The external form is the input-output form. That is, when you type 209, the characters 2, 0, and 9, in character code form (B2, B0, and B9, in hexadecimal), come into the computer. When your program displays 209 on the screen, it must again do so by outputting each of these three characters in turn.

The internal form is what is used in calculations, such as addition and subtraction. In this case 11010001 is the binary internal form, because 209 (decimal) is 11010001 (binary). In hexadecimal, this becomes D1. It also *happens* to be the character code for the letter Q, but that is irrelevant to this discussion.

If we want to write a program which lets us type "209+170" and then displays "379" (the sum of 209 and 170), for example, our program will normally do the following:

(1) Input the characters "209" and "170" (in external form).
(2) Convert them from external to internal form (this is called *input conversion*).

---

*In BASIC, this is also done, although the subroutines are part of the BASIC system and are called automatically when needed.

133

(3) Add them in internal form.

(4) Convert the result from internal form back to external form (this is called *output conversion*).

(5) Output the result (that is, "379").

Conversion to internal form is often called *conversion to binary*, and internal form is widely known as *binary form*. This is a misnomer, as the above tables show; *all* numbers in a computer are binary numbers. The internal form, however, expressed in binary, does represent the ordinary binary representation of a decimal number as given in section 2.

In sections 62 and 63 there are given two conversion routines, DECI (Decimal Input) and DECO (Decimal Output). At this point we will discuss only how these routines are used, since they contain instructions that we will study at a later time.*

The routine DECI is entered with the standard input buffer index in the X register. That is, if we have set INBUF EQU $0200 as usual, then X has to be set, before the JSR DECI, to a value (normally zero) which is such that LDA INBUF,X loads the first character of the input string. This allows DECI to be used when several numbers are given on one input line; normally, if we are reading a number starting at the beginning of the line, we would enter DECI with X set to zero.

When DECI exits, the converted decimal number will be in the A and X registers, with the upper half in A and the lower half in X; and the carry will be clear, unless the given number was too large (that is, larger than 65535). In that case the carry will be set (and the contents of A and X are meaningless).

The routine DECO is entered with the A and X registers containing a 16-bit number, as on exit from DECI. This number is converted to decimal and displayed, using COUT. An example of the use of DECI and DECO is given in Figure 15. Note that Figure 15 uses DECOZ, rather than DECO; this is an alternative, which starts the output on a new line (DECO continues on the current line).

There are two ways to make sure that the LISA system knows where the subroutines are. One is to include all the instructions of the subroutines with the program that calls them and assemble these all together. The other is to assemble them at different places; for example, DECI might be assembled at $0900 (by inserting ORG $0900 as the first statement of DECI) and similarly DECO at $0A00. If you do this, then DECI EQU $0900 and DECOZ EQU $0A00 should be included with the calling program, to tell it where DECI and DECOZ are.† Make sure, if you do this, that the subroutines are not so close together that they overlap.

Do not try to use these instructions (particularly PHA and PLA) in your own programs until you have studied them in detail; they must be used with care.

†Looking at Figure 22, section 63, we see that DECO starts at the eighth byte of this program because the PHA, JSR, and JMP take up a total of 7 bytes (see Table 4 in the Appendix). Thus, if DECOZ is assembled at $0A00, DECO will be at $0A07, and DECO EQU $0A07 should be included with any program in which JSR DECO is contained.

```
; THIS PROGRAM READS A NUMBER K AND DISPLAYS 2K
GETLNZ   EQU    $FD67     ; LOCATION OF GETLNZ ROUTINE
         ORG    $0800     ; START OF PROGRAM SECTION
PROG1    JSR    GETLNZ    ; READ A NUMBER
         LDX    #!0       ; ENTER INPUT CONVERSION WITH X = 0
         JSR    DECI      ;   (NUMBER STARTS AT BEGINNING OF LINE)
         BCS    PROG1     ; IF TOO LARGE, TRY AGAIN
         STA    IUPPER    ; INPUT CONVERSION EXITS WITH NUMBER
         STX    ILOWER    ;   IN A AND X -- STORE IT
         ASL    ILOWER    ; DOUBLE SHIFT OF ILOWER AND
         ROL    IUPPER    ;   IUPPER (MULTIPLICATION BY 2)
         LDX    ILOWER    ; ENTER OUTPUT CONVERSION WITH NUMBER
         LDA    IUPPER    ;   TO BE CONVERTED IN A AND X
         JSR    DECOZ     ; CALL OUTPUT CONVERSION

         (here we include either the subroutines DECI and DECO,
            or else EQU statements which specify where they are)
         ORG    $C100     ; START OF DATA SECTION
ILOWER   DFS    !1        ; LOWER END OF 16-BIT NUMBER, I
IUPPER   DFS    !1        ; UPPER END OF I
         END
```

Figure 15. Using Input and Output Conversion.

An APPLE subroutine which may be used along with output conversion is PRBL2 (the PRBL stands for "print blanks"), which prints *n* blanks, where *n* is entered in the X register. Thus, to print 10 blanks, you do an LDX #!10 followed by JSR PRBL2 (where PRBL2 EQU $F94A defines this subroutine in your program).

The subroutines DECI and DECO (and DECOZ) *use the registers for their own purposes*, just like RDKEY and GETLNZ (see section 25). After a JSR to any one of these subroutines, therefore, *do not* expect Y (for example) to have the same value it had before the JSR.

EXERCISES

1. What is the output of each of the following sequences of instructions, assuming that the input is the number 50? 100? 200? (Assume that DECI and DECOZ are as in this section; DIV is as in section 40; and GETLNZ is as in section 25.)

    *(a)
    ```
                                JSR    GETLNZ
                                LDX    #!0
                                JSR    DECI
                                INX
    ```

```
                              BNE     NEXT
                              CLC
                              ADC     #!1
                      NEXT    JSR     DECOZ
```

(b)
```
                              JSR     GETLNZ
                              LDX     #!0
                              JSR     DECI
                              CMP     #!0
                              BNE     NEXT
                              CPX     #!100
                              BNE     NEXT
                              TAX
                      NEXT    JSR     DECOZ
```

*(c)
```
                              JSR     GETLNZ
                              LDX     #!0
                              JSR     DECI
                              LDY     #!10
                              JSR     DIV
                              LDA     #!0
                              JSR     DECOZ
```

2. Write sequences of instructions to do each of the following. (Assume that DECI, DECOZ, DIV, and GETLNZ are as in the preceding exercise.)

(a) Read one number, store it in READ and READ+!1 (with bytes reversed), and display it.

*(b) Display the 8-bit quantity J times 200. (Use MULT.)

(c) Read one line which contains two numbers, one starting in column 1 and the other starting in column 7, and branch to NOTEQ if they are unequal. (The numbers may range from 0 to 65535.)

*3. What is wrong with the following program to output the numbers 1 through 10 (using DECOZ as in this section)?

```
                              LDX     #!0
                              STX     J
                      LOOP    INC     J
                              LDX     J
                              CPX     #!11
                              BEQ     DONE
                              JSR     DECOZ
                              JMP     LOOP
                      DONE    (next  instruction)
```

42. COMPLETE PROGRAMS

We are now ready to write a complete program. In the next eight sections, we will learn how to assemble, debug, and run such a program on the APPLE.

There is no instruction on the 6502 that *stops* the computer (as there is on many other computers). A *main program* on the APPLE customarily ends with an instruction called BRK ("break"), which jumps to a program called the *monitor,* discussed in section 47.*

Here is an example of a complete program; it reads text from the keyboard, terminated by a control-E, and stops (using BRK) with the A-register containing the number of times that the word AGE occurs as a separate word in what was typed:

```
RDKEY   EQU   $FD0C        ;  APPLE SUBROUTINE, RDKEY
CTRLE   EQU   $85          ;  CONTROL-E CHARACTER
        ORG   $0800        ;  START OF PROGRAM SECTION
        LDA   #!0          ;  INITIAL VALUE OF COUNT (NO.
        STA   COUNT        ;  OF OCCURRENCES OF "AGE") = 0
        JMP   L3           ;  SKIP FIRST TEST, FIRST TIME
L1      JSR   RDR          ;  READ ONE CHARACTER
L2      JSR   CAC          ;  CHECK FOR ALPHABETIC CHARACTER
        BCC   L1           ;  IF NOT, LOOK FOR "AGE" NOW
        LDX   #!3          ;    (THREE CHARACTERS IN "AGE")
L3      JSR   RDR          ;  READ ONE CHARACTER
        CMP   AGE-!1,X     ;  CHECK NEXT CHARACTER OF "AGE"
        BNE   L2           ;  IF UNEQUAL, CHECK ALPHABETIC
        DEX                ;  IF EQUAL, ARE THERE ANY MORE
        BNE   L3           ;    CHARS. OF "AGE" -- IF SO, CHECK
        JSR   RDR          ;  READ ONE MORE CHARACTER
        JSR   CAC          ;  IS THIS CHARACTER ALPHABETIC
        BCC   L1           ;  YES, GO BACK (NOT "AGE")
        INC   COUNT        ;  NO, INCREASE "AGE" COUNT
        JMP   L3           ;    AND READ NEXT CHARACTER
```

---

*You can also terminate a main program by JMP INIT (where INIT EQU $FB2F is specified). This also jumps to the monitor, but in a cleaner way.

```
RDR     STX    TEMP          ;  READ-CHARACTER SUBROUTINE
        JSR    RDKEY         ;  - - SAVE X, GET CHARACTER,
        LDX    TEMP          ;  RESTORE X AGAIN (SINCE RDKEY
        CMP    #CTRLE        ;  USES X ITSELF) - - IF UNEQUAL
        BNE    DONE          ;  TO CONTROL-E, THEN RETURN
        LDA    COUNT         ;  CONTROL-E - - LOAD COUNT INTO
        BRK                  ;  A-REGISTER AND STOP
CAC     CMP    #"A"          ;  CHECK ALPHABETIC CHARACTER
        BCC    CAC1          ;  SUBROUTINE - - IF LESS THAN
        CMP    #"Z"+!1       ;  "A" OR GREATER THAN "Z",
        RTS                  ;  SET CARRY (SUBROUTINE RETURNS
CAC1    SEC                  ;  WITH CARRY CLEAR IF ALPHABETIC
DONE    RTS                  ;  CHARACTER, AND SET OTHERWISE)
        ORG    $0900         ;  START OF DATA SECTION
AGE     ASC    "EGA"         ;  BACKWARD STRING "AGE"
TEMP    DFS    !1            ;  TEMPORARY STORAGE FOR X
COUNT   DFS    !1            ;  NO. OF OCCURRENCES OF "AGE"
        END
```

This is an *interactive* program; you type the input *while the program is running* (in contrast with *remote job entry* systems, mainly on large computers, which accept your typed input into a file *before* running your program, which then reads the file). If the text which you type into the above program is

```
THE AGENT OF THE MANAGER SAID THAT MY TEEN-AGE SON WAS UNDER
AGE, BUT MY DAUGHTER WAS OF SUFFICIENT AGE TO MANAGE THE STORE
```

(followed by control-E), the final value in the A-register is 3 (counting the AGE in TEEN-AGE, UNDER AGE, and SUFFICIENT AGE, but not the AGE in AGENT, MANAGER, or MANAGE).

When you write a complete program, be sure to check that the following has been done:

(1) All necessary EQU statements are given. (In the above program, RDKEY and CTRLE must be defined with EQU if they are used.)

(2) The program has a program section, starting with ORG, and a data section, starting with ORG (but see section 45 below).

(3) If you have any subroutines (such as RDR and CAC above), they end with RTS (note that CAC ends with RTS in two different places). If you have a main program, it ends with BRK (note that the BRK above is in the middle of the subroutine RDR, but it is still the end of the main program).

(4) All variables are declared. This means that every variable J in the program must have J DFS *n* or J BYT *n* or J ASC *message* or some other such declaration (see also sections 63 and 73) in the data section of the program. (Thus, in the program above, AGE, TEMP, and COUNT must be declared since they appear in the program section.)

(5) Subroutines save and restore registers where necessary. (The loop which starts at L3 involves the X register, but it also contains a call to RDR. As we learned in section 25, RDKEY uses X for its own purposes. Therefore, RDR *saves* X in a temporary location, here called TEMP, and then *restores* X after calling RDKEY. The result is that the value in the X register is always the same, *after* calling RDR, as it was beforehand. This property of calls to RDR is clearly needed in the loop starting at L3. Also see section 57 for a more general discussion of saving and restoring.)

(6) There is an END, which is the last statement in the program; and there is only one END.

EXERCISES

1. Give three reasons why the following program is not a complete program, as described in this section:

```
        ORG   $0800
DUMB    LDA   J
        SEC
        SBC   I
        JSR   COUT
        ORG   $0900
I       DFS   !1
J       DFS   !1
```

*2. Give three reasons why the following program is not a complete program, as described in this section:

```
        ORG    $0800
BAD     LDX    I
        JSR    WORSE
        STX    I
        BRK
        END
WORSE   INX
        END
```

3. Expand the following program into a complete program (with a data section starting at address 0B00):

```
        ORG    $0A00
KFIRST  JSR    GETLNZ
        LDA    INBUF
        STA    K
```

43. HAND ASSEMBLY

Debugging an assembly language program requires a thorough knowledge of the relation between assembly language and machine language. The surest way to get this knowledge is to *hand-assemble* a few programs—that is, to translate them from assembly language to machine language by hand.

We have already learned, in sections 10 and 27, all but one of the instruction formats of the 6502. These are:

(1) *One-byte instructions* (operation code only), such as INX.
(2) *Immediate data instructions*, that is, those which operate on *constants* (such as LDA #$64)—second byte is the constant. (The first byte of every instruction is *always* the operation code.)
(3) Instructions containing *16-bit addresses*, such as STX K—second and third bytes are the address (with bytes reversed).
(4) *Conditional branches*, such as BNE L7—second byte is the signed relative address (this, plus two, plus the address of the conditional branch, gives the address to branch to).
(5) Instructions containing *8-bit addresses*, such as LDA $33—second byte is the 8-bit address. (This is the one we have to take up later, in section 74.)

All of these, except the first and third, are two bytes long. The actual operation codes, in all cases, are given in Table 4 in the Appendix. (Note that Table 4 uses the letter Q for instructions of type (3) above, and the letter Z for those of type (5).)

Now consider a sample program, such as that of Figure 16(a). (This program does not have separate program and data sections; we will take up this subject further in section 45.) We will show how to hand-assemble it. The steps are as follows:

(1) Draw the lines of Figure 16(b). The left-hand column will eventually contain addresses, while the other columns will contain data (as in Figure 16(e)). *All the digits, in all the columns, are always in hexadecimal.* The important point here is to leave exactly the right amount of space for

140

```
      ORG    $0900
T     DFS    !100       ____
W     BYT    !100       ____  __
S1    LDA    #" "       ____  __ __
      LDX    W          ____  __ __ __
S2    CMP    T-!1,X     ____  __ __ __
      BNE    S3         ____  __ __
      DEX               ____  __
      BNE    S2         ____  __ __
S3 (next instruction)   ____
```

| (a) | (b) |

```
   0900                        0900
   0964   __                   0964   64
   0965   __ __                0965   A9 A0
   0967   __ __ __             0967   AE __ __
   096A   __ __ __             096A   DD __ __
   096D   __ __                096D   D0 __
   096F   __                   096F   CA
   0970   __ __                0970   D0 __
   0972                        0972
```

| (c) | (d) |

```
      ORG    $0900
T     DFS    !100       0900
W     BYT    !100       0964   64
S1    LDA    #" "       0965   A9 A0
      LDX    W          0967   AE 64 09
S2    CMP    T-!1,X     096A   DD FF 08
      BNE    S3         096D   D0 03
      DEX               096F   CA
      BNE    S2         0970   D0 F8
S3 (next instruction)   0972
```

| (e) |

Figure 16. Assembling a Program by Hand.

each instruction and piece of data (one space for each byte). Note that there are:

(a) *two* spaces for LDA #" " (it involves a constant);

(b) *three* spaces for LDX W (W has a 16-bit address);

(c) *three* spaces for CMP T−!1,X (T has a 16-bit address);

(d) *two* spaces for each BNE (conditional branch);

(e) *one* space for DEX (operation code only);

(f) *one* space for W BYT !100 (W is a single byte);

(g) and *no* spaces for T (since we do not know what is in T).

(2) Now fill in the first column, as in Figure 16(c). Note that:

(a) The *first* number is determined by the ORG statement.

(b) Every number, plus the number of spaces opposite it, gives the next number. (Thus 0965+2 gives 0967 because there are two spaces opposite 0965.) Note that for a DFS we must add the number of spaces involved (100 decimal, in this case, or hexadecimal 64).* Also do not forget that 0967+3 = 096A, not 0970.

(3) Next, fill in all the spaces *except those corresponding to addresses*, as in Figure 16(d). The spaces filled in will include the following:

(a) *Operation codes*, obtained from Table 4 in the Appendix. Remember to check the addressing mode when looking up the operation codes; for example, CMP T−!1,X has the operation code DD (not CD) because the address is indexed by X (and if it were indexed by Y, the operation code would be D9). Also remember not to use the Z options in Table 4 (such as CMP Z,X with operation code D5—use CMP Q,X instead) until we study zero-page instructions in section 74.

(b) *Constants (immediate data)* such as A0 (here the character code for " ", or the blank, obtained from Table 10 in the Appendix.)

(c) *Data declared by constant declarations*, such as W BYT !100, which contains 100 (decimal) or 64 (hexadecimal). Remember that all numbers in machine language are always written out in hexadecimal.

(4) Finally, fill in the addresses, as in Figure 16(e). In doing so, you will be referring to the addresses of labels that you have already calculated in the first column. (In this case the address of S1 is 0965, for example, because the assembly language statement with label S1 corresponds to the machine language statement with address 0965.) The addresses include:

(a) *Standard 16-bit addresses,* such as that of W. Always remember to reverse the bytes; this is 64 09 here, not 09 64.

---

*In LISA 1.5, there may be a bug in the listings of this first column. The bug does not affect the resulting machine language program, only the listings; and it is corrected in LISA 2.5.

(b) *Relative addresses*, calculated as in section 27. Here the first relative address is z where $096D+2+z = 0972$, so that z is 3. The second relative address is z where $0970+2+z=096A$, so that z is -8, or F8 in twos' complement form.

(c) *Standard 8-bit addresses* (see section 74).

(d) *Addresses with offsets*. In this case the address of T is 0900, so T$-$!1 represents $0900-1$ (in hexadecimal), which is 08FF. As always, we have to reverse these bytes, so the result is FF 08.

This concludes the process of hand assembly. You should go over it several times to make sure you understand it. Of course, hand assembly can always be checked by having the computer do it, as we will see in section 46.

EXERCISES

*1. Find three errors in the first stage of hand assembly (as in Figure 16(b)) illustrated below:

```
            ORG   $0800
    T       DFS   !100      ----
    N       DFS   !1        ---- --
    START   LDA   #" "      ---- -- -- --
            LDX   N         ---- -- -- --
    LOOP    STA   T-!1,X    ---- -- -- --
            DEX             ---- --
            BNE   LOOP      ---- -- -- --
```

2. Find two errors in the third stage of hand-assembly (as in Figure 16(d); the first two stages are correct in this case) illustrated below:

```
            ORG   $0800
    T       DFS   !100      0800
    START   LDX   #!16      0864   A2 16
    LOOP    TXA             0866   8A
            STA   T,X       0867   8D __ __
            DEX             086A   CA
            BNE   LOOP      086B   D0 __
```

*3. Find two errors in the fourth stage of hand-assembly (as in Figure 16(e); the first three stages are correct in this case) illustrated below:

```
            ORG   $0900
    T       DFS   !8        0900
    W       DFS   !1        0908
    START   LDA   W         0909   AD 09 08
            LDX   #!8       090C   A2 08
```

```
LOOP      CMP     T, X          090E    DD  00 09
          BEQ     DONE          0911    F0  05
          DEX                   0913    CA
          BNE     LOOP          0914    D0  F8
DONE (next instruction)         0916
```

44. DESK CHECKING AND WALKTHROUGHS

Debugging of any program—but most particularly, of an assembly language program—does not start by running it on the computer. It starts with *desk checking*, which is nothing more than sitting at your desk and checking over your work.

We all make errors in our programs. Even computer scientists with twenty years' experience make errors by the dozens. The difference between a good programmer and a poor one is not that the good one makes no errors, but rather, to a great extent, that the good one makes fewer *simple* errors.

We have already mentioned that an assembly language program should contain one comment for every instruction. A good method of desk checking consists of writing the program first without any comments, or with comments only where you have to remind yourself what you were doing, and then going through it once more and putting one comment on every line. Try to make the comments as easy to understand as you can. If you do this, you will often find bugs that would escape you if your comments were more obscure.

Some errors are *repeatable;* the same error will happen every time you run the program. Other errors are not repeatable; either a different error will happen each time, or else the program will run properly most of the time and make an error only every so often. A non-repeatable error must normally be found by desk checking because, when you try to find it on the computer, it usually disappears, only to reappear again later.

The most common kind of non-repeatable error happens when a variable is not initialized, or set to some starting value. In that case, the starting value will depend on what program (call it P) was running on the APPLE just before you started work on this one. If your variable has address α, then the program P left behind some quantity at the address α, which could be anything—an instruction code, data, or something left over from the program that was running before P. This is called *garbage*.

You should make a list of the kinds of errors you find yourself making. Every time you find an error, put it on your list and check for it next time you desk-check. Initialization checking of all variables should *always* be done.

Once you finish desk checking, *walk through* various parts of your program a few times. The walkthrough is a process which can best be illustrated by an example. The following steps are keyed to the letters in Figure 17, which shows a typical walkthrough:

(a) Here is the program; it finds the sum of several numbers. It has already been checked for initialization. The A and X registers and the carry flag are set (in steps 1, 2, and 3); the elements of T, as well as N, were presumably set before this program started.

(b) For this walkthrough, we take N to be 4. (Choices like this are usually necessary; otherwise, walkthroughs take far too long.) We start a table of variables, with N = 4 and A = 0 since we start at step 1 by loading A with zero.

(c) We do step 2, which loads X with 1. (Obviously, we don't construct a whole new table; we simply add X to the table of step (b), with the value 1, and similarly throughout.)

(d) We do step 3, and clear the carry C (that is, set it to zero).

(e) We do step 4 and set A to 0+T(X), or T(X). Now look at X in the table; it is 1, so T(X) is T(1). (Often you will find a bug at this point; in this case, though, we didn't.) Whenever a variable gets a new value, cross out the old value.

(f) We do step 5 and add 1 to X; so X is now 2.

(g) We do steps 6 and 7. Is X equal to N? Is 2 equal to 4? No; so we go back and do step 4 again. We set A to T(1)+T(X), and X is now 2, so this is T(1)+T(2). (You will find a bug here if you forgot to put INX in the program, or used DEX instead.)

(h) We do step 5 and add 1 to X; so X is now 3.

(i) We do steps 6 and 7. Is X equal to N? Is 3 equal to 4? No; so we do step 4 again. We set A to T(1)+T(2)+T(X), and X is 3, so this is T(1)+T(2)+T(3). (If we didn't choose N = 4 in this walkthrough, this would be a good time to start over, with N = 4, because otherwise the walkthrough would start to get monotonous.)

(j) We do step 5 and add 1 to X; so X is now 4.

(k) We do steps 6 and 7. Is X equal to N? Is 4 equal to 4? Yes; so we do step 8. We store A in SUM, so that SUM = T(1)+T(2)+T(3).

Is this what we wanted? Probably not (since T(4) is missing); so we have found a bug.

A good way to do walkthroughs is with a friend. As you walk through the program, see if you and your friend, between the two of you, can find bugs. Avoid this, however, if it tempts you to have your friend write your programs for you (or if it tempts your friend).

When you are done with desk checking and walkthroughs, do something else for a while; then, later, do them again just before sitting down at the APPLE. You will be surprised how many more errors you can find this way.

(a)	(1)		LDA	#!0
	(2)		LDX	#!1
	(3)		CLC	
	(4)	LOOP	ADC	T−!1,X
	(5)		INX	
	(6)		CPX	N
	(7)		BNE	LOOP
	(8)		STA	SUM

(b)	N 4	A 0		

(c)	N 4	A 0	X 1	

(d)	N 4	A 0	X 1	C 0

(e)	N 4	A ~~0~~ T(1)	X 1	C 0

(f)	N 4	A ~~0~~ T(1)	X ~~1~~ 2	C 0

(g)	N 4	A ~~0~~ ~~T(1)~~ T(1)+ T(2)	X ~~1~~ 2	C 0

(h)	N 4	A ~~0~~ ~~T(1)~~ T(1)+ T(2)	X ~~1~~ ~~2~~ 3	C 0

(i)	N 4	A ~~0~~ ~~T(1)~~ ~~T(1)+~~ ~~T(2)~~ T(1)+T(2)+T(3)	X ~~1~~ ~~2~~ 3	C 0

Figure 17. A Walkthrough. (Continued on p. 148)

	N	A	X	C
	4	0	~~X~~	0
(j)		~~T(1)~~	~~2~~	
		~~T(1)+~~	~~3~~	
		~~T(2)~~	4	
		T(1)+T(2)+T(3)		

	N	A	X	C	SUM
	4	~~0~~	~~X~~	0	T(1)
(k)		~~T(1)~~	~~2~~		+T(2)
		~~T(1)+~~	~~3~~		+T(3)
		~~T(2)~~	4		
		T(1)+T(2)+T(3)			

Figure 17. A Walkthrough. (Continued)

EXERCISES

1. The following program is supposed to set Y to the number of trailing
   blanks in the string INBUF; that is, the number of consecutive blanks
   immediately preceding the first carriage return ($8D). Walk through it
   with INBUF containing "2" followed by two blanks and a carriage
   return. Stop at the *point in the walkthrough* where the bug becomes
   clear.* Describe the bug and also give the table (similar to that of Figure 17(k)) up to this point.

```
               ORG    $0800
      CRET     EQU    $8D
      INBUF    EQU    $0200
      START    LDA    #CRET
               LDX    #$FF
      LOOP1    INX
               CMP    INBUF, X
               BNE    LOOP1
               DEX
               LDY    #!0
               LDA    #" "
      LOOP2    CMP    INBUF, X
               BNE    DONE
               INY
               JMP    LOOP2
      DONE     (next  instruction)
```

_____

*You may be able to find the bug by desk checking, rather than by walkthroughs; but answer these
exercises as if you were not.

*2. The following program is supposed to set SUM to the sum of all of the signed numbers T(1), T(2), ..., T(N) which are positive (ignoring those which are negative). Walk through it with N = 4, T(1) = 30, T(2) = −5, T(3) = −40, and T(4) = 15. As in exercise 1 above, stop when the bug becomes clear, describe the bug, and give the table. (The array T starts at T(1).)

```
        ORG    $0850
T       DFS    !100
SUM     DFS    !1
START   LDA    #!0
        STA    SUM
LOOP    LDX    N
        LDA    T−!1,X
        BMI    CONT
        CLC
        ADC    SUM
        STA    SUM
CONT    DEX
        BNE    LOOP
```

3. The following program is supposed to set MINALL equal to the minimum of all the unsigned numbers T(1), T(2), ..., T(N). Walk it all the way through to the end with N = 2, T(1) = 3, and T(2) = 5, and give the table at that point as before. Is there a bug? If so, what is it? (The array T starts from T(1).)

```
        ORG    $08A0
T       DFS    !200
MINALL  DFS    !1
N       DFS    !1
START   LDA    #!0
        STA    MINALL
        LDX    N
LOOP    LDA    T−!1,X
        CMP    MINALL
        BCS    CONT
        STA    MINALL
CONT    DEX
        BNE    LOOP
```

45. INTERMIXING, OVERWRITING, AND STARTING ADDRESS ERRORS

Strictly speaking, we can write an APPLE assembly language program *without* separate program and data sections—that is, with only one ORG statement, at the beginning—and put instructions and data together. (We can even leave out ORG entirely, in which case ORG $0800 is assumed.) Such *intermixing*, however, must be done in such a way that instructions never "run into" data. To see what this means, consider the following instructions and data:

```
0807   A9  4C              LDA    #$4C
0809   8D  0C  08          STA    L
080C                   L   DFS    !1
```

This kind of sequence *is wrong and should never be used*. To see why, consider the machine language form at the left. After the instruction at 0809 is done, the computer tries to do the instruction at 080C next. This means that the byte at 080C will be treated as an *operation code*, but this is not an operation code—it is the value of L. (We just stored $4C here with the STA instruction, and $4C, as an operation code, is a *jump* to the address given in the next two bytes—and who knows what that would do.)

After every instruction you must consider what the computer is going to do next. If the answer is "nothing"—the program is finished at this point—then the next instruction should be BRK, if it is a main program, or RTS, if it is a subroutine. (Data following BRK or RTS, of course, is quite permissible.)

Closely related to intermixing errors are *overwriting errors*. The instruction codes of any program are supposed to be constant; they stay in memory all the time that the program is being run.* If there is a mistake in a program which causes some quantity to be stored in any instruction code byte, that byte is said to be *overwritten*, or *destroyed*. (Many programmers also say "clobbered.")

Overwriting errors are much more common in assembly language than in any

---

*There are exceptions to this; see sections 78, 80, and 81.

150

other language. They do not become apparent, as you are debugging, until some later time (and possibly *much* later), when the program tries to do the clobbered instruction. Remember, just as with intermixing errors, that the computer executes *machine language only*—not assembly language. If LDX #!233 has the machine language form A2 E9, then the computer will load the X register with 233 only if it finds A2 E9 there. If it finds something else there, it will do some other instruction.

There are many possibilities. If the E9 is destroyed, then the X register is loaded with some number other than 233. If the A2 is destroyed, the instruction will be different. If you are lucky, the A2 will be overwritten with zero—the operation code for a BRK. If you are unlucky, the A2 will be overwritten with a *one-byte* instruction. The E9 will then be treated as the *operation code* of the next instruction.

As it happens, E9 is the operation code for SBC #*n*. The next byte after the E9—which is *really* an operation code—is now treated as *n*. When this sort of thing happens, the computer is said to be *out of alignment*. Note that if *n* is a one-byte instruction code, the computer is back in alignment again, but it has just done a few unwanted—and potentially harmful—instructions. If *n* is a two- or three-byte instruction code, the computer stays out of alignment (for the moment, at least).

The main lessons to be learned from all this are two. First, *when an assembly language program makes an error, the error might have been caused long earlier*, by an overwritten instruction. *Never* assume that you know the real cause of an error in an assembly language program; very often, it is caused by an error that happened earlier. (This is sometimes called a *propagated error.*)

Second, *be as sure as you possibly can, before starting to debug, that there cannot be any overwriting*. The most common cause of overwriting is storing data in an array with an index that is *out of range*—that is, too large or too small. If you set T(J) to something, where the array T runs from T(1) to T(100), and J happens to be greater than 100 or less than 1 at the time, you may overwrite an instruction of your program. If this is a kind of error which you make frequently, you can write some instructions to test every subscript just before it is used, to see if it is out of range. This slows down the program a bit but should speed up the debugging process considerably.

Data, as well as instruction codes, can be overwritten. If you have an array T, followed by some constant data (a character string, for example), and you write into T with an index out of range, you may destroy the character string. Later, when you want to display that character string (for example), strange characters may appear on the screen.

You can test whether any of your instructions have been overwritten, during debugging of your program, by using the Move and Verify commands of the APPLE monitor (see the end of section 48).

Still another related error concerns *starting addresses*. If your data section is given first, and you jump to the first address in the program, the computer will try to execute data as instructions, just as in intermixing errors. This problem can be avoided by giving the *program* section first; or by putting JMP START just before the data, and the label START just after it.

EXERCISES

*1.   Point out all intermixing errors in the following program. (Not all of the intermixed instructions and data in this program are erroneous.)

					ORG	$0B00
0B00	AD	03	0B	MIX	LDA	I
0B03				I	DFS	!1
0B04	D0	08			BNE	MIX2
0B06				J	DFS	!1
0B07	AD	06	0B		LDA	J
				COUT	EQU	$FDED
0B0A	4C	11	0B		JMP	MIX3
0B0D				K	DFS	!1
0B0E	20	ED	FD	MIX2	JSR	COUT
0B11	60			MIX3	RTS	
0B12				L	DFS	!1
					END	

2.   The following subroutine, which is presumably called several times during a run, sets T(1) through T(100) to the value 2. Suppose that instead of STA T−!1,X we had written STA T,X (causing an overwriting error). What is this error? (Describe it in detail, using the machine language form of the program as given.) At what time will this error affect the run, and in what way? (Ignore the effects of the other error, that is, the fact that the first byte of T will never be stored.)

					ORG	$0820
0820				T	DFS	!100
0884	64			N	BYT	!100
0885	AE	84	08	SUBR	LDX	N
0888	A9	02			LDA	#!2
088A	9D	1F	08	LOOP	STA	T−!1,X
088D	CA				DEX	
088E	D0	FA			BNE	LOOP
0890	60				RTS	

*3.   Answer the two questions of Exercise 2 above for the following subroutine, which sets T(1) through T(100) to the value 233.

```
                                        ORG   $0870
       0870                       T     DFS   !100
       08D4    A2   64            START LDX   #!100
       08D6    A9   E9                  LDA   #!233
       08D8    9D   6F   08       LOOP  STA   T-!1,X
       08DB    CA                       DEX
       08DC    D0   FA                  BNE   LOOP
       08DE    60                       RTS
```

46. THE LISA COMMANDS

Anyone who has ever used BASIC is familiar with BASIC *commands* (LIST, RUN, SAVE, and the like), as distinct from BASIC *statements* (N = I+J−K and the like). LISA also has commands, many of which you must become familiar with; but the fundamental ideas of LISA commands are a bit different.*

In BASIC, there are *line numbers*, which are in numerical order. Putting in a new line between line numbers *i* and *j* is merely a matter of choosing a line number between *i* and *j*. In assembly language, however, line numbers are not part of the language. LISA does use its own line numbers, but they are line numbers in a literal sense: the first line is always line number 1, the second is always line number 2, and so on.

Since there is never any line number 1½, or the like, this means that putting in new lines, when you are changing a program, is done by a command of its own: I (for "insert"). In the same way, *taking out* lines is done with the command D— for "delete." (The LISA *prompt character* ! asks you to type a command.)

You can use the command I *n* to insert any number of lines you want to, *before* line *n* (*not after* line *n*—watch this carefully). You can use I (all by itself) to insert any number of lines at the end of your program. In either case, when you are done inserting new lines, type *control-E return*.

You can use the command D *m* to delete line *m*. You can use D *m,n* to delete lines *m*, *m*+1, and so on up through (and including) *n*, all at once. If you want to *change* lines (that is, delete them and then insert something else in their place), then write M (for "modify") instead of D; that is, M *m* or M *m,n* depending on whether you are taking out one line or more than one.

LISA uses an old trick to make typing a *new* program look like a special case of *changing* a program. In fact, inserting new lines into a program which has nothing in it at all is exactly the same as typing a new program! So the first thing you do, as soon as you load LISA, is to type I (by itself) and then type in your

---

*We have omitted discussion of how to *start up* LISA because this differs from one APPLE configuration to the next; see your computer store for details.

new program. (Remember, however, that *every* command in LISA—even an I by itself—is followed by *return*.)

You will probably want to display your program, or parts of it, on the screen; this is called *listing*. You can type L (by itself) to list your whole program; or L *m* to list line *m*; or L *m,n* to list lines *m, m* + 1, and so on up through (and including) *n*. (You can also direct output to the printer, just as you would in BASIC, and use L to obtain *hard copy*—that is, a printer listing of your program.) When you think your program is ready to go, give it a *file name* (such as TEST7) and then *save* it on the disk, by typing SAVE followed by the file name (SAVE TEST7 in this case). You can have up to 30 characters in a file name, and it must start with a letter, just like a variable name.

You cannot run your program immediately, as you can in BASIC. You have to *assemble* it first—that is, you must have it translated from assembly language into machine language. The command ASM (for "assemble") does this. It will produce a listing on the screen of both the assembly language and the machine language form of your program. Normally, this listing is too large to fit on the screen, and LISA goes so fast that you cannot look at the listing without *typing a space*. This will stop the listing process; when you want LISA to continue, type another space. You can do this as often as you like.*

Many people make a large number of typing errors, and the APPLE provides several ways of correcting them. You can always use the *backspace key* (←) to back up and type something over. If you want to start the entire line over, type *control-X*. (These keys can also be used if you are typing input to a program which uses the subroutine GETLNZ of section 25.)

Suppose now that you have typed a long line with some characters in it that you do not want. You could, of course, type control-X, and then the whole line over again, as above; but then, possibly, you would make another similar typing mistake. LISA provides several special keys to allow you to fix mistakes without retyping a line.

First, backspace (←) back to the first character that you do not want, and now type control-K. This will pass over the character; further control-K's will pass over further characters. When you get to the first character that you *do* want, type → over and over again until you get to the end of the line.† The characters control-O, control-L, control-J, and control-K stand for "up," "down," "left," and "right," respectively; they move the cursor (which is blinking on the screen) in these directions. You can move the cursor anywhere on the screen you want to, by using these keys over and over. (Remember that control-O is *not* control-zero.)

---

*LISA 2.5 will stop the listing when an assembly error occurs.

†The APPLE has a *repeat key,* marked REPT. Holding down both this key and another key (for example, →) will have the same effect as if that other key was typed over and over again.

This also gives you a way of *inserting* characters into a line you have already typed. Backspace to the place you want to insert; use the control characters O, L, J, and K to move the cursor to a blank place on the screen; type the new characters; use the control characters again, as before, to move the cursor back to the next character position after the insertion; and finally type → over and over again until you get to the end of the line, just as in deletion.

EXERCISES

1. Suppose that the current LISA program, with line numbers given, is

1	LDA	P
2	STA	Q
3	LDA	R
4	STA	S

   What will each of the following sequences of LISA commands do (to the *original* program above)? Give the new LISA program for each answer (with line numbers in sequence, starting from 1).

   (a)   I 3

                                   STA   T

   *(b)   D 2,4

   (c)   M 2

                                   STA   T

2. Suppose that the current LISA program, with line numbers given, is as in the preceding exercise. Give a sequence of LISA commands (as short at possible) acting on the original program above to yield each of the following as the current LISA program:

   *(a)

1	LDA	M
2	STA	N
3	LDA	P
4	STA	Q
5	LDA	R
6	STA	S

   (b)

1	LDA	P
2	LDA	R
3	STA	S

   *(c)

1	LDA	P
2	STA	Q
3	LDA	R
4	STA	T

3. Suppose that the current LISA program, with line numbers given, is as in Exercise 1. What is displayed after the following sequence of LISA commands?

```
D 1
D 1
I 2
         STA    T
         LDA    U
M 3
         LDA    V
L
```

47. STEPPING AND TRACING

You are now ready to begin debugging, with the help of an APPLE program called the *monitor*. (The APPLE screen is also sometimes known as a monitor, but in this book the word "monitor" will always refer to the program which is at the heart of the APPLE system.)

To start working with the monitor, you type BRK (which is a LISA *command*, as well as being an instruction). The monitor displays * which is its prompt character (much like ! in LISA), asking you to type a *monitor command*. If your program starts at hexadecimal 0800, you can type 0800G (or 800G) and the monitor will go to your program (G stands for "go to") and execute it.*

Normally, you would not type 0800G unless your program was already working perfectly. Instead, you would use *stepping and tracing* (sometimes in conjunction with *breakpoint debugging*, to be taken up in the next section). To *step through* a program means to go through it one instruction at a time, or, as we say, one *step* at a time. At each step, the monitor displays:

(1) the *address* of the instruction;
(2) the *machine language form* of the instruction;
(3) the *assembly language form* of the instruction;
(4) the *contents of the registers* in hexadecimal, *after* this instruction is performed.

All this is done by typing S (for "step") instead of G. If we type 0800S (for example), the following might be displayed:

```
0800 -   AD  3C  08        LDA     $083C
A = 01  X = 00  Y = 5F  P = 30  S = F8
```

Here the instruction LDA $083C, which has the machine language form AD 3C 08, is itself at address 0800; the A register contains 1, the X register contains zero, and the Y register contains 5F in hexadecimal. (There are two further registers displayed, P and S, which we will study in sections 60 and 67, respectively.)

---

*Do *not* type $0800G, which will not work; integers in monitor commands are *always* in hexadecimal anyway, so the character $ is not used.

158

Note that LDA $083C was probably given in your program as LDA W or some other such instruction with a symbolic address (such as W). We presumably had W = 1, since the A register contains 1 after it was loaded with the value of W. When your program has been assembled, you can write down (from the assembly listing) the hexadecimal address of each variable. If you want to see what is in the byte with address 083C, just type 083C (followed by *return*) and this will be displayed in hexadecimal. This works for any address. In the same way, if you want to see what is in an entire array, say from address 0884 to 08DB, just type 0884.08DB (note the period) and all these bytes will be displayed in hexadecimal. This works for any two addresses.*

We can step as many times as we want to, by typing S several times. Thus 0800SSSSS would step five times, starting at the beginning of the program. Each step would be displayed, as above; so there would be five such displays on the screen, for a total of ten lines.

The letter S is preceded by the address where the stepping starts; but we can leave this out if we want to keep stepping from where we left off. Thus, for example, we could keep typing SSSSS over and over; and each time, five more steps of the program would be displayed.

The aim of stepping is to let you see whether your computations are taking place properly. You should be able to tell this by looking carefully at:

(1) the contents of the registers, at each step;
(2) which instructions you are actually doing;
(3) and, if necessary, the contents of cells and arrays of cells in the memory (by typing in their addresses, as above).

It is possible, during stepping, to lose track of where you are in your program. If you do this, and you have a displayed step with instruction address *xxxx*, type *xxxx*L to list the machine language and assembly language form of this instruction and the next few instructions (to fill up the screen). You should be able to match this up with your hard copy of the program.

Tracing is "unlimited stepping." Typing 0800T (for instance) has the effect of typing 0800 followed by an unlimited number of S's. Steps are displayed on the screen indefinitely; you can stop and start this by typing a space, just as with LISA listings (see the preceding section).†

After you have found some bugs in your program, get back to LISA from the

---

*This is often used to look at an *entire* program, including instructions and data; in this form, it is called a *dump*.

†On APPLE systems *without* the Language Card, but *with* the Autostart ROM, S and T may not work; however, you can use a step-and-trace program supplied, with instructions, on the diskette which accompanies this book (see p. 403).

monitor* and then type LOAD followed by the program name (in the example of the preceding section, LOAD TEST7). This brings the program back into main memory from disk, an operation known as *loading the program*. (Do not confuse this with loading a register, which is quite different.) You are now ready to use I, D, and M as in the preceding section, to fix bugs.

A generalized version of the LISA command LOAD allows you to combine several programs into one, if you have saved them all. Let us say that they are called PROG1, PROG2, PROG3, and so on. You LOAD PROG1 just as in the preceding section, and then you *append* the other programs. Thus AP PROG2 will append the second one; AP PROG3 the third one; and so on (AP stands for "append").

A description of all the LISA commands used in this book is given in Table 13 in the Appendix. A description of all the APPLE monitor commands used in this book is given in Table 14 in the Appendix. (For further monitor commands, refer to the APPLE manuals.)

EXERCISES

*1. Suppose that we are stepping through a program containing the following two instructions in sequence:

```
            LDY      # ! 100
            INY
```

and the following information is displayed, after one particular step (involving the first of these):

```
    0838-    A2  64           LDY   #$64
    A = 8D  X = 32  Y = 64  P = 30  S = F8
```

What would be displayed after the next step? (Assume that the P and S registers are unchanged.)

2. Suppose that we are stepping through the following sequence of instructions:

```
            LDA      ALPHA1
            STA      BETA1
            LDA      ALPHA2
            STA      BETA2
            LDA      ALPHA3
            BMI      ALFNEG
```

---

*This is done by typing 7003G (in LISA 1.5), 6003G (in LISA 2.5, 48K), or E003G (in LISA 2.5, 64K).

and the following information is displayed, after four steps:

```
08F4-    AD 31 09         LDA     $0931
  A=6F  X=00  Y=64  P=31  S=F4
08F7-    8D 6B 09         STA     $096B
  A=6F  X=00  Y=64  P=31  S=F4
08FA-    AD 32 09         LDA     $0932
  A=FF  X=00  Y=64  P=31  S=F4
08FD-    30 08            BMI     $0907
  A=FF  X=00  Y=64  P=B1  S=F4
```

What APPLE monitor command will now display the hexadecimal contents of the cell ALPHA2?

*3.   The following sequence of instructions is supposed to put into the Y register the number of one-bits in BETA. (It has a bug, however.)

```
              LDA    BETA
              LDX    #!8
              LDY    #!0
              ASL
       LOOP   BCC    LOOP1
              INY
              ASL
       LOOP1  DEX
              BNE    LOOP
```

As we are stepping through the program, the following are the last four steps displayed:

```
0920-    90 02            BCC     $0924
  A=D0  X=05  Y=03  P=30  S=F6
0924-    CA               DEX
  A=D0  X=04  Y=03  P=30  S=F6
0925-    D0 F9            BNE     $0920
  A=D0  X=04  Y=03  P=30  S=F6
0920-    90 02            BCC     $0924
  A=D0  X=04  Y=03  P=30  S=F6
```

Find the bug. How do the steps help you to do this? (Hint: Look at what happens to the A register.)

48. BREAKPOINT DEBUGGING

Stepping and tracing are fine for short programs and for programs which do not call subroutines like COUT, RDKEY, and the like; but for more general programs, *breakpoint debugging* is indicated.

A *breakpoint* is simply a point in a program at which you can stop, temporarily, to look at the contents of a few registers and cells in memory, and then continue. This is done by putting a break instruction (BRK, or hexadecimal 00) at the breakpoint, so that control is returned to the APPLE monitor system.

Breakpoint debugging depends on one further feature of the monitor, namely *changing* the contents of memory. In order to put *hh* (in hexadecimal) in the cell with address *xxxx*, we type *xxxx:hh* (or simply *:hh* if we have just looked at what was in cell *xxxx*). As before, remember never to type $ as part of *xxxx*. In order to put *aa*, *bb*, *cc*, and so on, into the array starting at address *xxxx*, we type *xxxx:aa bb cc* (and so on). This will put *aa* at address *xxxx*; *bb* at address *xxxx*+1; *cc* at address *xxxx*+2; and so on.

Suppose now that you want to *set a breakpoint* at the instruction whose address is *xxxx*. You type *xxxx* and when the system responds with *hh* you type :00 to put a zero (BRK) at that point. When your program gets to that point, it will do the instruction whose operation code is 00, that is, BRK; so it will go back to the monitor. To *remove* this same breakpoint, type *xxxx:hh* with the same *hh* as above (that is, the operation code that was at address *xxxx* before the breakpoint was set). Then *xxxx*G will start the program up again.

If you know where your program is going (what sequence of instructions it is doing next, at any time), then breakpoint debugging proceeds as follows:

(1) Pick an instruction which you think the computer will reach in a correct way; set a breakpoint there; and run the program up to this point. (If the program starts at *xxxx*, type *xxxx*G as usual and wait until BRK is executed, as described above.)

(2) Look at the registers and various cells in memory to see if the program seems to be working properly so far. If it isn't, go to Step 4 below; otherwise, remove the breakpoint you just set, and set another breakpoint,

picking a different instruction* to which you think the program will continue in a correct way.

(3) Start the program at the breakpoint you just removed, by typing *xxxx*G where *xxxx:hh* was used to remove the breakpoint. Note that this will continue with the first instruction that the computer did *not* perform, because it stopped at the last breakpoint. When the computer gets to the next breakpoint, go back to Step 2.

(4) You now know approximately where your error is. Up to breakpoint *a* (let us say) your program worked properly; whereas, at breakpoint *b*, it was not working right. If you can find the error by looking again at your hard copy, especially that particular section (and knowing, this time, what it is actually doing), then fix it and reassemble. Otherwise, set breakpoint *a* again, run the program from the beginning again up to breakpoint *a*, remove this breakpoint, and start stepping through the program, as in the preceding section.

If you do *not* know where your program is going—that is, if one of your bugs might be that it is doing the wrong instruction, or going to the wrong place—then do the steps outlined above with the following changes. In Step 1, pick *several* possible breakpoints, and set them; do the same thing in Step 2. Also in Step 2, remove *all* breakpoints that you are sure the program will not get to, when you start it up in Step 3; and look not only at the registers and memory, but at *which breakpoint you stopped at*, to make sure it is the one you expected at that point.

A problem arises in the breakpoint debugging of programs that use GETLNZ, which uses the input buffer starting at address 0200. The problem is that the APPLE monitor *also uses this same input buffer*, so that when you type commands (like SSSSS), these will overwrite the characters you have there. To get around this, write a loop which moves these characters to another array, and then put a breakpoint in your program *after* this loop is complete.

Sometimes, when you are using breakpoint debugging, you may enter an endless loop by mistake. In that case, hit the *reset key* (on some APPLEs, *control-reset*). This forces a break.

The Move and Verify commands, mentioned at the end of section 45 as a way of testing whether instructions have been overwritten, have the forms

$$cccc < aaaa.bbbbM \qquad \text{(Move)}$$
$$cccc < aaaa.bbbbV \qquad \text{(Verify)}$$

The Move command above moves your program, which takes up memory from

---

*If you want to set the *same* breakpoint as before, then remove the breakpoint, perform one *step* (using S), and then set the breakpoint again. The reason for this is left as exercise 2 below.

address *aaaa* through address *bbbb*, to a large unused area of memory starting at address *cccc*. The Verify command above, executed at some later time, checks that the two copies of your program are still the same. If not, then the locations where they are different will be displayed, together with the different contents in each such pair of locations. (You should check at this point whether it was actually the original or the copy that was overwritten.)

EXERCISES

1. An INY instruction is at hexadecimal location 0A03. Give the APPLE monitor command to:

   (a) Set a breakpoint at this location.
   *(b) Remove a breakpoint at this location.
   (c) Continue processing after breaking at this location.

*2. A programmer has set up a breakpoint in a large loop by writing BP1 BRK (where BP1 is a label) in the *assembly language* form of the loop and has run the program up to BP1. It is now desired to continue processing this program, starting immediately after BP1 and letting the computer go around the loop until it gets to BP1 again. The programmer can do this by typing *yyyy*G, where *xxxx* is the address of BP1 and *yyyy* = *xxxx*+1. Show that this *cannot* be done if the breakpoint was set at BP1 by *xxxx*:00 rather than by writing BRK in the assembly language form, unless a single step is taken as suggested in the text. (Hint: Try to specify, *precisely,* how you would go about doing this. There are several plausible ways, but none of them work.)

3. Suppose that someone who is learning programming asks you, "Can you put a breakpoint in a *data* byte, rather than an instruction byte?" How would you answer?

49. THE TELEPHONE LINE BREAK
PRINCIPLE AND BINARY SEARCH

We have noted that breakpoint debugging is used for programs that are too large to be debugged by stepping and tracing. For even larger programs, there is the *telephone line break principle*.

Imagine yourself setting out to repair a four-mile-long telephone line, in which there is a break somewhere (the insulation has worn through). You can start at one end of the line, and, every 100 feet or so, you can test it to see whether there is a break so far—that is, between where you are and the beginning of the line.

For a line four miles long, testing every 100 feet, you will need over 200 tests. There is a faster way, which proceeds as follows. Go two miles down the line, and test it. If the test works properly, you know that the break is in the last two miles of line. Otherwise, it is in the first two miles. Either way, you have now isolated two miles of line to test.

Now go *one* mile down this two-mile stretch, and test again. If this test works, then the break is in the second of these two miles; otherwise, it is in the first mile. Either way, you now have the break isolated to within one mile of line. Now go halfway into this mile of line, and keep on dividing the line in half, in this way.

The advantage of this method is that, in only nine tests (instead of over 200), you can get the problem isolated to within 100 feet. The idea works even if there is more than one break in the line; it finds the *first* break (the one closest to the end where you started), and then, if there are further breaks, you can repeat the process.

The same principle can now be used in debugging a program. Set your first breakpoint about halfway through the program. When you get there (if you do), check registers and memory to see if the program has worked properly so far. If so, you know that your first bug is in the second half of the program. Otherwise, it is in the first half of the program.

Either way, you have isolated one half of the program to work on. Now set a breakpoint about *halfway through that half*, run your program again, and check registers and memory again. In this way you can isolate your problem to about one-fourth of your program. Continue in the same way, dividing the program roughly in half each time, until you have isolated your problem to an area small enough to use ordinary breakpoint debugging or stepping and tracing.

As before, this method needs to be changed a bit if part of your problem is that your program is not going where it is supposed to. It may be that if you set a breakpoint halfway through a section of your program, the breakpoint will be missed entirely. Of course, this does isolate the problem; it is in the first half of that section. However, you can always set several breakpoints, just as in ordinary breakpoint debugging.

It is interesting that this same principle can be used to write a program to find a quantity Q among the elements T(1) through T(N) of a table. We could compare Q with T(1), then with T(2), and so on; but that is like trying to test every 100 feet of a telephone line. Suppose, however, that the elements of the table T are *sorted*. This means that they are in ascending order, so that T(1) is the smallest, T(2) is the next smallest, and so on. We can now find Q in the table by using a *binary search*, which works by repeatedly dividing the table T in half.

To start the binary search, we compare Q with T(N/2). If Q is *larger* than T(N/2), then Q must be T(J) for some J larger than N/2 (since the table is sorted). Thus Q is in the second half of the table. Otherwise, Q is in the first half of the table (again because the table is sorted). In either case, we have narrowed the search down to a table which is twice as small as the one we had before. Now we compare Q with the middle element of *that* table, and continue in the same way. This will be taken up further in section 86.

Remember never to try to *step through* (or trace through) an input or output subroutine (RDKEY, GETLNZ, COUT, or the like). For input, the stepping process gets in the way of typing the characters; for output, it interferes with the display of characters on the screen. (In any event, there are clearly no bugs in the APPLE monitor subroutines.)

EXERCISES

*1.   You have undoubtedly learned about *common logarithms* (to the base 10) and *natural logarithms* (to the base $e \simeq 2.71828$). In computer science, logarithms to the base 2 are quite useful; we have $\log_2 x = y$ where $2^y = x$. Thus the powers of 2, from 1 through 64, have logarithms as follows:

| | LOGARITHM |
NUMBER	(BASE 2)
1	0
2	1
4	2
8	3
16	4
32	5
64	6

and intervening numbers have intervening logarithms (thus $\sqrt{2} \simeq 1.414$ has logarithm 0.5, since $2^{0.5} = \sqrt{2}$.) Derive a formula, in terms of logarithms to the base 2, for the number of steps required to find a break in a telephone line of total length x feet to within an interval of y feet, by the method given in the text.

2. (a) The telephone line break principle cannot be used directly on a program consisting of one very large loop, executed a large number of times. Why not?
    (b) Describe a method of adding a few instructions to your program, which will allow the principle to be applied in the above case. (Instructions of this kind are known as *diagnostic instructions*.)

3. *(a) Derive a formula for the number of steps taken by a binary search of a table of size n, in terms of logarithms to the base 2. Assume that the search proceeds until the table, after having its size reduced many times, has length 2; and that two final steps are taken at this point, to check each of the two elements of that table. Explain, in words, how to interpret your formula if n is not a power of 2.
    *(b) Suppose that a binary search program was itself being debugged. In this case the considerations of exercise 2(a) above would *not* be important. Why not?

50. ASSEMBLY-LEVEL PATCHING

When you are correcting several errors in a program, you will normally assemble the program again after correcting each error or small group of errors. There is a problem in this, however, that arises when you do not have a printer handy, or if you are not making a separate hard copy every time you reassemble.

Suppose you are debugging the first assembly. In this process, you will need to know the addresses of various pieces of data and points in your program. If you have a printout of the assembly, this information will be on the printout. If not, you can write it down, little by little, as you debug.

For example, if LDA $08DA (displayed on the screen during stepping) corresponds to LDA R in your program, then you know that R has the address 08DA. If LDA R has the label BETA in your program, and LDA $08DA is given, in displaying the step, at the address 0838, then BETA is associated with the address 0838.

However, suppose that you reassemble and look for further bugs. Most of the information that you gained in this way will probably be lost. If you made a change in your program, involving insertion or deletion, then all the addresses coming *after* the change will not be the same as they were before. This is due to the way the assembler assigns locations in strict numerical order (except when there is an ORG pseudo-operation in the middle of the program).

There is a very old method of getting around these problems, known as *patching*. It was developed for computer systems on which assembly took a long time and incurred a high cost, so that programmers avoided reassembly for economic reasons. In those days, patching required the changes in a program to be translated *by hand* from assembly language into machine language. On the APPLE, however, we can do *assembly-level patching*, which is simpler, more foolproof, and requires no hand translation.

The basic idea of patching is concerned with putting a sequence of new instructions between the two instructions I_1 and I_2. Suppose first that I_1 is a *three-byte* instruction. Then patching proceeds as follows:

(1) Get back into LISA from the monitor (by typing 7003G or 6003G or E003G as directed at the end of section 47).

(2) List your program. If it does not list properly, load it again with the LOAD command (again as in section 47).

(3) Change instruction I_1 to a *jump* to a point *after the end* of your program (just before the END statement). Note that this replaces three bytes by three bytes, since JMP is also a three-byte instruction.

(4) At that point, write the instruction I_1, followed by the new instructions, followed by a jump to I_2. (These instructions are then called the *patch*.) All addresses of other instruction and data words should remain unchanged by this process.

(5) Reassemble and start debugging again.

If I_1 is not a three-byte instruction, we have to find another way to replace n bytes, before I_2, by another set of n bytes. Instead of one instruction I_1, take two or three instructions before I_2. If these total three bytes in length, replace them by a jump as in Step 3. If they total four or five bytes in length, replace them with a jump followed by one or two "nonsense" bytes (BYT !0 will do). These two or three instructions must also, of course, be put into the patch (in Step 4) instead of the single instruction I_1.

Patching is also used for taking out instructions. If one byte is to be taken out, replace it with NOP, a one-byte instruction which does nothing. (NOP stands for "no operation," and it is always pronounced "no op," never "nopp.") If two bytes are taken out, replace them with two NOPs. In fact, you can do this for any number of bytes, but it may be simpler to replace the first three bytes by a jump to the instruction after the deleted ones. (Then again, you may find this confusing.)

Never leave a working program with patches in it. As soon as you are sure that your program works, reassemble it one final time, taking the patches out and replacing them by what you would have written if you had not been interested in patching.

An interesting and true story about patching concerns the Apollo spacecraft, orbiting the moon, whose computer started registering an alarm and refusing to perform further calculations. The astronauts quickly found out that it was the alarm *signal* that was out of order, and giving a false error indication. A programmer, back on earth, wrote a patch in the error handling program, to test for that particular error and treat it as if it were not an error. This patch was actually done at the machine language level, and the changes to the machine language program were transmitted to the astronauts by voice—and the patched program got them safely back to earth.

EXERCISES

1. (a) Consider the following sequence of instructions:

```
             LDX     # ! 8
    LOOP     LDA     BITS−! 1, X
             LSR
             CMP     # $58
             BNE     ERROR
             JMP     PATCH1
    LOOP1    DEX
             BNE     LOOP
```

This makes reference to the following patch, at the end of the program:

```
    PATCH1   LDA     BITS−! 1, X
             LSR
             ROR     BIN
             JMP     LOOP1
```

Rewrite this program so as to remove the patch; that is, bring the instructions of the patch back inside the main body of instructions, at the point where they belong.*

   (b) What instructions and labels become unnecessary in the process of part (a) above?

*2. Write an assembly-level patch to insert the instructions

```
             BNE     BETA
             INC     Q+! 2
```

just before BETA, in the sequence

```
             LDA     P
             CLC
             ADC     Q
             BCC     BETA
             INC     Q+ ! 1
    BETA     STA     Q
```

Show both the patch and the modified sequence above.

---

*We may note that the point of the patch is to insert another LDA and LSR so that the carry flag, as set by the LSR (and overwritten by the CMP after the first LSR), can be used by the ROR.

*3. Write an assembly-level patch which will remove the ASL and insert a
     new ASL just after TYA in the sequence

```
              LDX     # ! 0
              LDY     # ! 0
    GAMMA     LDA     BITS−! 1 , X
              LSR
              TYA
              BCC     DELTA
              CLC
              ADC     # ! 1
    DELTA     ASL
              TAY
              INX
              CPX     # ! 8
              BNE     GAMMA
              STY     BIN
```

Show both the patch and the modified sequence above. Be very careful in
counting bytes, so that no instruction outside the patch has its address
changed.

PROBLEM 1 FOR COMPUTER SOLUTION

USING GETLNZ, MULT, DECI, AND DECOZ

At this point it is time to start writing programs on the computer.

Our first exercise will be, to a great extent, an exercise in typing, using the
editor, using the assembler, and correcting typing errors. There will be very
little actual programming.

You are to write a program which:

(1) Inputs a number, using GETLNZ and DECI.
(2) Stores this number and inputs a second number in the same way.
(3) Multiplies the two numbers, using MULT.
(4) Prints out the result, using DECOZ.
(5) Goes back to Step 1.

In doing this, it is assumed that you will be typing in the program MULT of
section 39 and the programs DECI and DECO of sections 62 and 63. *There is a
lot of typing involved in this, and that is done on purpose.* Typing in long programs which you have written, and then checking your own work to make sure
that you have done it right, is something that is *absolutely necessary* to you as a
programmer. Note that you must check every single instruction in MULT,
DECI, and DECO after you have typed it in.

After you have finished this program, make sure that you do not destroy the
file; you can use these three subroutines in further programming exercises in
this book.

51. CALLING LISA PROGRAMS FROM BASIC PROGRAMS

Once you have debugged a LISA program, you can adapt it in such a way that it becomes a subroutine, called by a BASIC program. This is done as follows:

(1) Start your LISA program with ORG $8000 followed by OBJ $0800 (OBJ stands for "object code"). When LISA assembles your (assembly language) *source code*, or *source program*, it will put your (machine language) *object code*, or *object program*, in memory, starting at address 0800 (this is what OBJ $0800 does). However, the program will not run until its instruction and data code bytes have been moved, in memory, to an area which starts at address 8000.* (We will see, in Step (5) below, why this is necessary.)

(2) At the start of your LISA program, write JSR IOSAVE (where IOSAVE EQU $FF4A is specified). This saves all the registers. At the end of your LISA program, write JMP IOREST (where IOREST EQU $FF3F is specified). This restores all the registers and returns. Remember to use JMP IOREST rather than JSR IOREST because IOREST itself will return. All this is necessary because *BASIC assumes that your LISA program saves and restores all the registers.*

(3) On the assembly listing, note the *last address* used by your object code. If your program has length not greater than 1000 (hexadecimal) bytes, this will be of the form 8*ddd*, and the last three digits, *ddd*, plus one,† will be the hexadecimal length *n* of your program.

---

*For example, if the source code contains LDA W where W is at location 8150—that is, 150 (hexadecimal) bytes after 8000—the object code form of this is AD 50 81. Suppose now that these three bytes have addresses 809C, 809D, and 809E. When LISA assembles this program, these three bytes (AD, 50, and 81) will be stored at 089C, 089D, and 089E, but *the bytes themselves do not change*; in particular, they do not become AD 50 09 (for the address 0950, or 150 bytes after 0800).

†Plus one because there are *n*+1 bytes, rather than *n* bytes, between the addresses 8000 and 8000+*n* (inclusive).

(4) Save your object code with the LISA command

<u>D</u>BSAVE *name*,A$800, L$*n*

where <u>D</u> stands for control-D; *name* is the name of the program; and *n* is the length, as above. The control-D means that an APPLE DOS (Disk Operating System) command is being executed. In this case, the command is BSAVE (which stands for "binary save"—here "binary" is again a misnomer, as before, since *all* numbers in a computer are in binary, but, as usual, it denotes integer and machine language program codes, as contrasted with character codes). The A means "address" (the starting address, at the moment, is $800, because this is where LISA put the program) and the L means "length."

(5) LISA programs normally use cells 0800 through 17FF. BASIC, however, uses these cells for other purposes. In fact, BASIC uses *all* available memory unless you tell it to do otherwise, with a HIMEM statement. The first statement of your BASIC program should be

1   HIMEM: 32767

This forces BASIC to use only the first 32K of memory (cells 0 through 32767, decimal, or 0 through 7FFF, hexadecimal). Your LISA program can now use memory starting at address 8000, as we have mentioned above. The *second* statement of your BASIC program should be

2   PRINT "<u>D</u>BLOAD *name*,A$8000"

where <u>D</u> and *name* are as before. In BASIC, *printing* a string beginning with control-D causes an APPLE DOS command to be executed. In this case, the command is BLOAD ("binary load," which loads a program that has been saved with "binary save"—remember that "to load a program" means to bring it back into main memory from disk). The A means "address," as before, and this time the program is being brought back, not into address $0800—where it was assembled by LISA—but into address $8000, where it will execute.

(6) To call your LISA program, use CALL 32768 in BASIC. (Note that *n*, in the CALL *n* statement in BASIC, *must* be decimal, not hexadecimal.)

(7) You may want your BASIC program to pass data to your LISA program, and vice versa. In that case, the first statement of your LISA program should be JMP START, followed by a few bytes of data, followed by START which is the first instruction of your program. The JMP   START takes three bytes, which means that the first *data* byte has *decimal* address 32771. The next few data bytes have decimal addresses 32772, 32773, and so on. The BASIC statement POKE *a,e* now puts *e* into the

cell with *decimal* address a; the statement $K = PEEK(a)$ puts into K what is in the cell with decimal address a. $PEEK(a)$ may also be used in expressions; one may write $K = K+PEEK(a)$, for example, to add to K what is in the cell with address a. To pass an *array* T of data between a BASIC program and a LISA program, determine the address of the array in the LISA program and convert this to a decimal number a. Now POKE $a+J,e$ into T(J) (assuming that T starts with T(0)); while $K = PEEK(a+J)$ puts T(J) into K. As before, PEEK $(a+J)$ may be used in more general expressions. The quantity e in POKE a,e and POKE $a+J,e$ may be a constant, variable, or an arithmetic expression (having a value v in the range $0 \leq v \leq 255$).

EXERCISES

1. Suppose that we were to call the subroutine MULT (as given in section 39) from a BASIC program. Since the BASIC program cannot load the *registers* of the 6502, let us assume that we have two bytes, MULTA and MULTX, which hold the A and X register contents, respectively, before and after the call to MULT. These are given immediately following the jump to START, as follows:

```
                    ORG    $8000
                    JMP    START
         MULTA      DFS    !1
         MULTX      DFS    !1
```

    (a) Give the assembly language statements required to call MULT in this situation, entering MULT with the A and X registers properly set, and properly using the quantities left in the A and X registers by MULT. (Remember to use IOSAVE and IOREST.)
    *(b) Give the BASIC statements required to set M = I*J in BASIC, using this assembly language subroutine. Assume that I, J, and M are 8-bit quantities.
    (c) Do part (b) above if I and J are 8-bit quantities, while M is a 16-bit quantity. Note that M must be reconstructed from its two halves, which are placed in MULTA and MULTX by the sequence given in the answer to part (a) above.

2. An array U in an assembly language program, with 100 elements ranging from U(1) to U(100), has the hexadecimal starting address 80E8.

    *(a) Write a FOR loop in BASIC which moves the elements T(1) through T(100) in the BASIC program into this array.

(b) Write a FOR loop in BASIC which moves the elements in this array back to T(1) through T(100).

*(c) Do part (a) above if T has 101 elements, ranging from T(0) through T(100).

3. Suppose that you have three assembly language programs, ALPHA, BETA, and GAMMA, all of which are called from the same BASIC program. You assemble your three programs in one assembly, and at the start of the assembly you write

```
ORG    $8000
JMP    ALPHA
JMP    BETA
JMP    GAMMA
```

What BASIC statement can now be used to call GAMMA from BASIC?

52. LOGICAL "AND"

We now proceed to discuss the rest of the instructions on the 6502.

There is an instruction called AND, which sets individual bits of the A register to zero. Most of the time, AND is used with a binary (or hexadecimal) constant called a *mask*. Zero-bits in the mask specify which bits are to be set to zero. Thus

$$\text{AND} \qquad \#\%01111110 \qquad \textit{or} \qquad \text{AND} \qquad \#\$7E$$

sets the first and last bits of the A register to zero.

AND is a *bit-by-bit* instruction. This means that each bit in the A register is determined, after the AND, solely by its old value and by the value of the corresponding bit in the mask.* Let us denote the kth bit in the mask by P_k, and the k-th bit in the A register by Q_k (before the AND) and by R_k (after the AND). Then R_k is determined as follows:

$$
\begin{array}{c|cc}
 & Q_k = 0 & Q_k = 1 \\
\hline
P_k = 0 & R_k = 0 & R_k = 0 \\
P_k = 1 & R_k = 0 & R_k = 1
\end{array}
\qquad \textit{or, abbreviating,} \qquad
\begin{array}{c|cc}
 & 0 & 1 \\
\hline
0 & 0 & 0 \\
1 & 0 & 1
\end{array}
$$

Those who know mathematical logic will recognize, in the table at the right, the truth table for logical "and" (which is why this instruction is called AND). If 0 means "false," and 1 means "true," then $R = P$ *and* Q is given by this table, because R is true ($= 1$) only if P and Q are both true.

AND sets the zero status flag, and this allows it to be used for testing individual bits in memory. Thus, for example, the sequence of instructions

```
LDA   Q
AND   #%00001000
BEQ   BZERO
```

---

*This is not true of addition, for example, where each bit in the A register is also influenced by the carry from the addition in the bit just to the right of it.

goes to BZERO if the fourth bit from the right in Q is zero. In that case, the fourth bit from the right in the A register will be zero, and all the other bits of the A register will be set to zero by the AND. Thus the A register will be zero, and the zero status flag, which is tested by BEQ, will be set.

AND is used, together with shifting, to load *fields* of individual bytes into the A register. A field is a part of a byte. For example, the diagram below shows a byte divided into three fields:

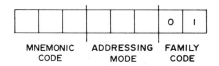

```
MNEMONIC    ADDRESSING   FAMILY
  CODE         MODE       CODE
```

This is the format of the operation codes of eight of the instructions on the 6502: LDA, STA, ADC, SBC, CMP, AND itself, and two instructions which we take up in the next two sections, ORA and EOR. Each of these eight instructions has a mnemonic code (000 through 111). The addressing mode (constant, indexed by X, indexed by Y, etc.) also has a three-bit code. Suppose we want to load the A register with the addressing mode of L5. We can write

```
LDA     L5          ; OPERATION CODE TO A-REGISTER
AND     #%00011100  ; MASK OUT MNEMONIC, FAMILY CODES
LSR                 ; SHIFT TO RIGHT-HAND
LSR                 ;   END OF A-REGISTER
```

The reason that we shift fields to the right-hand end of the register is that the number in the field (0 through 7 in this case) is then in the same format as the corresponding number in the entire register (binary 00000000 through 00000111, in this case). The instruction CMP #!5 can now be used, for example, to check whether the addressing mode is equal to 5. (Without the two LSRs, this would have to be CMP #!20). We could also shift *before* masking, thus:

```
LDA     L5          ; OPERATION CODE TO A-REGISTER
LSR                 ; SHIFT TO RIGHT-HAND
LSR                 ;   END OF A-REGISTER
AND     #%00000111  ; MASK OUT ALL BUT ADDR. MODE
```

Note that the mask has to be changed in this case. This example shows why a mask is called a mask; all fields except the one we are looking for are cleared, or *masked out*.

The preceding two uses of AND may be combined, to test whether a *field* is equal to zero. Thus

```
LDA   L5          ;  LOAD L5 AND MASK OUT ALL BUT
AND   #%00011100  ;  ADDR. MODE  − −  Z FLAG SET IF
BNE   NONZ        ;  RESULT (ADDR. MODE OF L5) = 0
```

goes to NONZ if the addressing mode field of L5 is not zero.

AND sets the sign status flag, as well as the zero status flag. Note, however, that AND #%01111111 does *not* produce the absolute value of a signed integer; if it is negative, it must be converted into its twos' complement.

The example of mnemonic code and addressing mode fields given above was adapted from Table 15 in the Appendix. *All* the operation codes of the 6502 are grouped into "families" like this.

EXERCISES

1. Take the logical AND of the following numbers of two hexadecimal digits apiece, by converting the numbers to binary, taking the logical AND, and converting the result back to hexadecimal. Show your work.

    *(a) 20 and 35.
     (b) F6 and C7.
    *(c) 55 and AA.

2. Take the logical AND of the following numbers of two hexadecimal digits apiece. Try to do the binary conversions in your head. (Express the results in hexadecimal.)

     (a) 35 and 0F.
    *(b) 72 and F0.
     (c) 94 and 81.

*3. Write a program to load the A register with the mnemonic code of L5 (the leftmost three bits) by shifting *left*, using ROL, and masking. (There is a slight trick to this one, based on the fact that ROL really rotates a nine-bit register, as explained in section 34.)

53. LOGICAL "OR"

To set individual bits of the A register to *one*, rather than zero, we have the instruction ORA. (You have undoubtedly noticed by now that every mnemonic on the 6502 has three letters, which is why A—for the A register—is on the end of ORA.)

In this case, *one-bits*, rather than zero-bits, in the mask specify which bits are to be set to one. Thus

ORA   #%10000001   *or*   ORA   #$81

sets the first and last bits of the A register to one. Like AND, ORA is used, most of the time, with a binary or hexadecimal constant (the mask).

ORA, like AND, is a bit-by-bit instruction. The determination of R_k from P_k and Q_k, as in the preceding section, is:

$$
\begin{array}{c|cc}
 & Q_k = 0 & Q_k = 1 \\
\hline
P_k = 0 & R_k = 0 & R_k = 1 \\
P_k = 1 & R_k = 1 & R_k = 1
\end{array}
\qquad \textit{or, abbreviating,} \qquad
\begin{array}{c|cc}
 & 0 & 1 \\
\hline
0 & 0 & 1 \\
1 & 1 & 1
\end{array}
$$

In mathematical logic, the table at the right is the truth table for logical "or," giving R = P *or* Q, because R is true (= 1) if either P or Q (or both) is true.

We have seen in section 24 that the leftmost bit of any character code which is displayed (using COUT) is always 1. The ORA instruction is often used (see section 73, for example) to set this bit to 1, if it is not known to be 1, before the given character code is displayed.

Just as AND may be used to *unpack* bytes, or break them up into fields, ORA may be used to *pack* fields back into bytes. This use of ORA depends on the fact that the logical "or" of any quantity Q with *zero* is Q itself. Suppose we have three bytes called MCODE, AMODE, and FCODE, which contain the mnemonic code, addressing mode, and family code respectively, as in the preceding section. Then we can put them back together, into a byte called OPCODE, in the following way:

```
LDA    MCODE      ; PUT MNEMONIC CODE IN A-REGISTER
ASL               ; SHIFT THIS CODE
ASL               ;    THREE BITS TO
ASL               ;       THE LEFT
ORA    AMODE      ; INSERT ADDRESSING MODE
ASL               ; SHIFT MNEMONIC CODE AND ADDRESSING
ASL               ;   MODE TWO MORE BITS TO THE LEFT
ORA    FCODE      ; INSERT FAMILY CODE
STA    OPCODE     ; RESULT IS THE OPERATION CODE
```

We could also add, instead of using ORA; but note that the carry would have to be cleared in that case. This use of ORA is quite common when we are dealing with the two 4-bit halves of a byte separately (see section 83).

ORA, like AND, sets the sign status flag. Note, as before, that ORA #%10000000 does not change a positive integer into its negative; this must be done by forming the twos' complement.

ORA also sets the zero status flag. If the mask is constant, the zero status flag is always cleared, indicating a non-zero result, except, possibly, if the mask is zero. We may note that ORA #$0 leaves the A register unchanged; so it may be used to set the zero and sign status flags from the current contents of the A register, if they had been altered by a preceding instruction not involving the A register (INX, DEX, ASL Q, and so on). Note also that AND #$FF accomplishes the same thing.

The fact that ORA sets the zero status flag may be used to test a 16-bit quantity for being zero. Thus

```
LDA    P
ORA    P+!1
BEQ    PZERO
```

goes to PZERO if the 16-bit quantity P is zero, because then, and only then, will the logical "or" of its two bytes be zero. The same trick works with quantities having 24 bits, 32 bits, and so on.

EXERCISES

1. Take the logical OR of the following numbers by converting them from hexadecimal to binary, taking the logical OR, and converting the result back to hexadecimal. Show your work.

    (a) 20 and 35.
    *(b) F6 and C7.
    (c) 55 and AA.

2. Take the logical OR of the following hexadecimal numbers. Try to do the binary conversions in your head.

   *(a) 35 and 0F.
    (b) 72 and F0.
   *(c) 94 and 81.

3. Write a program to form a byte P in memory out of two hexadecimal digits, LDIGIT (at the left) and RDIGIT (at the right). Assume that LDIGIT and RDIGIT are single-byte quantities, in the range from zero to 15.

54. LOGICAL EXCLUSIVE "OR"

Our third and last bit-by-bit instruction, EOR, is used to *change* individual bits in the A register—that is, to make them 1 if they are 0 and 0 if they are 1. Like AND and ORA, EOR is normally used with a constant binary or hexadecimal mask. The bits to be changed are one-bits in the mask; in this way, EOR is like ORA. Thus, for example,

EOR   #%00001111   *or*   EOR   #$0F

changes the rightmost four bits of the A register, while leaving the leftmost four bits unchanged.

In mathematics, "P or Q" includes the case that both P and Q might be true (as in the statement "$ab = 0$ if, and only if, either $a = 0$ or $b = 0$"). In ordinary English, "P or Q" *excludes* this case (as in the statement "Either Smith or Jones will win the election"). This so-called *exclusive OR* is sometimes used in mathematical logic, and it gives rise to our EOR instruction, because the determination of R_k from P_k and Q_k, as in the last two sections, is:

	$Q_k = 0$	$Q_k = 1$			0	1
$P_k = 0$	$R_k = 0$	$R_k = 1$	*or, abbreviating,*	0	0	1
$P_k = 1$	$R_k = 1$	$R_k = 0$		1	1	0

and this is the truth table for exclusive OR. (It is the same as the truth table for the ordinary or *inclusive* OR, except that, if P_k and Q_k are both 1, R_k is zero; that is, the case in which the two quantities are both true is excluded.) The exclusive OR of any quantity Q with zero is Q itself, just as with the inclusive OR.

EOR may be used in making *signed comparisons*. The instruction EOR #%10000000 (or EOR #$80) converts the signed quantity p, with $-128 \leq p \leq 127$, into the unsigned quantity $p+128$, with $0 \leq p+128 \leq 255$.* Every number in the signed range corresponds, in this way, to a number in the

---

*You may verify, by trying various examples, that adding 128 (binary 10000000) to *any* signed number is the same as changing its leftmost bit (to 1 if it is zero, or to zero if it is 1).

unsigned range. Furthermore, P < Q (signed) if and only if P+128 < Q+128 (unsigned), so that the sequence of instructions (for example)

```
LDA    Q                ;  LOAD Q (SIGNED)
EOR    #%10000000       ;  CONVERT TO Q+128 (UNSIGNED)
STA    TEMP             ;  SAVE Q+128
LDA    P                ;  LOAD P (SIGNED)
EOR    #%10000000       ;  CONVERT TO P+128 (UNSIGNED)
CMP    TEMP             ;  COMPARE WITH Q+128
BCC    LESS             ;  IF P+128 < Q+128, THEN P < Q
```

goes to LESS if P < Q, where P and Q are both signed. (Another way of doing signed comparisons is taken up in section 56.)

Of course, EOR #%10000000 does not convert a number into its negative. However, we can use EOR #%11111111 (or EOR #$FF) to convert a number into its *ones'* complement. We recall (see section 7) that the twos' complement is the ones' complement plus one; and this gives us a fast way to subtract the X register from a constant k—namely, take the ones' complement of $X-(k+1)$, since if this is z, then $z+1 = -(X-(k+1))$, so that $z = k - X$. If $k = 7$, we write

```
TXA            ;  CALCULATE X-8 AND THEN TAKE
SEC            ;    ONES' COMPLEMENT, GIVING
SBC    #!8     ;   Z WHERE Z+1 = -(X-8) = 8-X,
EOR    #$FF    ;   OR Z = (8-X)-1 = 7-X
```

EOR, done twice, "undoes itself"—the result of EOR n followed by another EOR n (for *any* value of n) is to leave the A register unchanged. In particular, EOR #%10000000 converts $p+128$ (unsigned) back to p (signed), as well as the reverse. This property of EOR may be used to perform *field replacement*; if the addressing mode field of OPCODE is to be replaced by the addressing mode field of OP2, for example, we could presumably write

```
LDA    OP2              ;  GET A-MODE FIELD OF OP2
AND    #%00011100       ;  (MASK OUT ALL OTHER FIELDS)
STA    TEMP             ;  AND SAVE IT
LDA    OPCODE           ;  GET OPCODE AND MASK OUT
AND    #%11100011       ;    ITS OLD A-MODE FIELD
ORA    TEMP             ;  INSERT NEW A-MODE FIELD
STA    OPCODE           ;  AND STORE UPDATED OPCODE
```

but we could save two instructions with this unusual trick:

```
LDA    OPCODE           ;  GET OLD OPCODE
EOR    OP2              ;  (A-MODE FIELD IS CLEARED AND
AND    #%11100011       ;  EOR-ED ONCE; ALL OTHER FIELDS
EOR    OP2              ;  ARE EOR-ED TWICE -- NO CHANGE)
STA    OPCODE           ;  STORE UPDATED OPCODE
```

Either EOR or ORA can be used in certain situations. In particular, all the uses of ORA which are commented INSERT in this section and the previous one could just as easily be EOR.

On a number of other computers, the "exclusive OR" instruction is given as XOR instead of EOR. LISA allows you to write XOR instead of EOR on the 6502, if you so desire.

EXERCISES

1. Take the logical exclusive OR of the following numbers by converting them from hexadecimal to binary, taking the logical exclusive OR, and converting the result back to hexadecimal. Show your work.

   *(a) 20 and 35.
    (b) F6 and C7.
   *(c) 55 and AA.

2. Take the logical exclusive OR of the following hexadecimal numbers. Try to do the binary conversions in your head.

    (a) 35 and 0F.
   *(b) 72 and F0.
    (c) 94 and 81.

*3. Write a program to branch to LEQ if the signed quantity P is less than or equal to the signed quantity Q. Your program should be *seven* instructions long. (Hint: see section 28.)

55. BIT TESTING

We have seen how individual bits of a byte can be tested by using AND. There is another instruction on the 6502* that does somewhat the same thing, namely BIT. The instruction BIT Q takes the logical AND of Q and the A register, and sets the zero status flag in the same way that AND Q does. Thus the instruction sequences

```
LDA   Q                    LDA   #%00001000
AND   #%00001000           BIT   Q
BEQ   BZERO                BEQ   BZERO
```

both go to BZERO if the fourth bit from the right in Q is zero.

The differences between AND and BIT are:

(1) BIT *cannot* be used with indexing.
(2) BIT *cannot* be used with a constant (such as BIT #$80).
(3) BIT *does not* change the A register. This property of BIT can be used to test Q against a "sliding mask" that starts as binary 00000001 and shifts to the left each time we test. Thus the following program is an alternative way of counting the one-bits in Q (see section 35):

```
        LDY   #!0       ; INITIAL VALUE OF BIT COUNT
        LDA   #!1       ; INITIAL VALUE OF MASK
TALLY   BIT   Q         ; TEST THIS BIT (DOES NOT
        BEQ   TALLY1    ;   CHANGE MASK) - - IF EQUAL
        INY            ;   TO 1, ADD 1 TO BIT COUNT
TALLY1  ASL            ; SLIDE THE MASK AND RETURN
        BCC   TALLY     ;   UNLESS MASK WENT INTO CARRY
```

If we add LDA Q to the first program in section 35 (as we must, in order to get an equivalent program), then the above program is 16 cycles slower, but one

---

*Relatively few computers other than the 6502 have an instruction like BIT. Almost all computers, by contrast, have instructions like AND, ORA, and EOR.

byte shorter. We can also use BIT when there are several quantities which must
be tested against the same mask. Thus

```
LDA    #$1      ;  SET UP MASK
BIT    C1       ;  TEST RIGHTMOST BIT
BNE    C1ODD    ;    OF C1
BIT    C2       ;  TEST RIGHTMOST BIT
BNE    C2ODD    ;    OF C2
```

goes to C1ODD if C1 is odd (rightmost bit equal to 1); otherwise it goes to
C2ODD if C2 is odd. We could, of course, do further bit tests with the same
mask.

(4) BIT Q sets the sign status flag to the sign of Q, *regardless of the sign of
the A register*. This makes BIT the *only* 6502 instruction that sets the zero and
sign flags according to the results of two different calculations. (Remember that
the zero status flag setting is taken from the logical AND of Q and the A register.) This property of BIT permits us to go to QNEG if Q is negative in still
another alternative way to those of section 28:

```
BIT    Q        ;  TEST THE SIGN BIT
BMI    QNEG     ;    OF Q
```

Note that this does not change the values of A, X, or Y, and can thus be used
even if A, X, and Y are all in use (or if their contents are unknown). The space
and time used by the above instructions are the same as those of the alternatives.

One further property of BIT is taken up at the end of the next section.

An unusual use of BIT allows you to save a byte or two when skipping over a
single two-byte instruction. Consider, for example, two programs, called P1 and
P2, which start with the following logic:

```
P1     ORA    #$40
       JMP    P1A
P2     ORA    #$20
P1A    JSR    SUB
```

Now suppose that we replace the three-byte JMP by the single byte $2C, the
operation code for BIT. The ORA at P2 has the machine language form 09 20.
Thus the BIT is interpreted as BIT $2009, and it performs a BIT instruction with
whatever is in cell 2009. *This does nothing* (except to the flags, which may be
ignored), and JSR SUB is the next instruction; the result, therefore, is effectively
the same as that of the JMP. Note that this sequence "goes out of alignment" (see
section 45) on purpose!

EXERCISES

1. The instruction BIT Q is like AND Q, except that AND Q puts the result in the A register, whereas BIT Q does not. What other pair of instructions on the 6502 has a similar property?

*2. What is wrong with the following program to count the number of negative elements of the array T, from T(1) through T(N)?

```
        LDX   N
        LDY   # ! 0
LOOP    BIT   T−! 1, X
        BPL   EPOS
        INY
EPOS    DEX
        BNE   LOOP
```

3. How much space and time does the sequence (given in the text)

```
        LDA   # $ 1
        BIT   C1
        BNE   C1ODD
        BIT   C2
        BNE   C2ODD
```

save, compared to its alternative (using AND)? Note that *time* will be saved only when the computer does *not* branch to C1ODD.

56. THE OVERFLOW STATUS FLAG

When we add two *unsigned* numbers, and the answer is too large to fit in one byte (that is, greater than 255), the carry flag is set. Similarly, when we subtract two unsigned numbers, and the answer is less than zero, this is indicated in the carry status flag (by clearing it, whereas it would be set otherwise).

When we add or subtract two *signed* numbers, however, the answer may also be too large, or too small, to fit in one byte as a signed number. This is called *arithmetic overflow*, or simply *overflow*.

Overflow is different from carry. For example, $100+100 = 200$ (decimal), and the operation of adding $100+100$ does not produce carry because 200 is less than 256; but it does produce overflow, because the range of signed numbers is from -128 to 127, and 200 is greater than 127.

Or consider $(-3)+5$. This *does* produce carry, because it is the same as the unsigned addition $253 + 5$, which produces a result that is greater than 255; but it *does not* produce overflow because $(-3)+5 = 2$, and 2 is well within the range (from -128 to 127) of the signed numbers on the 6502.

For this reason, *overflow has its own status flag* on the 6502. This is called V (not O, because, for example, O = 1 looks like "zero equals one"), and the branches on overflow clear and set reflect this designation:

BVC L	Branch to L on overflow flag clear
BVS L	Branch to L on overflow flag set

This concludes our study of conditional branch instructions. There are eight of them, based on four status flags (zero, sign, carry, and overflow), namely BEQ, BNE, BPL, BMI, BCC, BCS, BVC, and BVS.

The instructions ADC and SBC set the overflow flag if there is overflow and clear it if there is no overflow. Thus

```
LDA   P       ; ADD P AND Q, AND GO TO
CLC           ; OVER IF P+Q IS OUTSIDE
ADC   Q       ; THE SIGNED NUMBER RANGE
BVS   OVER    ; (-128 THROUGH 127)
```

goes to OVER if adding P and Q produces overflow. Note that ADC and SBC are *the only instructions*, of those which perform a calculation that might overflow (such as the increment, decrement, and shift instructions), *which affect this flag*. Especially important is the fact that *compare instructions do not affect the overflow flag*. (Table 3 in the Appendix shows the instructions which act on the overflow flag; these are marked with a V in the "Flags" column.)

In our discussion of signed comparisons in section 28, we noted that BPL and BMI cannot be used because, for example, if P is −29 and Q is 100, then P < Q and P−Q is negative (−129, to be specific), but the sign bit of this is positive. On the other hand, there is also overflow in this case because −129 is not in the range of signed numbers.

Suppose now that we want to branch to LESS if P < Q. It is not too hard to see that BMI will work as long as there is no overflow. Furthermore, if there *is* overflow, then either:

(a) the result is greater than 127, in which case the number is positive, but its sign is negative; or

(b) the result is less than −128, in which case the number is negative, but its sign is positive.

In other words, *the sign is always wrong in this case*; so we can use BPL, rather than BMI. (BPL also branches on zero, but in this case the result can never be zero.) This gives us another way to branch to LESS if P<Q, as signed numbers:

```
            LDA   P          ; CALCULATE P-Q IN THE
            SEC              ;   USUAL WAY AND SET THE
            SBC   Q          ;     SIGN AND OVERFLOW FLAGS
            BVS   OVSET      ; IS THE OVERFLOW SET
            BPL   GEQ        ; NO, TO GEQ IF P >= Q
            BMI   LESS       ;   AND TO LESS IF P < Q
    OVSET   BPL   LESS       ; YES, TESTS ARE BACKWARDS
    GEQ     (next instruction)
```

This is both shorter and faster than the alternative in section 54.

Just as we can clear the carry (CLC), we can clear the overflow flag; the instruction CLV does this. There is no instruction to set the overflow flag, however.

Overflow has an interesting theoretical property. The ADC instruction adds two binary numbers exactly as we did in section 3—from right to left. At each of the eight bit positions, there is the possibility of carry. In particular, at the leftmost bit position, there is the *carry out* (what goes into the carry flag) and the *carry in* (that is, the carry out of the second bit position from the left). It can now be shown that the overflow flag is set to the exclusive OR of this particular carry out and carry in. This simplifies the hardware of the 6502.

The final property of BIT, which we mentioned in the preceding section, is that BIT Q places the *second bit from the left* of Q (regardless of what is in the A register) into the *overflow* status flag. This gives us a fast way, using BVC or BVS, of testing this particular bit in a byte, if that is ever necessary.

EXERCISES

1. *(a) How much space is saved by the signed comparison program of this section, as compared with the alternative in section 54? Show your work.
    (b) How many cycles are saved by the signed comparison program of this section, if it goes to GEQ, as compared with the alternative in section 54? (Show your work. Note that there are two different cases in which the program of this section goes to GEQ. The total number of cycles is the same in both cases.)
    *(c) How many cycles, maximum and minimum, are saved by the signed comparison program of this section, if it goes to LESS, as compared with the alternative in section 54? (Show your work. Note that there are two different cases in which the program of this section goes to LESS. One of these takes more cycles than the other.)

2. *(a) Rewrite the program of this section in such a way that the first three instructions remain the same, but BVC OVCLR is the fourth instruction. Note that the action of this program, after the subtraction, may be expressed in the following table:

	OVERFLOW	
	CLEAR	SET
SIGN +	GO TO GEQ	GO TO LESS
SIGN −	GO TO LESS	GO TO GEQ

Make all further changes which are necessary in order that the old program and the new program do the same thing in all four cases.
    *(b) Are space requirements affected by this change?

3. (a) Using the table of exercise (2) above, rewrite the program of this section in such a way that the first three instructions remain the same, but

BMI NEG is the fourth instruction. Make all further changes which are necessary in order that the old program and the new program do the same thing in all four cases.

(b) Are space requirements affected by this change?

57. SAVED AND RESTORED VARIABLES

In this section and the next seven sections, we shall take up a number of fundamental facts about subroutines on the 6502.

There is a very common bug in writing subroutines which was alluded to briefly in sections 25, 34, and 42, and which we will now take up in its full generality. It may be illustrated as follows. Suppose we have a loop which calls SUB a total of N times:

```
        LDX  N        ; PUT COUNT IN X-REGISTER
LOOP    JSR  SUB      ; CALL SUB
        DEX           ; DECREASE THE COUNT
        BNE  LOOP     ; IF NON-ZERO, LOOP BACK
```

Let us look at this loop very carefully. First we load N; then we call SUB; then we decrease N by 1—at least we think we do. The problem is this: after the subroutine returns, and we do the DEX, *how do we know that N is still in the X register?*

If SUB is simple enough, it doesn't use the X register at all and there is no problem; but it might be that SUB has a loop of its own, and leaves the X register set to zero. In that case, DEX will set it to −1, and BNE will always branch. In other words, we have an endless loop. In general, if SUB uses the X register for its own purposes, problems of this sort may arise; they do not always give rise to endless loops, but they do normally cause wrong answers to be calculated. The same thing can happen with the Y register, of course; and it *does* happen with many common subroutines, such as RDKEY (as we noted in section 25).

How do we solve such problems? One way to do this was suggested in section 42. At the beginning of SUB, we *save* the X register (as, for example, by STX TEMP). At the end of SUB, just before we return, we *restore* the X register (as, in this case, by LDX TEMP). Whatever value X had at the beginning of SUB, that value is restored at the end, so that SUB acts as if it had not changed X at all. (For another method of saving and restoring, see sections 60 and 61.)

In any subroutine, we must consider the possibility of saving and restoring the various registers. This does *not* need to be done in any of the following cases:

(1) For a register which is *not used at all* in a subroutine. (For example, the subroutine MULT of section 39 does not use the Y register.)

(2) When a subroutine *returns data* (that is, exits with data in a register). The subroutine MULT, for example, is entered with two quantities to be multiplied in A and X and returns their product in A and X, so that A and X *must not* be restored to their initial values.

(3) When *the calling program assumes that a given register has been destroyed*. This happens quite often with RDKEY; if a call to RDKEY is in a loop, for example, the loop index *i* is kept in memory and decremented there (with DEC *i*).

On some computers (other than the 6502), every subroutine always saves and restores all the registers. Note, however, that data cannot be returned in registers if this is done.

Saving and restoring is often done in the middle of a program. With only three basic registers to work with, sometimes a program will run out of registers to use. If you need the X register, but the X register is already in use, *save* it (with STX TEMP); then use it; then restore it (with LDX TEMP). We should, of course, always consider alternatives to using registers, such as keeping a loop index in memory, as in point (3) above, and likewise shifting bytes in memory instead of in the A register.

If there is a register free, it can often be used for saving and restoring. Suppose we need to do a calculation in the A register, but there is something in the A register now which we will need later on. If the X register is free, we can save the A register there, with TAX, and restore it later with TXA. This is the fastest method of saving and restoring, whenever it is applicable. (See, for example, the final program of section 34.)

We say that a subroutine *preserves* a register if the contents of that register are the same at the end of that subroutine as they were at the beginning. This may be because the register was saved and restored, or simply because it was never used in the subroutine. Further examples of subroutines which do *not* preserve the registers include GETLNZ, of section 25 (and GETLN, of the exercises in that section), as well as the input and output conversion routines DECI, DECO, and DECOZ described in section 41.

EXERCISES

1. Consider the subroutine DIV of section 40. Should this subroutine save and restore any of the A, X, and Y registers? Why or why not?

*2. We have seen in section 39 that RTS in 6502 assembly language is like
     RETURN in BASIC or FORTRAN. There can be several RETURN state-
     ments in a BASIC or FORTRAN program. Similarly, there can be several
     RTS instructions in a 6502 program; but this is unlikely if the A, X, and Y
     registers are all saved and restored. Why? (Hint: consider saving space.)

 3. Consider the following subroutine:

```
            CALC        BIT     Q
                        BPL     CALCX
                        STA     TEMP
                        LDA     #!0
                        SEC
                        SBC     Q
                        STA     Q
                        LDA     TEMP
            CALCX       RTS
```

*(a) CALC sets Q equal to $f(Q)$, for what well-known function f?
 (b) When CALC is called, are the values of the A, X, and Y registers in
     the calling program preserved, whether Q was originally positive or
     negative? Why or why not?

58. RETURN ADDRESSES AND INDIRECT JUMPS

We have talked briefly about the JSR instruction (Jump to Subroutine, section 25) and the RTS instruction (Return from Subroutine, section 39). It is time to find out how they work. The basic idea which we must know about is that of a *return address*.

Consider Figure 18. Here we have a program P1, which calls a program P2 in three places. (The program P1 might be the main program, but it also might be another subroutine; we refer to it as the *calling program*, or the program that calls the subroutine P2.)

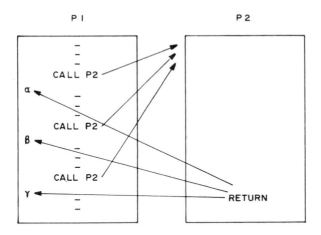

Figure 18. Calling a Subroutine More Than Once.

The *call* statement (JSR P2 on the 6502) clearly jumps, or branches, to P2. The *return* statement (RTS on the 6502) also jumps; but where does it jump? The first time that P2 is called, the return statement jumps to α. The second time, it jumps to β; while the third time, it jumps to γ.

How can we have a single instruction that can jump to any of three places? The answer involves the design of the *call* instruction, which not only jumps, but also calculates, and stores somewhere in memory, the *return address*. This is the address of the next instruction after the JSR. The first time that P2 is called, the return address is α. The second time, it is β; the third time, it is γ.

The return instruction now jumps to the return address, as this address is stored in memory. So, the first time, RTS would jump to α; the second time, it would jump to β; and, the third time, it would jump to γ, exactly as we wanted.

The next question is *where to store the return address*. Different computers have different answers to this question.

Some computers, such as the IBM 4300 series (and the older IBM 360 and 370), store the return address, not in memory at all, but in a *register*. The return instruction then returns to the address kept in this register. It is an *indexed jump*; it is as if we had JMP T,X in addition to LDA T,X on the 6502 (except that T would be zero in this case; we would add zero to the contents of the X register, and jump to the resulting location).

The 6502 does not have such an instruction, partly because the X and Y registers are only 8 bits long. Many other computers, however, have instructions like this.

Other older computers, such as the CDC 6000 series (made by Control Data Corporation), store the return address for a subroutine P2 at the beginning of P2. The return instruction from P2 then jumps to the address stored at the beginning of P2.

It is interesting to note that the 6502 does have an instruction which jumps to an address stored at a given location P2; it is JMP (P2) (the parentheses must be there). This is an *indirect jump*; it is said to use *indirect addressing* (which will be taken up further in sections 75 and 76). The address must be stored at P2 and P2 + !1,* with bytes reversed as usual.

Suppose, for the moment, that we wanted to use this instruction to end a subroutine. When we called the subroutine, we would have to store the return address at P2. Suppose the return address is CONT; then we would load the lower half of CONT and store it at P2, and then load the upper half of CONT and store it at P2 + !1. This may be done as follows, using another feature of LISA:

```
LDA    #CONT      ;  MOVE  ADDRESS  OF  CONT
STA    P2         ;    TO  B  (LOWER  HALF)
LDA    /CONT      ;  MOVE  ADDRESS  OF  CONT
STA    P2+!1      ;    TO  B  (UPPER  HALF)
```

---

*The calculation of P2 + !1 involves a 6502 hardware bug when the address of P2 is of the form $abFF; the calculated result will be $ab00 rather than $ac00, where $ac = ab + 1$.

For any address (or other 16-bit constant) J, #J denotes its right half and /J denotes its left half, in instructions which make reference to a constant. Of course, if J is an 8-bit unsigned constant, it can be thought of as a 16-bit constant whose left half is zero and whose right half is J itself; this is denoted by #J (as we have already seen). Note that /J, like #J, makes the instruction containing it into a *two-byte* (immediate data) instruction.

RTS, on the other hand, works in a different way. In fact, JSR stores the return address in a data structure known as a *stack*; and RTS gets the return address back out of the stack, and jumps to it. This method of keeping return addresses represents an advance by the 6502 (and other microcomputers), and, as we shall see, saves considerable time and space. In order to understand it more fully, we need some basic information about stacks.

EXERCISES

1. Suppose we did not have the instructions JSR and RTS on the 6502, and that, instead of calculating a return address and storing it in P2, as in the text, we called a subroutine with a code in the A register (1, 2, 3, etc.), indicating where the call took place. What does the subroutine need to do now, in order to return properly? Write out a sequence of instructions that might be used in this case, assuming four return addresses, ALPHA, BETA, GAMMA, and DELTA, and four codes, 1, 2, 3, and 4. (Note that the subroutine will probably be using the A register for its own purposes.)

*2. In BASIC, there is a statement

$$\text{ON } v \text{ GOTO } n_1, n_2, n_3, \ldots$$

which goes to n_1 if $v = 1$; to n_2 if $v = 2$; and so on. Suppose that you have a table of the addresses of n_1, n_2, and so on, arranged as a serial array JTABLE of two-byte quantities. Write a sequence of instructions on the 6502 which implements the above GO TO statement, assuming that v is in the A register.* (Ignore the possibility that v may be too large, or may be negative. Check to make sure you have the right offsets; see section 32.)

3. Suppose you are calculating $M = 15000/N$ by writing a program that calls DIV (from section 40). How is the process of writing this program made easier by using the / operator in LISA?

---

*For example, suppose that the A register contains 2. Then you want to go to n_2. The address of n_2 will be the *second* address in JTABLE; and your program, in this case, must take this address, move it to some other position (both bytes of it), and then do an indirect jump to this other position (call it IA). This will go to n_2 because it goes to the place whose address is currently at IA.

59. STACKS

We shall first learn about stacks in general, and then take up the specific hardware stack used in the 6502.

In the simplest applications—which are all we shall ever be concerned with, in this book—a stack is an array of variable size. Suppose we call our stack H and its size X. Then the elements of H can be considered as ranging from $H(0)$ through $H(X-1)$.

We can increase the size of the stack by setting $H(X)$ to some quantity A, and then adding 1 to X. This is called *pushing* A onto the stack. (See Figure 19.)

We can decrease the size of the stack by subtracting 1 from X. After we do this, $H(X)$ is usually moved back to A again. This is generally called *popping* A from the stack. On the 6502, it is known, more logically, as *pulling* (the opposite of pushing).

Both pushing and pulling can be done in BASIC:

```
H(X)  =  A        X  =  X-1
X  =  X+1         A  =  H(X)

Pushing A        Pulling A
```

or in 6502 assembly language, using the A and X registers:

```
STA  H, X         DEX
INX               LDA  H, X

Pushing A         Pulling A
```

Every stack has a certain maximum size, which we shall call *max*, and we always have $X < max$. On the 6502, we normally have $max = 256$, so that $X < 256$ or $X \le 255$—the largest permissible unsigned value of the X register under any conditions.

Now suppose that we have just pushed P3, P2, and P1, in that order, onto the stack. We say that P1 is at the *top* of the stack; P2 is the *second element down*, in the stack, and P3 is the *third element down*. Using what we have learned about offsets, we may note that

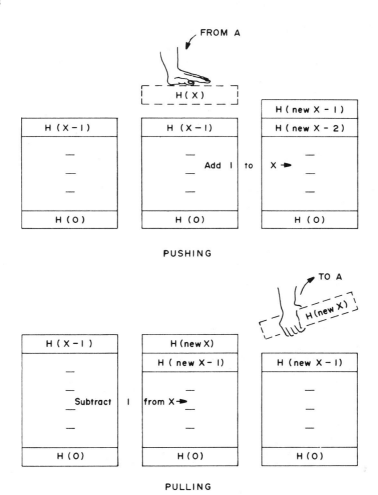

Figure 19. Pushing and Pulling.

LDA H−!1,X	loads P1 (the top of the stack);
LDA H−!2,X	loads P2 (the second element down);
LDA H−!3,X	loads P3 (the third element down);

and, in general, LDA H−!n,X loads the nth element down.

The presence of minus signs in the instructions above leads to the idea of *upside-down stacks*. In an upside-down stack called H, the bytes are not H(0), H(1), H(2), and so on, as above; instead, they are H(max−1), H(max−2), H(max−3), and so on down to H(X+1), with H(X) still the element *above* the top of the stack. Thus X is no longer the size of the stack. Instead, the size is z, where $max - z = X + 1$ (or $z = max - (X + 1) = max - 1 - X$). On the 6502, if $max = 256$, we have $z = 255 - X$; in other words, *the size of the stack is the ones' complement of what is in the X register* (see section 7).

Pushing and pulling would now be done as follows:

```
STA H, X          INX
DEX               LDA H, X
```

Pushing A   *Pulling A*

and if P3, P2, and P1 are pushed on such a stack, as above, then

```
LDA H+!1,X        loads P1 (the top of the stack);
LDA H+!2,X        loads P2 (the second element down);
LDA H+!3,X        loads P3 (the third element down);
```

and, in general, LDA H+!n,X loads the nth element down, and the minus signs have been replaced by plus signs.

Stacks can be used for saving and restoring. If we save several quantities by pushing them onto a stack, we can restore them later by pulling them from the stack.

Note that, when we pull something from a stack, there is *no* need to set the quantity at the top of the stack to zero (or any other special value). This is because, after pulling, this quantity will be *above* the top of the stack, and so its value will not matter. At some later time, the stack may become larger again; but, when this happens, a new value will be pushed into this quantity anyway.

The origin of the terms "pushing" and "popping" is interesting. They were first used by scientists at the RAND Corporation, near Los Angeles, where the cafeteria has a "well" for holding plates. When you took a plate off the top, the next one would pop up from inside the well. Every so often the cafeteria worker would come by with a stack of clean plates and push them down into the well. (In German computing literature, a stack is called a *Keller*, which means basement. Pushing and popping are apparently compared to throwing potatoes into the cellar and pulling them back out again!)

EXERCISES

*1. Modify the BASIC program of this section for pulling A from a stack H, so that it goes to 799 if there is nothing to pull—that is, if the stack is *empty*, or has no elements in it. (If the stack *becomes* empty, in the process of pulling A, do not go to 799.) Should this test be made before the two given BASIC statements, or after them? Why? (Hint: check carefully what happens when X = 0.)

2.   Modify the BASIC program of this section for pushing A onto a stack H, so that it goes to 899 if there is no room on the stack for what is being pushed— that is, if the stack is *full,* or has its maximum number of elements. (If the stack *becomes* full, in the process of pushing A, do not go to 899.) Assume that H is defined in BASIC by DIM H(n) and that this defines elements H(0) through H(n). Should this test be made before the two given BASIC statements, or after them? Why? (Hint: check carefully what happens when X = n.)

*3.   Suppose that the elements of a stack H are considered as ranging from H(1) through H(X), rather than from H(0) through H(X−1). How does this affect the pushing and pulling statements in BASIC? Formulate these in the simplest way (hint: what happens when you interchange the order of the two statements?). Ignore the checking for full and empty stacks suggested by the preceding two exercises. (The answer will indicate how pushing and pulling are in fact most often done in algebraic languages such as BASIC.)

60. STACK-ORIENTED INSTRUCTIONS

We shall now complete the explanation of how JSR and RTS work, and introduce four new instructions and one new register on the 6502.

The *hardware stack* of the 6502 is an upside-down stack, as described in the preceding section, having the *fixed addresses* 0100 through 01FF. It is associated with a special 8-bit register called the *stack pointer*. This is the register S which appeared in the stepping displays described in section 47.

The instruction PHA (Push A) pushes the A register onto the hardware stack. It does this by storing the A register in location 0100+S and then decrementing S. This is exactly what we did at the end of the last section, except that the stack pointer S replaces the X register.

The instruction PLA (Pull A) pulls the A register from the hardware stack, by incrementing S and then loading A from location 0100+S. Again, this is the same as before but with S taking the role of X.

Finally, JSR pushes, onto the hardware stack, the *return address* (minus one, to simplify hardware operations); and RTS pulls this back from the stack (and adds 1 back onto it), and goes to the resulting return address. Since addresses are 16-bit quantities, JSR pushes *two* bytes (the *high-order* byte first, so that the two bytes will appear in memory, as usual, with bytes reversed),while RTS pulls two bytes.*

The instructions PHA and PLA may be used for *saving and restoring* the A register. The X and Y registers may be saved by moving them to the A register first, and restored by moving them back. If we want to save all three registers A, X, and Y, we can write

---

*As an example, suppose that there are three bytes on the stack. Then these are in cells 01FF, 01FE, and 01FD, and the stack pointer contains FC. If cells 08B4, 08B5, and 08B6 contain the three bytes of the instruction JSR α, then the next instruction after this JSR starts in cell 08B7, so that 08B7 is the return address. If this JSR is now done, there will be *five* bytes on the stack, in cells 01FF, 01FE, 01FD, 01FC, and 01FB, and the stack pointer will be set to FA. The two new bytes on the stack are 08 (in cell 01FC) and B6 (in cell 01FB), because 08B6 is the return address (08B7, as above) *minus one*. If an RTS is now done, this 08B6 is pulled from the stack, and a jump is made to 08B6+1 or 08B7 (the return address); there are now three bytes on the stack, as before, so that the stack pointer is set to FC. (Note that this is FC, *not* 01FC; the stack pointer is 8 bits long.)

```
PHA      ;  SAVE  THE  A  REGISTER
TXA      ;  MOVE  X  TO  A
PHA      ;  (THIS  SAVES  THE  X  REGISTER)
TYA      ;  MOVE  Y  TO  A
PHA      ;  (THIS  SAVES  THE  Y  REGISTER)
```

at the beginning of the subroutine, and

```
PLA      ;  RESTORE  THE  Y  REGISTER
TAY      ;  MOVE  IT  BACK  TO  Y
PLA      ;  RESTORE  THE  X  REGISTER
TAX      ;  MOVE  IT  BACK  TO  X
PLA      ;  RESTORE  THE  A  REGISTER
```

at the end of the subroutine, just before RTS.

Note that if we save A, X, and Y, in that order, then Y will be at the top of the stack. When we restore, *we must restore Y first*; then X, and then A. In general, *if we save several quantities by pushing them, and restore them by pulling them, they have to be pulled in the reverse order of pushing.*

Stack-oriented call and return instructions such as JSR and RTS may be used directly in case there is more than one level of subroutine. Consider Figure 20, where we have a program P1 that calls a subroutine P2, and P2 itself calls a subroutine P3. The order of events here is as follows:

(1) P1 calls P2, and α (minus one) is pushed on the stack.
(2) P2 calls P3, and β (minus one) is pushed on the stack.
(3) P3 returns to P2. A return address is pulled from the stack, and this is β, because β is now at the top of the stack.
(4) P2 continues, after the call to P3, and then returns to P1. This time the return address which is pulled is α.

The same method works if there are four or more subroutines, each of which calls the next. Note that the return addresses are pulled in reverse order from the order in which they were pushed—and that this is exactly the order in which they are needed.

The instruction TSX moves the stack pointer to the X register. Once this has been done, then the instruction

```
LDA  STACK + ! 1, X         loads the top of the stack;
LDA  STACK + ! 2, X         loads the second element down;
LDA  STACK + ! 3, X         loads the third element down;
```

and so on, where STACK EQU $0100 has been specified.

The instruction TXS moves the X register to the stack pointer. This is the only way to load the stack pointer; typically, one loads a constant into the X register and then does a TXS. The user of a system such as that of the APPLE should not do this, however, since the system keeps track of the stack pointer itself. One exception to this is in decrementing the stack pointer without pushing anything onto the stack. The following sequence will do this:

```
TSX        ; MOVE STACK POINTER TO X
DEX        ; DECREASE IT BY 1 AND
TXS        ; RESTORE STACK POINTER
```

This concludes our study of transfer instructions on the 6502. There are six of them: TAX, TAY, TXA, TYA, TSX, and TXS.

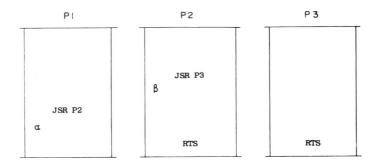

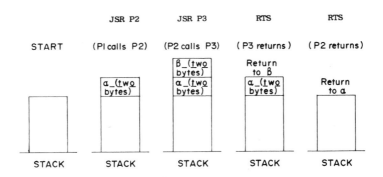

Figure 20. Two Levels of Subroutine Calls.

EXERCISES

1. The contents of the cells with addresses 01F0 through 01F7 are:

ADDRESS	CONTENTS
01F0	82
01F1	1F
01F2	D6
01F3	4B
01F4	53
01F5	79
01F6	08
01F7	EA

   (a) If the stack pointer contains F3, give the new contents of the stack pointer, and of the cells above, if a JSR at the address 08C1 is performed.

   *(b) If the stack pointer contains F4, give its new contents if RTS is performed.

   (c) To what address will the program jump if RTS is performed, with the stack pointer containing F4? Show your work.

2. The contents of the registers A, X, and Y are 1, 2, and 3 respectively. Give the new contents of the A register after each of the following sequences of instructions:

   *(a) TXA; PHA; TYA; PLA.
   (b) PHA; TXA; PHA; PLA; PLA.
   *(c) PHA; TXA; PHA; TYA; PHA; PLA; PLA.

3. Suppose that a programmer wished to save and restore the X register, inside a subroutine, by using the instructions TXS and TSX. Would this work? Why or why not?

PROBLEM 2 FOR COMPUTER SOLUTION
CHECKING AN ARRAY FOR DUPLICATIONS

Write a program to input several 8-bit quantities as decimal numbers, converting them with DECI, putting them into an array, and then checking to see whether any two of the quantities in the array are the same.

The last decimal number which you input should be followed by *two carriage returns*. This is the way in which your program determines that there is no more input.

If two of the quantities in the array are the same (say n), your program should type the message "n IS DUPLICATED"; otherwise, "NO DUPLICATIONS" should be printed. (Do *not* have your program print out the quotation marks.)

Note that it is *not* necessary to determine whether more than one quantity is duplicated. In the message "n IS DUPLICATED" the quantity n should be the *first* duplicated quantity, if there are several.

61. USING THE HARDWARE STACK

Subroutines are very common on microcomputers, even more so than on large computers, because memory space is so "tight" (that is, limited). Try not to repeat any sequence of more than four instructions in an assembly language program on a microcomputer; instead, make that sequence of instructions into a subroutine, and call it twice (or more).

Saving and restoring, in addition, are very common on the 6502, since it has so few registers. (The IBM 4300 series computers, by contrast, have 16 general purpose registers, not to mention the condition code, the floating point registers, and so on.) For both these reasons, it becomes imperative to know how to use the stack and the S register.

Do not, by the way, confuse the S register with the S *flag* (the sign status flag). The manufacturers of the 6502 refer to the S flag as the N flag, or the *negative status flag*, for this reason. Most programmers refer to it as the sign status flag, however, because other microcomputers (such as the Z-80) have such a flag. In this section we will use S to mean the stack pointer exclusively.

The bytes with addresses 0100, 0101, and so on, up through 0100+S, are called *available stack space*. These bytes can be used for future quantities to be put on the stack. The bytes with addresses 0100+S+1, 0100+S+2, and so on, up through 01FF, are the bytes which are actually *on* the stack. The top of the stack has address 0100+S+1.

The S register should have the same value, at the end of any subroutine, that it does at the start of that subroutine. The bytes that are on the stack at the start of the subroutine should be unchanged when that subroutine ends. These are the two basic properties of the stack as it is used in subroutines.

If PHA, PLA, and TXS are not used, these properties will normally be automatic. JSR decreases S by 2; RTS increases S by 2; so one JSR and one RTS leave S unchanged. Also, JSR stores the return address (minus one) by pushing it, and this does not affect any bytes that were on the stack before the JSR.

If PHA and PLA are used, the main point to remember is that *everything that is pushed must also be pulled*, and under *all* conditions. Otherwise, the specifications above will be violated (and, also, the return address will be wrong, when you do the RTS at the end of the subroutine).

A very important use of PHA and PLA is for saving and restoring. In fact, *saving with STA TEMP and restoring with LDA TEMP is almost never necessary*. Instead, we save with PHA and restore with PLA. Note that this is one cycle faster, and also saves four bytes, because PHA and PLA are one-byte instructions, while STA TEMP and LDA TEMP are three-byte instructions.

The combination of STA TEMP and CMP TEMP may be replaced by PHA and CMP $0100,X if you have previously done a TSX to put the stack pointer into the X register. However, you must do a PLA later on, even through the result in the A register is never used in your program (everything that is pushed must also be pulled).

The same kind of trick may be used to replace STA TEMP and ADC TEMP (or SBC TEMP, etc.). However, it is very often not worth the effort, because the X register is tied up by the TSX. (Another replacement for STA TEMP, in general, is discussed in section 80.)

Another very common trick in assembly language programming concerns a subroutine (call it P) which calls another subroutine (call it Q) and *immediately returns*. The two instructions JSR Q and RTS may be replaced by the single instruction JMP Q in this case. (The eventual return from Q, by RTS, serves here as the return from P.)

Still another common trick is often used when a subroutine "ends in the middle"—that is, when the last instruction of the subroutine is a JMP, which goes back to some internal loop, and there is a conditional branch, in the subroutine, to an RTS. In this case the conditional branch can easily go to the RTS of the *next* subroutine; and this subroutine might not need its own RTS at all, thus saving one instruction byte. (The instruction BNE DONE in the program of section 42 is an example of this.)

Stack overflow—the use of more than 256 bytes on the stack—is very uncommon on the 6502. Normally, in fact, we do not check for it. This causes no harm, since the stack will never overflow into any cells other than those with addresses 0100 through 01FF. (If the top of the stack is at cell 0100, and a byte is pushed into this cell, so that the stack becomes completely full, the stack pointer changes from 00 to FF. The next bytes would go in cells 01FF, 01FE, and so on.)

If you wish to test for stack overflow after pushing, or for the stack's being empty after pulling, you can do a TSX followed by CPX #$FF (note that the stack pointer contains hexadecimal FF when the stack is *either full or empty*). If you are in a subroutine, remember that the stack cannot be empty, since it will contain at least the return address.

EXERCISES

*1. Give a BASIC statement which corresponds to the following sequence of instructions:

```
          LDA     I
          PHA
          SEC
          SBC     J
          TAX
          PLA
          CLC
          ADC     T, X
          STA     K
```

(Here the array T starts from T(0).)

2. Give a sequence of instructions, not involving RTS, that is equivalent to RTS. (That is, it pulls two bytes from the stack, adds one to the 16-bit result, and jumps to that location.)

*3. What improvement in the subroutine

```
KSUBR     JSR     KINPUT
          JSR     KCALC
          JSR     KOUT
          RTS
```

is suggested by the text?

62. AN INPUT CONVERSION PROGRAM

We shall now give two detailed examples of the use of the hardware stack. These are the input and output conversion programs mentioned in section 41.

The input conversion program is shown in Figure 21. It uses the following method (like that of section 33):

1. Set N to zero.
2. Read a digit D. If the next character is not a digit, stop; N is the answer.
3. Set N = 10*N+D and go back to step 2.

For example, let the input characters be "125+". Then the successive values of N are:

(1) zero;
(2) 10*0+1, or 1;
(3) 10*1+2, or 12;
(4) 10*12+5, or 125.

The multiplication by 10 is done as in section 33, except that 16-bit quantities are being multiplied. Therefore, 16-bit addition is done as in section 15, and 16-bit shifting is done as in section 34. Conversion of each character from character code form to integer form is done as in section 33.

There is only one PHA instruction in this program. In keeping with the rule that everything pushed must be pulled, let us see where the A register is pulled. Three instructions after the PHA, there is a BCS. If this branches to DECIB, there is a pull (PLA) at that point. Otherwise, the PLA is two instructions past the BCS. Note that the PLA at DECIB has no purpose, in this case, other than to pull what was pushed.

Notice also the subroutine that starts at DECI4, to multiply N by two and check for overflow. If there is overflow, we want to exit from DECI since we cannot proceed further, but note that there are now *two* return addresses on the stack—one was put there when we entered DECI, and the other was put there when we entered DECI4.

```
; DECI -- DECIMAL INPUT
; ENTER WITH INBUF INDEX IN X
; I. E., LDA $0200,X LOADS FIRST
;   CHARACTER OF INPUT STRING
; EXITS WITH CARRY SET ON OVERFLOW
; I. E., NUMBER LARGER THAN 65535
; OTHERWISE, NUMBER IS IN A AND X
; UPPER HALF IN A, LOWER HALF IN X
; AND CARRY IS CLEAR
DECI9 EQU $0200        ; INPUT BUFFER
DECI  LDA #:0          ; PUT NUMBER N IN
      STA DECI6        ;   DECI6 AND A
DECI1 TAY              ; THEN DECI6 AND Y
DECIA LDA DECI9,X      ; GET A CHARACTER
      CMP #"9"+!1      ; DECIMAL DIGIT?
      BCS DECI3        ; NO, TOO LARGE
      SBC #"0"-!1      ; CONVERT, TEST
      BCC DECI3        ;   FOR TOO SMALL
      INX              ; TO NEXT CHAR.
      STA DECI7        ; SAVE DIGIT D
      TYA              ; N IN DECI6, A
      JSR DECI4        ; 2N IN DECI6, A
      STA DECI8        ; PUT 2N IN Y AND
      LDY DECI6        ;   DECI8
      JSR DECI4        ; 4N IN DECI6, A

      JSR DECI4        ; 8N IN DECI6, A
      ADC DECI8        ; CARRY IS CLEAR ON
      PHA              ;   EXIT FROM DECI4
      TYA              ; PUT 10N IN A AND
      ADC DECI6        ;   TOP OF STACK
      BCS DECIB        ; IF OVERFLOW, QUIT
      STA DECI6        ; PUT 10N IN
      PLA              ;   DECI6 AND A
      ADC DECI7        ; CALCULATE 10N+D
      BCC DECI1        ; IF CARRY SET, ADD
      INC DECI6        ;   1 TO LEFT HALF
      BNE DECI1        ; IF OVERFLOW, QUIT
      RTS              ;   WITH CARRY SET
DECI3 TYA              ; NON-NUMERIC CHAR.
      TAX              ; SO NUMBER IS DONE
      LDA DECI6        ; PUT N IN A AND X
      CLC              ; AND QUIT WITH
      RTS              ;   CARRY CLEAR
DECI4 ASL              ; DOUBLE SHIFT
      ROL DECI6        ;   (MULTIPLY BY 2)
      BCC DECI5        ; IF OVERFLOW, PULL
      PLA              ; TWO BYTES OF
DECIB PLA              ; RETURN ADDRESS
DECI5 RTS              ; QUIT
DECI6 DFS !1           ; TEMPORARY STORAGE
DECI7 DFS !1           ; DIGIT D
DECI8 DFS !1           ; TEMPORARY STORAGE
```

Figure 21. An Input Conversion Program.

Since we want to exit from DECI4 *and* from DECI, we must pull the DECI4 return address before doing an RTS. This is done in the two PLA instructions just before DECI5. (Note that *two* bytes must be pulled, in order to pull an address.) The same technique may be used whenever you wish to exit from more than one level of subroutine.

Many further techniques are used in this program. The subroutines DECI and DECI4 both exit with carry clear, unless overflow takes place. For DECI, this is due to the CLC instruction; for DECI4, the branch at BCC DECI5 is taken when there is no overflow, so the carry must be clear. This fact is used to justify not having a CLC before the first ADC; the carry is already clear.

As the program proceeds, the intermediate results are kept in many different places, to save time. As an example, consider the instructions STA DECI8 and LDY DECI6. These two instructions move a 16-bit quantity from one place (DECI6 and the A register) to another (the Y register and DECI8).

The RTS at DECI5 is shared between the subroutine at DECI4 and DECI itself (see the earlier BCS DECIB), as suggested at the end of the preceding section. Also note the TYA followed by TAX; to move a quantity from Y to X takes two instructions, since there is no instruction TYX (unfortunately) on the 6502.

Always remember, when using DECI, that it uses the registers for its own purposes, and does not save and restore them. The same is true of DECO and DECOZ, introduced in the next section.

We may note that the temporary variables in this program are called DECI6 and DECI8, rather than (say) TEMP1 and TEMP2. This sort of thing is quite common in programs, such as DECI, which are written to be included in other programs. If DECI used a variable called TEMP1, there might be trouble if it were included in a program which also used a variable called TEMP1. For one thing, the label TEMP1 would occur twice, which is an assembly error. Even if this were fixed, there would still be trouble if the other program stored something (call it z) in TEMP1, then called DECI, and then expected TEMP1 to still contain z, instead of what DECI had left there.

EXERCISES

1. In Figure 21, suppose that the PHA instruction had occurred *before* one or more of the JSR DECI4 instructions. What further change would this require in the error exit (through DECIB) from DECI4?

2. *(a) Suppose we have three subroutines P, Q, and R such that P calls Q and Q calls R. None of the subroutines uses PHA or PLA. Suppose now that, inside R, there is an error exit which returns to P. What must be done in the error exit to condition the stack properly for this return?

(b) Suppose that the error exit, above, returns to *the subroutine that called P*. What must be done in the error exit now?

3. *(a) In Figure 21, why is there no CLC before the second ADC?

   (b) Four instructions after DECIA, there is a branch to DECI3 on carry clear. If this branch is taken, the carry is clear. Why, then, is the CLC needed, three instructions later?

   *(c) Why is an SEC not needed just before the RTS that immediately precedes DECI3, since we need the carry to be set at this point?

63. AN OUTPUT CONVERSION PROGRAM

The output conversion program of section 41 is shown in Figure 22. It starts by dividing the given number by 10000, and obtaining a quotient Q and a remainder R. Note that, for example, 23456 divided by 10000 is 2, with remainder 3456. In general, the quotient will be the *first* digit, and the remainder will be the original number with the first digit removed.

The process above is then repeated three more times, dividing by 1000, by 100, and by 10. Four digits are obtained and printed out. At the end, the fifth digit, which is the remainder upon dividing by 10, is printed out.

We divide by using repeated subtraction. To divide by M by N in this way, we do the following steps (as in section 37):

1. Set Q = −1.
2. Add 1 to Q.
3. Subtract N from M.
4. If the result is non-negative, go back to step 2.
5. Add N to M, producing the remainder R.

For example, if M is 26, and N is 10, the values of Q and M go through the following stages:

(1) Q is −1, and M is 26.
(2) Q is 0, and M is 16.
(3) Q is 1, and M is 6.
(4) Q is 2 and M is −4; and we add 10 to M again, producing the remainder R = 6 (and the quotient Q is 2, which is correct).

The 16-bit subtraction uses the technique of section 17; the 16-bit addition uses the technique of section 15. Adding 1 to the quotient, as discussed above, is done directly in memory, as suggested near the end of section 57 (for loop counts). The constants 10, 100, 1000, and 10000 are kept in two parallel arrays of two-byte quantities, as studied in section 32. These use BYT, as studied in section 26, and a new constant declaration, HBY, or "high-order byte." Recall from section 26 that if we write BYT !1000 (for example), we will get a single byte consisting of the rightmost eight bits of the constant 1000. Writing HBY !1000 now gives us the *leftmost* eight bits of this same constant.

(There is also ADR, or "address," not used in DECO, which gives us an entire 16-bit constant with bytes reversed, as they would be in an address. Thus ADR n is the same as BYT n followed by HBY n.* Note that ADR n always gives *two* bytes, even if $n<256$, in which case the second of these two bytes is zero.)

Students very often tend to confuse BYT with EQU, and you should pause at this point to make sure you understand the difference. If we write N BYT !100 in our program, then LDA N loads 100; LDA #N would load the rightmost eight bits of the *address* of N, and is not often used. On the other hand, if we write N EQU !100 then LDA #N loads 100, while LDA N loads the contents of the byte with address 100. This is because LDA #N is the same as LDA #!100, while LDA N is the same as LDA !100. In both cases, !100 can be *directly substituted* for N in the instruction, because N is equivalent to !100—which is basically what N EQU !100 means. Note that you cannot set N EQU #!100—this is not allowed. Also, N BYT !100 puts a byte of data in the program, and is normally given in the data section, whereas N EQU !100 *does not put any data* in the program, and can go anywhere, intermixed with anything else.

The program DECO uses the byte at the top of the stack to keep a *partial* result—in this case, the left half of M, as above. This is pulled, subtracted, and then pushed again, using the sequence PLA-SBC-PHA. Later, it is pulled, *added*, and pushed again, using the sequence PLA-ADC-PHA.

If the top of the stack contains a partial result, this must be initialized by a push instruction. This is done at DECO; the initial contents of A are the upper half of the number to be converted. Note that DECOZ does this before calling CROUT, which destroys the contents of A (but not of X or Y).

What is pushed must also be pulled; and so the PHA at the start of the program must be "undone" with a PLA, in this case just before DECO5. To the programmer who does not thoroughly understand stacks, this PLA looks quite mysterious—it is just before the return, but DECO does not return anything, in particular, in the A register. The PLA does nothing but adjust the stack pointer so that the RTS will get the proper return address.

DECO does not print leading zeroes (see the end of section 3). Instead of 00614, it prints 614; instead of 00207, it prints 207. (Note that zeroes which are

---

*In LISA 2.5, you can write ADR i, j, k, . . . , which is the same as writing ADR i followed by ADR j followed by ADR k (and so on); also, there is another constant declaration, DBY, which is exactly like ADR except that the bytes are *not* reversed. Thus DBY ("double byte") n is the same as HBY n followed by BYT n. Finally, there is .DA (.DA #n like BYT n; DA /n is like HBY n; and .DA v is like ADR v if v is not preceded by # or /).

not leading, such as the zero in 207, are printed.) The only exception to this rule is the number 0, which prints as 0. DECO keeps a *leading-zero flag*, DECO9, which becomes non-zero as soon as a non-zero digit is encountered. As long as DECO9 is zero, no digits that are zero will be printed. (The choice of name of the flag DECO9 resembles that of the temporary locations DECI6 and DECI8 in the preceding section.) Note that the *single* instruction INC   DECO9 sets DECO9 to a non-zero value.

EXERCISES

1.   (a) In Figure 22, why is the SEC just before DECO2 not included in the DECO2 loop?
     *(b) Why is there no CLC before the first ADC?
     (c) At DECO3, it is noted that the carry is always set, so that ADC #"0"−!1 actually adds the character "0" to the A register. The reason that the carry is always set is that the preceding ADC was the last instruction that affected the carry; and this instruction *always sets* the carry. Why? (Hint: Look carefully at the logic of this program.)

2.   Suppose that N1 BYT !2 and N2 EQU !2 are specified in a program. Are the following statements true or false?

     *(a) ADC #N2 adds 2 (if the carry flag is clear) to the A register.
     (b) SBC #N1 subtracts 2 (if the carry flag is set) from the A register.
     *(c) CPY N2 compares the Y register with the number 2.

3.   Suppose that, for some reason, a partial result kept on the stack and updated with the sequence PLA-SBC-PHA did *not* need to be initialized. We would still, in this case, require a PHA at the start of the subroutine, and a PLA at the end. Why? (Hint: Consider the return address. Be specific about what goes wrong, and why.)

```
; DECO-- DECIMAL OUTPUT
; ENTER WITH 16-BIT NO. IN A AND X
; UPPER HALF IN A, LOWER HALF IN X
; PRINTS OUT THE NUMBER IN DECIMAL
; ENTER AT DECOZ TO START NEW LINE
DECOZ PHA                ; (CROUT USES A)
      JSR CROUT          ; CARRIAGE RETURN
      JMP DECOA          ; SKIP NEXT INST.
DECO  PHA                ; PUT NO. IN TOP OF
DECOA LDA #!0            ; STACK AND X
      STA DECO9          ; LEADING ZERO FLAG
      LDY #!4            ; 4 POWERS OF 10
DECO1 LDA #$FF           ; CURRENT DIGIT SET
      STA DECO7          ; TO -1, CARRY SET
      SEC                ; FOR SUBTRACTION
DECO2 INC DECO7          ; CURRENT DIGIT + 1
      TXA                ; SUBTRACT POWER OF
      SBC DECO5-!1,Y     ; TEN (16-BIT
      TAX                ; SUBTRACT) FROM
      PLA                ; NUMBER IN TOP
      SBC DECO6-!1,Y     ; OF STACK AND X
      PHA                ; IF NON-NEGATIVE,
      BCS DECO2          ; SUBTRACT AGAIN
      TXA                ; CARRY IS CLEAR
      ADC DECO5-!1,Y     ; HERE. ADD THIS
      STA DECO8          ; SAME POWER OF 10
      PLA                ; AND PUT RESULT
      ADC DECO6-!1,Y     ; IN TOP OF STACK
      PHA                ; AND DECO8
      INC DECO9          ; BUMP LEADING ZERO
      LDA DECO7          ; FLAG IF NON-ZERO
      BNE DECO3          ; DIGIT. OTHERWISE
      DEC DECO9          ; RESTORE FLAG, IF
      BEQ DECO4          ; ZERO, SKIP PRINT
DECO3 ADC #"0"-!1        ; CONVERT CHARACTER
      JSR COUT           ; (CARRY SET) PRINT
DECO4 LDX DECO8          ; PUT NO. IN TOP OF
      DEY                ; STACK AND X, DO
      BNE DECO1          ; NEXT POWER OF 10
      TXA                ; LAST DIGIT IN X
      CLC                ; CLEAR CARRY AND
      ADC #"0"           ; CONVERT CHARACTER
      JSR COUT           ; PRINT LAST DIGIT
      PLA                ; QUIT (MUST UNDO
      RTS                ; THE PHA AT START)
DECO5 BYT !10            ; TABLE OF POWERS
      BYT !100           ; OF 10. THIS IS A
      BYT !1000          ; SERIAL ARRAY OF
      BYT !10000         ; 16-BIT QUANTITIES
DECO6 HBY !10            ; THE LOWER HALVES
      HBY !100           ; ARE GIVEN FIRST,
      HBY !1000          ; THEN THE UPPER
      HBY !10000         ; HALVES
DECO7 DFS !1             ; CURRENT DIGIT
DECO8 DFS !1             ; TEMPORARY STORAGE
DECO9 DFS !1             ; LEADING ZERO FLAG
COUT  EQU $FDED          ; ONE CHARACTER OUT
CROUT EQU $FD8E          ; CARRIAGE RETURN
```

Figure 22. An Output Conversion Program.

64. ADVANTAGES OF HARDWARE STACKS

Why does the 6502 handle subroutine calls in such a seemingly complicated way? Why not just use the same method that the IBM 4300 or CDC 6000 series uses? The question is an important one, and deserves a detailed answer, which we can most easily express by means of an example.

Figure 23 shows a typical large program, consisting of a main program (S1) and some subroutines, each of which is represented by a box. If one of these programs calls another, this is represented, in the figure, by an arrow from the first box to the second box. Thus, for example S1 calls the subroutine S2; S2 calls S3; and S3 calls S4.

The main program and the various subroutines are grouped into *levels*. The first (or lowest) level consists of all the subroutines that do not call any other subroutines. The second level consists of subroutines that call only first-level subroutines. In the third level, a subroutine may call only those in levels 1 and 2; and so on.

Any program with a large number of subroutines may be diagrammed in this way, so long as no program calls *itself* as a subroutine (either directly or indirectly). The program of Figure 23 contains a main program and 39 subroutines, but there are only four levels; and this is typical of programs of this kind—the number of levels is considerably less than the number of subroutines.

Suppose now that every subroutine saves and restores the A, X, and Y registers. If we do not use a stack, we need three bytes in *every* subroutine for this, or a total of 39*3 = 117 bytes. If we use a stack, we need only three bytes for each *level* (not counting the top level), for a total of 3*3 = 9 bytes.

Why is this? Every time a subroutine on the third level is called, three bytes are pushed on the stack. When that subroutine returns, these bytes are pulled. When the next subroutine on the third level is called, *the same three bytes on the stack are re-used*. The same sort of thing happens on lower levels.

Similarly with return addresses, if we had a subroutine call instruction which put the return address in a fixed place in memory (instead of on the stack), then we would need one such fixed place (that is, two bytes) for *every* subroutine,

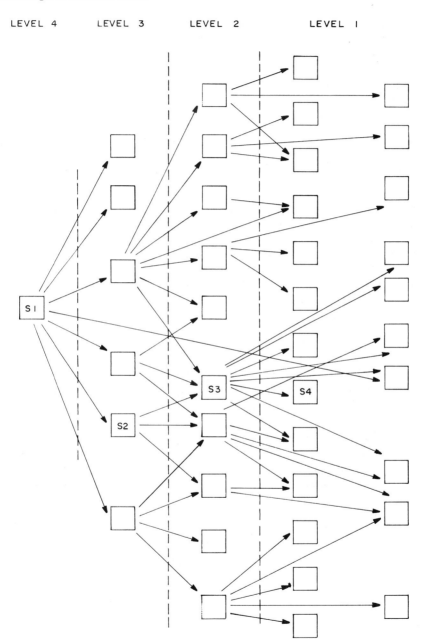

Figure 23. Several Levels of Subroutines.

for a total of 39*2 = 78 bytes.* With JSR, which pushes a return address on the stack, we only need two bytes for each level (not counting the *lowest* level, this time, because a lowest-level subroutine contains no JSR, by definition) or a total of 3*2 = 6 bytes.

The reason is much the same as before. Every time a subroutine on the third level is called, *the same two bytes* are used for the return address, namely the first two bytes on the stack. Again, as before, stack bytes are similarly re-used on lower levels.

Further space is saved because PHA and PLA are one-byte instructions. As we have seen, STA TEMP and LDA TEMP are three-byte instructions. The space savings in our example are typical; they become even greater when there are more subroutines, as happens quite commonly.

Still another advantage of hardware stacks has to do with writing a program that calls itself as a subroutine; this is known as a *recursive program*. Recursive programs are more common on large computers than on microcomputers, but it is interesting to note that a stack, or its equivalent, *must* be used in such a program. If P calls P, which calls P, and so on, *n* times, then *n* separate return addresses, at least (and normally saved and restored variables as well), must all be on the stack at one time.

EXERCISES

1. (a) In Figure 23, if each subroutine (including lowest level subroutines, but not the main program) saved the A, X, and Y registers by STA, STX, and STY, and loaded them by LDA, LDX, and LDY, how many bytes do all these instruction codes take?
    (b) How many bytes would the corresponding instruction codes take if a stack were used? (Note that, in this case, the sequence PHA-TXA-PHA-TYA-PHA saves the A, X, and Y registers, while the sequence PLA-TAY-PLA-TAX-PLA restores them. Also note that each subroutine, as in part (a) above, still has to contain these sequences.)

2. *(a) How many subroutine levels would it take, in Figure 23, to use up the *entire* stack, assuming that PHA and PLA are not used? (Remember that the lowest level subroutines do not use JSR.)

---

*Some computers have subroutine-call instructions which leave the return address in a register. This register must now be saved and restored by every subroutine which is at neither the highest nor the lowest level. In this case, 16*2 = 32 bytes would be used for this purpose, if the 6502 had such an instruction.

*(b) How many subroutine levels would it take to use up the entire stack if each subroutine (including lowest level subroutines, but not the main program) saved the A, X, and Y registers on the stack?

*3. We have noted that any program with a large number of subroutines may be diagrammed as in Figure 23, with each subroutine on some level, so long as no program calls *itself* as a subroutine. Why is this last restriction necessary? (Hint: Look carefully at the definition of subroutine levels.)

65. BCD NUMBERS AND DECIMAL MODE

In this section and the next three sections, we take up the last few instructions on the 6502: CLD, SED, CLI, SEI, RTI, PHP, and PLP. We will then go on to see how some of the instructions we studied earlier can be used in further ways.

We have considered *unsigned integers* (ranging from 0 to 255, in one byte) and *signed integers* (ranging from −128 to 127). There are also *binary-coded decimal*, or *BCD*, numbers, which range from 0 to 99.* A BCD number always has two digits, and each digit is contained in four bits of the given byte. Thus the bits 10010000 correspond to the BCD number 90, since the first digit (9) is 1001 in binary, while the second digit (0) is 0000 in binary. (The same bits, 10010000, would represent the unsigned integer 144, or the signed integer −112.)

BCD numbers look like hexadecimal numbers and, in fact, can sometimes be manipulated as such. Thus, for example, LDA #$25 loads hexadecimal 25, or binary 00100101, into the A register, and then this acts like the BCD number 25. In general, BCD *constants* are always written as if they were hexadecimal constants. (There are only 100 legal BCD numbers, and hexadecimal constants such as 7C, F9, and BA do not correspond to any BCD number.)

Let us now consider adding two BCD numbers. If the A register contains $25, as above, and we add another $25, we get $4A, or 01001010 in binary, but if 25 is a BCD, or binary-coded *decimal* number, we want to get the answer 50 (as a BCD number, or binary 01010000). The way we do this is to use a flag called the *decimal mode flag*.

Like the carry flag, the decimal mode flag can be set (to 1) or cleared (set to zero) by means of instructions:

CLD	Clear decimal mode flag
SED	Set decimal mode flag

---

*On certain older computers, BCD refers to a character coding scheme, similar to ASCII, but encoding each character in six bits intead of eight.

Normally, this flag is clear. When it is set, *the instructions ADC and SBC add or subtract BCD numbers and produce a BCD result.* Note that this applies *only* to ADC and SBC, not to increment, decrement, or shift instructions.

The carry flag works in the usual way when decimal mode is on (that is, when the decimal mode flag is set). If the carry flag is set, then ADC adds an extra 1 (as a BCD number). If the result r is less than 100 (in BCD), the carry flag is cleared; otherwise, it is set, and the A register is set to $r-100$. Similarly, if the carry flag is *clear* (indicating a borrow status), then SBC subtracts an extra 1 (as a BCD number). If the result r is greater than or equal to zero, the carry flag is set; otherwise, it is cleared (indicating borrow status) and the A register is set to $r+100$.

The zero, sign, and overflow flags are *not* set in usable ways by ADC and SBC when the decimal mode is on.* You cannot add or subtract in decimal mode and follow this with a BEQ, BNE, BPL, BMI, BVC, or BVS, for this reason. Also, the A register is set, but not in a usable way (and computation is *not* halted), if the two quantities being added in decimal mode with ADC, or subtracted in decimal mode with SBC, are not both valid BCD numbers.

If we subtract a decimal number n from zero, with the decimal mode on, we get its *tens' complement*, or $100-n$. Signed decimal numbers can be represented in tens' complement notation, just as ordinary signed integers are represented in twos' complement notation. This, however, is very rare.

Loop counts are almost never kept as BCD numbers. This is because a loop count is normally changed with an increment or decrement instruction; as we have seen, these instructions are not affected by decimal mode.

Two BCD numbers, however, may be *compared*, using CMP, CPX, or CPY. This is true even though these three instructions are unaffected by decimal mode. The reason is that the relations ("less than," "greater than," and so on) between the two 8-bit quantities remain the same whether these are treated as ordinary unsigned numbers or as BCD numbers.

There are no instructions resembling BCC and BCS that test whether the decimal mode flag is on or off. (This can be done indirectly, however; see section 67.) Many programmers make it a practice to start *all* main programs with CLD (Clear Decimal Mode), just in case the previous user of the machine left the decimal mode on.

Note that a left shift, in decimal mode, does *not* multiply by 2. If you want to multiply a BCD number by 2, add it to itself, in decimal mode. (Four shifts to the right, however, will divide a BCD number by 10.)

---

*For example, if A = 99 (in BCD), then adding 1 sets A equal to zero, but it does *not* set the zero flag.

EXERCISES

1. Add the following BCD numbers with the decimal mode on, and also with the decimal mode off. In each case, give *both* the BCD answer and the final setting of the carry flag.

   (a) 39 and 39
   *(b) 77 and 76
   (c) 92 and 94

2. Subtract the following BCD numbers with the decimal mode on, and also with the decimal mode off. In each case, give *both* the BCD answer and the final setting of the carry flag.

   *(a) 61 minus 49
   (b) 23 minus 58
   *(c) 14 minus 81

3. Suppose that the byte EIGHT contains the constant 8. Then the program (executed with the decimal mode *off*)

```
              LDA   K
              LSR
              BIT   EIGHT
              BEQ   BETA
              SEC
              SBC   #!3
     BETA     STA   K
```

   divides the BCD number K by two. How does it work? Explain in detail. (Hint: If the BCD number is *ab*, consider two cases—where *a* is even and where *a* is odd.) Specifically, why does the constant 3 appear in the SBC instruction?

66. PACKED STRINGS

Why do we use BCD numbers at all? The reason has to do with *multi-digit* BCD numbers, and their use in devices, such as calculators, in which computation with decimal digits is required.

Consider a number with 8 decimal digits, such as 93,000,000. We can keep this number in 8 bytes, with one character code (for a digit) in each byte, as follows:

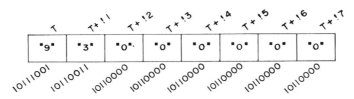

Or we can *pack* it into 4 bytes, with *two* digits (that is, one BCD number) in each byte, as follows:

T	T + !1	T + !2	T + !3
10010011	00000000	00000000	00000000
9 3	0 0	0 0	0 0

This is known as a *packed string*, in contrast to the *unpacked string* of the preceding illustration. In general, an *n*-byte packed string consists of 2*n* decimal digits, and these may be *unpacked* into a 2*n*-byte number, consisting of character codes for digits.

Suppose now that we wish to add two J-byte packed strings. Using decimal mode, we can add them *two digits at a time*, from right to left—first the rightmost two digits of each string, then the next two, and so on. This takes advantage of the fact that the carry flag is used and set by ADC to support multi-digit addition whether the decimal mode flag is on or off.

Conversion of packed strings to unpacked form, or of unpacked strings to packed form, is simple and fast. We merely convert one byte to two, or two

225

bytes to one, and then repeat this J times, for J-byte packed strings. Conversion of either packed or unpacked strings to *binary* (internal) form, however, or the reverse, is much more time-consuming. We saw in sections 62 and 63 some conversion routines of this kind; and these were restricted to *two-byte* quantities in internal form. In the general, multi-byte case, the two-byte additions and subtractions in these routines become multi-byte additions and subtractions, which slows them down considerably.

This suggests to us why BCD numbers and packed strings are used. Consider, for example, a calculator. It has a display consisting of decimal digits, and a keyboard where numbers may be entered, also in decimal-digit form. It also contains a microcomputer which can be directed to add the number punched in at the keyboard to the contents of the display. If this were done in internal binary form, the input number would have to be converted into this form, and the answer would have to be converted back to a string of decimal digits. It is much easier and faster to keep all numbers in the calculator as packed strings, and to add them in the way described above.

Note that a decimal number expressed in two bytes does *not* have these bytes reversed; if the bytes are D and D+!1, then D is the high-order byte and D+!1 the low-order byte. The same is true, of course, for more than two bytes; the first is always the high-order byte, and the last is the low-order byte.

Unpacked strings may also be added directly, but care must be taken. In adding 5 and 7, for example, we are really adding their character codes, or B5 and B7 (hexadecimal). This may be done by subtracting B0 from the second of these codes, and then adding. If the result (B5+07=BC, in this case) is greater than B9 (the character code for 9), then 10 is subtracted (resulting in B2, in this case) and a carry preserved for the next addition, going from right to left.

EXERCISES

*1.   Write a program to convert an unpacked string B, of length K, into the corresponding packed string N. Assume that B DFS !100 and N DFS !50 are used to define B and N, and that K ($\leq$ 100) is an even number. Use a loop ending with DEX and BNE.

2.   Write a program to print out a packed string of length M, using COUT. Make sure that the character code for each digit (not the digit itself) is output. Use a loop ending with INY, CPY M, and BNE.

*3.   Write a program to add the J-byte number at N1 to the J-byte number at N2, to produce a J-byte number at N3. (Remember that the bytes are *not* reversed.)

67. THE STATUS REGISTER

There is one more register on the 6502, called the *status register*. It is also sometimes called the *flag register*, because it is nothing more than the various status flags, all combined into one register, as follows:

S	V		B	D	I	Z	C

We have already met the sign flag (S), the overflow flag (V), the decimal mode flag (D), the zero flag (Z), and the carry flag (C). The *break flag* (B) is set to 1 whenever there is a break; the *interrupt flag* (I) is discussed in the next section.

Other names for the status register are the *program status word,* * or the PSW, or simply the P register; it appears as the P register in the stepping displays (see section 47). There are no transfer instructions on the 6502 which move the P register (as we shall call it) to any of the other registers, or vice versa. Instead, *the P register can be pushed and pulled,* just like the A register. The instructions which do this are:

> PHP   Push P register (status register)
> PLP   Pull P register (status register)

The easiest way to move the P register to the A register is therefore PHP followed by PLA. This can be reversed, by PHA followed by PLP, moving the A register to the P register.

We have already seen that there is no single instruction which branches on the setting of the decimal mode flag. It is possible to do this in four instructions, however, as follows:

```
PHP                 ; MOVE P REGISTER INTO STACK
PLA                 ; AND THEN BACK TO A
AND   #%00001000    ; LOOK AT ONLY THE FOURTH
BNE   ALPHA         ;  BIT FROM THE RIGHT  (D)
```

---

*This terminology is borrowed from IBM, although the program status word on IBM computers is much larger, and contains much more information, than that of the 6502.

This branches to ALPHA on decimal mode set. The same sort of thing could be done with any of the other flags, of course, although it would not be necessary in most cases.

The existence of the P register solves a tricky problem associated with decimal mode. Suppose you have turned the decimal mode on for the purposes of a subroutine. When the subroutine is finished, do you turn the decimal mode off again? This depends on whether the calling program had the decimal mode on; and you have no way of knowing this.

One solution, of course, is to use the sequence of instructions above, at the start of the subroutine. This allows you to record the fact that the decimal mode was on (or off) and to take the proper action at the end of the subroutine; but a better method is just to save the P register, with PHP, at the start of the subroutine and restore it, with PLP, at the end. Now you can turn decimal mode on and off all you want to, inside the subroutine.

PHP and PLP are also used to save and restore other flags. Suppose you have computed a value of the carry flag which you will need later on in your program. In the meantime, though, you have to do some shifting, which will destroy the carry flag. Save it with PHP; then shift; then restore it again with PLP. The same sort of thing works with any other flag.

During debugging, you can check the various flag settings by noting the P register contents in the stepping display. Suppose, for example, that you have an instruction which is supposed to clear the overflow flag. If the line P=75 appears in the stepping display after this instruction is executed, you have an error. This is because 75 (hexadecimal) is 01110101, in binary; and, referring to the diagram above, we see that the overflow flag (V) is 1 in this case, being the second bit from the left.

EXERCISES

1. Give a single instruction on the 6502 which branches under the same conditions as each of the following:

    (a)
    ```
                    PHP
                    PLA
                    AND     #$40
                    BNE     ALPHA
    ```

    *(b)
    ```
                    PHP
                    PLA
                    AND     #$2
                    BEQ     ALPHA
    ```

(c)

```
        PHP
        PLA
        AND    #$80
        BNE    ALPHA
```

2. Give a single instruction on the 6502 which sets or clears a flag in a way that is equivalent to each of the following:

*(a)

```
        PHP
        PLA
        AND    #$BF
        PHA
        PLP
```

(b)

```
        PHP
        PLA
        ORA    #$8
        PHA
        PLP
```

*(c)

```
        PHP
        PLA
        AND    #$FE
        PHA
        PLP
```

3. A program starts with PHP followed by PHA, and ends with PLP, PLA, and RTS, in that order. This is almost surely wrong. Why? (If this one is not obvious, walk it through, as this was discussed in section 44.)

68. INTERRUPTS

There are times, while a program is running, that something happens which needs the computer's immediate attention. This might be a keyboard input; or a disk operation; or a button pushed by a user who is playing a computer game; or an early warning signal that there is going to be a power failure in a millisecond or so. In any of these cases, the 6502 can be configured in such a way that an *interrupt* occurs in the program being run. When this happens, the computer calls a special kind of subroutine, called an *interrupt routine*, which does whatever is appropriate in the given situation. When the interrupt routine is finished, the computer goes back to what it was doing before.

There are three kinds of interrupts on the 6502. The first kind is called an IRQ interrupt; the address of the corresponding interrupt routine is kept in cells FFFE and FFFF (with bytes reversed). This means that when the user pushes a button, for example, the computer stops whatever it is doing, looks in cells FFFE and FFFF, in which there will be an address α, and calls the interrupt routine, which starts at address α. (IRQ simply means "interrupt request.")

The APPLE has its own IRQ interrupt routine, at an address which it keeps in cells FFFE and FFFF. You cannot change this address, because these two locations—and, indeed, all locations from C100 through FFFF—are reserved for the APPLE system, and are normally in read-only memory, or ROM, which means that they cannot be changed (see section 78 for a further discussion of ROM). The APPLE's IRQ interrupt routine calls a subroutine whose address is kept in locations 03FE and 03FF; this is normally the address of still another APPLE monitor routine, but you *can* change this address (because locations 03FE and 03FF are not in ROM). This means that you *can* write your own interrupt routines on the APPLE, but you do not have to, and most programmers ordinarily do not.

There is a basic difference between an ordinary subroutine and an interrupt routine. After an ordinary subroutine returns, the contents of the registers may be unchanged or not, depending on the programmer's intentions. Many subroutines do save and restore the registers, but, as we have seen, many others, such as our MULT and DIV, do not. After an interrupt routine returns, however, the contents of the registers—*including the status flags*—*must* be unchanged, because we have no way of knowing what the computer was doing when the interrupt happened.

The subroutine call, made by the interrupt, *itself pushes the status register, exactly as if PHP had been done*. There is then a new return instruction:

RTI   Return from Interrupt

which *pulls* the status register and then does a subroutine return. Note that we must use RTI, rather than PLP and RTS, to return from an interrupt subroutine; this is because the return address, *and not the return address minus one* (as with JSR), is pushed by the interrupt subroutine call. Therefore RTI does *not* add one to the pulled return address, as RTS does.

The entire interrupt system can be turned off, or *disabled*, by means of a status flag, the *interrupt status flag*, whose values are 0 if the interrupt system is *on*, and 1 if it is *off*. Two instructions set and clear the I flag, as this flag is called:

CLI   Clear I (Turn Interrupt System On)
SEI   Set I (Turn Interrupt System Off)

The interrupt subroutine call *turns the interrupt system off*, exactly as if SEI had been done. This is so the interrupt routine does not, itself, get interrupted.* This is done *after* the P register is pushed, however; so when the RTI pulls the P register, the interrupt system will be turned back on again, or *enabled*, since the interrupt status flag (in the P register) is presumably equal to zero. (On many microcomputers other than the 6502, you must do the equivalent of a CLI just before returning from an interrupt subroutine.)

Some interrupt subroutines do not return (with RTI) at all. In particular, pressing the *reset key* on the keyboard, as when getting out of an endless loop, causes an interrupt; and the APPLE allows you to proceed with debugging at this point, rather than doing an RTI, which would simply put you back in the endless loop. Reset interrupts are the second kind of 6502 interrupts; the interrupt subroutine address for them is in cells FFFC and FFFD.

There are interrupts that cannot be turned off, even by SEI. These are called *non-maskable interrupts*, or NMI interrupts. This is the third kind of 6502 interrupt; the interrupt subroutine address for it is kept in cells FFFA and FFFB. A power failure warning interrupt should be non-maskable; you want it to be able to interrupt even another interrupt routine. The APPLE NMI interrupt routine calls a subroutine whose address is kept in locations 03FC and 03FD; as with IRQ

---

*This is in contrast to some computers on which interrupt subroutines *can* get interrupted; specifically, each interrupt has a *priority*, and higher priority interrupts can interrupt lower-priority interrupt subroutines.

interrupts, this allows you, as an APPLE user, to write your own NMI interrupt
routine, although normally you would not do so.

EXERCISES

*1. Suppose that the following quantities are contained in the stack of the
     6502, with values given in hexadecimal:

ADDRESS	CONTENTS
01F0	A7
01F1	D4
01F2	55
01F3	26
01F4	B1
01F5	3C
01F6	08
01F7	9E

The instruction LDA #!0, at locations 0832 and 0833, is now executed,
after which the P register contains 31 and the S register contains F3. At
this point, an interrupt occurs. Give the new contents of the stack locations above, as well as the contents of the P and S registers, at the start of
the interrupt routine. Justify your answer. (Remember that the interrupt
system will be turned off, and this must be reflected in the new P register
contents.)

 2. Suppose that locations 01F0 through 01F7 are as in the statement of exer-
     cise 1 above, and that the P and S registers contain B7 and F3 respec-
     tively. At this point, an RTI is executed. Give the new contents of the P
     and S registers, and specify the address to which the RTI branches. Justify
     your answer.

*3. Suppose that a three-byte instruction at locations 08B0, 08B1, and 08B2
     is executed. If an interrupt now occurs, the return address which is put
     into the stack is not always 08B3. Why not?

69. INPUT INSTRUCTIONS

Every computer has instructions to perform input and output. On the APPLE, all input-output is done by means of subroutines, such as RDKEY and COUT; but we should know a little about the instructions which these subroutines use.

It is important to note that *you will not, and cannot, be held responsible for learning how to write input-output subroutines yourself* on the 6502, until you learn quite a bit about microcomputer *hardware*—far more than is given in this book.* This is because the specific instructions used in such subroutines depend on the way in which the 6502 is connected to the keyboard, the screen, the printer, and so on—*and this varies,* very widely, *from one 6502-based system to another.* Thus the APPLE, the ATARI 800, and the VIC-20, for example, have separate and different input-output subroutines, and each of these is found only on its own particular system. We can only specify the general principles of input-output on the 6502.

First of all, input-output on any microcomputer is normally done *one character at a time.* If you want to input several characters (such as in a subroutine like GETLNZ), *you have to write a loop,* containing instructions to read a single character. (This is in contrast to the situation on many large computers in which a single input instruction causes the input of an entire array.)

Reading a single character normally consists of the following steps:

(1) Test to see whether the person sitting at the keyboard has typed a new character.
(2) If not, return to step 1.
(3) Read the new character.

Step 3 above is done by loading, into the A register, a location which we will call INDATA ("input data"), that has a *fixed address* (just as the stack has the fixed addresses 0100 through 01FF). The computer[†] is wired in such a way that

---

*For a good reference on the hardware of the 6502, see L. Leventhal, *6502 Assembly Language Programming,* Berkeley: Osborne/McGraw-Hill, 1980.
[†]*Not* the APPLE. See the explanation on the following page.

loading this particular address causes a new character to be input. (The specific address can be wired in an arbitrary way, and varies from one 6502-based system to another.)

Step 1 above is done by loading, into the A register, *another* location with a similar fixed address, which we will call INSTAT ("input status"). The computer is wired in such a way that loading this address causes the loading of the contents of a *status register associated with the keyboard* (do not confuse this with the P register). One bit of this status register is the *ready flag.* When a new character has been typed, the ready flag is set (by the circuitry of the keyboard—*not* by your program). When the new character is read, as in step 3 above, the ready flag is cleared (again automatically—not by your program).

Finally, step 2 above is done with a bit test and branch (see section 52). Thus a typical program to read a character might be:

```
IWAIT   LDA   INSTAT        ; GET INPUT STATUS
        AND   #%00000001    ; LOOK AT RIGHTMOST BIT
        BEQ   IWAIT         ; IF STILL 0, KEEP TRYING
        LDA   INDATA        ; IF 1, GET A CHARACTER
```

We emphasize, however, that this is only a *typical* program, because many details can be different depending on how the given 6502 system is wired. Among these are:

(1) The specific locations of INSTAT and INDATA.
(2) *Which* bit of INSTAT (in the above case, it is the rightmost bit) is the ready flag.
(3) Whether 1 means "ready" and 0 means "not ready" (as in the above example) or vice versa.
(4) Whether the scheme above is used at all. In another version of this scheme, each character which is input is only seven bits long, and the eighth (leftmost) bit is used as the ready flag. Here there is only one special location in memory; if this is called INDATA, and the value 1, as before, in the leftmost bit signifies a ready status, the instructions

```
IWAIT   LDA   INDATA    ; GET BOTH DATA AND STATUS
        BPL   IWAIT     ; PROCEED ONLY IF STATUS = 1
```

perform the same function, in this context, as the preceding instructions did in their context. This is the scheme used by the APPLE, where INDATA is hexadecimal C000.
(5) Other hardware considerations of an arbitrary nature. On the APPLE, for example, there is an operation called "clear keyboard strobe" which must take place *immediately following* the reading of any character. For internal APPLE hardware reasons, BIT $C010 performs this function; it

clears the sign bit of INDATA, so that it will signify "not ready" until another key is pressed. Still another arrangement involves the ready status, not as a flag, but as an *interrupt*. When a new character is typed, an interrupt occurs, as described in the preceding section. The interrupt routine then reads a character and puts it in an array of characters to be processed later by the program that is currently running.

Various other microcomputers, such as the Z-80, have separate instructions to input a character. On the 6502, however, this is always done by wired-in load instructions, as above—a scheme that is often known as *memory-mapped input-output*. The use of ready flags, as above, is often referred to as *handshaking*.

EXERCISES

*1. Expand the first sequence of input instructions given in this section into a primitive version of GETLN, the APPLE monitor subroutine that gets a line of input (including a terminating carriage return) and puts it in cells 0200 through $0200+n$, where the line contains n characters plus the carriage return. (Ignore the fact that the actual GETLN subroutine in the APPLE monitor allows for backspacing and retyping, and do not start by outputting a carriage return, as GETLNZ does.)

*2. Rewrite the first sequence of input instructions given in this section, so as to save one byte. (Hint: Use a shift.)

3. (a) Suppose that, on the APPLE, the ready flag (the leftmost bit of INDATA) were 0 for "ready" and 1 for "not ready," instead of the reverse. In the instructions

```
IWAIT   LDA   INDATA   ; GET BOTH DATA AND STATUS
        BPL   IWAIT    ; PROCEED ONLY IF STATUS = 1
```

we would then replace BPL by BMI. If we did this, what bug would still remain in the given sequence? (Hint: See Tables 9 and 10 in the Appendix.)

(b) How can this bug be fixed?

70. OUTPUT INSTRUCTIONS

There are many resemblances between input and output instructions on the 6502. Like input, output is done one character at a time. As with input, there are no instructions on the 6502 that are exclusively used for output. Instead, an output instruction is normally a *store* instruction that stores into a cell with a certain fixed address.

The analogy between loading and storing, on the one hand, and input and output, on the other, is an important one. In fact, in the study of computer hardware, loading a register is often called *reading from memory*, and storing a register is often called *writing into memory*.

Let us consider, for a moment, output to a device such as a printer. Such a device always has a certain maximum speed; for example, this might be 30 characters per second. Since ten bits are sent for each character (eight for the character itself, and two more for synchronization purposes), this is 300 bits per second, or 300 *baud* (named for Baudot, a French scientist, just as the *volt* is named for Volta, and the *farad* for Faraday).

Thirty characters per second is one character every 34,100 cycles (since 34,100 = 1,023,000/30, and there are 1,023,000 cycles per second, as we mentioned in section 36). After one character is sent, the computer must wait 34,100 cycles to send the next one.

If the computer has nothing else to do, the easiest way to wait for 34,100 cycles (or any other number) is with a *wait loop*. This is simply a loop that does nothing, over and over again. A typical wait loop on the 6502 is

```
          LDA   L      ;  SET THE COUNT
          STA   I      ;   I EQUAL TO L
    L1    LDA   M      ;  SET THE COUNT
          STA   J      ;   J EQUAL TO M
    L2    LDA   N      ;  SET THE COUNT
          STA   K      ;   K EQUAL TO N
    L3    DEC   K      ;  DO NOTHING BUT DECREASE
          BNE   L3     ;     THE COUNT AND LOOP BACK
          DEC   J      ;  DECREASE THE SECOND
          BNE   L2     ;     COUNT AND LOOP BACK
          DEC   I      ;  DECREASE THE FIRST
          BNE   L1     ;     COUNT AND LOOP BACK
```

This waits for approximately 8*L*M*N cycles (actually, 8*L*M*N + 15*L*M + 15*L + 8 cycles). The value of this is 34,100 cycles if we take L = 12, M = 6, and N = 57.

The APPLE monitor has a wait loop of its own. The instruction JSR WAIT (where WAIT EQU $FCA8) waits for $(26+27k+5k^2)/2$ cycles, where k is the initial content of the A register. You can wait for slightly less than 34,100 cycles by loading the A register with 114 (decimal) and then calling WAIT.

Wait loops are not the only way to produce output in a timed way. Many output devices will send a signal after the proper amount of time has gone by, and they are ready to receive a new character. This signal goes into an *output ready flag* in a status register. Output ready flags and input ready flags arise in completely different ways, but they are treated in exactly the same way by the programs that use them; you wait until the device is ready, and then either input (by loading) or output (by storing). Thus, assuming that we have two special locations ODATA and OSTAT (like INDATA and INSTAT of the preceding section), and that the *second* bit from the right (this time) in OSTAT is the ready flag, with the value 1 meaning "ready," we might proceed as follows:

```
OWAIT   LDA   OSTAT        ; GET OUTPUT STATUS
        AND   #%00000010   ; LOOK AT 2ND BIT FROM RIGHT
        BEQ   OWAIT        ; IF STILL 0, KEEP TRYING
        STX   ODATA        ; IF 1, OUTPUT A CHARACTER
```

where the character to be output is in the X register. As with input, the output ready signal can, in more complex systems, cause an interrupt rather than setting a flag.

When we have a loop in an assembly language program that is inside another loop, which may be in turn (as in our wait loop above) inside still another loop, and so on, these are called *nested loops*, just as in BASIC or FORTRAN.

Just as with input, the APPLE uses a non-standard scheme for output. The characters to be output on the APPLE screen are placed in certain fixed memory locations. The actual display of these characters on the APPLE screen is done by a part of the APPLE computer system which is completely hidden from the user. In practice, COUT and other such monitor subroutines place character codes in the proper fixed memory cells.

EXERCISES

1. Under the conditions of the output sequence of instructions at the end of this section, what is the shortest way of outputting a character in the A register, if the X and Y registers are in use for other purposes? Illustrate by writing a sequence of instructions. (Note that

```
OWAIT    LDA    OSTAT
         AND    #%00000010
         BEQ    OWAIT
         STA    ODATA
```

will not work, because the STA will *always* store the final contents of OSTAT, since this is loaded into the A register by LDA.)

*2. In the wait loop of this section, how long does the loop wait if L, M, and N are all zero? (Hint: There is a trick to this one, which can be widely used in other situations. Walk the program through carefully if you do not see the trick.)

3. Modify the second *input* sequence of instructions of the preceding section, so that it becomes an output sequence. Assume that the character to be output is in the A register. (Note that the obvious modification, namely

```
OWAIT    LDA    ODATA
         BPL    OWAIT
         STA    ODATA
```

will not work. Why not?)

PROBLEM 3 FOR COMPUTER SOLUTION
16-BIT HEXADECIMAL CONVERSION

Write a program to input four hexadecimal digits, convert them to a 16-bit quantity in memory, and output this quantity in decimal, using DECOZ (use your copy of DECOZ from Problem 1).

The input should be done with GETLNZ. Remember that GETLNZ uses the A, X, and Y registers for its own purposes.

If any of the four digits which you input is *not* the character code for a digit (0 through 9) or A through F, your program should print out the message BAD INPUT and try again.

After you output the converted number, loop back to read another hexadecimal quantity.

71. QUEUES AND POLLING

The real power of ready flags is that they can be used to support *simultaneous input, processing, and output*. You can be typing characters; the computer can be making calculations; and other characters can be displayed or typed, all at the same time.

When you type characters in, you might type them too fast for the computer to use right away. It has to save them somewhere, and use them later. In the same way, the computer might produce output characters too fast for the output device (faster than 30 characters per second, for example); so these characters have to be saved somewhere, and used later by the output device. Both these problems may be solved by means of data structures known as *queues*.

In a queue, you always want to put characters (or other data) into the queue in a certain order and then use them, later, *in that same order*. The *first* character to be put in is the first character to come out; this is abbreviated as First In, First Out, or FIFO. This makes a queue different from a stack, for example. When we put bytes on a stack in some order, we always remove them in the *reverse* order, as we saw in section 60. The *last* character to be put in is the first character to come out, in this case; this is abbreviated as Last In, First Out, or LIFO.*

Figure 24 shows how to implement a queue of characters as an array called Q. This array has length m, and goes from Q(0) through Q($m-1$). Characters are put into the queue at the rear, and leave the queue at the front. (The meaning of "queue" is "a waiting line"; you can think of people waiting for groceries, or for tickets, and getting in line at the rear of the queue, waiting for a while, and then leaving at the front of the queue.)

If the queue of Figure 24 is an *input queue*, then characters (in this case the message ALL THE WAY AROUND THE RING) are typed as input, inserted at the rear of the queue in order, and then later used by the computer, by removing them in this same order from the front of the queue. If this is an *output queue*, then the computer outputs ALL THE WAY AROUND THE RING into the rear

---

*There is also GIGO (Garbage In, Garbage Out), which is a computer version of Murphy's Law. If your input data are incorrect—"garbage"—then the output you produce will also be garbage.

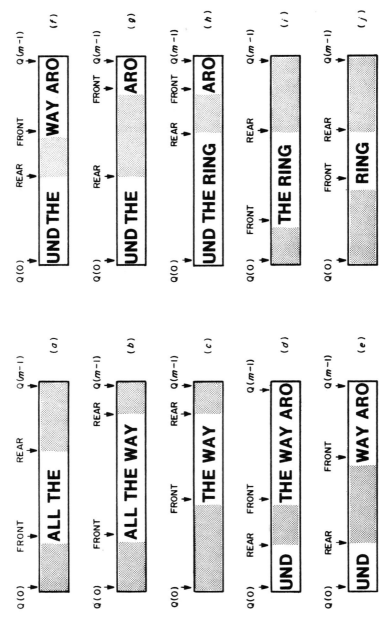

Figure 24. A Queue Implemented in an Array.

of the queue; the output device (such as the printer) then displays these characters, in the same order, by removing them from the front of the queue.

This method of setting up a queue is often known as a *ring buffer*, or a *circular array*, because you can think of the array Q as endless—the next character after Q($m-1$) is Q(0). (The stack, on the 6502, is also a circular array, because the stack pointer increments from $FF to zero, and decrements from zero to $FF.)

We will now show how to do simultaneous input, processing, and output. Let us first consider processing—that is, reading and writing characters, with subroutines ICHAR and OCHAR, which are analogous to RDKEY and COUT on the APPLE. We have *two* queues, an input queue and an output queue. It should be clear from Figure 24 that ICHAR *removes* one character from the front of the input queue, while OCHAR *inserts* one character at the rear of the output queue.

For simultaneous input and output, there are two possibilities. One is to use interrupts. When a character is typed, an interrupt occurs; the interrupt routine (call it QIN) then *inserts* the new character at the rear of the input queue. Similarly, when a character is printed and 1/30 of a second (for example) has gone by, an interrupt occurs, and the interrupt routine (call it QOUT) *removes* one character from the front of the output queue.

This kind of interrupt requires extra hardware, at extra cost, and there is another way to do the same job without interrupts, using a technique called *polling*. This also involves QIN and QOUT; but this time, these are called by a *polling routine,* which simulates what is done by the interrupt hardware.

A polling routine is a routine (call it POLL) that is called, at a high rate of speed (normally, over 1000 times per second) by the program being executed. Its purpose is to *poll* the ready flags, or test whether any of them is set. In this case, there are two ready flags—one for input and one for output. If neither of the ready flags is on, POLL simply exits. If the input ready flag is on, POLL calls QIN; if the output ready flag is on, POLL calls QOUT.

In order for polling to work, it is essential that POLL be called "often enough." There must never be any substantial period of time (half a second, say) during which POLL is not called. Otherwise, for example, you could type two characters during that period of time, and the *first* of these characters would never be put into the input queue, because that can only be done by POLL.

The easiest way to implement POLL is to have it called, by the program being executed (and by every one of its subroutines), at *every labelled instruction*. This works because there is always a very short period of time (a few microseconds) between execution of labelled instructions. In particular, whenever a branch or a jump is taken, it goes to a labelled instruction, where there is another call to POLL. Note that, *almost* all the time, POLL is very fast (since it just checks two flags, finds neither of them set, and exits); so the calls to POLL do not slow processing down to any significant extent.

EXERCISES

*1.   A queue, like a stack, can be *empty* (that is, have no elements in it).
      Describe the modifications which have to be made to ICHAR and QOUT
      to handle the case of an empty queue.

 2.   In Figure 24(a), the bytes of the queue appear to range from Q(FRONT)
      through Q(REAR). However, they are often kept in Q(FRONT) through
      Q(REAR-1) instead. Can you think of a good reason why? (Hint: Write
      a sequence of instructions to test whether the queue is empty.)

*3.   Just as there are upside-down stacks, so there are *upside-down queues*,
      which may be thought of exactly as pictured in Figure 24 except that Q(0)
      becomes Q(m), and Q($m-1$) becomes Q(1). Can you think of a good rea-
      son why a queue should be upside down? (Hint: Consider saving space
      and time.)

72. THE SPEAKER AND REAL-TIME PROGRAMMING

The APPLE has another form of output, called the *speaker*, which will introduce us to a new style of programming. The speaker is memory-mapped, like all input-output on the APPLE; it uses the special cell with address $C030. We usually write

SPKR   EQU $C030

Unlike the case of character input-output, however, *any* instruction (a load, store, or whatever) which refers to SPKR will produce speaker output, which is a barely noticeable click. We can then, for example, produce a musical note as a series of clicks. Let us learn how to do this.

There is a musical note known as A-440; on the piano, it is the A above middle C. The designation A-440 means that anything which vibrates 440 times per second will produce that particular note. What we will do is to make the APPLE produce a click on the speaker 440 times per second. This will be done as follows:

(1) Produce a click.
(2) Wait for approximately 1/440 of a second.
(3) Go back to step 1.

How many cycles are there in 1/440 of a second? Since one second is 1,023,000 cycles (see section 36), the answer is 1,023,000/440, or 2325. However, the click (if we use a load) takes four cycles, and step 3 takes three, leaving 2318 cycles for step 2.

We now need a subroutine, like the wait loops of section 70, which produces a delay of 2318 cycles. One way to write such a subroutine is as follows:

(1) Divide 2318 by 256, giving 9 and a fraction. We will therefore wait for 10 microseconds in a loop which is executed slightly fewer than 256 times.
(2) Divide 2318 by 10, giving 231 with a remainder of 8. We will therefore load register X with 231 (two cycles) and use up 10 cycles in the loop, as, for example, with LDA-BEQ-DEX-BNE, a total of 231 times (2310 cycles; actually 2309, because the BNE takes only 2 cycles instead of 3, the last time through the loop, because it does not branch).
(3) This makes 2311 cycles; and a BEQ which branches (three cycles),

together with two NOPs at two cycles apiece, complete the sequence at 2318 cycles. The complete loop is now as follows:

```
A440      LDA    SPKR      ; PRODUCE A CLICK
          LDX    #!231     ; START THE WAIT LOOP
A440L     LDA    #!0       ; WAIT FOR 10 CYCLES
          BEQ    A440C     ;  (2 + 3 +
A440C     DEX              ;   2 + 3) AND
          BNE    A440L     ; LOOP BACK
          BEQ    A440N     ; USE UP SEVEN
A440N     NOP              ;  MORE CYCLES WITH
          NOP              ;  BEQ-NOP-NOP
          JMP    A440      ; AND LOOP BACK
```

Of course, this loop is endless; if we wanted to play this particular note for only a limited period of time, we would have to insert further statements. These would *themselves* take a certain amount of time, and this would have to be taken into account when calculating constants such as 231, as above.*

Programs like this are an example of *real-time programming*, where the purpose is *not* to calculate anything, but rather to cause a certain sequence of events to happen at certain calculated intervals of time. Another very common example of this, although the APPLE does not have it, is the *seven-segment display*. This typically consists of seven *light-emitting diodes*, or LEDs, which allow you to display any digit from 0 to 9 by turning some of them on and leaving some of them off, as follows:

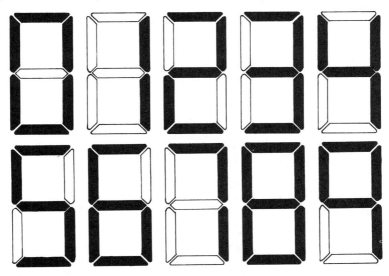

---

*The APPLE has a subroutine BELL1 (with BELL1 EQU $FBD9) which produces an 0.1 second "beep" on the speaker, using these techniques. This is useful as a primitive signal from the APPLE to the user.

(Here the shaded areas are "on" and the unshaded areas are "off.") Each light-emitting diode is turned on by loading a special cell, just as the speaker is clicked, but once the LED is on, it does not stay on; it starts to fade out in approximately 1 millisecond (1000 microseconds). Therefore an LED must be *pulsed*, like the speaker; that is, our program must refer to the special cell for the LED at least once every 1000 microseconds.

Digital watches use seven-segment displays. Many of them use *liquid crystal displays* (LCDs), an improvement over LEDs, but the seven segments are still there.

EXERCISES

1. A louder note may be produced on the speaker by giving two clicks in a row (that is, LDA SPKR twice) and then waiting as before. Specify the changes to the A-440 program so that this may be done while continuing to use exactly 2325 cycles in the loop.

*2. Specify the changes to the A-440 program to produce C-512, which is the C on the piano just above A-440. Show your work. Can you do this by changing only the constant loaded into the X register and the instructions after the loop? (Note that 512 does not go evenly into 1,023,000, so you will have to use an approximation.)

3. Suppose that the segments in a seven-segment display are given letter designations as follows:

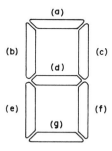

Suppose now that a subroutine is written, which is entered with a quantity in the A register in the following format:

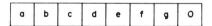

The subroutine will test each of these bits, and light the corresponding LED if the given bit is 1. The digit 0, for example, involves LEDs *a, b, c, e, f,* and *g* (see the diagrams in the text), and the subroutine is therefore entered with binary 11101110, or hexadecimal EE, in the A register. Give the corresponding hexadecimal contents of the A register for each of the remaining digits, 1 through 9.

73. FURTHER STRING
DECLARATIONS

In section 26, we studied the declaration ASC, which permits us to define an ASCII string in which each character has its high-order bit equal to one (with the string enclosed in double quotes). However, LISA has several other ways of declaring strings, each one involving a different pseudo-operation.

The pseudo-operation INV produces a character string that can be displayed on the screen in what is called "inverse mode" on the APPLE, or "black-on-white" as opposed to "white-on-black." This mode is much used, for example, in VISICALC, a very popular APPLE program. Writing

```
        INV     "ENTER THE FIRST NUMBER"
```

produces the 22 characters in the string ENTER THE FIRST NUMBER with first two bits of each character set to 00, which the APPLE interprets as inverse mode (see Tables 9 and 10 in the Appendix).

The APPLE monitor subroutine call JSR SETINV ("set inverse mode") provides another way to display inverse mode characters. After SETINV has been called, any character, even if its first two bits are not zero, will be displayed by JSR COUT in inverse mode. The APPLE is returned to normal mode by JSR SETNRM ("set normal mode"). The definitions of SETINV and SETNRM are

```
        SETINV  EQU     $FE80
        SETNRM  EQU     $FE84
```

The pseudo-operation BLK produces a character string that can be displayed on the screen in what is called "blinking mode" or "flashing mode" on the APPLE; this alternates between normal and inverse mode. (The cursor that normally appears on the APPLE screen is a blank, in blinking mode.) Writing

```
        BLK     "ENTER THE FIRST NUMBER"
```

produces the characters in the string ENTER THE FIRST NUMBER with the first two bits of each character set to 01, which the APPLE interprets as blinking mode (see Tables 9 and 10 in the Appendix).

247

Many programmers like to keep strings in such a way that the length of a string can be deduced from its form. LISA provides two pseudo-operations for this—DCI and STR. DCI (''define characters immediate'') defines a string in which the *last* character has its *leftmost* bit different from the leftmost bits of all the other characters in that string. Hence we can write

```
          LDX   #$FF          ; STARTING VALUE OF X = -1
LOOK      INX                 ; MOVE TO NEXT CHARACTER OF
          LDA   MSG4,X        ;  STRING, AND LOAD IT
          ORA   #%10000000    ; SET LEFTMOST BIT TO ONE FOR
          JSR   COUT          ;  DISPLAY, AND DISPLAY IT
          LDA   MSG4,X        ; IF LEFTMOST BIT WAS 1, MORE
          BMI   LOOK          ;  CHARS. IN STRING -- GET THEM
```

where COUT EQU $FDED is given, and MSG4 is defined by

```
          MSG4    DCI    "ENTER THE FIRST NUMBER"
```

and ENTER THE FIRST NUMBER will be displayed. Note that if ENTER THE FIRST NUMBER had been given in *single* quotes, the leftmost bit of the last character would have been 1, not zero.

STR (meaning simply ''string'') gives a string preceded by a single byte which gives its length. In LISA 1.5, the leftmost bit of this length byte *is the same as those of the rest of the string,* and, in particular, is equal to 1 for a string given in double quotes. We can write

```
          LDA   MSG7          ; GET LENGTH BYTE AND SET ITS
          AND   #%01111111    ;  LEFTMOST BIT TO ZERO
          TAX                 ; LENGTH OF STRING NOW IN X
          LDY   #!0           ; (FIRST CHAR. IS AT MSG7+!1)
WATCH     INY                 ; MOVE TO NEXT CHARACTER OF
          LDA   MSG7,Y        ;  STRING, AND LOAD IT
          JSR   COUT          ; DISPLAY THIS CHARACTER
          DEX                 ; DO THIS N TIMES, WHERE N IS
          BNE   WATCH         ;  THE LENGTH OF THE STRING
```

where COUT EQU $FDED is given, and MSG7 is defined in LISA 1.5 by

```
          MSG7    STR    "ENTER THE FIRST NUMBER"
```

and ENTER THE FIRST NUMBER will again be displayed (but note the AND, which is necessary). In LISA 2.5, the length byte is a full eight bits, and the first three instructions above may be replaced by the single instruction LDX MSG7.

Finally, there is HEX, which allows you to specify the individual hexadecimal digits in a string. Thus, if we write

```
          MSG1    HEX    C5CED4C5D2A0D4C8C5A0
                  HEX    C6C9D2D3D4A0CED5CDC2C5D2
```

we get the string ENTER THE FIRST NUMBER just as before (refer to Figure 11, section 24). The main use of HEX, however, is to specify hexadecimal digits that do not correspond to characters (in normal mode). Note that HEX uses no quotes or dollar signs.

EXERCISES

1. In each case, give a single use of either INV or BLK which is equivalent to the given sequence.

   *(a)

	BYT	$4B
	BYT	$79

   (b)

	BYT	$0B
	BYT	$39

2. In each case, give a single use of either DCI or STR which is equivalent to the given sequence. (Assume LISA 1.5.)

   (a)

	BYT	$D3
	BYT	$D4
	BYT	$CF
	BYT	$50

   *(b)

	BYT	$83
	BYT	$D9
	BYT	$C5
	BYT	$D3

*3. Give a *single* use of HEX which is equivalent to the following sequence. (Note that only three bytes, not five, are specified. See section 63.)

	BYT	!10
	BYT	$3456
	HBY	$3456

74. ZERO-PAGE INSTRUCTIONS

Think of the memory of the 6502 as being like a book; it is made up of 256 parts, called *pages*, and each page contains 256 characters (or bytes). The pages are numbered from 00 to FF in hexadecimal. Page *ab* contains the bytes, or cells, with addresses *ab*00 through *ab*FF.

Using this terminology, *page one* is the stack, since the stack extends from address 0100 to 01FF, as mentioned in section 60. Page two is the buffer INBUF, used in the subroutines GETLN and GETLNZ, as mentioned in section 25.

The most important page, however, is *page zero*. Every cell in page zero has an address which is really only eight bits long (00 to FF); and there exists a whole set of instructions which use eight-bit (that is, one-byte) addresses, instead of 16-bit addresses. These are called *zero-page instructions*.

Almost every instruction on the 6502 which involves a 16-bit address has a counterpart which involves an 8-bit (page zero) address. In fact, there are only four exceptions to this rule, as follows:

(1) Zero-page instructions allow indirect addressing in many cases; this will be taken up in the next two sections.

(2) Aside from indirect addressing, zero-page instructions *cannot be indexed by Y* (except for LDX and STX). This is no great loss, because 16-bit addresses can always be used in this case (and page zero is not a good place to store arrays, anyway).

(3) STX Z,Y and STY Z,X may be used if Z is a zero-page address. (We have already seen that they *cannot* be used otherwise.)

(4) JMP and JSR can go to 16-bit addresses only. (Again, this is no great loss; every zero-page address is also a 16-bit address.)

The greatest advantage of page zero is that it saves both time and space, as we can see from Table 4 in the Appendix, where *the notation Z denotes a zero-page instruction*. Thus ADC Q takes 4 cycles and 3 bytes, whereas ADC Z (the zero-page equivalent of ADC Q) takes only 3 cycles and 2 bytes. The same is true for LDA, STA, and many other instructions.

Thus, for example, in the first program of section 33, we can save two bytes and two cycles (one of each for the STA, and one of each for the ADC) by putting TEMP in page zero. Likewise, in the second program of section 33, we can save two bytes and $2n$ cycles, where n is the number of digits in the number being input. Note that the loop is done n times, and we save two cycles each time; but only two bytes are saved (STA TEMP and ADC TEMP appear only *once* each, in this program).

The APPLE system uses almost all of page zero itself, since so much time and space are saved. If you are constructing your own 6502-based system, you should do the same. On the APPLE, however, you cannot use page zero indiscriminately; otherwise, you might *overwrite* some of the data used by the APPLE monitor, LISA, and BASIC in page zero. If you do that, then at some later time, when you are using the APPLE monitor, LISA, or BASIC, or when you use subroutines such as RDKEY or COUT, these may very easily behave in unpredictable ways.

Fortunately, cells 19 through 1F are unused by the APPLE monitor, LISA, and BASIC. We can thus use these cells for variables such as TEMP, in the example above. A variant of EQU (see section 25), called EPZ (Equate to Page Zero), is used for setting these up. Thus by writing

```
TEMP      EPZ      $1F
TEMP2     EPZ      $1E
TEMP3     EPZ      $1D
```

in your program, you can use TEMP, TEMP2, and TEMP3 as page-zero locations, so that STA TEMP2, for example, uses an 8-bit address. (If EQU were used instead of EPZ, then STA TEMP2 would have a 16-bit address, even though one byte of that address would be zero.)

Many page-zero locations have special meanings, on the APPLE, that are available to users. For example, location $33 is the *prompt character*—the character which appears on the screen when you are supposed to type some input. The LISA assembler stores ''!'' in location $33, and it is this which makes ! the prompt character in LISA. If you wish to write your own system, with its own prompt character ($ for example), you can store this in location $33 at the start of your system.

The APPLE system subroutine GETLN, which we met in section 25 (exercise 3), outputs the prompt character to the screen and then calls GETLN1, another system subroutine which may be used (like GETLN) to input a line, but *without* giving a prompt character. Thus JSR GETLN is equivalent to the sequence

```
LDA      PROMPT
JSR      COUT
JSR      GETLN1
```

where GETLN1 EQU $FD6F and PROMPT EPZ $33 have been specified.

Indexing in page zero *stays in page zero*. For example, even though $A0+A0 = 140$ (hexadecimal), the zero-page instruction LDA $A0,X loads the A register with the contents of cell 0040 (*not* cell 0140) if the X register contains hexadecimal A0.

EXERCISES

1. *(a) How many cycles (maximum and minimum), and how many bytes, would be saved in the subroutine MULT of section 39, if MDATA1 and MDATA2 were kept in page zero? Show your work. (Do not do the *whole* analysis twice; look only at the instructions that are different in the two cases. Remember that if k cycles are saved in a loop which is done n times, this makes a total of kn cycles saved.)
    *(b) How many cycles (maximum and minimum), and how many bytes, would be saved in the subroutine DIV of section 40, if DDATA1 and DDATA2 were kept in page zero? Show your work. (As in part (a), do not do the whole analysis twice.)

2. Can it save any cycles, or any bytes, to put some of the *instructions* of a program in page zero? Why or why not?

3. We saw in section 60 that, if we move the stack pointer to the X register with TSX, then LDA $0101,X loads the A register with the quantity on top of the stack. It thus follows that STA $00FF,X stores the A register in a cell which is not currently in the stack (being "above the top of the stack"). This STA instruction, however, *cannot* be made into a zero-page instruction. Why not?

75. PRE-INDEXED INDIRECT ADDRESSING

In section 58, we considered indirect jumps such as JMP (B), which use an address which is itself stored in memory. This is a special case of *indirect addressing*, a concept used by a great number of computers both large and small.

A "load Z" instruction with indirect addressing, for example, loads a register with a quantity R, where Z contains the address of R. A "store Z" instruction with indirect addressing stores a register in the cell R, where Z, as before, contains the address of R.

It is possible for an instruction to use *both* indirect addressing and indexing. There is some question, however, as to which ought to be done first. If the indexing is done first, then a "load Z,*index*" instruction, with indirect addressing, would load R, where the address of R would be found by a "load Z,*index*" instruction with ordinary, or *direct, addressing*.

On the other hand, if the indirect addressing is done first, then a "load Z,*index*" instruction, with indirect addressing, would be like "load R,*index*" where the address of R is found at Z.

The 6502 is unusual in that it features *both* these kinds of indirect addressing. However, they are subject to a number of restrictions, as follows:

(1) *All indirect addresses must be in page zero.* This makes indirect addressing more useful in the APPLE system, which uses almost all of page zero, than in APPLE user programs.

(2) *Pre-indexed indirect addressing* (indexing first) *uses the X register only; post-indexed indirect addressing* (where the indirect addressing comes first) *uses the Y register only*.

(3) Except for JMP—which we have already studied—*indirect addressing without indexing at all cannot be used.* We can set either X or Y to zero (much like setting the carry flag to zero before ADC, in order to do an add without carry); or we can use another trick, explained at the end of the next section. JMP is also an exception to rule (1) above.

(4) *Indirect addressing with indexing can be used only with the family of instructions we studied in section 51*; namely, LDA, STA, ADC, SBC, CMP, AND, ORA, and EOR.

The notation (Z,X) is used for pre-indexed indirect addressing. Thus LDA (ALPHA,X) loads the A register with R, where LDA ALPHA,X would load the A register with the lower half of the *address* of R, and LDA ALPHA+!1,X would load the A register with the upper half of that same address.

Under these same conditions, STA (ALPHA,X) would store the A register in R; CMP (ALPHA,X) would compare the A register to R and set the status flags accordingly; and so on.

Pre-indexed indirect addressing depends very strongly on how page zero is used. This is because, in order to use it, you need *several* addresses, all in page zero, which you can index by means of the X register.

The best use for pre-indexed indirect addressing is in calling *subroutines with parameters*. For example, suppose we have a FORTRAN subroutine LOGAND (I, J, K) which sets K to the logical AND of I and J. We can then CALL LOGAND(M1, M2, M3) in FORTRAN, for example, and this will set M3 to the logical AND of M1 and M2.* In assembly language, if M1, M2, and M3 are single-byte data, we do a JSR LOGAND *preceded* by LDX #MSEQ where

```
MSEQ        ADR     M1
            ADR     M2
            ADR     M3
```

has been specified, *in page zero* (see section 63 for ADR). The subroutine LOGAND is now

```
LOGAND    LDA     (0,X)    ;  LOGAND(I, J, K) LOADS I,
          AND     (2,X)    ;    DOES A LOGICAL AND WITH
          STA     (4,X)    ;    J, STORES THE RESULT IN
          RTS              ;    K, AND EXITS
```

For example, AND (2,X) starts by adding 2 to the 8-bit address of MSEQ (which is in the X register), producing MSEQ+!2; but the address of M2 is at MSEQ+!2 and MSEQ+!3, so that AND M2 is effectively done.

A sequence of addresses such as that given at MSEQ is known as a *calling sequence*. At some later time, you can load X with the zero-page address of a different calling sequence, and call LOGAND(M4, M5, M6), for example. In order to use this technique effectively on the 6502, however, you have to have large amounts of zero-page memory available; such memory is most likely to be

---

*This feature of FORTRAN has no counterpart in BASIC.

available if you are constructing your own 6502-based system, independently of the APPLE.

Another use for pre-indexed indirect addressing is as follows. Suppose that your system has several addresses kept in page zero, but not necessarily in an array. You can use data at any one of these addresses by loading the corresponding zero-page address into the X register and then doing LDA (0,X) (or STA, ADC, and so on).

The indexing done in pre-indexed indirect addressing stays in page zero, just as in the preceding section. Thus, if the X register contains $A0, then LDA ($A0,X) uses an indirect address in cells $40 and $41—*not* in cells $0140 and $0141.

EXERCISES

1.   Suppose that Z has the zero-page address 1A, while the X register contains 4. What addresses in memory must have the contents 09 and 14, respectively, in order for STA (Z,X) to store the A register at location 0914?

*2.   Write a subroutine EXCH(B1, B2) which exchanges the contents of the bytes B1 and B2. Assume that the addresses of B1 and B2 are given in zero-page locations CS, CS+!1, CS+!2, and CS+!3, where LDX #CS followed by JSR EXCH calls EXCH(B1, B2). Use pre-indexed indirect addressing to load and store B1 and B2. Do not use the Y register.

3.   Suppose that you are writing a subroutine ADD16(Q1, Q2, SUM) which adds the 16-bit quantities Q1 and Q2 to form the 16-bit quantity SUM. You would like to write it along the lines of the preceding exercise. That is, LDX #CS followed by JSR ADD16 should call ADD16(Q1, Q2, SUM), where the addresses of I, J, and K are kept in zero-page locations CS through CS+!5. What difficulty will arise in writing such a subroutine? (Hint: Try writing it and see.)

76. POST-INDEXED INDIRECT ADDRESSING

The notation (Z),Y is used for post-indexed indirect addressing. Thus LDA (Z),Y is like LDA R,Y where the address of R is kept, with bytes reversed, at the zero-page locations Z and Z + !1. Under the same conditions, STA (Z),Y is like STA R,Y; ADC (Z),Y is like ADC R,Y; and so on.

The difference in notation between (Z,X) and (Z),Y can be remembered as follows: in (Z,X) we do indexing first (producing Z,X) and then indirect addressing (producing (Z,X)); in (Z),Y we do indirect addressing first (producing (Z)) and then indexing (producing (Z),Y).

Post-indexed indirect addressing is used when a subroutine has a parameter which is the name of an *array*, such as a character string. For example, let DISPL(S) be a subroutine which displays the character string S. We set aside a place in page zero (call it ADRS) for the address of S. Now, to display the string T (for example), we first put the address of T into ADRS, as follows:

```
LDA    #T        ;  MOVE  ADDRESS  OF
STA    ADRS      ;    T  INTO  ADRS
LDA    /T        ;      (LOWER  HALF  FIRST,
STA    ADRS+!1   ;      THEN  UPPER  HALF)
```

(For the notations #T and /T, see section 58.) The subroutine DISPL can now be just like the first subroutine of section 25, except that LDA (ADRS),Y is used instead of LDA T,Y (and has the same effect). In general, (ADRS),Y is used instead of T,Y to make indexed reference to the array whose name is the subroutine parameter.

This technique requires only two cells in page zero; and thus it is used much more often than the corresponding technique with pre-indexed indirect addressing, which requires many cells in page zero.

Post-indexed indirect addressing is useful in *list processing* on the 6502. A *list node* L of *length* n consists of the n bytes L, L+!1, and so on, up through L+!n−!1. A *pointer to the list node* L consists of two bytes (say L2 and

L2+!1) which contain the address of L. A *simple list* of *length k* consists of k list nodes $L_1, \ldots, L_k$, each of which contains two bytes (say L_i and $L_i + !1$) which are a pointer to the next node, or zero if this is the last node. (Zero is not the address of any list node.)

Now suppose that the zero-page locations PTR and PTR+!1 are a pointer to the list node L_i (or, as we say, they *point* to L_i). Then the sequence

```
LDY    #!3
LDA    (PTR),Y
```

(for example) loads the A register with byte 3 of L_i (the first byte of L_i being byte zero). If the first two bytes of each node point to the next node, as above, then the sequence

```
LDY    #!0      ;  SET UP Y TO LOAD LOWER
LDA    (PTR),Y  ;  HALF OF POINTER
PHA             ;  SAVE THIS LOWER HALF
INY             ;  INCREASE Y SO WE CAN LOAD
LDA    (PTR),Y  ;  UPPER HALF OF POINTER
STA    PTR+!1   ;  STORE IN PTR (UPPER HALF)
PLA             ;  RESTORE LOWER HALF OF
STA    PTR      ;  POINTER AND STORE IN PTR
```

sets PTR and PTR+!1 to point to the next node.

Either kind of indirect addressing may be used with the corresponding register (X or Y) set to zero, to give the effect of indirect addressing without indexing. Post-indexed indirect addressing is slightly faster (five cycles instead of six) if used in this way. However, it is best just to use whatever index register happens to be free, and to use Y if they are both free. In some cases, X (or Y) may be *known to be zero,* as after a loop ending with DEX and BNE.

Faster indirect addressing without indexing can be done if we use the following trick. Suppose that L and L+!1 are our two locations in page zero. Keep L itself set to zero at all times. Now, in order to indirectly address a cell P with hexadecimal address *abcd,* store *ab* into L + !1 and *load Y* with the constant *cd*. If this is done, L and L+!1 will contain the two-byte quantity *ab*00, and LDA (L),Y will load the variable whose address is *ab*00+*cd*, or *abcd*. That is, LDA (L),Y will load P; and, in the same way, STA (L),Y will store P, and so on. The instructions

```
LDY    /P
STY    L+!1
LDY    #P
```

will store *ab* into L+!1 and load Y with *cd*, as indicated above.

EXERCISES

*1. Suppose that the contents of the zero-page locations Z and Z+!1 are 9
     and 8 respectively. What must be done in the Y register in order for STA
     (Z),Y to store the A register at location 0908? (Be careful. There is a
     trick to this one.)

 2. Write a subroutine MSGOUT to display a message, one character at a
     time (using COUT as in section 25). Assume that the address of the mes-
     sage to be displayed is in the zero-page locations MSG and MSG+!1. The
     message itself consists of a length byte followed by a string to be dis-
     played; that is, if MSG and MSG+!1 contain the 16-bit quantity α, then
     cells α+!1 through α+!n, for some n, contain the n bytes of the message,
     and cell α contains n itself.

*3. Suppose that we tried to eliminate the PHA and the PLA from the final
     program of this section, by writing

```
          LDY    # ! 0
          LDA    (PTR) , Y
          INY
          STA    PTR
          LDA    (PTR) , Y
          STA    PTR+ ! 1
```

     This would not work. Why not?

77. LONG ARRAYS

Since the X register is only eight bits long, and similarly for the Y register, we can make an indexed reference to no more than 256 bytes of any array, as we saw in section 13. A *long array*, on the 6502, is an array of more than 256 bytes. We shall now study how to do indexing in long arrays.

Suppose we do LDX J followed by LDA T,X to make reference to T(J). The instruction LDA T,X adds the 16-bit address of T to the 8-bit quantity J. In a long array, J will be a 16-bit quantity. What we have to do is to add this to the 16-bit address of T, using 16-bit addition as discussed in section 15. This gives us the address of T(J), and now we can use post-indexed indirect addressing, as in the preceding section, thus:

```
LDA    #T        ;  ADD  THE  ADDRESS  OF  T
CLC             ;  (WITH  CARRY  INITIALLY  CLEAR)
ADC    J         ;  TO  THE  16-BIT  QUANTITY  J
STA    ZP        ;  (KEPT  WITH  BYTES  REVERSED)
LDA    /T        ;  AND  PUT  THE  RESULT  IN  THE
ADC    J+!1      ;  ZERO-PAGE  LOCATIONS
STA    ZP+!1     ;  ZP  AND  ZP+!1
LDY    #!0       ;  THEN  USE  POST-INDEXED  INDIRECT
LDA    (ZP),Y ;  ADDRESSING  (WITH  Y = 0)
```

We can improve this slightly by using one of the tricks of the preceding section. The LDY #!0 is eliminated; the STA ZP becomes TAY; and ZP is kept equal to zero at all times. Thus, as before, if *abcd* is the hexadecimal address of T(J), then *ab*00 is kept at ZP and ZP+!1 (with bytes reversed); *cd* is kept in Y; and LDA (ZP),Y loads the byte at address *ab*00+*cd* = *abcd*.

Suppose now that we wish to *increment* an index in a long array. We cannot just increment Y; we must increment the 16-bit quantity contained in Y and ZP+!1 (if the improvement above is used), and similarly for *decrementing* such an index. Using the methods of section 30, the instruction sequences would be

	INY		TYA
	BNE BETA		BNE BETA
	INC ZP+!1		DEC ZP+!1
BETA	(next instruction)	BETA	DEY

Index Increment   *Index Decrement*

Note that we are again using the fact that transfer instructions such as TYA set the zero (and the sign) flag.* Actually, there is a single exception to this rule; TXS does not affect any flags.

Constant subscripts in long arrays are used in exactly the same way they are in short arrays. If we have an array T of size 10000, starting with T(0), and we wish to load T(5000) into the Y register, we can use LDY T+!5000 just as we use LDY T+!50 for a short array, to load T(50) into the Y register.

Parallel long arrays and *serial long arrays* may be used. In a serial array of two-byte quantities, we multiply our indices by 2, as indicated in section 32; and in a serial *long* array, this involves a 16-bit shift, as we studied these in section 34. Note that, for example, four parallel arrays of 256 bytes each are still short arrays and may be manipulated as such, even though there is a total of 1,024 bytes in the four arrays.

Offsets, in a similar way, are the same for long as for short arrays. In the instructions above which add J to the address of T, if we wished to use an offset of -1, we would be adding J to the quantity which is one less than the address of T. This can be done by replacing #T and /T by #T$-$!1 and /T$-$!1 respectively, in these instructions. Note that the # and / apply to *entire* expressions; thus, for example, /T $-$!1 means /(T $-$!1), and not (/T) $-$ 1. (We never actually use parentheses in such expressions in LISA, however.)

In this way we can handle, in a long array, all of the kinds of expressions with offsets that we studied in sections 23 and 32. This includes arrays T starting with T(1), or with some other T(k) for $k \neq 0$; expressions of the form T($e+k$) or T($e-k$), where k is a (possibly 16-bit) constant; and offsets in serial long arrays.

EXERCISES

1. Give a BASIC statement which corresponds with each of the following sequences of assembly language instructions. Assume that T is a long array of 8-bit quantities, which starts at T(0); that ZP and ZP+!1 are zero-page locations, with ZP set to zero; and that J and K are 16-bit quantities.

---

*If the improvement of the preceding page is *not* used, then INY and DEY, here, become INC ZP and DEC ZP respectively.

(a)
```
        LDA    J
        CLC
        ADC    K
        TAY
        LDA    J+!1
        ADC    K+!1
        PHA
        TYA
        CLC
        ADC    #T
        TAY
        PLA
        ADC    /T
        STA    ZP+!1
        LDA    (ZP),Y
        STA    W
```

*(b)
```
        LDA    #T
        CLC
        ADC    J
        TAY
        LDA    /T
        ADC    J+!1
        STA    ZP+!1
        LDA    (ZP),Y
        INY
        BNE    ALPHA
        INC    ZP+!1
ALPHA   STA    (ZP),Y
```

(c)
```
        LDA    #T
        CLC
        ADC    K
        TAY
        LDA    /T
        ADC    K+!1
        STA    ZP+!1
        LDA    (ZP),Y
        CLC
        ADC    #T
        TAY
        LDA    /T
        ADC    #!0
        STA    ZP+!1
        LDA    #!0
        STA    (ZP),Y
```

*2. How many bytes, and how many cycles, are saved if the specified improvement is made to the first program of this section? Show your work. (Remember that the cells ZP and ZP + !1 are in page zero.)

3. Write a loop which sets T(J) = 0 if J is even and 1 if J is odd, for all elements T(J) of the long array T of N elements. Set T(0) first, then T(1), and so on through T(N), where N is a two-byte quantity (note that N+1 different elements are set). Use post-indexed indirect addressing, with the zero-page locations ZP and ZP+!1; assume that ZP is permanently set to zero. For loop control, move the two-byte quantity N to a two-byte quantity N1, and decrease N1 until it becomes zero, using the sequence

```
DEC    N1
BNE    ALPHA
DEC    N1 + !1
BNE    ALPHA
```

Note that there is a problem with this sequence, because the two-byte number N1 becomes zero only if N1+!1 was zero *before* decrementing, not afterwards. However, this can be fixed by *incrementing* N1 + !1 when this is initialized, unless N1 = 0 (if the two-byte quantity N1 is not to be used for any purpose other than counting).

78. ADDRESS MODIFICATION

We shall now introduce a fascinating trick which can often be used to save space and time in programs written for the 6502. It has several forms, and many uses, although it also has a couple of disadvantages. We will consider it initially as part of an improved method of processing long arrays.

Consider the following subroutine, in both assembly language and machine language form (LELA stands for Load Element of Long Array):

```
0840    AD FE 10        LELA    LDA     ARRAY
0843    EE 41 08                INC     LELA+!1
0846    D0 03                   BNE     LELA1
0848    EE 42 08                INC     LELA+!2
084B    60              LELA1   RTS
```

What happens when we call LELA? The first element of ARRAY, at address 10FE, is loaded, and then we increment LELA+!1. Where is that? It is *one of the instruction bytes*—specifically, the one containing FE. After incrementation, it contains FF. Since this is not zero, we branch to LELA1, and return.

Now suppose we call LELA again. Cells 0840, 0841, and 0842 now contain AD, FF (*not* FE), and 10. What happens? Remember that it is the *machine language* form that is executed—not the assembly language form. The instruction AD FF 10 loads the A register with the *second* element of ARRAY, at address 10FF. Now we increment LELA+!1 again, from FF to zero, and, since this is zero, we also increment LELA+!2, from 10 to 11. Thus cells 0840, 0841, and 0842 now contain AD, 00, and 11. (The sequence INC-BNE-INC is the 16-bit increment, from section 30.)

The third time we call LELA, we will do the instruction AD 00 11, which loads the *third* element of ARRAY; and so on. Every time we call LELA, it loads an element of ARRAY and *advances itself* so that the next element is loaded the next time. Furthermore, because of the 16-bit increment, this works on *long* arrays as well as short ones.

This is called *address modification*. We are modifying, or changing, the address in an instruction; in this case, we are adding one to it. We can also modify an address by *storing* into it; for example, we can set up the initial contents (FE and 10) of this same address by executing

```
LDA    #ARRAY     ;  RIGHT-HAND 8 BITS OF
STA    LELA+!1    ;    ADDRESS OF ARRAY
LDA    /ARRAY     ;  LEFT-HAND 8 BITS OF
STA    LELA+!2    ;    ADDRESS OF ARRAY
```

If LELA has been called several times, the above sequence sets up LELA to *start over again*, at the beginning of the array.

Now for the disadvantages. First, we have to remember to do the above sequence *at the start of our program, as part of the initialization*. It is very easy to forget this, or to think that it is not necessary because the array is processed only once; but, if our program later becomes a subroutine, which is called more than once, then the array will be processed more than once, and each time it has to start over at the beginning.

The other disadvantage is more serious. It has to do with the two kinds of memory in microcomputer systems. There is ordinary memory, usually called, for historical reasons, "random-access memory" or RAM; and there is *read-only memory*, or ROM. We mentioned in section 70 that "reading from memory" and "writing to memory" are terms used in computer hardware for what we have been calling *loading* and *storing*. Read-only memory, then, is memory that can be *loaded*, but cannot be *stored*.

ROM is more expensive than RAM, but it is often used to protect a program (such as the monitor) from being overwritten by a bug in a user's program. You can put in ROM any bytes that you are never going to store into; this includes any constant data that you have, and it also includes almost all the instructions of your programs. However, an instruction like the one at LELA cannot go into ROM, because you are storing into it (and also incrementing it, a process that includes storing a new value). The same is true of any instruction whose address is modified.

The APPLE uses RAM for user programs (although it uses ROM for the instruction codes of BASIC and the monitor). You will, therefore, have no difficulty using address modification on the APPLE. Even in systems which are implemented mostly in ROM, there is always a certain amount of RAM; and there is usually enough RAM in any system to keep a few subroutines that use address modification, like LELA. Only the subroutines themselves need to be in RAM; the initialization and calling instructions can be anywhere in ROM.

The address in our modified instruction is a *dummy address*; it is "stored over" by the initialization, and so it does not need to be given as ARRAY. Instead of LDA ARRAY we might write LDA MODIFY (where MODIFY EQU $FFFF or any other 16-bit address) to remind us that this is a modified address. Also, we could replace LDA by STA, which would give us a subroutine to *store* the A register in the "next byte" of a long array.

EXERCISES

*1.   Give a sequence of assembly language instructions, using address modification, which sets W = T(J), where T is a long array and J is a 16-bit quantity. Use the same idea as in the preceding section, but with address modification (and the dummy address MODIFY) rather than page zero.

  2.   Give a sequence of instructions which changes "load T(J)" to "load T(J−1)" at the instruction with the label L. (Hint: see section 30.)

*3.   An alternative way of writing the LELA program of this section is to change the first two instructions to

           LELA   LDA   ARRAY, Y
                   INY

with the Y register initialized to zero; that is, LDY #!0 replaces the instructions

           LDA   #ARRAY
           STA   LELA+!1

which initialize LELA+!1 (and this location is no longer modified). Discuss the advantages and disadvantages of this alternative scheme.

79. SUBROUTINE PARAMETERS

Address modification is useful in many other situations besides that of process-ing long arrays. One of the most important has to do with subroutine parame-ters. In MULT and DIV we have seen that up to three bytes can be given to a subroutine, and returned from the subroutine, in the registers. When there are more parameters than this, however, or when an array name is a parameter, other techniques must be used.

Suppose first of all that we have a subroutine with one parameter, which is the name of an array. The address of this array will be assumed to be entered in the A and X registers, with the upper half in A and the lower half in X. That is, we might call G(U) by

```
        LDA     /U
        LDX     #U
        JSR     G
```

Now suppose that G is defined, in general, as G(T), where T is U this time, but T might be something else the next time that G is called. (We refer to T as a *for-mal parameter*, and to U as the corresponding *actual parameter*.) Suppose that ALPHA is the label of an instruction which makes reference to T, such as

```
ALPHA       LDA     MODIFY,X
```

Then, at the beginning of the subroutine G, we perform

```
        STX     ALPHA+!1
        STA     ALPHA+!2
```

Note that X, the lower half of the address, goes first, while A, the upper half, goes second (since the bytes are reversed).

If there are *several* instructions in G which make reference to T, then we must have instructions which store A and X in every one of these. The collec-tion of STA-STX pairs at the beginning of the program is the *preamble* to the program. In general, a preamble is that part of the initialization of a subroutine that puts actual parameter addresses wherever they are needed.

Now suppose that G has two parameters, T1 and T2, both of which are names of arrays. For example, G might be a program which moves the array T1 to the array T2. We have two addresses, of two bytes each, to be given, or *passed*, as we say, to the subroutine by its calling program; and three registers, A, X, and Y, are not enough. One solution is to *push* the addresses of T1 and T2 onto the stack before calling G, as follows:

```
LDA   /T1    ; ADDRESS OF T1 TO
PHA          ;   STACK (UPPER HALF)
LDA   #T1    ; ADDRESS OF T1 TO
PHA          ;   STACK (LOWER HALF)
LDA   /T2    ; ADDRESS OF T2 TO
PHA          ;   STACK (UPPER HALF)
LDA   #T2    ; ADDRESS OF T2 TO
PHA          ;   STACK (LOWER HALF)
JSR   G      ; RETURN ADDRESS TO STACK
```

The subroutine G must now pull these quantities from the stack. First it pulls the return address and saves this in X and Y; then it pulls the four address bytes and modifies addresses accordingly (remembering that these bytes are pulled in the reverse order of pushing); finally, it pushes the return address back on the stack, so that a proper RTS may be made. Note that everything pushed is subsequently pulled, although the four address bytes are pushed in the calling program and pulled in the subroutine.

For a subroutine G to move N bytes from T1 to T2, we may proceed as in Figure 25. Of course, N might also be a parameter, in which case the preamble would be further expanded. (The same address modification techniques, clearly, work for both single-variable parameters such as N and array parameters such as T1 and T2.)

EXERCISES

1. Explain why STA BETA+!1 comes before STA BETA+!2 in Figure 25.

*2. Write a subroutine ARRAY0(T, N) which sets T(1) through T(N) to zero. The subroutine should be entered with the value of N in the Y register and the address of T in A and X (upper half in A, lower half in X). Thus, for example, to set U(1) through U(16) to zero, one should be able to write

```
LDA   /U
LDX   #U
LDY   #!16
JSR   ARRAY0
```

Use address modification, and decrement the index in the Y register.

G	PLA		; LOW ORDER BYTE OF
	TAX		; RETURN ADDRESS TO X
	PLA		; HIGH ORDER BYTE OF
	TAY		; RETURN ADDRESS TO Y
	PLA		; LOW ORDER BYTE OF
	STA	BETA+!1	; ADDRESS OF T2 TO BETA
	PLA		; HIGH ORDER BYTE OF
	STA	BETA+!2	; ADDRESS OF T2 TO BETA
	PLA		; LOW ORDER BYTE OF
	STA	ALPHA+!1	; ADDRESS OF T1 TO ALPHA
	PLA		; HIGH ORDER BYTE OF
	STA	ALPHA+!2	; ADDRESS OF T1 TO ALPHA
	TYA		; PUT THE RETURN ADDRESS
	PHA		; BACK ON THE STACK,
	TXA		; PUSHING IN THE REVERSE
	PHA		; ORDER OF PULLING
	LDX	#!0	; INITIAL VALUE OF INDEX
ALPHA	LDA	MODIFY,X	; MOVE ONE BYTE FROM THE
BETA	STA	MODIFY,X	; 1ST ARRAY TO THE 2ND
	INX		; TO NEXT BYTE TO BE MOVED
	CPX	N	; WAS THIS THE LAST BYTE
	BNE	ALPHA	; IF NOT, LOOP BACK
	RTS		; END OF SUBROUTINE

Figure 25. A Subroutine with a Preamble.

3. Modify the subroutine of Figure 25 in such a way that it expects the address of T1 on the stack, and the address of T2 in the A and X registers. (This is a hybrid of the two methods of this section.) That is, G should be called by

```
LDA    /T1
PHA
LDA    #T1
PHA
LDA    /T2
LDX    #T2
JSR    G
```

80. IMMEDIATE DATA MODIFICATION

Address modification is concerned with addresses in three-byte instructions, but we can also modify *constant data* in *two-byte* instructions. If we do so, we can save considerable amounts of memory in APPLE programs. In fact, as we shall see, *there is very little reason, in APPLE user programs, to have separate data bytes at all, except for those which are in arrays.*

Suppose we have a data byte called M. There will be at least one instruction, making reference to M, other than a store instruction. Suppose, for the moment, that this is a load instruction (LDA M). Change this instruction to a constant load of zero (LDA #!0) with a label (such as LOADM), and *keep M itself in the second byte of this instruction.*

When you store M, you will store it at LOADM+!1. This is an *immediate data modification*; it changes the immediate data in the instruction at LOADM. This could be done by

STA   LOADM+!1

but another, and more easily understood, notation for the same instruction is STA M where M has been defined at the end of your program by

M   EQU   LOADM+!1

All instructions in your program which make reference to M, except for LOADM, will now make reference to the second byte of the instruction LOADM. This saves two bytes—the byte M itself, and another byte which is saved because LOADM has been changed from a three-byte to a two-byte instruction. It also saves two cycles each time the instruction at LOADM is done, because this has been changed from a four-cycle to a two-cycle instruction. For maximum savings of this kind, you should choose LOADM to be that instruction (with immediate addressing), making reference to M, which is executed most often.

Two-byte data can be handled in the same way, although the two bytes of a

16-bit quantity Q are no longer Q and Q + !1. With every such quantity Q, there will normally be *two* instructions with immediate addressing which act on the two halves of Q. These are now *both* changed to instructions which make reference to constants. Figure 26 shows this process applied to the first of the two byte comparison sequences of section 29. The two bytes are now called QHI and QLO, and referred to as such in other instructions.

Saving and restoring, if the restoring is done by other than a load, is made faster by immediate data modification. Instead of STA TEMP and ADC TEMP as at the beginning of section 33, write STA TEMP and TEMPL ADC #!0 where TEMP EQU TEMPL + !1 is inserted at the end of your program to define TEMP. This saves two cycles every time the instruction sequence is done, as well as two bytes of memory.

The instructions that have immediate addressing on the 6502 are LDA, LDX, LDY, ADC, SBC, CMP, CPX, CPY, AND, ORA, and EOR. This implies that immediate data modification is *not* applicable to certain data bytes, such as those which are stored and decremented only (a loop count, for example), or stored and shifted only.

Immediate data modification is very seldom an improvement over keeping data bytes in page zero, if you have the space in page zero to do this. Even a simple sequence such as the one above, involving STA TEMP and ADC TEMP,

```
                LDA    P+!1      ;  COMPARE UPPER HALF OF P
                CMP    Q+!1      ;    TO UPPER HALF OF Q
                BNE    DECIDE    ;  IF NOT EQUAL, DECIDE
                LDA    P         ;  COMPARE LOWER HALF OF P
                CMP    Q         ;    TO LOWER HALF OF Q
        DECIDE  BCC    LESS      ;  GO TO LESS IF P < Q
```

(a)

```
                LDA    P+!1      ;  COMPARE UPPER HALF OF P
        D1      CMP    #!0       ;    TO QHI (KEPT IN 2ND BYTE)
                BNE    DECIDE    ;  IF NOT EQUAL, DECIDE
                LDA    P         ;  COMPARE LOWER HALF OF P
        D2      CMP    #!0       ;    TO QLO (KEPT IN 2ND BYTE)
        DECIDE  BCC    LESS      ;  TO LESS IF P < (QHI,QLO)
        QHI     EQU    D1+!1     ;  SPECIFY WHERE QHI IS KEPT
        QLO     EQU    D2+!1     ;  SPECIFY WHERE QLO IS KEPT
```

(b)

Figure 26. Immediate Data Modification.

is normally not improved (in either space or time) by immediate data modification if TEMP had been kept in page zero. One exception to this is if the ADC is in a loop, done n times, while the STA is not; in this case n cycles are saved by the ADC, while only one extra cycle is taken by the STA.

The uses of EQU in this section are normally kept at the *end* of a program. This is because, when a label such as LOADM or TEMPL is part of an expression used in EQU (on the right-hand side), this label must have been defined *before* the EQU (that is, the EQU must appear *after* the labeled instruction or data). Otherwise, we could write (for example)

```
P       EQU     Q+!1
Q       EQU     P−!1
```

and trying to determine what Q and P actually are would send LISA itself into an endless loop! An expression such as Q+!1 above, appearing in an EQU before Q is defined, is known as a *forward reference,* and these are not permitted by the LISA system.

EXERCISES

1. Consider the following program, which stores in NEQUAL the number of elements of the serial array T of two-byte quantities that are equal to the two-byte quantity in A and X:

```
                STA     J+!1
                STX     J
                LDY     #!0
                LDX     #!200
        ALPHA   LDA     T−!2,X
                CMP     J
                BNE     BETA
                LDA     T−!1,X
                CMP     J+!1
                BNE     BETA
                INY
        BETA    DEX
                DEX
                BNE     ALPHA
                STY     NEQUAL
```

*(a) Specify the changes to instructions in this program if immediate data modification is used for the two bytes of J. Call these two bytes JUPPER and JLOWER, and define each of them by EQU. (See the hint to exercise 1(a), section 74.)

*(b) How many cycles (maximum and minimum), and how many bytes, are saved if this is done? Show your work.

(c) How many cycles (maximum and minimum), and how many bytes, would be saved if the two bytes of J were kept in page zero (and address modification is *not* used)? Show your work.

2. *(a) Specify the changes to instructions in the subroutine DIV of section 40 if immediate data modification is used for DDATA1 and DDATA2.

(b) How many bytes, and how many cycles (maximum only), are saved if this is done? How does this compare with the savings when DDATA1 and DDATA2 are kept in page zero, as in exercise 1(b) of section 74?

*3. Of the various data bytes in the input and output conversion programs of sections 62 and 63, there is *one* (other than those in the tables at DECO5 and DECO6) which *cannot* be implemented with immediate data modification. Which one is it, and why?

PROBLEM 4 FOR COMPUTER SOLUTION
MULTI-PRECISION MULTIPLICATION

Write a program which accepts, as input, two unsigned integers of *arbitrary* length, typed in on one line each, and produces, as output, the result of multiplying them.

Your program should have two arrays (call them M1 and M2) for the digits of the two numbers to be multiplied, and another array (call it M3) for the product. It should store one decimal digit of each number (the decimal digit itself, *not* the character code for this decimal digit) in one byte of the corresponding array. It should use a method similar to the one we are all familiar with from grade school, to multiply these numbers. When you multiply two digits, you get a two-digit number; you carry the first digit and bring down the second one. (Do *not* use MULT from the text. Either use repeated addition—3 × 8 is 8+8+8, for example—or else construct some tables first and then use table lookup.)

As before, use GETLNZ to input each of the numbers to be multiplied, and make sure that you remember about GETLNZ using the A, X, and Y registers for its own purposes. Print out the product after you are done, and then go back to read another pair of numbers.

81. RELATIVE ADDRESS MODIFICATION

Relative addresses, as well as immediate data, can be modified. One use we can make of this is to implement the *computed GO TO statement* of FORTRAN, or the ON . . . GOTO statement of BASIC. Thus, for example, either of the two statements

```
ON K GOTO 11, 12, 13, 14, 15        (BASIC)
GO TO (11, 12, 13, 14, 15), K       (FORTRAN)
```

goes to 11 if K = 1, to 12 if K = 2, to 13 if K = 3, to 14 if K = 4, and to 15 if K = 5.

Suppose now that K is in the X register, and that the labels 11, 12, 13, 14, and 15 are represented, in assembly language, by L11, L12, L13, L14, and L15, respectively. Then we might write

```
DEX             ; IF K = 1,
BEQ    L11      ;   GO TO L11
DEX             ; IF K = 2,
BEQ    L12      ;   GO TO L12
DEX             ; IF K = 3,
BEQ    L13      ;   GO TO L13
DEX             ; IF K = 4, GO TO
BEQ    L14      ;   L14, OTHERWISE
BNE    L15      ;   GO TO L15
```

This takes 14 bytes* and either 5, 9, 13, 17, or 19 cycles, depending on the value of K, with 12.6 cycles as the average. (Of course, we are assuming here that K actually is between 1 and 5.)

Now let us see how we can improve this by using a modified relative address, in an instruction called MODREL, of the form

```
MODREL    BNE    *
```

---

*Note the use of BNE (which always branches, here), rather than JMP (see section 27). If JMP were used, this sequence would take 15 bytes.

which will be modified into a branch to any of L11, L12, L13, L14, and L15; and all the relative addresses needed here are kept in a table. Let the instruction immediately following MODREL have the label MODR1; then MODR1$+r = b$, where r is the relative address corresponding to the branch address b, and this implies that $r = b-$MODR1. Our table of relative addresses may therefore be defined by

```
RELADS    BYT    L11 − MODR1
          BYT    L12 − MODR1
          BYT    L13 − MODR1
          BYT    L14 − MODR1
          BYT    L15 − MODR1
```

Our computed GO TO statement may now be implemented as follows, under the same assumptions as before:

```
          LDA    RELADS−!1,X    ;  LOAD RELATIVE ADDRESS FROM
          STA    MODREL+!1      ;   TABLE AND STORE IT
MODREL    BNE    *              ;  GO TO MODIFIED ADDRESS
MODR1     (next instruction)
```

Note that we can't use JMP for the modified address, because JMP takes an ordinary, 16-bit address. We have to use a conditional branch; but what happens if the condition is not satisfied? The use of BNE solves our problems quite nicely. Let us suppose, for example, that K is 3. We load RELADS+2 (that is, RELADS$-1+3$) into the A register. This is L13$-$MODR1, and it is presumably not zero, so that, after we store this number (call it r) in the second byte of MODREL, the BNE actually branches; and, by the rules of relative addressing, it branches to MODR1$+r = $ MODR1$+($L13$-$MODR1$) = $ L13, which is where we want to go.

(What is delightful about this trick is that it works even if the BNE does not branch. This will happen only if the relative address is zero; but, by the rules of relative addressing, such a BNE *would go to the next instruction anyway*—even if it did branch. This is quite common, in fact, since L11, for example, could follow MODREL immediately. In this case, the label MODR1 should appear on a line by itself. In LISA this is done by writing a *colon* after the label; thus MODR1: is written in this case.)

The implementation above takes 13 bytes, eight for the instructions and five for the table. It takes 11 cycles, or 10 if the BNE does not branch, as noted above. Hence this is a better implementation of the computed GO TO with respect to both space and time. In general, if there are five or more branch instructions in a computed GO TO, both space and time are saved by relative address modification.

Of course, we have to make sure that the calculated relative addresses are all in the proper range (from -128 to 127). If this is not the case, one can branch to a jump (JMP) instruction, which has an arbitrary 16-bit jump address. It should also be mentioned that the computed GO TO may also be implemented by using an indirect address, taken from a jump table; this, however, would require *two* bytes, rather than just one, to be stored. Still another alternative involves *pushing* this two-byte address, and then using RTS to pull it and jump to it.

EXERCISES

*1. We have noted above that the relative address modification program of this section takes 10 or 11 cycles, as opposed to an average of 12.6 cycles for the alternative. Can you think of any circumstances under which this is *not*, in fact, an improvement? How common would you expect those circumstances to be, in practice?

2. Suppose that all the branches, in the program of this section, go *forward*. Under these circumstances, is there another conditional branch instruction which could be used instead of BNE? If so, is it an improvement over BNE? Why or why not?

3. Consider the following program, which uses relative address modification:

```
              STX     BRANCH+ ! 1
              LDA     Q
    BRANCH    BNE     *
              LSR
              LSR
              LSR
              LSR
              LSR
              LSR
              LSR
              STA     Q
```

*(a) Explain in words what this does. Assume that the X register contains an integer from 0 through 7.
(b) What happens if the BNE does not branch? Is what happens in this case "correct" in some sense?
*(c) How much time does this algorithm take, for each value of X from 0 through 7, if the BNE does in fact branch? Show your work.

82. ARRAYS OF STRINGS

It is quite common for a program to work with a large number of character strings, which are kept in an array. These might be names and addresses of people; or, possibly, names and addresses (in the technical sense) of variables in a program.

If all the strings in an array have the same length, then we can use techniques we have already learned. For example, if every string is three characters long, we have an array of three-byte quantities, like the arrays of two-byte quantities that we studied in section 32. Most of the time, however, this will not be the case. Names tend to have widely varying lengths, whether they are the names of people or of program variables.

In general, *an array of strings is a long array.* Even if there are fewer than 256 strings, and even if no string has a length greater than 256, it is quite unlikely that the total number of characters in *all* the strings can be restricted, in real applications, to be not greater than 256.

Suppose that we keep all our strings in sequential order, and precede each string by its length, as follows:

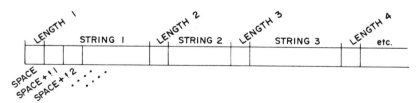

in an array called SPACE. Suppose that we have another array called T, such that T(J) contains some information that we are keeping about string J. (To make things easier, we will assume that T is an ordinary, short array of bytes.)

Let us now consider the process of searching through all these strings, to find one which is the same as another string called NAME which is kept in the same way—that is, preceded by its length. At the end of this process, if N is equal to string J, we wish to leave J in the X register. This will make it easy, for example, to look at the associated information T(J).

We will use post-indexed indirect addressing, and keep the address of the *beginning* of the current string in the two zero-page locations ZP and ZP + !1. The instructions LDA (ZP),Y and CMP NAME,Y will then serve to compare one character of the current string with one character of the string called NAME. Here Y starts at the length of NAME and decreases to zero. (If the length of the current string is not the same as the length of NAME, the strings *cannot* be equal, and we do not even bother comparing them.)

If the strings are not the same, then we add the length of the current string, *plus one* (because of the length byte), to the two-byte quantity in ZP and ZP + !1. This will set these two locations to the address of the beginning of the next string. We are always looking at string J, where J is in the X register; and, every time through the loop, we compare the X register with NSTR, the total number of strings. If they are equal, then NAME is not in our array of strings, because these range from string zero through string NSTR−1. In this case we can put NAME into the array, if we want to, and update NSTR.

At the beginning of the program, we must put the address of the array SPACE into the zero-page locations, so as to initialize them for treatment of string zero. The resulting program is shown in Figure 27. Note that we are using a new kind of loop here, in which the comparison (with CPX) takes place at the *beginning* of the loop. This has the consequence that, if NSTR is zero, the loop is not done at all. (In most loops, the loop is done once, even if the loop count is zero.) The program jumps to FOUND if the given string is found, and to NOTF otherwise; if it jumps to FOUND, then NAME is equal to string J, where J is in the X register.

Suppose now that we wished to find the J-th string, where J has just been calculated. Using the method described above, we would have to look through all strings from the first through the J-th, and this takes quite a bit of time. For this reason, our method should be used only when we look through our strings in order (string 1, string 2, and so on). Another more general method of keeping arrays of strings is discussed in section 85.

EXERCISES

1. Specify the changes to the program of Figure 27 if, instead of a maximum number of strings called NSTR, we keep an extra zero-byte after the end of the last string. (To the program, this looks like another length byte, except that it is zero.)

*2. Specify the changes to the program of Figure 27 if there is another array, called LB, which contains all the length bytes. (Thus LB(J) is the length of the J-th string, and this length byte is *not* contained in the array called SPACE.) Note that ZP and ZP+!1 should contain the address of the byte

before the first byte of the current string, just as before, even though this
is no longer a length byte. (Assume that the string NAME is still preceded
by its own length byte.)

3. Specify the changes to the program of Figure 27 if there are no length
bytes; instead, each string is terminated by a zero-byte. (Note that this
does *not* resemble the zero-byte of exercise 1 above; NSTR is still
required.) You may assume that the place in the program where "we are
done—NAME is string J" has the label DONE. This time, assume that
NAME is *not* preceded by a length byte; and keep the address of the *first
byte* of the current string (rather than this address minus 1) in ZP and
ZP+!1 and move *forward*, rather than backward, through NAME during
the comparison. (Start the loop at ALPHA with INY.)

```
        LDX   #$FF       ; SET STRING INDEX TO −1
        LDA   /SPACE     ; SET THE ZERO-PAGE LOCATIONS
        STA   ZP+!1      ;   ZP and ZP+!1 TO BE THE
        LDA   #SPACE     ;   ADDRESS OF STRING ZERO
        STA   ZP         ;   (THE FIRST ADDRESS OF SPACE)
LOOP    INX              ; INCREASE THE STRING INDEX
        CPX   NSTR       ; IF EQUAL TO THE TOTAL NUMBER
        BEQ   NOTF       ;   OF STRINGS, GO TO NOT-FOUND
        LDY   #!0        ; GET THE LENGTH OF THIS STRING
        LDA   (ZP),Y     ;   (NEED Y=0 FOR THIS INSTR.)
        CMP   NAME       ; IF UNEQUAL TO THE LENGTH OF
        BNE   PROC1      ;   NAME, STRINGS CANNOT BE =
        TAY              ; INITIALIZE Y TO STRING LENGTH
ALPHA   LDA   (ZP),Y     ; COMPARE A CHARACTER OF STRING
        CMP   NAME,Y     ;   X WITH A CHARACTER OF NAME
        BNE   PROC       ; IF NOT =, STRINGS ARE NOT =
        DEY              ; IF =, PROCEED TO NEXT CHAR.
        BNE   ALPHA      ; ARE THERE ANY MORE CHARACTERS
        BEQ   FOUND      ; IF NOT, STRING HAS BEEN FOUND
PROC    LDY   #!0        ; RELOAD LENGTH OF STRING X
        LDA   (ZP),Y     ;   (NEED Y=0, JUST AS ABOVE)
PROC1   CLC              ; ADD 1 TO LENGTH OF STRING X
        ADC   #!1        ;   (TO PASS OVER LENGTH BYTE)
        ADC   ZP         ; ADD TO ADDRESS IN ZP AND
        STA   ZP         ;   ZP+!1, SO THIS BECOMES THE
        BCC   LOOP       ;   STARTING ADDRESS OF THE NEXT
        INC   ZP+!1      ;   STRING IN THE ARRAY −− THEN
        BCS   LOOP       ;   BRANCH BACK TO LOOP
```

Figure 27. A Program to Search an Array of Strings.

83. ARRAYS OF HEXADECIMAL DIGITS

In section 32, we considered arrays of quantities, each of which is two bytes long. We can also consider arrays of quantities, each of which is *half* a byte long. Half a byte is sometimes called a *nybble*. (Half a bite of food is called a nibble of food.) A nybble, then, is four bits, or one hexadecimal digit (or one *decimal* digit in a packed string, as in section 66).

If we have an array of nybbles, then storing each nybble in a separate byte wastes a considerable amount of space. If we have *two* arrays, T1 and T2, of hexadecimal digits, we can keep T1(J) in the first four bits of T(J), and T2(J) in the second four bits of T(J), for an array T of bytes. The elements T1(J) and T2(J) may then be obtained by shifting and masking. In what follows, however, we will assume that we have *one* array of hexadecimal digits, two of which are kept in each byte.

Suppose that H1 is such an array. Byte 0 of H1 contains H1(0) and H1(1); byte 1 of H1 contains H1(2) and H1(3); and so on, as in Figure 28. In general, byte k of H1 contains H1($2k$) (in its first four bits) and H1($2k+1$) (in its second four bits).

BYTE 0	H1(0)	H1(1)
BYTE 1	H1(2)	H1(3)
BYTE 2	H1(4)	H1(5)
	$\vdots$	$\vdots$
BYTE k	H1($2k$)	H1($2k+1$)
	$\vdots$	$\vdots$

Figure 28. A Serial Array of Hexadecimal Digits.

Now suppose that the A register contains J, and that we want to load H1(J). We saw in section 32 that we would have to multiply J by 2 first if we had an array of two-byte quantities. For an array of nybbles, we have to *divide* J by 2 first. Moreover, we have to have some way of knowing whether to look at the first four bits of the resulting byte, or at the second four bits.

Fortunately, we can do this efficiently because LSR not only divides the A register by 2 but also shifts its rightmost bit into the carry flag, as we saw in section 31. Note that the rightmost bit of any integer indicates whether it is even or odd. Thus H1(J) may be loaded, under these conditions, as follows:

```
          LSR                      ; DIVIDE J BY 2
          TAY                      ; LOAD BYTE CONTAINING H1(J)
          LDA    H1,Y              ;   AND PRESERVE THE CARRY FLAG
          BCC    ALPHA             ; LEFT OR RIGHT HAND 4 BITS
          AND    #%00001111        ; RIGHT HAND 4 BITS (CARRY IS
          BCS    BETA              ;   SET SO THIS ALWAYS JUMPS)
ALPHA     LSR                      ; LEFT HAND 4 BITS - -
          LSR                      ;   MOVE THESE TO RIGHT
          LSR                      ;   (CLEARS LEFT HAND 4
          LSR                      ;   BITS AT THE SAME TIME)
BETA      (next instruction)
```

Like any array, an array of hexadecimal digits is most commonly processed in order from beginning to end. The following subroutine stores a hexadecimal digit in such an array and advances to the next one, so that it can be called *n* times to store the digits H2(0) through H2(*n*−1) in that order. The subroutine keeps a byte index into the array H2 in the Y register, and it also keeps a flag, called HFLAG; if this is zero, the next nybble is stored in the left-hand four bits of the next byte, while if it is equal to −1, the next nybble is stored in the right-hand four bits:

```
HSTORE    INC    HFLAG            ; ADD 1 TO HFLAG - -  IF IT
          BNE    HST1             ;   WAS -1, IT IS NOW ZERO
          ORA    H2,Y             ; INSERT LEFT HAND 4 BITS
          STA    H2,Y             ; STORE IN CURRENT BYTE
          RTS                     ;   AND QUIT
HST1      ASL                     ; SHIFT LEFT HAND 4 BITS
          ASL                     ;   TO LEFT, AND
          ASL                     ;   STORE THEM IN
          ASL                     ;   THE FOLLOWING BYTE
          INY                     ;   (INCREASE BYTE INDEX,
          STA    H2,Y             ;   THEN STORE)
          LDA    #$FF             ; PUT -1 BACK IN HFLAG FOR
          STA    HFLAG            ;   NEXT TIME HSTORE IS CALLED
          RTS                     ;   AND QUIT
```

Here HFLAG and the Y register must be initialized, as by

```
LDY    # ! 0         ;  STARTING VALUE OF THE
STY    HFLAG         ;    INDICATOR IS ZERO,
DEY                  ;    AND THAT OF Y IS −1
```

An alternative way of keeping a flag like HFLAG is by using its *rightmost bit only*. The flag can now be changed from zero to one, *or vice versa*, with the single instruction INC HFLAG (or DEC HFLAG); it may be tested by shifting it into the carry flag (with LDA HFLAG and LSR) and then doing a BCC or BCS.

The APPLE monitor has three subroutines for printing nybbles: JSR PRHEX prints one nybble (the right-hand nybble) from the A register; JSR PRBYTE prints two nybbles from the A register; and JSR PRNTAX prints four nybbles, two from the A register and then two more from the X register. These may be declared in a LISA program by

```
PRHEX     EQU     $FDE3
PRBYTE    EQU     $FDDA
PRNTAX    EQU     $F941
```

EXERCISES

*1. Specify the changes to HSTORE which would be made if HEX2 were a long array. Use address modification; remember that both STA instructions, as well as ORA, must have modified addresses. (Hint: First determine *at what point*, in the program, the address modification must take place.)

2. The letters E, T, A, O, I, N, S, H, R, D, L, and U are the 12 most common letters in English words. Suppose that we have a file composed entirely of words (such as a word processing file). We may decrease the amount of space necessary to keep this file by translating it into a nybble code. In this code, the blank corresponds to the nybble 0; each of the 12 letters above corresponds to one of the nybbles 1 through 12; and any other character that may occur in the file corresponds to one of the nybbles 13, 14, or 15, followed by a further nybble which denotes the specific character involved. (Note that there are 61 legal codes: 0 through 12; 13-0 through 13-15; 14-0 through 14-15; and 15-0 through 15-15.) Describe, in words, the operation of a program to translate a file into this form. Assume that the file is contained entirely in memory, as an array C, starting with C(1), and that the new file is also entirely in memory, and is formed by using the subroutine HSTORE of this section. Also assume that the original file ends with a zero-byte, and that, in the new form, it

ends with the code 15-15. Specify explicitly all calls to HSTORE and to the initialization of HSTORE.

*3. Write a subroutine, using PRBYT, which is equivalent to PRNTAX. Try to use as few instructions as possible. (Hint: see the end of section 61. Note that PRBYT does not use the X register.)

84. SORTING

The word "sorting" has a very specific meaning in computing. To sort means to put a collection of data in some order; normally, *ascending order*, from the smallest to the largest.

Suppose we have a collection of numbers: 212, 312, 213, 202, 415, 617, 305. These are kept in an array T, with T(1) = 212 and T(7) = 305. We wish to arrange them into ascending order: 202, 212, 213, 305, 312, 415, 617. In this order, they can go in another array U, with U(1) = 202 and U(7) = 617. Or we can have an *in-place sort*, in which case the data go back in the array T, with T(1) = 202 and T(7) = 617.

The easiest way to do in-place sorting is as follows. Go through T and look at *pairs* of adjacent numbers: T(1) and T(2), then T(2) and T(3), and so on, up through T(6) and T(7), in this case. For each pair, if the numbers in the pair are *in order*—that is, $T(J) \le T(J+1)$—leave them there. Otherwise, *interchange* them; that is, set T(J) = T(J+1) and vice versa.

When you have finished one *pass* through the array (starting with T(1) and T(2), and ending with T(N−1) and T(N), where N = 7 in this case), go back and do another pass. Keep doing passes until you can go through one whole pass without making any interchanges; that is, each pair, T(J) and T(J+1), is in order. At that point, you are done.

In BASIC, this might be done as follows:

```
10      J = 1
20      K = 0
30      IF T(J) <= T(J+1) THEN 80
40      Z = T(J)
50      T(J) = T(J+1)
60      T(J+1) = Z
70      K = 1
80      J = J+1
90      IF J <> N THEN 30
100     IF K <> 0 THEN 10
```

The variable K is a *flag*. Every time we do an interchange (lines 40 through 60), we set K = 1 (line 70). At the beginning of every pass, we set K = 0 (line 20). If we can get through a whole pass without doing an interchange, then K will still be zero (line 100).

The variable Z is used because we cannot just set $T(J) = T(J+1)$, and $T(J+1) = T(J)$, in order to do an interchange. If we did that, we would give $T(J)$ and $T(J+1)$ the same value, when we want them to have each other's values.

The test at line 90 is peculiar because it skips the last case on purpose. That is, J is equal to 1, 2, 3, and so on up through $N-1$, but J is never equal to N. This is because, when $J = N-1$, we are comparing $T(J)$ and $T(J+1)$; that is, $T(N-1)$ and $T(N)$. This is the last comparison to be made.

The same sorting program, done on a serial array T of two-byte quantities (which would be necessary to keep a number as large as 617), is shown in Figure 29. Note that the flag K is now either zero (meaning "no interchanges"), or non-zero, and that it is set to a non-zero value by adding 1 to it. The variable J has been assigned to the X register (actually, 2J is kept in X, and ranges from 2 to 2N). The variable Z, in the BASIC program, is not needed in the LISA program, since we can interchange two quantities by using two registers (as we noted first in section 8). Note the offsets carefully; since T starts from $T(1)$, the element $T(J)$ is accessed by $T-!2,X$ (lower half) and $T-!1,X$ (upper half) if 2J is in the X register. The element $T(J+1)$ is then accessed by T,X (lower half) and $T+!1,X$ (upper half), under these same conditions.

A flag like K, meaning "there has been an interchange" if it is *not* equal to zero, is called a *logical flag*, and is said to be *true* if it is non-zero and *false* if it is zero. LISA allows you to use BFL (Branch on False) instead of BEQ, and BTR (Branch on True) instead of BNE, if you so desire. In particular, we could replace BNE ALPHA by BTR ALPHA as the final instruction in Figure 29.

EXERCISES

1. The way in which K is used as a flag in Figure 29 is open to the objection that it is possible to set K to zero by adding 1 to it (if it is equal to 255). However, in the program of Figure 29, this can never happen. Why not?

*2. In the BASIC program of this section, why is the test made for $T(J) \le T(J+1)$, rather than $T(J) < T(J+1)$? (Hint: Consider a very simple case, with $N = 2$ and $T(1) = T(2)$, and walk it through.)

3. Specify the changes to Figure 29 if immediate data modification is used. How many bytes are saved if this is done? (Hint: Clearly the variables in the array T cannot be treated as immediate data. What other variables in this program can be so treated?)

```
                LDA   N         ; CALCULATE 2*N (SERIAL ARRAY
                ASL             ;   OF N TWO-BYTE QUANTITIES
                STA   TWON      ;   IS 2*N BYTES LONG)
ALPHA           LDX   #!0       ; STARTING FLAG VALUE IS ZERO
                STX   K         ; STARTING INDEX VALUE IS 2
                LDX   #!2       ;   (THAT IS, 2*J, WHERE J = 1)
BETA            LDA   T+!1,X    ; COMPARE T(J+1) WITH T(J)
                CMP   T-!1,X    ;   WHERE 2*J IS IN X REGISTER
                BNE   DECIDE    ;   COUNTING ELEMENTS OF T FROM
                LDA   T,X       ;   T(1) THROUGH T(N). IF T(J+1)
                CMP   T-!2,X    ;   IS GREATER OR EQUAL (T(J)
DECIDE          BCS   GAMMA     ;   LESS OR EQUAL), SKIP AHEAD
                LDA   T,X       ; NOTE THIS MUST BE REDONE IF WE
                LDY   T-!2,X    ;   TOOK THE BCS BRANCH ABOVE.
                STA   T-!2,X    ;   HERE WE INTERCHANGE, LOWER
                TYA             ;   HALVES FIRST (NOTE THAT Z
                STA   T,X       ;   IS NOT NEEDED).
                LDA   T-!1,X    ; NOW DO THE UPPER HALVES. NOTE
                LDY   T+!1,X    ;   THAT WE CAN LOAD Y, INDEXED,
                STA   T+!1,X    ;   BUT NOT STORE Y, INDEXED (EX-
                TYA             ;   CEPT IN PAGE ZERO), SO INSTEAD
                STA   T-!1,X    ;   WE -TYA- AND STORE A, INDEXED.
                INC   K         ; SET THE FLAG (TO NON-ZERO)
GAMMA           INX             ; ADD 2 TO THE INDEX (FOR THE
                INX             ;   NEXT TWO-BYTE QUANTITY)
                CPX   TWON      ; IF 2*J <> 2*N (I. E., J <> N),
                BNE   BETA      ;   THEN DO THE NEXT PAIR
                LDA   K         ; IF K <> 0 (THERE HAVE BEEN IN-
                BNE   ALPHA     ;   TERCHANGES), DO ANOTHER PASS
```

Figure 29. Sorting an Array of Two-Byte Quantities.

85. ALPHABETIZING

Alphabetizing a list of names may be thought of as a variation of sorting.

To make this easier to see, suppose that the two-byte quantities which were sorted in Figure 29 are thought of as two-*character* quantities. Notice that we start by comparing the bytes at the left. If these are unequal, then this is the only comparison we make. If they are equal, then we compare the bytes at the right.

This, however, is exactly how we would compare two-character quantities with respect to *alphabetical* order. Consider, for example, the quantities ME, OH, and MY. When comparing ME and OH, we compare only the M and the O; the M comes first, so ME comes before OH. The same thing happens when comparing MY and OH (even though H comes before Y). When comparing ME and MY, the M's are the same, and so we compare E and Y. Since E comes first, ME comes before MY.

Even the comparison of the individual character codes corresponds to alphabetical order. For example, E comes before Y, and we can test this by noting that the character code for Y is D9 (hexadecimal), and the character code for E is C5, which is *less* than D9.*

Comparing two strings which are more than two characters long is now an extension of this idea. We compare the first characters, then the second characters, then the third characters, and so on, of the two strings. As soon as we get to a pair of characters which are not equal, then we base our decision on those two characters. Thus with the words LEONINE and LEOPARD, we base our decision on the fourth characters, N and P, of the two words. Since N comes before P, LEONINE comes before LEOPARD.

Special care must be taken if the two strings have different lengths. You must compare *m* characters, where *m* is the *smaller* of the two lengths. If these characters are all equal, then the *shorter* string always comes first. Thus with BOUGH and BOUGHT, BOUGH comes first, after the first five characters of

---

*This is true whether a signed or an unsigned comparison is made, since the leftmost bits of the character codes of *all* the alphabetic characters are the same—an important property of the ASCII character code.

the two strings have been compared. Similarly with IRANIAN and IRAN, IRAN comes first.

Let us now consider the alphabetizing process as a variation on the BASIC program of the preceding section. *The only line that has to be changed is line number 30*; this should be changed to some equivalent of the following: "If T(J) precedes T(J+1) in alphabetical order, or if T(J) = T(J+1), go to 80." The rest of the logic of this BASIC program is exactly the same as before.

In the assembly language program of Figure 29, this means that the six statements from BETA to DECIDE, which correspond to line number 30 of the BASIC program, should be changed to the sequence of Figure 30. A number of special tricks, used in this sequence, need to be explained.

The basic idea is to use an *address table*. We still have a serial array T of two-byte quantities, as in Figure 29; but, this time, the two-byte quantities are the *addresses* of strings. The strings themselves are kept as in section 82, but we never interchange the characters in the strings—only the addresses. At the end of the program, we will have a table of addresses of strings in ascending order.

```
           LDA    T, X          ; USE ADDRESSES IN ADDRESS
           STA    ZP1           ;   TABLES, FOR T(J) AND
           LDA    T+!1, X       ;   T(J+1), TO SET UP THE
           STA    ZP1+!1        ;   ZERO PAGE LOCATIONS,
           LDA    T+!2, X       ;   ZP1 AND ZP2, WHICH WILL
           STA    ZP2           ;   THEN CONTAIN THE STARTING
           LDA    T+!3, X       ;   ADDRESSES OF THE TWO
           STA    ZP2+!1        ;   STRINGS TO BE COMPARED.
           LDY    #!0           ; START WITH LENGTH BYTES
           LDA    (ZP2), Y      ; COMPARE THE TWO LENGTH
           CMP    (ZP1), Y      ;   BYTES TO GET THE SMALLER
           BCC    SMALR         ;   AND PUT IT IN A-REGISTER
           LDA    (ZP1), Y      ; RECORD IF THE SECOND WAS
SMALR      ROR    LFLAG         ;   SHORTER (LFLAG SIGN = 0)
           TAX                  ; MINIMUM LENGTH TO X
CCHAR      INY                  ; MOVE TO NEXT CHARACTER
           LDA    (ZP2), Y      ; COMPARE ONE CHARACTER OF
           CMP    (ZP1), Y      ;   EACH STRING. IF THEY ARE
           BNE    DECIDE        ;   UNEQUAL, READY TO DECIDE
           DEX                  ; DO THIS M TIMES, WHERE
           BNE    CCHAR         ;   M IS THE MINIMUM LENGTH
           LDA    LFLAG         ; IF SECOND WAS SHORTER, IT IS
           BPL    EXCH          ;   LESS, SO OUT OF ORDER
DECIDE     BCS    GAMMA         ; IF SECOND >=, NOT OUT OF ORDER
EXCH       (next instruction)
```

Figure 30. Alphabetizing an Array of Strings.

(The *addresses* themselves will not be in ascending order; rather, the first address, at T and T+!1, will be the address of the string that comes first, alphabetically, and so on.)

Two zero-page locations, ZP1 and ZP2 (each two bytes long), are used. The first step is to compare the lengths of the two strings, and the smaller length is put in the X register, as the loop count. At the same time, *we save the carry flag* (from the compare) in the sign of LFLAG. This is done by rotating LFLAG to the right, which rotates the carry flag into the leftmost bit of LFLAG.

Now we compare M characters, where M is the loop count as above. If these are not all equal, we can make a decision at DECIDE, just as before. If they are all equal (correspondingly), we have three cases:

(1) The lengths of the two strings were equal. In that case the two strings are equal, and we want to go to GAMMA.
(2) The first string was shorter. In that case the first string precedes the second one; so the two strings are in order, and again we want to go to GAMMA.
(3) The second string was shorter. Note that this is the case in which the carry flag that was saved, above, will be zero (in the other two cases, it will be 1). In that case the second string precedes the first one; so the two strings are out of order, and we want to do an exchange. Thus, at this point, we go to EXCH (that is, we exchange) if LFLAG is *positive or zero*; that is, if its sign flag (the saved carry flag) is zero.

EXERCISES

1. Just before CCHAR in Figure 30, after we have calculated the minimum length, there is a TAX. Why don't we just calculate the minimum in the X register, using LDX and CPX instead of LDA and CMP?

2. Instead of ROR LFLAG, why can't we just use PHP (saving the entire P register, including the carry flag) and then, later on, PLP (which restores the P register) and BCC EXCH, instead of LDA LFLAG and BPL EXCH?

3. Suppose that, in the four instructions just preceding SMALR in Figure 30, we changed the ZP2 to a ZP1, and the two instances of ZP1 to ZP2.

   *(a) Would the same quantity be calculated at SMALR?
   *(b) What problem would arise later, just before DECIDE?

86. SEARCHING A SORTED ARRAY

An important reason for keeping arrays sorted is that searching is speeded up by a considerable amount, especially when the arrays are large. We shall now show how to perform this fast searching on the 6502, using the idea of *binary search* which we discussed briefly in section 49.

We will assume that we are looking for some quantity V in an array called T, with indices from T(1) through T(N), where N is a variable. The basic idea of this search is to keep dividing the table in half. At every stage, we are looking at only a part of the table, which is T(FIRST) through T(LAST). Initially, this is the whole table, so that FIRST is 1 and LAST is N.

The table is divided in half by taking the average of FIRST and LAST; we may call this average MIDDLE. We now see if V is in the first part of the table, from T(FIRST) through T(MIDDLE). We do this by testing whether V is greater than T(MIDDLE); if it is, then, *because the table is sorted*, V must be in the second part of the table (from T(MIDDLE+1) through T(LAST)), if it is in the table at all. Otherwise, it is in the first half of the table.

In either case, FIRST and LAST must be updated. If V belongs in the first part of the table, from T(FIRST) through T(MIDDLE), then MIDDLE becomes the new LAST, and FIRST stays the same. If V belongs in the second part of the table, from T(MIDDLE+1) through T(LAST), then MIDDLE+1 becomes the new FIRST, and LAST stays the same.

We keep dividing the table in half, in this way, until the size of the table has been reduced to 1. When this happens, FIRST and LAST will be equal. At this point, V is either equal to T(FIRST), or it is not in the table at all.

A program to perform this search on the 6502, assuming that T is a table of unsigned 8-bit quantities, is given in Figure 31. Since the array T starts with T(1), offsets are used as in section 23, and T−!1,X rather than T,X appears when reference is made to the X-th element of T. The program has two exits; if V is not in the table, the program exits to L4, while if V is in the table, the program exits to L5 with the table index in the X register.

Calculating the average of FIRST and LAST involves a trick which is quite useful whenever an average must be calculated. Of course, we add FIRST and LAST, and then divide by 2, using a shift. The problem is that FIRST+LAST might be greater than 255; if it is, then the carry flag will be set, while otherwise this flag will be cleared. The trick is to divide by 2 using ROR instead of LSR. This shifts the carry flag into the leftmost bit of the A register, which, in this case, is exactly what we need.

We test V greater than T(MIDDLE) by testing T(MIDDLE) less than V, using the carry flag, as suggested in section 28. This program may be easily adapted to searching two parallel arrays S and T for a 16-bit quantity in V and $V+!1$, by changing the two comparisons to 16-bit comparisons as indicated in section 29; that is, immediately following the TAX, we write

```
LDA   S-!1,X      ;  COMPARE T(MIDDLE)
CMP   V+!1        ;  WITH V  - -
BNE   DECIDE      ;  UPPER HALVES FIRST
```

(where DECIDE is the BCC, as in section 29); and immediately following the LDX, we write

```
LDA   S-!1,X      ;  COMPARE T(FIRST)
CMP   V+!1        ;  WITH V  - -
BNE   L4          ;  UPPER HALVES FIRST
```

The loop is executed n times for a table of size 2^n. For a table of size k, the number of times that the loop is executed is *the logarithm of k to the base 2*, rounded up to the nearest integer; if this number is n, then $2^{n-1} < k \leq 2^n$, by the fundamental properties of logarithms. (In your further study of computer science you will quite often encounter logarithms to the base 2; for example, there are methods of sorting n numbers in $n \log_2 n$ steps. See also the table of logarithms in the exercises to section 49.) It is remarkable that this particular loop takes 42 cycles, regardless of whether the BCC goes to L2 or not, and provided the BNE actually branches back to L1. For a table of size 2^n, the total number of cycles is in fact $42n+27$, plus one extra cycle if V is actually in the table.

We may note that the line L1 LDA FIRST may actually be eliminated from this program (and the label L1 moved down to the CLC), reducing the cycle time above to $38n+27$. This is because FIRST is already in the A register, whether we enter from STA FIRST or from BNE L1, since LDA FIRST appears just before BNE L1. Further improvements in the program are suggested in the exercises.

Searching sorted tables in this way works well when the tables are *constant*. When a table changes during the run of a program, particularly when it is constructed as the program proceeds, this method is not necessarily as good, because keeping a table sorted while it is growing is a time-consuming process.

```
            LDA   N         ;  SET  INITIAL  VALUE
            STA   LAST      ;    OF  LAST
            LDA   #!1       ;  SET  INITIAL  VALUE
            STA   FIRST     ;    OF  FIRST
    L1      LDA   FIRST     ;  TAKE  AVERAGE  OF  FIRST
            CLC             ;    AND  LAST  BY  COMPUTING
            ADC   LAST      ;    (FIRST+LAST)/2  = MIDDLE
            ROR             ;  SHIFT  IN  CARRY  (IF
            TAX             ;    MIDDLE  >  127)  - -  TO  X
            LDA   T-!1,X    ;  IS  T  (MIDDLE)  <  V  - -  IF
            CMP   V         ;    SO,  V  BELONGS  IN
            BCC   L2        ;    SECOND  HALF  OF  TABLE
            STX   LAST      ;  FIRST  HALF  OF  TABLE,  SO
            BCS   L3        ;    UPDATE  LAST  AND  BRANCH
    L2      INX             ;  SECOND  HALF  OF  TABLE,  SO
            STX   FIRST     ;    UPDATE  FIRST
    L3      LDA   FIRST     ;  DO  ALL  THIS  AGAIN  UNLESS
            CMP   LAST      ;    TABLE  SIZE  IS  NOW  1  - -
            BNE   L1        ;    THAT  IS,  FIRST  = LAST
            LDX   FIRST     ;  IS  T  (FIRST)  = V  - -  IF
            LDA   T-!1,X    ;    NOT,  THEN  V  IS  NOT  IN
            CMP   V         ;    THE  TABLE  AT  ALL.  IF  SO,
            BEQ   L5        ;    THEN  ITS  INDEX  IS  IN  X
    L4      (not  found)
            . . . . . . . . . . .
    L5      (found,  index  in  x)
```

Figure 31. A Program to Search a Sorted Array.

EXERCISES

*1. Consider the instruction at L3 in the program of Figure 31. Can this be replaced by TXA? Explain.

2. In the program of Figure 31, can the label L1 be placed on the ADC instruction? Why or why not?

*3. In the program of Figure 31, can the LDX FIRST be eliminated? Why or why not?

87. TWO-DIMENSIONAL ARRAYS

In many versions of BASIC, we can use array elements such as T(I,J), if we have declared T by a DIM T(m,n) statement for some integers m and n. The same is true in FORTRAN, although DIM is replaced here by the word DIMENSION (or INTEGER, REAL, or the like). An array such as T is called a *two-dimensional array*.

If we have an m-by-n two-dimensional array, as above, then mn is the total number of elements in the array. In assembly language, we reserve this many elements, by means of DFS, just as with one-dimensional arrays. For example, for a 10-by-15 array T of single-byte quantities, we would write T DFS !150 (since $150 = 10 \times 15$).

There is now a problem, however, as to how to make reference to T(I,J). We cannot put I in the X register and J in the Y register, for example; we have to calculate a single quantity, and put it in either X or Y. What is this quantity, and how is it calculated? There are actually two well-known ways to calculate it, one based on the FORTRAN language, and the other based on the language PL/I.

In PL/I, the order of the elements in an m-by-n array T is T(1, 1), T(1, 2), and so on up through T(1, n); then T(2, 1); then T(2, 2), and so on through the array. In FORTRAN, on the other hand, the order is T(1, 1), T(2, 1), and so on up through T(m, 1); then T(1, 2); then T(2, 2), and so on. Thus, in FORTRAN, the order of these elements follows through the *columns* of the two-dimensional array, whereas in PL/I it follows through the *rows* of this array (see Figure 32). We speak of a *column representation* in FORTRAN, and a *row representation* in PL/I.

In assembly language, we can use either a column or a row representation, whichever we like. Suppose that we have just calculated I and J, and we wish to use an instruction like LDA T,X to load T(I, J). Then the quantity that we must calculate and put in the X register is

$$(I-1)*n+(J-1) \qquad \text{(row representation)}$$
$$(J-1)*m+(I-1) \qquad \text{(column representation)}$$

for an m-by-n array T. We call the above formulas the *index formulas* for the two representations; the quantity in the X register is the *index* of T(I, J).

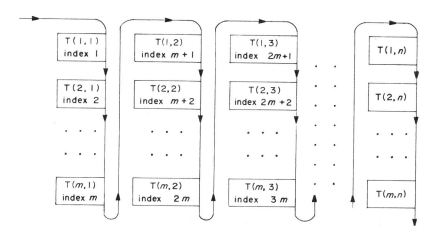

(a) Column representation of a two-dimensional array T

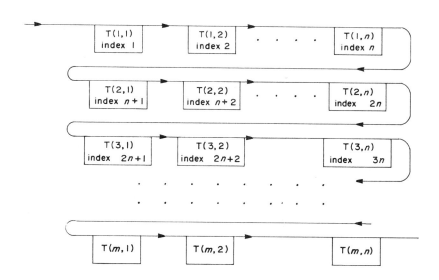

(b) Row representation of a two-dimensional array T

Figure 32. Two-Dimensional Array Representations.

Let us see how these work. In the row representation, for T(1, 1), we have
I = 1, J = 1, and (I−1)*n+(J−1) = 0. This is correct, because if the X register contains zero, then LDA T,X loads T, or, in other words, the *first* byte
of the array T, which is T(1, 1). For T(1, J), in general, we have
(I−1)*n+(J−1) = J−1; thus if J = 5, the index is 5−1, or 4. Again, this is
right since the cell T+!4 will contain T(1, 5).

For T(2, 1), we have I = 2, J = 1, and (I−1)*n+(J−1) = n. The first row,
from T(1, 1) through T(1, n), takes up the first n cells of the array, and so the
next cell would have the address T + n. Thus the index is again correct in this
case. In the same way, we can check that the formula (I−1)*n+(J−1) works in
all cases.

In the column representation, for T(1, 1), we have I = 1, J = 1, and
(J−1)*m+(I−1) = 0. This is correct for the same reason as before. This time,
for T(I, 1), in general, we have (J−1)*m+(I−1) = I−1; thus if I = 7, the index
is 7−1, or 6. This is right because the cell T+!6 will contain T(7, 1). For
T(1, 2), we have I = 1, J = 2, and (J−1)*m+(I−1) = m; the first column,
from T(1, 1) through T(m, 1), takes up the first m cells of the array, and so the
next cell has address T+m. As before, we can continue, if we wish, and check
the formula in other cases.

Both of our formulas may be generalized in a number of ways. If T is an *m*-
by-*n* serial array of *k*-byte quantities, rather than single-byte quantities, then all
indices, as above, are multiplied by *k*. If T starts from T(0, 0), rather than from
T(1, 1), the index formulas turn out to be

> I*n+J   (row representation)
> J*m+I   (column representation)

These are the same as the previous formulas, except that 1 is not subtracted. In
fact, it is not too hard to figure out that the 1 in T(1, 1) is what is subtracted in
those formulas.

It might seem that index calculation is unacceptably slow on the 6502,
because of the multiplication. However, we can easily multiply by a *constant* (*n*
or *m*) by setting up a table of multiples of that constant, and then doing table
lookup as in section 36.

The formulas for an array T starting at T(1, 1) may also be rewritten as

> I*n+J−(n+1)   (row representation)
> J*m+I−(m+1)   (column representation)

and the constant *n*+1, or *m*+1, may be subtracted from T, as noted in section 23, so that only I*n+J or J*m+I needs to be calculated and placed in an
index register. For example, for a 10-by-10 array, we have n+1 = m+1 = 11,

so that a reference to T−!11,X (such as LDA T−!11,X) will be a reference to T(I,J) if I∗n+J (or, respectively, J∗m+I) is in the X register.

EXERCISES

1. Give a BASIC statement (assuming 8-bit data) which is equivalent to each of the following sequences of assembly language instructions. Assume that T is a 10-by-10 array of single-byte quantities, given in a column representation starting with T(1,1), and that TENS is a 10-byte table of multiples of 10, from TENS(1) = 10 through TENS(10) = 100.*

   *(a)
   ```
                   LDA   T+!37
                   STA   U
   ```

   (b)
   ```
                   LDX   L
                   LDA   TENS−!1,X
                   CLC
                   ADC   K
                   TAX
                   LDA   V
                   STA   T−!11,X
   ```

2. Using an indexed DEC instruction, and *not* using the MULT subroutine of section 39 (but rather TENS as in the preceding exercise), write a sequence of instructions on the 6502 which sets T(I, J) = T(I, J) − 1, assuming that T is a 10-by-10 array of single-byte quantities, starting at T(1, 1), and given in:

   *(a) a column representation;
   (b) a row representation.

3. Suppose that an index has been calculated, according to one of our formulas, and placed in the X register in order that we can make reference to T(I, J) in some instruction Z, where the array T is as in exercise 1 above. It is now desired to make reference to T(I, J+1), using this same instruction Z. What change must be made to the X register, if the array T is given in:

   (a) a row representation?
   *(b) a column representation?

---

*Check your answers to make sure that they contain no expressions of the form T(e). Remember that T is a two-dimensional array, and can appear only in expressions of the form T(f, g).

88. 16-BIT SIGNED NUMBERS

The integers which are processed in BASIC are always signed, and are very often 16 bits long. Signed 16-bit integers may be processed in assembly language, using some simple extensions of techniques we have already learned.

In section 7, we mentioned that addition, or subtraction, of signed 8-bit quantities is the same as that of unsigned 8-bit quantities. Let us see why this is so. Suppose that P and Q are d-bit signed numbers, with corresponding unsigned values P′ and Q′. (If $P \geqslant 0$, then P′ = P; if $P < 0$, then $P' = P+2^d$; and similarly for Q.) The result of adding P′ and Q′ (call it S) is $P'+Q'$ if the carry is zero, and $P'+Q'-2^d$ if the carry is 1. If R = P+Q, and R has corresponding unsigned value R′, we must show that R′ = S. There are six cases, as follows:

Sign of P	+	+	+	−	−	−
Sign of Q	+	−	−	+	+	−
Sign of R	+	+	−	+	−	−
Carry	0	1	0	1	0	1
P′ =	P	P	P	$P+2^d$	$P+2^d$	$P+2^d$
Q′ =	Q	$Q+2^d$	$Q+2^d$	Q	Q	$Q+2^d$
R′ =	R	R	$R+2^d$	R	$R+2^d$	$R+2^d$
P′+Q′ =	R	$R+2^d$	$R+2^d$	$R+2^d$	$R+2^d$	$R+2\cdot2^d$
S =	R	R	$R+2^d$	R	$R+2^d$	$R+2^d$

In each case, we can see that R′ = S.

We now note that the proof does not depend on the value of d. What is true for 8-bit quantities is also true for 16-bit quantities; in other words, *signed 16-bit quantities may be added, using the method of section 15, or subtracted, using the method of section 17.*

This does not work, however, for multiplication. We can see this even with 8-bit integers; if we multiply a by $-b$, we are really multiplying a by $256-b$ (unsigned) and getting $256a-ab$, when what we want is 256^2-ab, because this is the twos' complement representation of $-ab$ as a 16-bit quantity.

Multiplication of signed quantities a and b, in general, proceeds as follows:

(1) Set c equal to the exclusive OR of the signs of a and b. (Thus $c = 0$ if and only if a and b have the same sign.)

(2) Set $\alpha = a$; if a is negative, set $\alpha = -a$.
(3) Set $\beta = b$; if b is negative, set $\beta = -b$.
(4) Multiply α by β, producing γ.
(5) If c is zero, the answer is γ; if $c = 1$, the answer is $-\gamma$. (The same scheme works for division.)

Negation of a signed 16-bit quantity proceeds in the same way as negation of a signed 8-bit quantity; we subtract it from zero (as a 16-bit quantity).

Comparison of two 16-bit signed numbers starts by comparing the left halves of the two numbers as signed 8-bit quantities. Either the method of section 54 or that of section 56 may be used. If the two left halves are equal, then the right halves are compared as *unsigned* quantities. (Remember that the leftmost bit of the right half of a 16-bit signed quantity does not function as a sign.)

Conversion of an 8-bit signed quantity to a 16-bit signed quantity proceeds by loading the left half of the 16-bit quantity with zero for a positive quantity, and with all one bits ($FF) for a negative quantity, as mentioned in section 12.

Addition of an 8-bit signed quantity U to a 16-bit quantity V may be performed without converting U as in the preceding paragraph. Suppose that we add U, as an *unsigned* quantity, to V as in section 19. If U is a negative number $-k$, then we calculate $V+256-k$ where we want $V-k$, so our answer is off by 256. This can be fixed by testing U beforehand and, if it is negative, subtracting 1 from the *left half* of V, a process that decreases V by 256; we can then proceed with the process of section 19. The following program does this:

```
        LDA   U        ; LOAD 8-BIT QUANTITY U
        BPL   L7       ; IF NEGATIVE, DECREASE V BY
        DEC   V+!1     ; 256 (V HAS BYTES REVERSED)
L7      CLC            ; NOW ADD U TO THE
        ADC   V        ;   RIGHT HALF OF V
        BCC   L8       ; IF THIS PRODUCES CARRY, ADD
        INC   V+!1     ;   1 TO THE LEFT HALF OF V
L8      STA   V        ; STORE NEW RIGHT HALF OF V
```

Similar techniques may be used to process signed n-byte quantities for $n > 2$. In particular, when we compare two such quantities, we compare their leftmost bytes as signed 8-bit integers, and all their other bytes, if necessary, as unsigned 8-bit integers.

EXERCISES

1. What is the smallest 16-bit signed integer? What is the largest 16-bit signed integer? (Express these as decimal integers, not as expressions involving a power of 2.)

*2. Write a program to compare two 16-bit signed integers U and V, branching to LESS if U < V. Use the method of section 56 for the required signed comparison.

3. Write a program to *subtract* an 8-bit *signed* integer U from a 16-bit quantity V, kept with bytes reversed, without converting U to 16-bit form. Use a variation on the method of the final program of this section.

89. NEGATIVE INDEXING

In section 22 we saw that loops in which the X register starts at N and goes down to zero are faster than those in which it starts at zero and goes up to N. This is because the sequence DEX-BNE is faster than the sequence INX-CPX-BNE. There is a technique, which we call *negative indexing*, that speeds up loops in which the index must, for some reason, start at zero and go up to n. It works only when n is a *constant*.

All quantities in the X and Y registers are always treated as *unsigned*, for the purposes of indexing. It is possible to load the signed number -1 into the X register; but this is the bit pattern 11111111, which is treated as the unsigned number 255. If you had an array T which went from $T(-5)$ to $T(5)$ (which is possible in the language PASCAL, for example), and you put -1 in the X register, then LDA T,X would *not* load $T(-1)$; it would try to load $T(255)$ (which does not exist).

Negative indexing is a way of using negative numbers as indices and then compensating for the problem mentioned above by the use of still another new kind of offset. We will illustrate it for $n = 6$, with an array T having values from $T(1)$ through $T(6)$.

First let us see what happens if we start at $T(6)$ and go down to $T(1)$. The successive values of the X register are 6, 5, 4, 3, 2, and 1. Using negative indexing, the successive values of the X register appear to be -6, -5, -4, -3, -2, and -1. Actually, the 6502 treats them as if they were 250, 251, 252, 253, 254, and 255.

Let us consider the first of these indices, namely 250. When the X register contains 250, we want it to refer to $T(1)$, which would be loaded into the A register by LDA T since it is the first byte of the array T. This can also be accomplished by LDA T$-$!250,X since the address of T, *minus* 250, *plus* 250, is simply the address of T again.

The second index is 251, and when this is in the X register, we want to refer to $T(2)$, which is kept in the cell T+!1. Instead of LDA T+!1 we could again use LDA T$-$!250,X since the address of T, *minus* 250, *plus* 251, is the address of T plus one. It is not hard to see, in fact, that the single instruction LDA T$-$!250,X will always load $T(k)$ into the A register, where the k-th index is contained in the X register.

Let us now use this idea in an example. Consider the following program to search T(1) through T(6) for the first byte T(J) which is equal to B:

```
         LDX    #!0      ;   START AT FIRST BYTE OF T
         LDA    B        ;   ALWAYS KEEP B IN A-REG.
LOOP     CMP    T,X      ;   IS B EQUAL TO T(X−250)
         BEQ    FOUND    ;   IF SO, WE ARE DONE
         INX             ;   MOVE TO NEXT BYTE OF T
         CPX    #!6      ;   AND LOOP BACK UNLESS X
         BNE    LOOP     ;     WAS 5, NOW 6 (FOR T+!5)
```

Using negative indexing, this can be rewritten as

```
         LDX    #!256−!6 ;   START AT FIRST BYTE OF T
         LDA    B        ;   ALWAYS KEEP B IN A-REG.
LOOP     CMP    T−!250,X ;   IS B EQUAL TO T(X−250)
         BEQ    FOUND    ;   IF SO, WE ARE DONE
         INX             ;   MOVE TO NEXT BYTE OF T
         BNE    LOOP     ;   LOOP BACK UNLESS X = 0
```

Note that we have only four instructions in the loop instead of five. *This is the main point of negative indexing*—to enable you to take a CPX (or CPY) instruction out of a loop, and to use the fact that INX (or INY) sets the zero status flag so that you can follow it immediately by BNE, just as you would with DEX (or DEY).

You *cannot* use negative indexing if the loop count n is a variable, because you need the address expression $T+n−!256$; if n is a variable, this cannot be used. You *should not* use negative indexing unless timing is crucial; that is, unless it really matters to you that you are saving those two cycles (for the compare instruction) every time through the loop. Negative indexing is too easy to get wrong, and must not be used indiscriminately.

Some examples of what can go wrong are as follows. You cannot write LDX #!−6 at the beginning of the loop if you are using LISA 1.5, which does not accept this (LISA 2.5 does). If the original loop had INX at the beginning, you must rewrite it to put INX at the end, and then you must be careful that your indices and your initial X value are not off by one. The expression $T−!250$ in the CMP instruction of our example may be rewritten as $T+!6−!256$ to emphasize the constant 6; but it may not be rewritten as $T−!256+!6$, which LISA, for its own reasons, interprets as $T−(!256+!6)$, which is not the same thing. In general, *two or more operators should be avoided* in an address expression, unless all of them (with the possible exception of the last) are plus signs.

EXERCISES

1. Suppose that we wished to delete T(50) from the array T of 200 bytes. In order to do this, we move T(51) to T(50); then T(52) to T(51); and so on,

the last byte being moved from T(200) to T(199). This is done as follows:

```
            LDY     #!50
LOOP        INY
            LDA     T, Y
            STA     T−!1, Y
            CPY     #!200
            BNE     LOOP
```

*(a) Rewrite this loop in such a way that the INY comes just before the CPY. Do not increase the total number of bytes in the loop. (Carefully walk through the result to make sure that it does the same thing as the original loop.)

 (b) Rewrite the new loop so as to use negative indexing. Use an LDY instruction of the form LDY #!256−n. (Carefully walk through the result, as in part (a) above.)

*(c) How many bytes, and how many cycles, are saved if this is done? Show your work.

2. The loop of exercise 1 above *cannot* be written to go in the reverse direction through the array (from T(200) down to T(51)), with DEY and BNE at the end. Why not? (If this is not obvious to you, walk through the first two or three iterations of the loop.)

*3. Consider a loop which searches an array T for an element E. If E is not equal to $T(k)$ for any k, $1 \leq k \leq N$, then the program increments N by 1 and sets $T(N) = E$, for the new value of N. Could such a program be improved by using negative indexing? Why or why not?

90. TAPE PARITY

Input-output on tapes is not totally reliable. Every so often, a bit will be transmitted as zero when it should be one (this is called *dropping a bit*) or as one when it should be zero (this is called *adding a bit*).

We will now discuss the use on the 6502 of an old trick which allows for errors of this kind, as long as they are not too frequent, to be automatically corrected. This trick has been around for over twenty years; it is called *vertical and horizontal parity checking*.

It is assumed that we are writing onto a tape a collection of n bytes, called a *block*. If more than n bytes are to be written, they are written as several blocks, each of n bytes in length. The scheme will now correct all bit dropping and bit adding, as long as *no more than one* such error occurs in each block.

The number n is variable, and may be adjusted according to the reliability of the tape. For example, 1000 bytes might be written as ten blocks of 100 bytes each ($n = 100$). However, if this leads too often to more than one error in a block, we can try writing those same 1000 bytes as 100 blocks of ten bytes each ($n = 10$).

Think of the bytes in the block as being arranged along the tape as in Figure 33. We now calculate an extra row of bits and an extra column of bits, as shown in the figure. These are written on tape along with the given block. When we read the tape back in, then checking this extra row and extra column will allow us to correct errors.

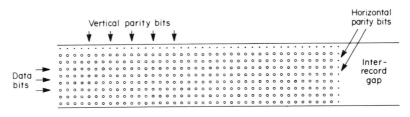

Figure 33. Arrangement of Bits on a Tape.

The bits in the extra row are the *vertical parity bits*. Each one is so chosen that the total number of one-bits in its column will be an odd number. The bits in the extra column are the *horizontal parity bits*; each one is so chosen that the total number of one-bits in its *row* will be odd.

We want these numbers to be odd, rather than even, because we want there to be at least one one-bit in each row and column. On certain computers, many of them obsolete (remember that this is an *old* trick), the one-bits are recorded, while the zero-bits are not; so a one-bit every so often is required to help synchronize the tape drive.

Mathematically speaking, if a row or column has an odd number of one-bits, we say that it has *odd parity*, or that its *parity is 1*. Otherwise, it has *even parity*, or its *parity is zero*. The parity of a row or column may be found as we did in section 35, by counting the one-bits; but there is a faster way, which depends on the fact that *taking the exclusive OR of a collection of bits will always yield its parity* (zero or one). This is because zero-bits do not affect the exclusive OR, while each one-bit changes the exclusive OR from zero to one or from one to zero, exactly as the successive integers, 1, 2, 3, and so on, alternate between being even and odd.

For the byte of horizontal parity bits, we take the exclusive OR of all the bytes to be sent; then, because we want the total number of one-bits in a row to be odd, rather than even, we take one more exclusive OR, namely with all one-bits ($FF). The result is the *parity of the block* of bytes that are sent. For each vertical parity bit, we take the exclusive OR of all the bits in one byte (which might be the byte of horizontal parity bits), together with an extra one-bit, for the same reason as above.

Suppose now that *one* of the bits in this block is either dropped or added. Suppose this bit is in row x and column y. Then when we read the tape in again, row x will have its parity wrong; the parity of this row will be zero, rather than one. Similarly, column y will have its parity wrong. All the other rows and columns will have correct parity.

This shows us how parity checking may be used to correct errors. When we read the tape in, we check the parities of all the rows and columns. If they are all correct, we assume that there has been no error. If one row and one column have the wrong parity (say row x and column y) then we look at the bit which is in row x and column y, and change it (to zero if it is one, or to one if it is zero).

It is important to note that *the one bit which is wrong might be one of the parity bits*. However, this does not matter, because the vertical parity bits themselves form a row, and this can be row x, as above; while the horizontal parity bits form a column, and this can be column y.

If there are two errors in a block, then more than one row, or more than one column, or both, will have wrong parity. In this case we cannot *correct* the error, but we can at least *detect* the fact that there has been an error. For this reason, the above scheme has been called a *single error correction, double error detection* scheme.

EXERCISES

1. The following program calculates the parity of the byte in the A register, and puts it in the rightmost bit of A:

    ```
                STA    B
                LDX    # ! 7
        LOOP    LSR
                EOR    B
                DEX
                BNE    LOOP
    ```

    *(a) How many bytes (including the data byte B), and how many cycles, does this program take? Show your work.

    *(b) In which bit of which register does this program keep the partial result (the exclusive OR of the first few bits)? Explain. (Hint: Walk through the routine, with %abcdefgh in the A register, where each of *a* through *h* is either 0 or 1. Keep track of the contents of *each bit* of the A register during the walkthrough, using the hyphen to denote the exclusive OR; thus *a-b-c* denotes the exclusive OR of *a*, *b*, and *c*.)

2. The following program also puts the parity of the byte in A into the rightmost bit of A:

    ```
                STA    B
                LSR    B
        LOOP    EOR    B
                LSR    B
                BNE    LOOP
    ```

    (a) How many cycles (maximum and minimum), and how many bytes (including the data byte B), does this program take? Show your work.

    (b) Answer exercise 1 above, part (b), for this program.

3. Suppose that the parity of a block, written to tape, is the 8-bit word BW. Suppose that the parity of this same block, read back from tape, is the 8-bit word BR. What is the easiest way to determine which bit in BR is wrong, if BR ≠ BW?

PROBLEM 5 FOR COMPUTER SOLUTION
FORMATTING A PARAGRAPH

Write a program which accepts, as input, a paragraph containing a total of no more than 256 characters; puts these characters into an array; and then outputs the array with a maximum of 27 characters per line, *without splitting up a word* (unless it is hyphenated). Thus if the input is

```
FROM NORTH AMERICA, IT'S EASY TO WING YOUR WAY SOUTH
TO THE CARIBBEAN. TRAVEL AGENTS WHO KEEP
UP-TO-THE-MINUTE SCHEDULES CAN INFORM YOU ABOUT
SPECIAL STOPOVER PRIVILEGES.
```

then the output will be

```
FROM NORTH AMERICA, IT'S
EASY TO WING YOUR WAY SOUTH
TO THE CARIBBEAN. TRAVEL
AGENTS WHO KEEP UP-TO-THE-
MINUTE SCHEDULES CAN INFORM
YOU ABOUT SPECIAL STOPOVER
PRIVILEGES.
```

Note that the first line is 24 characters long, and you can't put the first two letters of EASY on this line, because that would split up the word EASY; the next line is exactly 27 characters long; and so on. The hyphenated word UP-TO-THE-MINUTE could be split after any of the hyphens.

For extra credit, you may use long-array techniques to extend this program to handle paragraphs of over 256 characters.

Your program should use GETLNZ rather than RDKEY, for the usual reasons (that is, GETLNZ allows you to correct mistakes on a single line as you type).

91. THE APPLE DISK OPERATING SYSTEM

We have seen, in chapter 51, how to use the APPLE DOS (Disk Operating System) commands BSAVE and BLOAD. There are several other DOS commands, however, that can be used both in BASIC programs and in LISA programs. For example, DELETE *f* removes *f* from the disk; it is useful if you are about to run out of space on a diskette.

It may be that you have studied some of the DOS commands as part of a course in APPLE BASIC. We will assume, however, that you have not, and give an introduction to a very few of the most commonly used DOS commands. Further DOS commands may be studied in the APPLE DOS manual.

A disk operating system works with *files* on disk. A file consists of data which is put on the disk and then brought back into main memory, or *loaded,* at some later time. A file has a *name*, as we have seen, and every file on the disk must normally have a name different from that of every other file on the disk.

The commands BSAVE and BLOAD work with *binary files*. A binary file can also be saved and loaded directly from a LISA program. This is done by writing the same commands from assembly language that we did from LISA and from BASIC. If the command is DBSAVE LDATA,A$8C00,L$200 as in section 51 (to save 512—or hexadecimal 200—bytes starting at address 8C00 on a file called LDATA), one writes

```
          LDX   #$FF      ;   START CHARACTER INDEX AT −1
   LOOP   INX             ;   INCREASE CHARACTER INDEX
          LDA   BSMSG,X   ;   GET NEXT CHARACTER OF MSG
          CMP   #CRET     ;   IS IT A CARRIAGE RETURN
          BEQ   DONE      ;   IF SO, WE ARE FINISHED
          JSR   COUT      ;   IF NOT, OUTPUT IT
          JMP   LOOP      ;   AND GET THE NEXT ONE
   DONE   JSR   COUT      ;   OUTPUT THE CARRIAGE RETURN
```

with CRET EQU $8D and COUT EQU $FDED as usual, and with

```
   BSMSG   BYT   $84         ;   CONTROL-D
           ASC   "BSAVE LDATA,A$8C00,L$200"
           BYT   CRET        ;   CARRIAGE RETURN
```

(note that what follows the A *must* be a number, either in decimal or hexadecimal). The point here is that whenever a control-D is output as the first character of a line, the remaining characters, up to the carriage return, are treated by the APPLE as a DOS command. In general, a string of characters terminated by a carriage return is called a *record*. GETLNZ, for example, reads one record.

Besides binary files, APPLE DOS handles *text files*, which are composed of records as described above. A binary file, as we have seen, is saved and loaded all at once; a text file, however, is written and read *one character at a time*. This is done through the same monitor subroutines that we use to read characters from the keyboard, or display them on the screen. We have to tell the APPLE system, however, what file we are working with before we do this.

Before we work with any file, with the name *fname*, we must *open* it and specify whether we are reading or writing. The DOS command OPEN *fname* opens the file; the DOS command READ *fname* specifies that the file is to be read; and the DOS command WRITE *fname* specifies that the file is to be written. Opening a file is an initialization operation; it is done once at the beginning of any program that works with the file.

Note that READ and WRITE *do not* actually read and write. This is done by monitor subroutines. For example, RDKEY reads one character; COUT writes one character; and GETLN reads one line into the input buffer starting at cell 0200. We have used GETLNZ, which outputs a carriage return before calling GETLN. On the screen, this is useful, because the new line will be displayed starting at the left-hand end of the screen; but for disk input it is unnecessary, and GETLN is used instead.

If you are working with more than one file, then start your program with the DOS command MAXFILES *n* where you are working with a total of *n* (≤ 9) files.* Then open each file separately, as before. The commands READ and WRITE (without OPEN) will now switch the reading and writing back and forth among the files. If you have been reading file α, and you now wish to read file β, give the READ β command; and similarly for writing.

Whether you are working with one file, or more than one, you must *close* all your files with the DOS command CLOSE at the end of your program. CLOSE *fname* closes the file whose name is *fname*. All the DOS commands given above are given from a LISA program in the same way as the BSAVE command was given near the start of this section.

When you are using RDKEY and COUT for disk operations, you can simultaneously use KEYIN for keyboard input, and COUT1 for screen output. KEYIN and COUT1 work just like RDKEY and COUT, except that they do not read or write to disk. The defining EQU statements for them are:

Do not issue this command, however, while in LISA.

```
KEYIN   EQU   $FD1B
COUT1   EQU   $FDF0
```

EXERCISES

*1.   Modify the program of this section so that it becomes a general DOS command execution subroutine DOSCOM, called by loading the address of the given DOS command string into the A and X registers (upper half in A, lower half in X) and then calling DOSCOM. Thus, for example,

```
LDA   /BSMSG
LDX   #BSMSG
JSR   DOSCOM
```

should perform the DOS command BSAVE LDATA,A$8C00,L$200 (where BSMSG is as given in the text). Use post-indexed indirect addressing, with the two zero-page locations ZP and ZP+!1; do not save and restore any registers. Assume that CRET and COUT are defined as usual.

*2.   Do exercise 1 above, but using address modification instead of post-indexed indirect addressing. Do not use the Y register. Use MODIFY.

3.   (a)   What does the following instruction sequence do (the *sequence*, not the individual instructions), assuming that DOSCOM is as above, with CRET, RDKEY, and COUT defined as usual, and assuming that CTRLE (control-E) signifies the end of a file?

```
        LDA   /OPEN1
        LDX   #OPEN1
        JSR   DOSCOM
        LDA   /READ1
        LDX   #READ1
        JSR   DOSCOM
        LDA   /OPEN2
        LDX   #OPEN2
        JSR   DOSCOM
        LDA   /WRITE2
        LDX   #WRITE2
        JSR   DOSCOM
LOOP    JSR   RDKEY
        CMP   #CTRLE
        BEQ   DONE
        JSR   COUT
        JMP   LOOP
```

```
DONE     JSR    COUT
         LDA    /CLOSE
         LDX    #CLOSE
         JSR    DOSCOM
         RTS
OPEN1    BYT    $84
         ASC    "OPEN F1"
         BYT    CRET
READ1    BYT    $84
         ASC    "READ F1"
         BYT    CRET
OPEN2    BYT    $84
         ASC    "OPEN F2"
         BYT    CRET
WRITE2   BYT    $84
         ASC    "WRITE F2"
         BYT    CRET
CLOSE    BYT    $84
         ASC    "CLOSE"
         BYT    CRET
```

(b) What improvement may be made at the end of the sequence of
     instructions above? (Hint: see the end of section 61.)

92. MORE ON TEXT FILES

Besides reading and writing text files with your own user programs, you can also read them, change them in a number of standard ways, and write them back to disk, using a special kind of program called an *editor*.

The most important use of editors is in making changes to *programs*. The LISA commands, in fact, such as I and D, that we studied in section 46, are part of a system known as the LISA editor. Similarly, BASIC commands such as LIST, RUN, SAVE, and the like, are part of the BASIC editor. These editors have a limited number of commands, and were originally written to handle one specific kind of file.

More general editors (such as PIE, for example, which runs on the APPLE) have not only been written for manipulation of arbitrary text files, but also provide many commands which are not found in the LISA or BASIC editors. For example, you can search through a text file for all occurrences of a character string (such as HIM) and replace it with another character string (such as HIM OR HER). Also, you can take an existing part of your file and move it to a different part of your file.

A general text editor is not always better than a special-purpose editor such as the LISA editor. For example, the LISA editor, since it is always working with LISA programs, can catch syntax errors in these programs. Also, the LISA editor is faster than PIE.

The LISA editor does not keep LISA programs in the same format, on disk, that PIE or other editors do. However, LISA provides a facility whereby a LISA program can be written out as a *text file* (rather than a binary file, as would be done by the SAVE command) so that these editors can process it. This is done through the LISA command W (for "write"), used as an alternative to SAVE. Instead of SAVE TEST7 (for example) one types W TEST7 to put the current LISA program out on a text file, with the name TEST7.

In order to *read* a text file back into LISA, the LISA editor makes use of a trick, which takes a bit of explaining. As we have seen, the LISA command $\underline{\underline{D}}$ (control-D), followed by an APPLE DOS command, executes that command. As it happens, there is an APPLE DOS command, EXEC f, which reads a text file f and treats each line of this file as if it were typed at the keyboard. If you type EXEC TEST7 as an APPLE DOS command, the lines of the file TEST7 are treated as further APPLE DOS commands, as they would be at that point in your work with the APPLE if you typed them in; this accounts for the name EXEC, or "execute a file of commands." (This is like the "catalogued procedure" facility of large IBM computer systems.)

The LISA command DEXEC f, however, will treat each line of the file f as if it had been typed at the keyboard *while in LISA*, since the LISA system is now expecting another LISA command. Now suppose that the first line of f were I (the LISA insert command), and that the remainder of f were a LISA program. Then DEXEC f would act like an insert command, followed by lines to be inserted—in other words (at the beginning of the editing process) it would do the equivalent of reading in the file f.

The trick mentioned above involves the W command, which writes out a text file, but with one extra line, INS (a variation of I, the insert command) at the beginning. The command DEXEC f now reads this file back in. Actually, DEXEC f is analogous to AP f ("append f"), rather than LOAD f, because, if you have been working on another LISA program, the insertion process described above will insert the lines from the text file *after* that program. To prevent this, you can type the LISA command NEW (exactly like the BASIC command NEW) to start over with a new program, before typing DEXEC f. Of course, this would not be needed at the start of the editing process, which is when you usually would be loading a file. Also note that, after executing DEXEC f, you must type *control-E return,* which always terminates a group of inserted lines.

Listings from LISA assemblies can also be made into text files, using another trick. The LISA pseudo-operation DCM "c" (for "disk command c") causes c to be executed as a DOS command during the final phase of assembly. Note that this is a *pseudo-operation*, not a LISA command; you put it in your LISA program. Specifically, suppose that you want a listing file called LIST3. The first two lines of your LISA program should be DCM "OPEN LIST3" and DCM "WRITE LIST3" and you should have DCM "CLOSE LIST3" just before the END statement in your LISA program. When the OPEN and WRITE commands are executed, further output, which would normally go to the screen, goes to the file LIST3, and so that is where the listing will go.

Partial listings can be produced by the pseudo-operation NLS ("no list") in LISA, which causes the remainder of the LISA program not to be listed (either to a file or to the screen) until it is "undone" by the LISA pseudo-operation LST ("list"). A listing file can also be sent to the printer, in which case the LISA pseudo-operation PAG ("new page") can be used to start this printed file on a new page. Many programmers use PAG at the beginning of every subroutine in a long LISA program.*

---

*In LISA 2.5, there is TTL ("title"); TTL "s" cause the string s to appear as a title at the top of *each page* of the listing.

EXERCISES

*1.   Why is the command <u>D</u>EXEC *f* required in order to load a text file? Why
       doesn't LOAD *f* work? Explain.

2.   Suppose that we gave the pseudo-operations

```
DCM     "OPEN LIST1"
DCM     "WRITE LIST1"
DCM     "OPEN LIST2"
DCM     "WRITE LIST2"
```

      at the start of a LISA program, in order to produce *two* copies of the list-
      ing, on the files LIST1 and LIST2. This, in fact, would not work. Why
      not, and what would actually happen?

*3.   What appears on the screen when the following program is assembled?
       (Note that LST itself does not appear on the screen, whereas NLS does.)

```
LDA     P1
STA     P2
NLS
LDA     P3
STA     P4
LST
LDA     P5
STA     P6
BRK
END
```

93. SIMULATORS

Suppose that you have an APPLE which has replaced an obsolete computer. After selling or throwing out the obsolete computer, you find yourself with some good working programs for it, written in assembly language. Is there any way you can run these programs on the APPLE? Every computer has its own machine language, so you will not be able to run them directly; but you might be able to run them indirectly, using a special program called a *simulator*.

A simulator, in general, is a program that allows you to run, on machine X, a program written for machine Y. In this case, machine X is the 6502. Let us suppose that machine Y has n different instructions, with operation codes k_1, $k_2, \ldots, k_n$. Then the simulator is basically a program with n subroutines, one for each k_i.

The simulator starts by loading the given program into the memory of machine X. It now looks at the operation code of the first instruction of the program. Suppose that this is k_j; then the simulator calls its jth subroutine, whose job is to do what this particular operation code specifies.

Suppose that machine Y has a register, called the Q register, which is 32 bits long. Suppose that the instruction with operation code k_j is a "store Q" instruction. That is, it stores the Q register into some area of memory, which we shall call C, and C is also 32 bits long. Then, in the simulator, there will be set aside four special bytes of the memory of the 6502, to represent the Q register, and four bytes for each 32-bit word like C. The jth subroutine, as called above, will then move the four bytes of Q to the four bytes of C, one byte at a time.

Other subroutines of the simulator will perform similar functions. The machine Y will probably have many registers, like any machine does. Each of these will correspond to a *simulated register* such as the four bytes of Q as above. The main memory of machine Y will correspond to *simulated main memory*, and for each address α in machine Y there is a corresponding simulated main memory cell whose address, in the 6502, may be computed from α (although it is not necessarily equal to α).

The last thing that the jth subroutine does is to move the simulator on to the next instruction. This is because the simulator is going to *simulate*, or execute in simulated mode, one instruction after the next in the program written for machine Y, in the order in which machine Y would have executed these instructions. To do this, the jth subroutine modifies the *simulated program counter*, which is another collection of bytes like the other simulated registers.

In our example involving the "store Q" instruction, if the simulated program counter contains β, then the jth subroutine will add 1 to β (or sometimes some other small integer k, if "store Q" is a k-word or k-byte instruction). If instead of "store Q" we had "jump to L," then the corresponding subroutine would put the address of L in the simulated program counter. Conditional branching can also be simulated, by a combination of the above two techniques. After the jth subroutine is finished, then the main program of the simulator will use the simulated program counter to find the operation code of the next instruction.

Index register operations can also be simulated. The question here is which cell of the simulated main memory to make reference to. The address of this cell is normally part of the instruction indicated by the simulated program counter; but, if there is indexing in an instruction, we add to it the contents of the simulated index register. This is all done by the *main program* of the simulator, so that the n subroutines can use this information.

Simulation, as you might expect, is very slow. Typically, a program is slowed down by a factor of about 100 when it is simulated. Hence simulation should not be used unless it is absolutely necessary.

Simulation may be used, not only for obsolete computers, but for new computers that do not have much software yet, or before they are actually available. In this case, machine Y is the new computer, and machine X is the existing computer on which a simulator is written. In this case there is also often written an assembler, running on machine X, which produces programs for machine Y. This is called a *cross-assembler*, in contrast to an ordinary assembler which produces programs for the same machine on which it runs.

Simulation may also be used with a machine language which does not correspond to any existing computer language. An example is SWEET16, a machine language for a 16-bit machine that was never built. There is, however, a widely used simulator for SWEET16 that runs on the 6502 (and specifically on the APPLE).

Some computers simulate other computers *all* the time. Many models of the IBM 370, for example, consist of computers which are actually far simpler than the IBM 370, but which simulate it, using a simulator built into the hardware. This is called *microprogramming* (and is *not* to be confused with *microcomputing*, that is, the use of a microprocessor such as the 6502). A microprogrammed computer often simulates other computers, using other simulators (called *emulators* in this case), which are likewise built into the hardware.

EXERCISES

*1. Suppose that the UNIVAC 1110, a large computer, is being simulated on the 6502. Each address on the 6502 is the address of an 8-bit quantity, called a byte, and, in much the same way, each address on the 1110 is the address of a 36-bit quantity, called a *word* (not to be confused with an English word). Each simulated 36-bit word is expressed in five bytes on the 6502 (since $5 \times 8 = 40$ bits are sufficient to contain it). An area α of $5x$ bytes is used in the 6502 in order to simulate a UNIVAC 1110 memory area of x bytes which starts at the 16-bit address β on the 1110. To simulate the 1110 instruction L A5,N ("load A5 with N"), the five bytes with addresses p through $p+4$, representing the contents of the cell with address N, must be moved to the five bytes of the simulated register A5. Give a formula for p in terms of N, α, and β.

2. In the situation above, suppose that the simulated instruction is L A5,T,A1 ("load A5 with T(k), where k is in the index register A1"). Give a formula for p in terms of N, α, β, and k.

3. *(a) The UNIVAC 1110, as described in exercise 1 above, has one instruction per 36-bit word. Suppose that the instruction having address y is simulated in the cells having addresses q through $q+4$, and the simulated program counter contains q. In what way should the simulator modify this program counter after simulating L A5,N as above?

    (b) Answer the same question as above if the simulated program counter contains y, rather than q. (Note that the simulated program counter can contain either the actual 1110 address or the corresponding address in the 6502; this is a design decision to be made in designing the simulator.)

94. INTERPRETERS

An *interpreter* is like a simulator, except that, instead of running programs written in machine language for some machine Y, it runs programs written in some other language L. This might be BASIC, FORTRAN, PASCAL, or the like.

The operation of an interpreter is in many ways like that of a simulator. There is, in particular, something like a simulated program counter; but instead of indicating the address of a machine language instruction, this counter indicates the address at which the current *statement* in the language L is kept in memory.

Suppose now that there are *n* statement types in the language L. (In BASIC, these might be IF, GO TO, FOR, and the like.) There are now *n* subroutines of the interpreter, one for each statement type, just as there were *n* subroutines of a simulator, one for each of *n* different instructions in machine language.

An interpreter keeps a list of all variables in the program being interpreted. This list is used by the *n* subroutines as described above. For example, suppose that the current statement is $J = K + 3$. This is an assignment statement; so the subroutine which handles assignment statements would be called. This subroutine would add 3 to the quantity in K (in the list of variables) and store the result in J (in this same list). Note that the interpreter is itself a program, and might have its own variables called J and K; but these have nothing to do with the J and K in the program being interpreted.

An interpreter also keeps a list of *labels* and their corresponding addresses. If the program being interpreted has a statement GO TO 100, and the statement with label 100 is now in the computer at address α, then the label 100 will be kept in the label list, associated with the address α. When GO TO 100 is interpreted, the subroutine which processes GO TO statements will look up 100 in the list and will determine from this that α is to be placed in the simulated program counter. Separate from the list of labels is the list of *keywords* (in BASIC, these are IF, READ, DATA, DIM, and the like—in general, any words that have special meanings in the language). In some languages, keywords are *reserved*—that is, it is not allowed to use a keyword as an identifier.

We are now, finally, in a position to answer a very important question which was left unanswered in your study of BASIC. All microcomputers process

BASIC, and you can pretend that they are "BASIC machines" in the sense that they "know" BASIC directly. In fact, however, they don't. *The only language that a computer "knows" directly is its own machine language.* Whenever you are working with a microcomputer in BASIC, almost all the time you are actually working with an interpreter, as described above. (You might also be working with a *compiler*, which will be described in the next section.)

Interpreters differ according to how they keep, in memory, the programs they interpret, or the *source programs*. A *pure interpreter* keeps the source program in memory exactly as it appears externally. Thus if J=K+3 appears in the source program, the character string "J=K+3" appears in memory. A *semi-interpreter* translates the source program into an *intermediate language*, and the program is interpreted in this form. An intermediate language is to an interpreter what a language like SWEET16 is to a simulator—there are no machines which process it directly, but it is still quite easy for the interpreter to process it indirectly.

It is common, in an intermediate language, to replace variable names by their indices in a table. A pure interpreter cannot interpret J=K+3 without first looking up J and K in its tables, which is a time-consuming process. However, if J is the fifth variable in the program, and K is the sixth variable, then J and K would be replaced by 5 and 6, respectively, in the intermediate language. This makes it much easier for the semi-interpreter to interpret this statement, because there is no table lookup to do. (The constant 3 would also be replaced by some index in a table.)

Another characteristic of semi-interpreters is that all the keywords in the source program are translated into indices in the list of keywords; these indices are often called *tokens*. This again makes the semi-interpreter's job easier; a pure interpreter has to look up every keyword, every time it interprets a statement. This is particularly wasteful when the statement is in a loop, so that it will be done many times and therefore interpreted many times.

Interpreters, like simulators, are slow. On microcomputers, however, this often does not matter; as we have mentioned earlier, computer time on a microcomputer is usually so cheap as to be almost free.

EXERCISES

1. Suppose that GO TO is the only keyword in a given language which begins with the letter G. Can a pure interpreter for that language determine whether a given statement, being interpreted, is a GO TO statement by looking only at its first character? Explain.

*2.   Suppose that a statement in some language starts with the characters
       "A=B*C" (followed possibly by some other characters). Suppose that A,
       B, and C are all known to be simple (unsubscripted) variables. Should a
       pure interpreter for this language look up the values of B and C in its
       tables, and multiply them, as soon as it has looked at the first five charac-
       ters of this statement, as above? Explain.

 3.   In a semi-interpreter, when J=K+3 is interpreted, no table lookup takes
       place, as we noted in the text; but, when J=K+3 is translated from the
       source language to the intermediate language, J and K must be looked up
       in a table of variables. It might seem that this process compares unfavor-
       ably with that of a pure interpreter, since both kinds of interpreter perform
       table lookup at some point, while with the semi-interpreter there is the
       extra time for translation into the intermediate language. However, this is
       not necessarily the case. Explain why not.

95. ASSEMBLERS AND COMPILERS

By now you might well be wondering how a program like LISA is written.

An assembler processes a program P written in assembly language into a program Q in machine language. You can think of the assembler as reading the input P and producing the output Q. Most assemblers actually write out Q, although LISA leaves Q in memory to be executed; it can be written out, using the SAVE feature of LISA, if you want it to be. The program P is called the *source program*; the program Q is called the *object program*.

The main job of an assembler is in translating each assembly language statement into its machine language counterpart. There are two parts to this job. The first has to do with the operation codes and is quite easy. There is a table, in the assembler, of all mnemonics and their corresponding operation codes. When TYA occurs in the program P, the assembler looks up TYA in the table, gets the corresponding operation code (98, in hexadecimal) and puts it in the program Q.

Sometimes, on the 6502, there is more than one operation code for a given mnemonic. In that case the assembler must look at the rest of the given assembly language statement. Thus if the statement is STA T − !2,Y then LISA looks at the comma and the Y, notes that there are no parentheses around T − !2 (if there were, then the operation code would be 91), and calculates the operation code as 99.

The second part of the job, as above, is calculating the addresses. For example, STA T−!2,Y has the address 08BE (or, with bytes reversed, BE 08) if 08C0 is the address of T. This part is a bit harder than the first part, because we might not know the address of T yet. For example, T DFS !100 might come later on in the source program P, so we have not read it yet.

In order to take care of this part of the job, most assemblers are written in at least two parts, or *passes*. In the first pass, the assembler reads P as input, but does not produce Q yet. Instead, it constructs a *symbol table* in memory. This is a table of all identifiers (such as T) together with their corresponding addresses. In the final pass, the assembler reads P *again* as input, and this time it produces Q, with help from the information in the symbol table.

An assembler has a simulated program counter, much like a simulator does, but it is used in a different way. When the assembler reads an ORG *z* statement, the simulated program counter C is set to z. Every time the assembler reads an instruction or a data declaration, which would take up k bytes in Q, it adds k to C. Every time it comes to a *labeled* instruction, or a labeled data declaration, it puts the given label in the symbol table (in the first pass), together with *the current value of C*, which is then the address associated with that label.

Besides calculating operation codes and addresses, the assembler must do various miscellaneous jobs in connection with assembly language instructions. On the 6502, this includes calculating relative addresses for conditional branch instructions. It also includes calculating immediate data in hexadecimal form; for example, if LDA #!100 is contained in P, then the 100 must be converted to its hexadecimal form, or 64, before being inserted in Q.

Assemblers must also process the *pseudo-operations* in the source program P. Here the operation of an assembler is vaguely like that of a simulator. If there are n different pseudo-operations, then the assembler has n subroutines, one for each pseudo-operation. We have already seen that the subroutine which processes ORG k statements loads the simulated program counter with k.

A *compiler* is like an assembler, except that where an assembler has assembly language source programs, a BASIC compiler (for example) has BASIC source programs. In both cases, the object programs are in machine language. A compiler, however, is most often compared to an *interpreter*, because, although they are very different kinds of programs, compilers and interpreters are two ways of doing the same thing—namely, running a program written in some language such as BASIC.

Compilers are very long and complex programs, and they take quite a bit of time to run—sometimes longer than an interpreted program would take. In such a case it is clearly better to interpret than to compile. Also, many microcomputer systems are too small to support a compiler; there is no way to fit the compiler into the available memory space. On the other hand, an object program always runs much faster, after being compiled, than the corresponding source program would if it were interpreted. If a program is going to run for a long time, therefore, it is better to use a compiler, if you have one, than to use an interpreter.

One language that is almost always compiled, rather than interpreted, is FORTRAN. Before microcomputers were developed, FORTRAN, rather than BASIC, was the most common algebraic language, and it is still used more than BASIC on large computers such as the IBM 4300 series.

A *disassembler* is a program which converts a *machine* language program into its *assembly* language counterpart. These are useful if you are analyzing someone else's object program, although they can never be entirely satisfactory, for a number of reasons. (For one thing, they must choose variable names arbitrarily.)

EXERCISES

*1. Consider the table of mnemonics in an assembler. Is there any reason for this to be a sorted array? Explain.

 2. Consider the symbol table in an assembler. Is there any reason for this to be a sorted array? Why is this situation different from that of the preceding exercise? Explain. (Hint: see section 86.)

*3. Suppose you had a program which translated a BASIC program into its *assembly* language counterpart. Could this be used in a method of executing a BASIC program, as an alternative to the use of an interpreter? Explain.

96. STRUCTURED PROGRAMMING

How can we learn to write programs more efficiently? This general question has occupied the minds of computer scientists for a considerable amount of time. It includes both writing more efficient *programs* and making the *program-writing process* more efficient. Sometimes these goals conflict; as we saw in section 37, programmer time trades off with memory space and program time, and a program that is itself very efficient may take an unacceptably long time to write.

One way to write programs more efficiently is to be more organized. We are all familiar with "organized" and "disorganized" people; and often a person is organized in one area and disorganized in another. The reason that many people are not as efficient as they could be, when they are programming, is that they set about the task in too disorganized a way. There has been a considerable amount of work done on how to organize, or *structure*, the programming process better, and there have been many, sometimes conflicting, notions of what *structured* (or "organized") *programming* ought to be like.

One point that was noticed very early in the study of structured programming is that too many programmers use only the simple statements of any given programming language. They use assignments, IF statements in their simplest form (IF *condition* THEN GO TO *label*) and input-output, and don't use subroutines, iteration (such as the FOR statement in BASIC) and the more general forms of IF statement that are available in some languages (such as IF *condition* THEN *statement-1* ELSE *statement-2*). All these more complex statements can be simulated, or "faked up," in terms of simpler statements, but the result is usually a program that is much more difficult to understand than it should be.

The Dutch computer scientist E. W. Dijkstra put it this way: "For a number of years I have been familiar with the observation that the quality of programmers is a decreasing function of the density of GO TO statements in the programs they produce."* The reason for this is that the more complex statements of a language, which are more often used by better programmers, can always be simulated in terms of constructions involving GO TO statements, as shown in

---

*E. W. Dijkstra, "*Go-To Statement Considered Harmful*," Communications of the ACM 11, 3 (March 1968), pp. 147–148.

322

Figure 34. It follows immediately that poorer programmers will always use more GO TO statements in their programs.

The four *structured programming statements* of Figure 34 have found their way into many programming languages, in one form or another (Figure 34 shows their PASCAL form).[†] In assembly language, of course, we do not have these statements; but we can always write a program in a higher-level language first, using structured programming, if that makes it easier for us to understand it, and then hand-translate the resulting program into assembly language.

Dijkstra goes on to say: "I became convinced that the GO TO statement should be abolished from all 'higher level' programming languages (i.e. everything except, perhaps, plain machine code)." Upon Dijkstra's advice, this was tried, by a number of people, and the consensus today is that it doesn't work; there are *some* GO TO statements (most of them dealing with error conditions) that are easier to understand than the corresponding "structured" forms of them.

Another method of organizing yourself to program better is *top-down design*. This is similar to the process of writing an outline for a term paper. You lay out, on one sheet of paper, all the things you want your program to do, and then

STRUCTURED PROGRAMMING STATEMENT	INFORMAL MEANING	CORRESPONDING SEQUENCE OF ASSIGNMENTS AND CONDITIONAL BRANCHES
IF C THEN S1 ELSE S2	If the condition C is true, then do the statement S1; otherwise do the statement S2	IF C THEN GO TO m; S2; GO TO n; m: S1; n:
WHILE C DO S	As long as the condition C remains true, keep repeating the statement S (zero or more times)	GO TO n; m: S; n: IF C THEN GO TO m;
REPEAT SEQ UNTIL C	Repeat the sequence of statements SEQ (one or more times) until the condition C becomes true	m: SEQ; IF NOT C THEN GO TO m;
CASE K OF 1: S1; 2: S2; 3: S3; . . . . m; Sm	Do the statement S$_i$ (only) if the value of K is i, where i is any of 1, 2, ... , m.	IF K $<>$ 1 THEN GO TO n_2; S1; GO TO n; n_2: IF K $<>$ 2 THEN GO TO n_3; S2; GO TO n; n_3: IF K $<>$ 3 THEN GO TO n_4; S3; GO TO n; n_4: . . . . n_m: IF K $<>$ m THEN GO TO *error*; Sm; n:

Figure 34. Structured Programming Statements.

[†]In PASCAL, a label is followed by a colon, and a statement (usually) by a semicolon; thus m: S; denotes the statement S, having the label m.

expand each of these into a subroutine or section of code. If you want to, you can write your main program to look exactly like an outline; it is nothing more than a sequence of subroutine call statements, one for each line of the outline, with perhaps a very few iteration and error-checking statements thrown in. Many programmers find it much easier to understand their own programs if they write them in this way.

Still another device used in organizing yourself to be a more efficient programmer is the walkthrough, as we described it in section 44. Walkthroughs are even more effective when they are done in a group, with all the programmers in the group ready to discover bugs in the program that is being walked through.

Finally, there is an organizational device: the designation of the best programmer in any given programming group as the *chief programmer*. This sounds much easier than it is in practice, because very often the best programmer is not a natural leader, whereas other programmers in the same group may be natural leaders. It is a continuing, and important, organizational task to insure that the programmers in a group respect the authority of the chief programmer on a continuing basis and do not try to manipulate the design of the program against the wishes of the chief programmer.

EXERCISES

1. In each of the following cases, derive the corresponding sequence of assignments and conditional branches, as in the right-hand column of Figure 34:

    *(a) IF C THEN REPEAT Q1 UNTIL D ELSE S
     (b) WHILE C1 DO IF C2 THEN S1 ELSE S2

2. In each of the following cases, derive a corresponding structured program as in the preceding exercise, without using any GO TO statements:*

    *(a)   IF C1 THEN GO TO $m2$;
                                GO TO n;
                                m: S2;
                                n: IF C2 THEN GO TO m;
                                GO TO $n2$;
                                $m2$: S1;
                                $n2$:

---

*Note an important difference between PASCAL and many other languages with respect to labels. In Part (a), m: is a label, and IF is not; yet IF starts in column 1. This would not be permissible in assembly language, but is so in PASCAL. The PASCAL system can tell that IF is not a label; among many other things, it is not followed by a colon.

(b)
```
m:  IF  C1  THEN  GO  TO  m2;
S2;
GO  TO  n;
m2:  S1;
n:  IF  NOT  C2  THEN  GO  TO  m;
```

3. In each of the following cases, give a sequence of instructions on the 6502 which corresponds to the specified stuctured programming statement:

*(a) IF C1 THEN S1 ELSE WHILE C2 DO S2

(b) REPEAT IF C1 THEN S1 ELSE S2 UNTIL C2

97. BINARY AND HEXADECIMAL FRACTIONS

So far, all the numbers which we have learned how to process in the 6502 have been integers. How do we represent fractions in the binary or hexadecimal system? One way is by using an extension of what are informally called "decimals," or *decimal fractions*.

How do we calculate the value of a decimal like .738? It is certainly 738/1000, but why 1000 rather than 100 or 10000? Because there are *three* digits in 738, and 10 to the *third* power is 1000. We can use this same idea in the binary system. Thus .101 represents 5 (that is, 101 in binary) divided by 8 (which is 2 to the third power, since there are three digits in 101); in other words, ⅝. We refer to .101 as a *binary fraction* (by analogy with decimal fractions); the first 16 binary fractions, together with zero, are shown in Figure 35. The period in .101 is known as the *binary point* (by analogy with "decimal point").

We are familiar with the idea that certain decimal fractions *terminate*, whereas others do not. Thus ¾ is 0.75, because ¾ = 75/100; but ⅓ is the *unending* (or *non-terminating*) *decimal fraction* 0.333333 . . . . (and so on indefinitely). The same thing happens with binary fractions; in fact, the binary fraction 0.01010101 . . . . (and so on indefinitely) represents ⅓.

Given an unending decimal like .736736736 . . . . (and so on indefinitely), we can convert it to a fraction by dividing the repeating part (736 in this case) by $10^d - 1$, where d is the number of digits in the repeating part. In this case we obtain 736/999 (remember that .736 by itself would be 736/1000). A similar rule holds with binary fractions; thus .01 is ¼ (that is, 1 over the *second* power of 2, since there are *two* digits in .01) and therefore .01010101 . . . . (and so on indefinitely) is ⅓, since $3 = 2^2 - 1$.

(Why don't we represent ⅓ in the computer as the two integers 1 and 3, and then add, subtract, multiply, and divide fractions according to the rules we learned in elementary school? Because we would have to keep reducing our answers to lowest terms, which turns out to be very time-consuming. Besides, many of the numbers we wish to work with, such as π, do not correspond exactly to any fraction.)

Some of the fractions which terminate in the decimal system do not terminate in the binary system. For example, 3/16 is .0011 in binary, and, by the above rule, 3/(16−1), or 3/15, is .001100110011 . . . . (and so on indefinitely); but 3/15 reduces to ⅕, which, in the decimal system, corresponds to the *terminating* decimal 0.2 (since ⅕ = ²⁄₁₀).

In addition to decimal fractions like 0.75, there are more general numbers, like 3.25, in the decimal system, which have both an integer part and a fractional part. The same is true in the binary system; for example, 11.01 is the binary representation of 3.25.

Suppose now that we want to express 11.01 as a 16-bit quantity in the computer. We can decide, if we want to, that the first 10 of our 16 bits are for the integer; then comes the binary point, as noted above; and finally come 6 bits for the fraction. Thus 11.01 would be represented as 0000000011.010000 in this way.

In any such representation, there is always a question as to where to put the binary point. In the representation above, since we put the binary point after the first 10 bits, we can represent numbers from 0 (that is, 0000000000.000000) through $1023^{63}\!/_{64}$ (that is, 1111111111.111111). If this is too large a range, we can put the binary point somewhere else, say after the first seven bits. This would give us a range from 0 through (almost) 128, and it would give us more fractions between every pair of consecutive integers.

The answer to our question seems to be that we can put the binary point anywhere we want to, but, once we put it somewhere, it is *fixed* at that position for the purposes of addition and subtraction. That is, we can make calculations like

$$
\begin{array}{rr}
0110010000.110010 & 0100111011.011100 \\
+0011010110.100111 & -0001001101.101100 \\
\hline
1001100111.011001 & 0011101101.110000
\end{array}
$$

by adding or subtracting our 16-bit quantities *as integers*. This, however, is only because the binary points "line up"; if they did not, we would have to shift one number or the other until they did line up. For this reason, the above representation is called a *fixed-point representation*.

Negative numbers may be represented in a fixed-point representation by taking the twos' complement in the usual way. If this is done, the range of numbers in the first representation above becomes from −512 (that is, 1000000000.000000) through $511^{63}\!/_{64}$ (that is, 0111111111.111111).

There are also *hexadecimal fractions,* containing hexadecimal digits (thus .8 is ½, .C is ¾, and so on, as in Figure 35). These can be converted to binary fractions by expressing each hexadecimal digit as four binary digits, just as we did with hexadecimal integers in section 4. Conversion from binary to hexadecimal fractions also works the same way as it does with integers.

BINARY	DECIMAL	HEXADECIMAL
.0	0	.0
.0001	$\frac{1}{16}$	.1
.001	$\frac{1}{8}$	.2
.0011	$\frac{3}{16}$	.3
.01	$\frac{1}{4}$	.4
.0101	$\frac{5}{16}$	.5
.011	$\frac{3}{8}$	.6
.0111	$\frac{7}{16}$	.7
.1	$\frac{1}{2}$	.8
.1001	$\frac{9}{16}$	.9
.101	$\frac{5}{8}$	.A
.1011	$\frac{11}{16}$	.B
.11	$\frac{3}{4}$	.C
.1101	$\frac{13}{16}$	.D
.111	$\frac{7}{8}$	.E
.1111	$\frac{15}{16}$	.F
1.0	1	1.0

Figure 35. Binary and Hexadecimal Fractions.

EXERCISES

1. What fraction a/b (for *decimal* integers a and b) corresponds to each of the following unending binary fractions? (Give the fraction in lowest terms, in each case.)

   (a) .101010 . . . . .
   *(b) .10011001 . . . . .
   (c) .100100 . . . . .

2. Give the closest approximation to each of the following fractions as an unsigned fixed-point number of the form $bb.bbbbbb$ (that is, in 8 bits with the binary point between bits 6 and 5, counting from the right as bit zero):

   *(a) $\frac{4}{5}$
   (b) $2\frac{6}{7}$
   *(c) π

3. Decimal fractions of the form $k/10^n$ are terminating; but there are certain decimal fractions (1/5, for example) which are terminating but which are not (at least in lowest terms) of the form $k/10^n$. Are there any *binary* fractions which are terminating, but which are not of the form $k/2^n$ in their lowest terms? Why or why not?

98. REAL NUMBERS AND FLOATING POINT

A fixed-point representation, such as those of the preceding section, cannot normally handle certain very large and very small numbers (such as 6.061×10^{23} or 6.626×10^{-27}) that occur in calculations. In order for a computer to process real numbers, an alternative representation, known as *floating point*, is generally used.

The basic idea behind floating point is that we need three pieces of information to specify a general real number such as 6.626×10^{-27}:

(a) the *sign* (whether it is positive or negative);
(b) the *exponent* (that is, the power of ten, or -27 in this case, although in floating-point format this is actually a power of 2—or sometimes 16— rather than 10);
(c) and the *fraction* (that is, 6.626, which is not really a fraction, but in floating point we express it as a fraction, which we always can do; that is, we can write $.6626 \times 10^{-26}$ instead of 6.626×10^{-27}, and here .6626 is a fraction, that is, less than 1).

Since this is all the information we need to express a real number, all we need to do now is to specify a format. There are various floating-point formats; the following is the "short format" of large IBM computers such as the 4300 series:

(1) Each real number is specified in four bytes.
(2) The leftmost bit of the first byte is the sign; 0 means positive and 1 means negative, just as with integers.
(3) The rest of the first byte is the exponent.
(4) The other three bytes are the fraction.
(5) The exponent is a power of 16 (this is unusual; in most floating-point formats, it is a power of 2).
(6) The fraction is treated as a 6-digit hexadecimal fraction between .100000 and .FFFFFF (if it is less than .100000, we use the relation $.0xxxxx \times 16^n = .xxxxx0 \times 16^{n-1}$, repeatedly if necessary, to *normalize* the fraction, or put it in the above range).

(7) The exponent, in the range from -64 to 63, is *biased* by adding 64 to it; this puts it in the range from 0 to 127. Thus an exponent of e is actually represented as $e + 64$. (This is like biasing an electronic circuit by adding a constant positive voltage in such a way that the voltage will always remain positive, no matter how it fluctuates.)

The reason for biasing is that, as long as two floating-point numbers are *normalized* (that is, have normalized fractions in the sense of (6) above), the one with the larger exponent will always be larger. Hence we can compare two floating-point numbers by comparing their exponents, and then comparing the fractions if the exponents are equal. When we compare the exponents, biasing effectively converts a signed comparison into an unsigned comparison, much as was done in section 54. In fact, the bias is constructed in the same way that it was in that section; that is, it consists of 1 followed by a string of zeroes.

Figure 36 shows the floating-point representations of 2, 48, -2^{28}, and $1/512$, in the format above. Note how the exponent causes the actual position of the binary (or hexadecimal) point to "float" through the fraction (and sometimes off to the left or off to the right), which is why this format is called floating-point.

The number zero is expressed in floating point with a fraction of zero; the sign and the exponent do not matter in this case, but it is customary to make them zero as well. Note that a floating-point number, in the above format, *can* be changed into its negative by changing only one bit (the sign bit), unlike the case of twos' complement integers. (There are other common floating-point formats for which this is not the case.)

EXERCISES

1. Express each of the following real numbers as a normalized floating-point number, in the format given in the text (use hexadecimal, and express each quantity as 8 hexadecimal digits):

    *(a) $\frac{3}{8}$
     (b) $-11\frac{1}{2}$
    *(c) 2^{113}

2. In each case below, give the (decimal) real number whose expression in the floating-point format of the text is given in hexadecimal as:

     (a) BF140000 (express as a fraction in lowest terms)
    *(b) 42650000
     (c) 1F000400 (express as a power of 2)

*3. One of the numbers in the preceding exercise is not normalized. Which one is it? Express this number in normalized form.

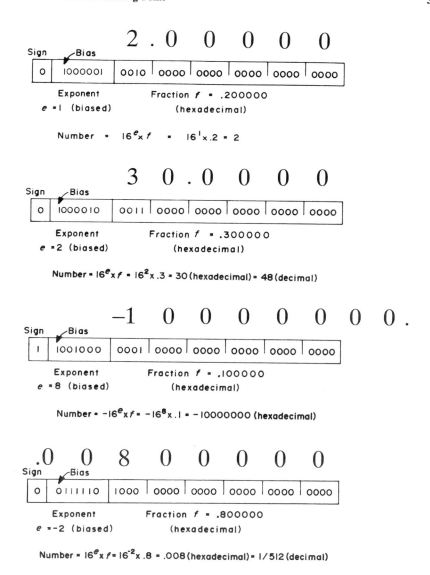

Figure 36. Floating Point Representation of Real Numbers.

99. FLOATING-POINT OPERATIONS

Once we have some numbers represented in floating-point format, what do we do with them? The answer, on the 6502, is that we *call subroutines* to add them, subtract or multiply or divide them, convert them to integer form and vice versa, and read them in or put them out. These subroutines are somewhat like the integer multiplication and division subroutines that we introduced in sections 39 and 40.

It should be mentioned that, on large computers such as the IBM 4300 series, there is, in fact, a single instruction which adds two floating-point numbers; and the same is true for subtraction, multiplication, and division. This is actually not nearly as much of a convenience as it would seem. Instead of one instruction (floating-point multiply), you have one instruction (JSR, which calls the floating-point multiplication subroutine), and so on, throughout your program. Also, you pay a tremendous amount for having floating-point instructions, because the computers which have them are so much more expensive than microcomputers such as the 6502.

Multiplication and division of floating-point numbers are actually easier than addition and subtraction. A floating-point number with sign s, exponent e, and fraction f may be expressed as $s \times b^e \times f$, where b is the base (16, for the floating-point format of the preceding section) and s, the sign, is taken as 1 for positive numbers and -1 for negative numbers. The product of $s_1 \times b^{e_1} \times f_1$ and $s_2 \times b^{e_2} \times f_2$ is $(s_1 \times s_2) \times (b^{e_1} \times b^{e_2}) \times (f_1 \times f_2)$, and $b^{e_1} \times b^{e_2}$ may be expressed as $b^{e_1 + e_2}$. It follows that, to multiply two floating-point numbers, all we have to do is to *multiply* the signs, *add* the exponents, and *multiply* the fractions. The result might not be normalized—the fraction .3 times itself gives .09 (for example)—but if it is not normalized, the normalization rule of the preceding section has to be applied only once.

In a similar way, dividing $s_1 \times b^{e_1} \times f_1$ by $s_2 \times b^{e_2} \times f_2$ gives $(s_1/s_2) \times (b^{e_1}/b^{e_2}) \times (f_1/f_2)$, and b^{e_1}/b^{e_2} may be expressed as $b^{e_1 - e_2}$. Hence in this case we would *divide* the signs, *subtract* the exponents, and *divide* the fractions. Again the answer might not be normalized—the fraction .F divided by .1 gives F in hexadecimal, for example—but, again, the normalization rule has to be applied only once (in the reverse direction from the above).

The reason that addition and subtraction are harder is concerned with the *shifting* that takes place when the binary points do not line up. We recall that, for example,

$$235.9 \qquad = \qquad \begin{array}{r} 235.9 \\ + \ \ 2.359 \\ \hline 238.259 \end{array}$$
$$+2.359$$

and, in general, whenever we add two decimal fractions, we have to shift one of them over so that the decimal point lines up with that of the other one. We saw from Figure 36 that the binary point in a floating-point number "floats" one position to the right each time the exponent is incremented by one. Hence if the difference between the exponents is z, then the smaller number is shifted z places to the right—in this case, z hexadecimal digits, or $4z$ bits—before addition. The same is true of subtraction.

The signs of two floating-point numbers being added or subtracted determine whether the operation to be performed is actually an addition or a subtraction. If the signs are unequal, then what was specified as an addition becomes a subtraction, and vice versa.

Subtraction is the one floating-point operation for which the normalization rule might have to be applied more than once. For example, the hexadecimal subtraction

$$\begin{array}{r} .532684 \\ - .532271 \\ \hline .000413 \end{array}$$

produces a fraction which has three leading zeroes, so that the normalization rule must be applied three times.

Always remember that floating-point numbers are only approximations of real numbers, and a succession of floating-point operations can easily tend to make the approximations even worse. This is especially true of subtraction, even though it might seem to be an exact operation (as above). If the first fraction above is off by one in the last position, so that the answer becomes .000412 or .412000 $\times$ 16^{-3}, this is off by 1000 (hexadecimal), rather than off by one. Addition, multiplication, and division of floating-point numbers may produce erroneous results even when the numbers being added, multiplied, or divided are themselves exact.

Real numbers are often used in statistical calculations, which make use of random numbers. The APPLE keeps a 16-bit random number, with bytes reversed, in cells RNDL and RNDH ("random, low" and "random, high," with RNDL EPZ \$4E and RNDH EPZ \$4F). Every time RDKEY is called, these locations act like a spinning roulette wheel, adding 1 over and over (ignoring carry) until a key is pressed, at which point the roulette wheel stops, and the number in these locations has been randomly selected.

EXERCISES

1. Explain in words how the floating-point numbers 42FF0000 and 41100000 are added, and how the result is produced. Check your work by converting each of these quantities into a real number, adding these real numbers, and converting the result back to normalized floating-point form.

*2. Explain in words how the floating-point numbers 41200000 and 41300000 are multiplied, and how the result is produced. Check your work by converting each of these quantities into a real number, multiplying these real numbers, and converting the result back to normalized floating-point form.

3. Let Q be the real number whose floating-point form is 50800000 (in hexadecimal). What happens, in the computer, when we perform the computation (Q+1)−Q? What point, noted in the text, does this example illustrate?

100. TYPELESS PROCESSING

We are now, finally, in a position to clear up a mystery that was left hanging in section 7. In that section we took up the fact that *all* data in a computer—signed integers, unsigned integers, character codes, or whatever—is encoded in binary, as one or more bytes. It follows that when we are given one or more bytes, representing a particular piece of data in some program, *there is no way to tell whether this is supposed to represent an integer, a real number, or something else*, except by understanding the program. This is a fundamental fact about data in any computer.

We know, however, that there are programming languages in which real numbers and integers can be intermixed in computations. This seems to be inconsistent with what we have just said. Suppose that we are using an interpreter, as described in section 94. Now consider the calculation of A+B, where A and B can be either integers or real numbers. If they are real numbers, the interpreter has to call a floating-point addition subroutine. If they are integers, it has to add them as integers. How can it possibly decide which one of these to do, if there is no way to tell a real number from an integer?

We note, first of all, that our difficulty depends on the fact that A and B can be integers and then, later on, real numbers *in the same run of the same program*. In some languages, such as FORTRAN, every real variable in a program remains real throughout that program, and the same is true for integers, so decisions like those discussed above can always be made. (In some versions of BASIC, all integers are kept in the computer as real numbers. This slows down the BASIC system, because now *all* addition has to be done in floating point; but it does allow the BASIC system to make this kind of decision.)

The general answer to the above problem is known as *typeless processing*. In typeless processing, every variable in a program has a *type code*, which is kept in memory along with the value of the variable. There are many kinds of type codes for a variable V; the simplest is possibly the following:

> TCV = 0   means that V is currently an integer
> TCV = 1   means that V is currently a real number

Both the value of V and the value of TCV may change as the program is running. If V is an integer, for example, and becomes real, then TCV is set to 1.

The addition of two numbers A and B, with type codes TCA and TCB as above, now proceeds as follows:

(1) If TCA = TCB = 0, add A and B as integers.
(2) If TCA = TCB = 1, add A and B as real numbers.
(3) If TCA = 1, but TCB = 0, add A and CONVR(B) as real numbers, where CONVR(B) is the real number corresponding to the integer B (CONVR means "convert to real").
(4) If TCA = 0, but TCB = 1, add CONVR(A) and B as real numbers.

It might appear that typeless processing is wasteful of both space and time, because of all the type codes and the testing, as above, that must take place every time we do an operation, even as simple as adding. However, there are many programs which run so fast, and take up such a small portion of available memory, that the extra convenience of typeless processing becomes worth its cost.

In more general typeless processing, there will be more than two types. In some languages, "integer" and "integer array" are different types; indeed, a single integer array of dimension n is a different type from a single integer array of any other dimension $m \neq n$. In LISP, a list processing language, "list" is a type, and "atom" (which includes integers) is another type. In SNOBOL, a string processing language, "integer" is one type and "string" is another.

EXERCISES

*1. In some versions of BASIC, there are three kinds of variables: real variables, whose names contain letters and digits only; integer variables, whose names end in the % character; and string variables, whose names end in the $ character. Is typeless processing appropriate for such a version of BASIC? Why or why not?

2. In the programming language APL, variable names may represent arrays, and there are array operations on these variables. Thus, for example, if A and B are array names, then setting A equal to A+B is equivalent to setting $A(k)$ equal to $A(k)+B(k)$, for all k in the range of these arrays. Likewise, setting A equal to A,B (using the comma as an operator like +) is equivalent to setting A equal to the concatenation of the arrays A and B; if A contains m elements and B contains n elements, then the new array value of A will contain $m+n$ elements. Assuming that all array elements are integers, is typeless processing appropriate for this language? Why or why not?

*3. Suppose that the quantity J, in the 6502, has a type code TJ. If TJ = 0, then J is an unsigned 8-bit quantity. If TJ = 1, then J is an unsigned 16-bit quantity, kept with bytes reversed as usual. The quantity K, in the same way, has the type code TK. Explain, in words, how typeless processing would be used to set $J = J+K$ under these circumstances. (There are four cases to consider. Note that the operation of addition does not, in itself, change the type code of J.)

PROBLEM 6 FOR COMPUTER SOLUTION
EIGHT QUEENS

Our final problem is one which is considerably easier than it looks. Consider the chessboard below, with eight queens on it:

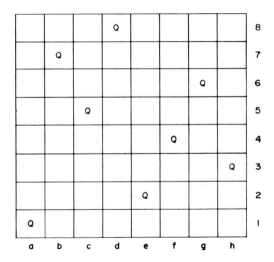

No two of these queens attack each other, meaning (by the rules of chess) that no two of them are on the same row, column, or diagonal row. Finding positions like this is not at all easy, by hand; your task is to find all of them (there are 92, in fact) by computer.

In such a position there is clearly one and only one queen in each row, 1 through 8 (otherwise two queens would attack each other along a row). Hence we can make a table:

ROW	1	2	3	4	5	6	7	8
COLUMN	a	e	h	f	c	g	b	d

for the above position, and refer to it as "position *aehfcgbd*." The trick is to generate all such positions *in alphabetical order*. (We will use "generate" to mean "find and display.") All the positions starting with a (like *aehfcgbd*) are generated first; then all those starting with b; and so on. Within those starting with a, we would start with those that started with aa or with ab, if there were any, which there are not, because a queen in row 2 and column a or b would attack a queen in row 1 and column a. (There are no positions starting with ac or ad either, but this takes much longer to figure out.)

What we now have to do is to number the *diagonal* rows also. There are 15 diagonal rows from upper left to lower right (let us call these rows of type P), and 15 more from upper right to lower left (let us call these rows of type Q). So we set up two arrays, P and Q, of length 15, both initialized to zero. Whenever we place a queen on the board, in row x of type P and row y of type Q, we set $P(x)$ and $Q(y)$ to 1, to indicate that these two diagonal rows are now occupied. Before we do this, we test whether $P(x)$ or $Q(y)$ was already 1; if so, we cannot place this queen since we already have another one on the board that would attack it. When this same queen is *removed* from the board, $P(x)$ and $Q(y)$ are set back to zero.

The program now proceeds as follows. Place a queen on the board in row 1 and column a (going through the diagonal row logic above). Now generate all positions starting with a (see the next paragraph). When this is done, *remove* the queen from row 1 and column a and place it back in row 1 and column b, and proceed to generate all positions starting with b (in the same way). Keep on doing this until you have generated all positions.

To generate all positions starting with a, try to place the next queen on each of the columns a, b, c, and so on, in turn, and row 2. The first one which is possible is c. Now generate all positions starting with ac in exactly the same way: move to row 3 and try each column one at a time. If you are on row i and you run out of columns, then go back to row $i-1$ (actually, *decrease* i by 1 and then go back to row i, for the new i), *remove* the queen that is in that row (unless the new $i = 0$, in which case the program is finished), and try to place a queen in the next position in that row, after the position it was in.

When you have generated a good position, like the one in the diagram above, display it (using COUT), and then proceed forward from that position, *exactly* as if you had failed to find a good position. It might pay you to write this program in BASIC first and debug it that way (make sure that you generate a total of 92 positions) and then rewrite it in assembly language.

APPENDIX

LIST OF TABLES

Table 1
BASIC in Terms of FORTRAN, PL/I, and Pascal

ASSIGNMENT	$v = e$ where v is a variable and e is an expression. Like $v = e$ in FORTRAN; like $v = e$; in PL/I; like $v: = e$ in PASCAL. BASIC does not use semicolons or colon-equals.
BLANKS	Unlike FORTRAN (and APPLE BASIC), standard BASIC does not ignore *all* blanks. Blanks may not appear inside a variable name. (In assembly language, blanks can appear *only* where they are explicitly allowed.)
CONDITIONAL STATEMENTS	IF c THEN n (where n is a line number—see below) Like IF (c) GOTO n in FORTRAN; like IF c THEN GOTO n; in PL/I (see GO TO below); like IF c THEN GOTO n in PASCAL. IF c THEN s (where s is a statement) Like IF (c) s in FORTRAN; like IF c THEN s; in PL/I; like IF c THEN s in PASCAL.
CONSTANTS	Except in some extended versions of BASIC, *no* difference between integer and real constants. There are also string constants (which we will not consider here).
END	As far as we are concerned, like END in FORTRAN, PL/I, or PASCAL.
GOSUB	GOSUB n is like CALL S in FORTRAN or PL/I, or S (by itself) in PASCAL, where S starts at line n. BASIC has *no* subroutine parameter facility.
GOTO	Like GOTO in FORTRAN, PL/I, or PASCAL, except that in PL/I one writes GO TO v where v is a *label* (see LINE NUMBERS, below), and GO TO is not discouraged in BASIC as it is in PASCAL.
INPUT-OUTPUT	INPUT and PRINT statements, with which we will *not* be concerned here.
ITERATION	FOR $v = m$ TO n followed by a group of statements g followed by NEXT v—Like DO k $v = m,n$ followed by g (having final statement number n) in FORTRAN. Like DO $v = m$ TO n; g; END; in PL/I. Like FOR $v: = m$ TO n DO BEGIN g END .า PASCAL. There is also FOR $v = m$ TO n STEP j in BASIC, but we shall not be concerned with this variation.
LINE NUMBERS	*Must be in sequence* in BASIC. Otherwise they are like statement numbers in FORTRAN or labels in PASCAL, or labels (except that in BASIC they are *integers*) in PL/I.
RELATIONAL OPERATORS	$<$ $>$ $<=$ $>=$ $=$ $<>$—Like .LT. .GT. .LE. .GE. .EQ. .NE. in FORTRAN; like LT GT LE GE $=\neg=$ in PL/I.
RETURN	Like RETURN in PL/I (except that there is no RETURN (e) facility) or FORTRAN. (In PASCAL, one returns from a subroutine by executing its last statement.)
VARIABLE NAMES	*One or two characters only,* except in extended versions of BASIC. Arrays declared with DIM $v(s)$, like DIMENSION $v(s)$ in FORTRAN, VAR v; ARRAY [range] OF t in PASCAL, or DCL $v(s)$ in PL/I.

Table 2

Hexadecimal-Decimal and Decimal-Hexadecimal Conversion

	Fourth Digit	Third Digit	Second Digit	First Digit		Fifth Digit	Fourth Digit	Third Digit	Second Digit	First Digit
0	0	0	0	0	0	0	0	0	0	0
1	4096	256	16	1	1	2710	3E8	64	A	1
2	8192	512	32	2	2	4E20	7D0	C8	14	2
3	12288	768	48	3	3	7530	BB8	12C	1E	3
4	16384	1024	64	4	4	9C40	FA0	190	28	4
5	20480	1280	80	5	5	C350	1388	1F4	32	5
6	24576	1536	96	6	6	EA60	1770	258	3C	6
7	28672	1792	112	7	7	11170	1B58	2BC	46	7
8	32768	2048	128	8	8	13880	1F40	320	50	8
9	36864	2304	144	9	9	16F90	2328	384	5A	9
A	40960	2560	160	10						
B	45056	2816	176	11			**Decimal to Hexadecimal**			
C	49152	3072	192	12						
D	53248	3328	208	13						
E	57344	3584	224	14						
F	61440	3840	240	15						

Hexadecimal to Decimal

To convert B7DC to decimal, look up:

B under Fourth Digit	—	45056
7 under Third Digit	—	1792
D under Second Digit	—	208
C under First Digit	—	12
Then add. Answer is	—	47068

To convert 47068 to hexadecimal, look up:

4 under Fifth Digit	—	9C40
7 under Fourth Digit	—	1B58
6 under Second Digit	—	3C
8 under First Digit	—	8
Then add. Answer is	—	B7DC

Example

Table 3
Names, Meanings, and Flag Settings of 6502 Instructions

Section Number	Sets Flags	Mnemonic		Name and Meaning
15	ZSCV	ADC	v	ADD WITH CARRY Sets $A=A+v+C$
52	ZS	AND	v	LOGICAL AND Sets $A=A$ *and* v
31	ZSC	ASL	v	ARITHMETIC SHIFT LEFT Sets $v=2*v$ (if v missing, sets $A=2*A$)
19	none	BCC	L	BRANCH ON CARRY CLEAR Goes to L if $C=0$
19	none	BCS	L	BRANCH ON CARRY SET Goes to L if $C=1$
20	none	BEQ	L	BRANCH ON EQUAL Goes to L if $Z=1$
55	ZSV	BIT	v	BIT TEST Calculates A *and* v (logical AND); sets Z; sets S and V to leftmost two bits of v, respectively
28	none	BMI	L	BRANCH ON MINUS Goes to L if $S=1$
20	none	BNE	L	BRANCH ON NOT EQUAL Goes to L if $Z=0$
28	none	BPL	L	BRANCH ON PLUS Goes to L if $S=0$
42	B	BRK		BREAK Goes to the monitor
56	none	BVC	L	BRANCH ON OVERFLOW CLEAR Goes to L if $V=0$
56	none	BVS	L	BRANCH ON OVERFLOW SET Goes to L if $V=1$
15	C	CLC		CLEAR CARRY Sets $C=0$
65	D	CLD		CLEAR DECIMAL MODE Sets $D=0$
68	I	CLI		CLEAR INTERRUPT FLAG Sets $I=0$ (*enables* interrupts)
56	V	CLV		CLEAR OVERFLOW FLAG Sets $V=0$
20	ZSC	CMP	v	COMPARE (WITH A) Calculates $A-v$; sets flags
20	ZSC	CPX	v	COMPARE WITH X Calculates $X-v$; sets flags
20	ZSC	CPY	v	COMPARE WITH Y Calculates $Y-v$; sets flags
9	ZS	DEC	v	DECREMENT MEMORY Sets $v=v-1$
9	ZS	DEX		DECREMENT X Sets $X=X-1$
9	ZS	DEY		DECREMENT Y Sets $Y=Y-1$
54	ZS	EOR	v	EXCLUSIVE OR Sets $A=A$ *eor* v

Continued on next page

Table 3—*Continued*

Section Number	Sets Flags	Mnemonic	Name and Meaning
9	ZS	INC v	INCREMENT MEMORY Sets $v=v+1$
9	ZS	INX	INCREMENT X Sets $X=X+1$
9	ZS	INY	INCREMENT Y Sets $Y=Y+1$
20	none	JMP L	JUMP Goes to L (direct or indirect)
25	none	JSR L	JUMP TO SUBROUTINE Calls L
8	ZS	LDA v	LOAD A Sets $A=v$
8	ZS	LDX v	LOAD X Sets $X=v$
8	ZS	LDY v	LOAD Y Sets $Y=v$
31	ZSC	LSR v	LOGICAL SHIFT RIGHT Sets $v=v/2$ (unsigned; if v missing, sets $A = A/2$)
50	none	NOP	NO OPERATION Does nothing
53	ZS	ORA	LOGICAL OR Sets $A=A$ *or* v
60	none	PHA	PUSH A Saves A on the stack
67	none	PHP	PUSH P Saves P on the stack
60	ZS	PLA	PULL A Restores A from stack
67	*all*	PLP	PULL P Restores P from stack
34	ZSC	ROL v	ROTATE LEFT Sets $v=2*v+C$ (if v missing, sets $A = 2*A + C$)
34	ZSC	ROR v	ROTATE RIGHT Sets $v=(256*C+v)/2$ (if v missing, sets $A=(256*C + A)/2$)
68	*all*	RTI	RETURN FROM INTERRUPT Returns to program being run from an interrupt routine
39	none	RTS	RETURN FROM SUBROUTINE Returns to calling program from subroutine
17	ZSCV	SBC v	SUBTRACT WITH CARRY Sets $A=(A-v)+(1-C)$
17	C	SEC	SET CARRY Sets $C=1$
65	D	SED	SET DECIMAL MODE Sets $D=1$
68	I	SEI	SET INTERRUPT FLAG Sets $I=1$ (*disables* interrupts)
8	none	STA v	STORE A Sets $v=A$
8	none	STX v	STORE X Sets $v=X$
8	none	STY v	STORE Y Sets $v=Y$
18	ZS	TAX	TRANSFER A TO X Sets $X=A$
18	ZS	TAY	TRANSFER A TO Y Sets $Y=A$
60	ZS	TSX	TRANSFER SP TO X Sets $X=SP$
18	ZS	TXA	TRANSFER X TO A Sets $A=X$
60	none	TXS	TRANSFER X TO SP Sets $SP=X$
18	ZS	TYA	TRANSFER Y TO A Sets $A=Y$

(For machine language forms and instruction times, see Table 4)

Table 4
Assembly and Machine Language Forms and Instruction Timing

(CONVENTIONS: L and Q have address *abcd*; Z has address 00*ef*; *n* has hexadecimal value *gh*; *jk* satisfies $AI + 2 + jk = AL$, where AI = address of this instruction, and AL = address of L)

Assembly Language	Number of Cycles[3]	Machine Language	Assembly Language	Number of Cycles[3]	Machine Language
ADC Q	4	6D *cd ab*	CMP #*n*	2	C9 *gh*
ADC Z	3	65 *ef*	CMP Q, X	4^1	DD *cd ab*
ADC #*n*	2	69 *gh*	CMP Q, Y	4^1	D9 *cd ab*
ADC Q, X	4^1	7D *cd ab*	CMP (Z, X)	6	C1 *ef*
ADC Q, Y	4^1	79 *cd ab*	CMP (Z), Y	5^1	D1 *ef*
ADC (Z, X)	6	61 *ef*	CMP Z, X	4	D5 *ef*
ADC (Z), Y	5^1	71 *ef*	CPX Q	4	EC *cd ab*
ADC Z, X	4	75 *ef*	CPX Z	3	E4 *ef*
AND Q	4	2D *cd ab*	CPX #*n*	2	E0 *gh*
AND Z	3	25 *ef*	CPY Q	4	CC *cd ab*
AND #*n*	2	29 *gh*	CPY Z	3	C4 *ef*
AND Q, X	4^1	3D *cd ab*	CPY #*n*	2	C0 *gh*
AND Q, Y	4^1	39 *cd ab*	DEC Q	6	CE *cd ab*
AND (Z, X)	6	21 *ef*	DEC Z	5	C6 *ef*
AND (Z), Y	5^1	31 *ef*	DEC Q, X	7	DE *cd ab*
AND Z, X	4	35 *ef*	DEC Z, X	5	C6 *ef*
ASL	2	0A	DEX	2	CA
ASL Q	6	0E *cd ab*	DEY	2	88
ASL Z	5	06 *ef*	EOR Q	4	4D *cd ab*
ASL Q, X	7	1E *cd ab*	EOR Z	3	45 *ef*
ASL Z, X	6	16 *ef*	EOR #*n*	2	49 *gh*
BCC L	3^2	90 *jk*	EOR Q, X	4^1	5D *cd ab*
BCS L	3^2	B0 *jk*	EOR Q, Y	4^1	59 *cd ab*
BEQ L	3^2	F0 *jk*	EOR (Z, X)	6	41 *ef*
BIT Q	4	2C *cd ab*	EOR (Z), Y	5^1	51 *ef*
BIT Z	3	24 *ef*	EOR Z, X	4	55 *ef*
BMI L	3^2	30 *jk*	INC Q	6	EE *cd ab*
BNE L	3^2	D0 *jk*	INC Z	5	E6 *ef*
BPL L	3^2	10 *jk*	INC Q, X	7	FE *cd ab*
BRK	7	00	INC Z, X	6	F6 *ef*
BVC L	3^2	50 *jk*	INX	2	E8
BVS L	3^2	70 *jk*	INY	2	C8
CLC	2	18	JMP L	3	4C *cd ab*
CLD	2	D8	JMP (L)	5	6C *cd ab*
CLI	2	58	JSR L	6	20 *cd ab*
CLV	2	B8	LDA Q	4	AD *cd ab*
CMP Q	4	CD *cd ab*	LDA Z	3	A5 *ef*
CMP Z	3	C5 *ef*	LDA #*n*	2	A9 *gh*

Continued on next page

Table 4—*Continued*

Assembly Language		Number of Cycles[3]	Machine Language	Assembly Language		Number of Cycles[3]	Machine Language
LDA	Q, X	4[1]	BD *cd ab*	ROR		2	6A
LDA	Q, Y	4[1]	B9 *cd ab*	ROR	Q	6	6E *cd ab*
LDA	(Z, X)	6	A1 *ef*	ROR	Z	5	66 *ef*
LDA	(Z), Y	5[1]	B1 *ef*	ROR	Q, X	7	7E *cd ab*
LDA	Z, X	4	B5 *ef*	ROR	Z, X	6	76 *ef*
LDX	Q	4	AE *cd ab*	RTI		6	40
LDX	Z	3	A6 *ef*	RTS		6	60
LDX	#*n*	2	A2 *gh*	SBC	Q	4	ED *cd ab*
LDX	Q, Y	4[1]	BE *cd ab*	SBC	Z	3	E5 *ef*
LDX	Z, Y	4	B6 *ef*	SBC	#*n*	2	E9 *gh*
LDY	Q	4	AC *cd ab*	SBC	Q, X	4[1]	FD *cd ab*
LDY	Z	3	A4 *ef*	SBC	Q, Y	4[1]	F9 *cd ab*
LDY	#*n*	2	A0 *gh*	SBC	(Z, X)	6	E1 *ef*
LDY	Q, X	4[1]	BC *cd ab*	SBC	(Z), Y	5[1]	F1 *ef*
LDY	Z, X	4	B4 *ef*	SBC	Z, X	4	F5 *ef*
LSR		2	4A	SEC		2	38
LSR	Q	6	4E *cd ab*	SED		2	F8
LSR	Z	5	46 *ef*	SEI		2	78
LSR	Q, X	7	5E *cd ab*	STA	Q	4	8D *cd ab*
LSR	Z, X	6	56 *ef*	STA	Z	3	85 *ef*
NOP		2	EA	STA	Q, X	5	9D *cd ab*
ORA	Q	4	0D *cd ab*	STA	Q, Y	5	99 *cd ab*
ORA	Z	3	05 *ef*	STA	(Z, X)	6	81 *ef*
ORA	#*n*	2	09 *gh*	STA	(Z), Y	6	91 *ef*
ORA	Q, X	4[1]	1D *cd ab*	STA	Z, X	4	95 *ef*
ORA	Q, Y	4[1]	19 *cd ab*	STX	Q	4	8E *cd ab*
ORA	(Z, X)	6	01 *ef*	STX	Z	3	86 *ef*
ORA	(Z), Y	5[1]	11 *ef*	STX	Z, Y	4	96 *ef*
ORA	Z, X	4	15 *ef*	STY	Q	4	8C *cd ab*
PHA		3	48	STY	Z	3	84 *ef*
PHP		3	08	STY	Z, X	4	94 *ef*
PLA		4	68	TAX		2	AA
PLP		4	28	TAY		2	A8
ROL		2	2A	TSX		2	BA
ROL	Q	6	2E *cd ab*	TXA		2	8A
ROL	Z	5	26 *ef*	TXS		2	9A
ROL	Q, X	7	3E *cd ab*	TYA		2	98
ROL	Z, X	6	36 *ef*				

For flag settings and the meaning of each instruction, see Table 3; for explanations of the addressing modes, see Table 8; for maching language forms in numerical order, see Table 5.

[1]Plus one if addition of index to address causes carry into high order byte of address.

[2]Minus one if the instruction does not branch; plus one if addition of signed relative address causes the high-order byte of the address to increase or decrease by 1.

[3]One cycle ≃ 0.9775 microseconds; 1,023,000 cycles = 1 second.

Table 5
6502 Instructions—Machine Language in Numerical Order

(CONVENTIONS: L and Q have address *abcd*; Z has address 00*ef*; *n* has hexadecimal value *gh*; *jk* satisfies AI + 2 + *jk* = AL, where AI = address of this instruction, and AL = address of L)

Machine Language	Assembly Language		Machine Language	Assembly Language	
00	BRK		45 *ef*	EOR	Z
01 *ef*	ORA	(Z, X)	46 *ef*	LSR	Z
05 *ef*	ORA	Z	48	PHA	
06 *ef*	ASL	Z	49 *gh*	EOR	#*n*
08	PHP		4A	LSR	
09 *gh*	ORA	#*n*	4C *cd ab*	JMP	L
0A	ASL		4D *cd ab*	EOR	Q
0D *cd ab*	ORA	Q	4E *cd ab*	LSR	Q
0E *cd ab*	ASL	Q	50 *jk*	BVC	L
10 *jk*	BPL	L	51 *ef*	EOR	(Z) , Y
11 *ef*	ORA	(Z) , Y	55 *ef*	EOR	Z, X
15 *ef*	ORA	Z, X	56 *ef*	LSR	Z, X
16 *ef*	ASL	Z, X	58	CLI	
18	CLC		59 *cd ab*	EOR	Q, Y
19 *cd ab*	ORA	Q, Y	5D *cd ab*	EOR	Q, X
1D *cd ab*	ORA	Q, X	5E *cd ab*	LSR	Q, X
1E *cd ab*	ASL	Q, X	60	RTS	
20 *cd ab*	JSR	L	61 *ef*	ADC	(Z, X)
21 *ef*	AND	(Z, X)	65 *ef*	ADC	Z
24 *ef*	BIT	Z	66 *ef*	ROR	Z
25 *ef*	AND	Z	68	PLA	
26 *ef*	ROL	Z	69 *gh*	ADC	#*n*
28	PLP		6A	ROR	
29 *gh*	AND	#*n*	6C *cd ab*	JMP	(L)
2A	ROL		6D *cd ab*	ADC	Q
2C *cd ab*	BIT	Q	6E *cd ab*	ROR	Q
2D *cd ab*	AND	Q	70 *jk*	BVS	L
2E *cd ab*	ROL	Q	71 *ef*	ADC	(Z) , Y
30 *jk*	BMI	L	75 *ef*	ADC	Z, X
31 *ef*	AND	(Z) , Y	76 *ef*	ROR	Z, X
35 *ef*	AND	Z, X	78	SEI	
36 *ef*	ROL	Z, X	79 *cd ab*	ADC	Q, Y
38	SEC		7D *cd ab*	ADC	Q, X
39 *cd ab*	AND	Q, Y	7E *cd ab*	ROR	Q, X
3D *cd ab*	AND	Q, X	81 *ef*	STA	(Z, X)
3E *cd ab*	ROL	Q, X	84 *ef*	STY	Z
40	RTI		85 *ef*	STA	Z
41 *ef*	EOR	(Z, X)	86 *ef*	STX	Z

Continued on next page

Table 5—*Continued*

Machine Language	Assembly Language		Machine Language	Assembly Language	
88	DEY		C1 *ef*	CMP	(Z, X)
8A	TXA		C4 *ef*	CPY	Z
8C *cd ab*	STY	Q	C5 *ef*	CMP	Z
8D *cd ab*	STA	Q	C6 *ef*	DEC	Z
8E *cd ab*	STX	Q	C8	INY	
90 *jk*	BCC	L	C9 *gh*	CMP	#*n*
91 *ef*	STA	(Z), Y	CA	DEX	
94 *ef*	STY	Z, X	CC *cd ab*	CPY	Q
95 *ef*	STA	Z, X	CD *cd ab*	CMP	Q
96 *ef*	STX	Z, Y	CE *cd ab*	DEC	Q
98	TYA		D0 *jk*	BNE	L
99 *cd ab*	STA	Q, Y	D1 *ef*	CMP	(Z), Y
9A	TXS		D5 *ef*	CMP	Z, X
9D *cd ab*	STA	Q, X	D6 *ef*	DEC	Z, X
A0 *gh*	LDY	#*n*	D8	CLD	
A1 *ef*	LDA	(Z, X)	D9 *cd ab*	CMP	Q, Y
A2 *gh*	LDX	#*n*	DD *cd ab*	CMP	Q, X
A4 *ef*	LDY	Z	DE *cd ab*	DEC	Q, X
A5 *ef*	LDA	Z	E0 *gh*	CPX	#*n*
A6 *ef*	LDX	Z	E1 *ef*	SBC	(Z, X)
A8	TAY		E4 *ef*	CPX	Z
A9 *gh*	LDA	#*n*	E5 *ef*	SBC	Z
AA	TAX		E6 *ef*	INC	Z
AC *cd ab*	LDY	Q	E8	INX	
AD *cd ab*	LDA	Q	E9 *gh*	SBC	#*n*
AE *cd ab*	LDX	Q	EA	NOP	
B0 *jk*	BCS	L	EC *cd ab*	CPX	Q
B1 *ef*	LDA	(Z), Y	ED *cd ab*	SBC	Q
B4 *ef*	LDY	Z, X	EE *cd ab*	INC	Q
B5 *ef*	LDA	Z, X	F0 *jk*	BEQ	L
B6 *ef*	LDX	Z, Y	F1 *ef*	SBC	(Z), Y
B8	CLV		F5 *ef*	SBC	Z, X
B9 *cd ab*	LDA	Q, Y	F6 *ef*	INC	Z, X
BA	TSX		F8	SED	
BC *cd ab*	LDY	Q, X	F9 *cd ab*	SBC	Q, Y
BD *cd ab*	LDA	Q, X	FD *cd ab*	SBC	Q, X
BE *cd ab*	LDX	Q, Y	FE *cd ab*	INC	Q, X
C0 *gh*	CPY	#*n*			

For flag settings and the meaning of each instruction, see Table 3.

For assembly language instructions in alphabetical order, see Table 4.

For explanations of the addressing modes, see Table 8.

Table 6
LISA Pseudo-Operations and Extended Mnemonics

	Pseudo-Operation		Section of This Text	Description (*Note:* {label} means an optional label; *label* means a required label; otherwise, no label)
{label}	ADR	*a*	63	Puts the 16-bit quantity *a* (with symbolic addressing) in memory, with bytes reversed (right-hand byte, then left-hand byte).
{label}	ASC	*s*	26	Puts the string *s* in memory, with the leftmost bit of each byte equal to 0 if *s* is "*cccc...c*" and to 1 if *s* is "*cccc..c*".
{label}	BFL	*k*	83	Branch on false to the label *k*; equivalent to BEQ *k*.
{label}	BGE	*k*	28	Branch to the label *k* on greater-or-equal; equivalent to BCS *k*.
{label}	BLK	*s*	73	Puts the string *s* in memory, with the leftmost two bits of each byte set to 01 (*blinking* mode—characters "blink" on the screen).
{label}	BLT	*k*	28	Branch to the label *k* on less-than; equivalent to BCC *k*.
{label}	BTR	*k*	83	Branch on true to the label *k*; equivalent to BNE *k*.
{label}	BYT	*a*	26	Puts the rightmost 8 bits of the 16-bit quantity *a* (with symbolic addressing) into memory.
{label}	DCI	*s*	73	Puts the string *s* in memory, with the high-order bit of its last byte different from that of the rest of the string (see ASC).
	DCM	"*c*"	92	DOS commands *to LISA* (DCM "OPEN *F*" and DCM "WRITE *f*" at start, DCM "CLOSE" just before END, produce *f* as a *disk listing file*).
{label}	DFS	*n*	11,13	Reserves *n* bytes for the variable or array labelled by *label* at this point (and does not set them to any initial values).
	END		11	Last statement in a program (one and only one END in a program).
label	EPZ	*a*	74	Sets *label* equivalent (see EQU below) to *a* in page zero.
label	EQU	*a*	25	Sets *label* equivalent to *a*. ("Equivalent" means: wherever *label* appears, the program acts as if *a* had been substituted for *label*.)
{label}	HBY	*a*	63	Puts the leftmost 8 bits of the 16-bit quantity *a* (with symbolic addressing) into memory.
{label}	HEX	*h*	73	Puts the string *h* of hexadecimal digits (*not* in quotes) in memory, two hexadecimal digits in each byte.
{label}	INV	*s*	73	Puts the string *s* in memory, with the leftmost two bits of each byte set to 00 (*inverse* mode—black on white).
	LST		92	Turns on the listing option (normally on; see NLS).
	NLS		92	Turns off the listing option, so that assembled instructions will not be listed, unless and until LST is specified.
	OBJ	*a*	51	Specifies program to be assembled into memory at the address *a*, normally $0800, regardless of origin (see ORG).
	ORG	*a*	11	Specifies program to start at the address *a* when it is executed. (May be assembled somewhere else, with OBJ, and moved later.)

Continued on next page

Table 6—*Continued*

	Pseudo-Operation		Section of This Text	Description (*Note*: {label} means an optional label; *label* means a required label; otherwise, no label)
	PAG		92	Page eject for printer listings. Will skip to the top of the next page if you are assembling to the printer.
{label}	STR	*s*	73	Puts the string *s* in memory, preceded by a 7-bit length accompanied by the high-order bit of the rest of the string (LISA 1.5), or an 8-bit length (LISA 2.5; see ASC).
{label}	XOR	*v*	54	Exclusive OR with *v*; same as EOR *v* options for *v* are the same as those for EOR *v*).

Table 7
Meanings of Special Characters in LISA

Character		Section of This Text	Description
Asterisk	*	30	Current location. (ALPHA BEQ *+!5 is equivalent to ALPHA BEQ ALPHA +!5)
Backspace	←	46	For backing up over characters, to correct a mistake.
Colon	:	81	Follows a label if *nothing else* follows that label on this line.
Comma	,	13	For indexing (,X means index register X; ,Y means index register Y)
Control-O,J,K,L		46	These characters allow the cursor to be moved around the screen for correcting mistakes.
Dollar sign	$	8	Precedes a hexadecimal number ($80 means 80 in hexadecimal, or 128 in decimal)
Exclamation point	!	8	Precedes a decimal number (!128 means 128 in decimal, or 80 in hexadecimal)
Hyphen (minus)	−	12,23	Subtraction (if T is the cell with address n, then $T - !k$ is the cell with address $n - k$)
Number sign	#	8	Immediate addressing (LDA #n means load the *number* n, or the lower half of the 16-bit constant n)
Parentheses	( )	58,75,76	Indirect addressing (JMP (L) or *op* (Z,X) or *op* (Z),Y where *op* is LDA, STA, ADC, SBC, CMP, AND, ORA, or EOR)
Percent sign	%	8	Precedes a binary number (%10000000 means 10000000 in binary, or 80 in hexadecimal, or 128 in decimal)
Plus sign	+	12,23	Addition (if T is the cell with address n, then $T+!k$ is the cell with address $n + k$)
Quotes (double)	"	24	"*cccc...* " is the string *cccc...c* with double " replaced by single " and leftmost bit of each byte = 1; "*c* is shorthand for # "*c*"
Quotes (single)	'	24	'*cccc...c*' is the string *cccc...c* with double ' replaced by single ' and leftmost bit of each byte = 0; '*c* is shorthand for # '*c*'
Repeat	REPT	46	Holding down any key k and REPT together produces *kkkk...*
Retype (right arrow)	→	46	After correcting mistakes, allows you to retype the rest of the (presumably correct) characters on the line.
Semicolon	;	18	Blank followed by semicolon (or semicolon in column 1) precedes a *comment* (ignored by the assembler)
Slash	/	58	High order immediate addressing (LDA /n means load the upper half of the 16-bit constant n)
Space	(blank)	19	One *or more* spaces precede and follow the mnemonic code on each line (and the semicolon if it is used)

Table 8
6502 Instructions—Explanations of Addressing Modes

Addressing Mode Symbol	Name	Section of This Text	Description
L(JMP, JSR)	Absolute	27	Jump is to the cell with address *abcd*, where *cd* is the second and *ab* the third byte of the instruction.
L (other)	Relative	27	Branch is to the cell with address *pqrs*+2+*jk*, where this instruction is at addresses *pqrs* and *pqrs*+1, and *jk* is the *signed* integer at address *pqrs*+1.
#*n*	Immediate	8	Refers to the number in the second byte of the instruction.
None	Implied or accumulator	10	No reference required; or, in the case of shifts, the A register is shifted.
Q	Absolute (extended)	8	Refers to the contents of the cell with address *abcd*, where *cd* is the second and *ab* the third byte of the instruction.
(Q)	Indirect (not indexed)	58	Refers to the contents of the cell with address *pqrs*, where cell *abcd* (as above) contains *rs* and cell *abcd*+1 contains *pq*.
Q,X	Absolute, indexed by X	13	Refers to the contents of the cell with address *abcd*+*xx*, where *abcd* is as above and *xx* is in the X register.
Q,Y	Absolute indexed by Y	13	Refers to the contents of the cell with address *abcd*+*yy*, where *abcd* is as above and *yy* is in the Y register.
Z	Zero page (direct)	74	Refers to the contents of the cell with address 00*ef*, where *ef* is the second byte of the instruction.
Z,X	Zero page, indexed by X	74	Refers to the contents of the cell with address 00*ef*+*xx*, where *ef* is as above and *xx* is in the X register.
(Z,X)	Pre-indexed indirect	75	Refers to the contents of the cell with address *pqrs*, where cell 00*ef*+*xx* (with *ef* and *xx* as above) contains *rs* and cell 00*ef*+*xx*+1 contains *pq*.
Z,Y	Zero page, indexed by Y	74	Refers to the contents of the cell with address 00*ef*+*yy*, where *ef* is as above and *yy* is in the Y register.
(Z),Y	Post-indexed indirect	76	Refers to the contents of the cell with address *pqrs*+*yy*, where cell 00*ef* (with *ef* as above) contains *rs*, cell 00*ef*+1 contains *pq*, and *yy* is in the Y register.

This table explains the notations used in Tables 4 and 5. Note that X and Y must be the letters X and Y themselves, while L, Q, and Z may be replaced by any label.

Table 9
APPLE Character Codes—Letters and Digits

Character	Character Codes					Character	Character Codes		
	Normal	Control	Inverse	Blinking	Lower case (optional)		Normal	Inverse	Blinking
A	C1	81	01	41	E1	0	B0	30	70
B	C2	82	02	42	E2	1	B1	31	71
C	C3	83	03	43	E3	2	B2	32	72
D	C4	84	04	44	E4	3	B3	33	73
E	C5	85	05	45	E5	4	B4	34	74
F	C6	86	06	46	E6	5	B5	35	75
G	C7	87	07	47	E7	6	B6	36	76
H	C8	88	08	48	E8	7	B7	37	77
I	C9	89	09	49	E9	8	B8	38	78
J	CA	8A	0A	4A	EA	9	B9	39	79
K	CB	8B	0B	4B	EB				
L	CC	8C	0C	4C	EC				
M	CD	8D	0D	4D	ED				
N	CE	8E	0E	4E	EE				
O	CF	8F	0F	4F	EF				
P	D0	90	10	50	F0				
Q	D1	91	11	51	F1				
R	D2	92	12	52	F2				
S	D3	93	13	53	F3				
T	D4	94	14	54	F4				
U	D5	95	15	55	F5				
V	D6	96	16	56	F6				
W	D7	97	17	57	F7				
X	D8	98	18	58	F8				
Y	D9	99	19	59	F9				
Z	DA	9A	1A	5A	FA				

Control Characters with Alternative Meanings

Backspace	88	Control-H
Bell	87	Control-G
Carriage return	8D	Control-M
Escape	9B	Control-[[1]
Left arrow	88	Control-H
Right arrow	95	Control-U

[1]See Table 10.

Table 10
APPLE Character Codes—Special Characters

	Character	Normal	Control	Inverse	Blinking
Ampersand	&	A6		26	66
Apostrophe	'	A7		27	67
Asterisk	*	AA		2A	6A
At-sign	@	C0	80	00	40
Backslash	\	DC	9C		
Circumflex	^	DE	9E		
Colon	:	BA		3A	7A
Comma	,	AC		2C	6C
Division	/	AF		2F	6F
Dollar sign	$	A4		24	64
Equals	=	BD	3D	7D	
Exclamation point	!	A1		21	61
Greater than	>	BE		3E	7E
Hyphen	–	AD		2D	6D
Left bracket	[	DB	9B		
Left parenthesis	(	A8		28	68
Less than	<	BC		3C	7C
Minus sign	–	AD		2D	6D
Number sign	#	A3		23	63
Percent sign	%	A5		25	65
Period	.	AE		2E	6E
Plus sign	+	AB		2B	6B
Question mark	?	BF	3F	7F	
Quote (double)	"	A2		22	62
Quote (single)	'	A7		27	67
Reverse slash	\	DC	9C		
Right bracket	]	DD	9D		
Right parenthesis	)	A9		29	69
Semicolon	;	BB		3B	7B
Slash	/	AF		2F	6F
Space	(blank)	A0		20	60
Underline	_	DF	9F		

(For backspace, bell, carriage return, escape, and left and right arrow, see Table 9.)

Table 11
APPLE Monitor Subroutines and Other Special Locations

Name	Hexa-decimal Address	Section of this Text	May Overwrite Registers	Description
BELL1	$FBD9	72	A,X	Gives a "beep" on the APPLE's speaker (1/10 of a second).
COUT	$FDED	25	none	Outputs the A register as a single character (normally to the screen; this assignment can be changed).
COUT1	$FDF0	91	none	Outputs the A register as a single character to the screen (only).
CROUT	$FD8E	25[1]	A	Outputs a carriage return ($8D).
GETLN	$FD6A	25[1]	A,X,Y	Outputs a prompt character (normally * but kept in PROMPT—see below) and then reads one line (see GETLN1).
GETLN1	$FD6F	74	A,X,Y	Reads into INBUF (see below) one line of input characters terminated by (and including) a carriage return; length returned in X.
GETLNZ	$FD67	25	A,X,Y	Outputs a carriage return and then calls GETLN (so the new line appears on the screen *starting at the left*).
INBUF	$0200	25	—	Standard input buffer; array of 256 characters.
INIT	$FB2F	42	—	Start of monitor; JMP INIT may be used to terminate a main program.
IOREST	$FF3F	51	all	Restores registers A,X,Y, and P (*not* S), saved by IOSAVE
IOSAVE	$FF4A	51	A,X	Saves registers A,X,Y,P, and S in cells $45 through $49.
KEYIN	$FD1B	91	A,X,Y	Reads one character into the A register from the keyboard.
PRBL2	$F94A	41	X	Outputs *n* blanks with COUT, where *n* is entered in the X register (if the X register is entered with zero, *n* = 256).
PRBYTE	$FDDA	82	A	Outputs the A register as two hexadecimal digits.
PRHEX	$FDE3	82	A	Outputs the A register (rightmost four bits only) as one hexadecimal digit.
PRNTAX	$F941	82	A	Outputs the A register as two hexadecimal digits, and then the X register as two hexa-decimal digits.

Continued on next page

(To call any of the above subroutines, with name r and hexadecimal address h as specified, write JSR r and then somewhere in your program with r EQU h to define the subroutine.)
[1]In the Exercises.

Table 11—*Continued*

Name	Hexa-decimal Address	Section of this Text	May Overwrite Registers	Description
PROMPT	$0033	74	—	Location of prompt character printed by GET-LN (see above).
RDKEY	$FD0C	25	A,X,Y	Reads one character into the A register (normally from the keyboard; this assignment can be changed).
RNDH	$004F	99	—	Random number (high-order byte); recalculated every time RDKEY is called.
RNDL	$004E	99	—	Random number (low-order byte); recalculated every time RDKEY is called.
SETINV	$FE80	73	Y	Set inverse mode for COUT (so that characters will be displayed black-on-white instead of white-on-black).
SETNRM	$FE84	73	Y	Turns off the inverse mode for COUT (see SETINV).
SPKR	$C030	72	—	Speaker location (for giving clicks to produce musical tones).
STACK	$0100	60	—	(Hardware) stack; array of 256 characters.
WAIT	$FCA8	70	A	Waits $(26 + 27k + 5k^2)/2$ microseconds, where k is entered in the A register.

Table 12
Register, Flag, and Memory Capabilities and Flag Settings

Name	Type	Number of Bits	Section of this Text	Instructions Which Use This Capability
A	Register	8	6	Move, LDA STA TAX TAY TXA TYA PHA PLA; Operations, ADC SBC AND ORA EOR; Compare, CMP; Shift, ASL LSR ROL ROR
B	Flag	1	67	Set, BRK; Restore, PLP RTI
C	Flag	1	15	Clear, CLC; Set, SEC; Test, BCC BCS; Operations, ADC SBC; Shift, ASL LSR ROL ROR; Compare, CMP CPX CPY; Restore, PLP RTI
D	Flag	1	65	Clear, CLD; Set, SED; Operations, ADC SBC; Restore, PLP RTI
I	Flag	1	68	Clear, CLI; Set, SEI; Operations, BRK and interrupts; Restore, PLP RTI
Memory bytes		8	6	Operations, INC DEC; Shift, ASL LSR ROL ROR; Move, STA STX STY; Using memory, LDA LDX LDY ADC SBC AND ORA EOR BIT
N	(See S)			
P	Register	8	67	Save, PHP; Restore, PLP RTI (See S, V, D, I, B, Z, C)
PC	Register	16	27	Branches, BCC BCS BEQ BNE BPL BMI BVC BVS; Jumps, JMP JSR BRK; Return, RTI RTS
S	Flag	1	28	Move, LDA LDX LDY TAX TAY TXA TYA TSX PLA; Operations, ADC SBC AND ORA EOR INC INX INY DEC DEX DEY; Compare, CMP CPX CPY BIT; Test, BPL BMI; Shift, ASL LSR ROL ROR; Restore, PLP RTI
S	Register	8	60	Call, JSR; Return, RTI RTS; Move, PHA PHP PLA PLP TXS TSX
Stack bytes		8	59	Call, JSR; Move, PHA PHP; Using stack, RTI RTS PLA PLP
V	Flag	1	56	Clear, CLV; Test, BVC BVS; Operations, ADC SBC BIT; Restore, PLP RTI
X	Register	8	6,13	Move, LDX STX TAX TXA TSX TXS; Operations, INX DEX; Compare, CPX; Indexing ADDR,X ZPAGE,X (ZPAGE,X)
Y	Register	8	6,13	Move, LDY STY TAY TYA; Operations, INY DEY; Compare, CPY; Indexing ADDR,Y (ZPAGE),Y; STX ZPAGE,Y
Z	Flag	1	20	Move, LDA LDX LDY TAX TAY TXA TYA TSX PLA; Operations, ADC SBC AND ORA EOR INC INX INY DEC DEX DEY; Compare, CMP CPX CPY BIT; Test, BEQ BNE; Shift, ASL LSR ROL ROR; Restore, PLP RTI

Continued on next page

Table 12—*Continued*

FLAG SETTINGS BY INSTRUCTIONS

C	Additive carry, ADC; subtractive carry (complement of the borrow status), SBC CMP CPX CPY; leftmost bit of shifted register, ASL ROL; rightmost bit of shifted register, LSR ROR
S	1 if signed result less than zero; 0 if signed result greater than or equal to zero*
V	Arithmetic overflow (see section 56), ADC SBC; second bit from the left of v, BIT v
Z	1 if result equal to zero; 0 if result unequal to zero

*For BIT v, the "result," *in this case,* is v itself, not (A *and* v)

Table 13
LISA Commands (Editing, Assembling, Saving Files, Etc.)

Command Name	Section of This Text	Description of LISA Command
AP *f*	47	Loads (see LOAD) the program whose file name is *f* and *appends* it to the end of the current program in memory.
ASM	46	Assembles the current program. (On error, after noting the error, type C *return* to continue, or A *return* to quit.)
BRK	46	Break (goes from LISA to the monitor).
ctrl-D *c*	92	Executes the DOS command *c*. (Ctrl-D EXEC *f* loads a file *f* written by W *f* instead of by SAVE *f*.)
D *n*	46	Deletes the line with line number *n*; renumbers the current file in sequence.
D *m,n*	46	Deletes the lines with line numbers *m*, *m*+1, . . . , *n*; renumbers the current file in sequence.
I *m*	46	Inserts the following lines (terminated by control-E *return*) before line number *m*; renumbers the file in sequence.
L	46	Lists (normally, displays on the screen) your entire program.
L *m*	46	Lists (normally, displays on the screen) the line with line number *m*.
L *m,n*	46	Lists (normally, displays on the screen) the lines with line numbers *m*, *m*+1, . . . , *n*.
LOAD *f*	47	Loads (brings into main memory from disk) the program whose file name is *f*.
M *m*	46	Modifies (changes) line *m* (equivalent to L *m* followed by D *m* followed by I *m*).
M *m,n*	46	Modifies (changes) lines *m*, *m*+1, . . . , *n* (equivalent to L *m,n* followed by D *m,n* followed by I *m*).
NEW	92	Starts LISA with a new program.
SAVE *f*	46	Saves (brings out of main memory onto disk) your program and gives it the file name *f*.
W *f*	92	Like SAVE except that the disk file *f* is a *text file*, so that it can be read by a BASIC program (see ctrl-D *c*).

(For the APPLE monitor commands, see Table 14.)

Table 14
Monitor Commands (For Debugging, Checking of Overwriting, Etc.)

Command Letter	Format of Command	Section of this Text	Description of Monitor Command
None	*xxxx*	47	Displays cell *xxxx* as two hexadecimal digits.
Colon	*xxxx*:*hh*	48	Puts *hh* (these two hexadecimal digits) in cell *xxxx*.
	xxxx:*hh* *h2* (etc.)	48	Puts *hh* in cell *xxxx*, *h2* in cell *xxxx* + 1, and so on (as many as desired).
G	*xxxx*G	47	Goes to a program at cell *xxxx*.
L	*xxxx*L	47	Lists the assembly language and machine language program (20 instructions) starting at *xxxx*.
M	*xxxx*<*yyyy*.*zzzz*M	45	Moves *yyyy* to *xxxx*,*yyyy* + 1 to *xxxx* + 1, etc.; *zzzz* is the last byte moved.
Period	*xxxx*.*yyyy*	47	Displays cells *xxxx*,*xxxx* + 1, ...,*yyyy* as two hexadecimal digits each.
S	*xxxx*S	47	Goes to a program at cell *xxxx*, but does (and displays) only a single step of this program.
	*xxxx*SSSSS (etc.)	47	Goes to a program at a cell *xxxx*, but does (and displays) only as many steps as there are S's.
	SSSSS (etc.)	47	Does (and displays) as many steps as there are S's, from where the APPLE monitor last left off.
T	*xxxx*T	47	Goes to a program at cell *xxxx* and displays all its steps (up to a break).
V	*xxxx*<*yyyy*.*zzzz*V	45	Compares *yyyy* with *xxxx*, *yyyy* + 1 with *xxxx* + 1, etc.; *zzzz* is the last byte compared.

Table 15
Families of Operation Codes on the 6502

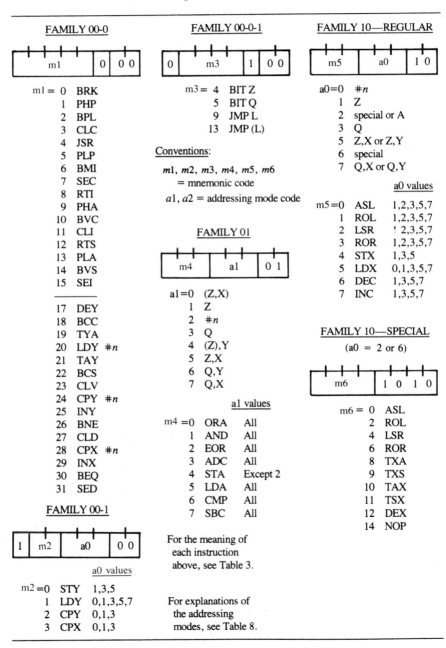

FAMILY 00-0

| m1 | | 0 | 0 0 |

ml = 0   BRK
     1   PHP
     2   BPL
     3   CLC
     4   JSR
     5   PLP
     6   BMI
     7   SEC
     8   RTI
     9   PHA
    10   BVC
    11   CLI
    12   RTS
    13   PLA
    14   BVS
    15   SEI

    17   DEY
    18   BCC
    19   TYA
    20   LDY #n
    21   TAY
    22   BCS
    23   CLV
    24   CPY #n
    25   INY
    26   BNE
    27   CLD
    28   CPX #n
    29   INX
    30   BEQ
    31   SED

FAMILY 00-1

| 1 | m2 | a0 | 0 0 |

a0 values

m2 =0   STY   1,3,5
     1   LDY   0,1,3,5,7
     2   CPY   0,1,3
     3   CPX   0,1,3

FAMILY 00-0-1

| 0 | m3 | 1 | 0 0 |

m3 = 4   BIT Z
     5   BIT Q
     9   JMP L
    13   JMP (L)

Conventions:

m1, m2, m3, m4, m5, m6
    = mnemonic code

a1, a2 = addressing mode code

FAMILY 01

| m4 | a1 | 0 1 |

a1 =0   (Z,X)
     1   Z
     2   #n
     3   Q
     4   (Z),Y
     5   Z,X
     6   Q,Y
     7   Q,X

a1 values

m4 =0   ORA   All
     1   AND   All
     2   EOR   All
     3   ADC   All
     4   STA   Except 2
     5   LDA   All
     6   CMP   All
     7   SBC   All

For the meaning of
each instruction
above, see Table 3.

For explanations of
the addressing
modes, see Table 8.

FAMILY 10—REGULAR

| m5 | a0 | 1 0 |

a0 =0   #n
     1   Z
     2   special or A
     3   Q
     5   Z,X or Z,Y
     6   special
     7   Q,X or Q,Y

a0 values

m5 =0   ASL   1,2,3,5,7
     1   ROL   1,2,3,5,7
     2   LSR   1,2,3,5,7
     3   ROR   1,2,3,5,7
     4   STX   1,3,5
     5   LDX   0,1,3,5,7
     6   DEC   1,3,5,7
     7   INC   1,3,5,7

FAMILY 10—SPECIAL
(a0 = 2 or 6)

| m6 | 1 0 1 0 |

m6 = 0   ASL
     2   ROL
     4   LSR
     6   ROR
     8   TXA
     9   TXS
    10   TAX
    11   TSX
    12   DEX
    14   NOP

ANSWERS TO STARRED EXERCISES

NOTE: Some of the exercises involve writing programs, and, for these, the answers given are only suggested answers, since programs can clearly be written in many ways to do the same thing. For the same reason, no answers at all are given for the Problems for Computer Solution.

1-1. (b) FIFTEEN INCHES.
1-2. (a) MEET ME BEHIND THE FENCE.
      (c) WILL YOU GO OUT WITH ME?
2-1. (a) 1100100.
      (c) 10000000.
2-2. (b) 140.
2-3. I AM LEARNING ABOUT COMPUTERS.
3-1. (b) 11000.
3-2. (a) 10011.
      (c) 11110.
4-1. (a) 64.
      (c) 1000.
4-2. (b) 291.
4-3. AFABCAB4DAD.
5-1. (b) D6AA.
5-2. (a) 215.
      (c) 41F.
6-1. (b) No (larger than 256).
6-2. (a) A = 1, X = 0. (256 in binary is 0000000100000000, and, of these 16 bits, the first eight, or 00000001, would go in the A register; the others, or 00000000, would go in the X register.)
      (c) A = 39, X = 16 (decimal).
6-3. $2^{12}-1$ or 4095.
7-1. (b) 00110110.
7-2. (a) −24.
      (c) −125.

8-1.   (a)

LDA	B3
STA	B5

(Here, as in the next two exercises, we may substitute X, or Y, for A throughout.)

(c)

LDA	#!0
STA	Z

8-2.   (b) W = 50 and W2 = 50 (or W = 50 and W2 = W)

8-3.

LDA	P
LDY	Q
STA	Q
LDA	R
STY	R
STA	P

(Many other solutions are possible.)

9-1.   (b) INC F4

9-2.   (a) K3 = K4−1

(c) J = S

C = S+1   (or C = J+1)

10-1.

```
080B A9 00
080D 8D DA 08
```

10-3.   M = 3

N = 3 (or N = M)

11-2.

	ORG	$08D0	
	LDA	#$50	(or LDA #!80)
	STA	C	
	ORG	$08FA	
C	DFS	!1	
	END		

12-1.

```
09C0 A9 00
09C2 8D 82 09
09C5 8D 80 09
09C8 8D 81 09
```

12-3.

```
0840 A9 00
0842 8D 59 08
0845 A9 64
0847 8D 58 08
```

13-1.   (b)

LDA	J
STA	T+!6

13-2. (a) $U(J) = T(J)$

(c) $U(M) = U(M) - 1$

14-1. (a)

$$\begin{array}{ll} (5A) & (C3) \\ +\underline{(3A)} & \underline{(2F)} \\ (94) & (F2) \end{array}$$

14-2. (1) Add c and f to get i, and note the carry.

(2) Add b and e and the carry, if any, to get h, and note the carry from this operation.

(3) Add a and d and the carry, if any, to get g.

15-1. (a)

```
LDA   K5
CLC
ADC   K6
STA   J
```

(c)

```
LDX   J
LDA   U, X
CLC
ADC   #!5
STA   T, X
```

15-2. (b) $W = N1 + 32$

15-3.

```
LDA   V1
CLC
ADC   V2
STA   V3
LDA   V1+!1
ADC   V2+!1
STA   V3+!1
LDA   V1+!2
ADC   V2+!2
STA   V3+!2
```

16-1. (a) No, because the answer is positive.

(b) No, because the answer is zero.

(c) Yes, because the answer is negative.

16-3. (a) 1, and the carry will be set.

17-1. (b)

```
LDA   P            or    LDA   P
CLC                      SEC
ADC   #!9                ADC   #!9
LDX   L                  LDX   L
SEC                      SBC   R, X
SBC   R, X               STA   S9
STA   S9
```

17-2. (a) $H = T(J) - T(3)$

(c) $U(I) = 160 + T(I) - U(I)$

18-1. (a)
```
                              LDA   I
                              CLC
                              ADC   J
                              TAX
                              LDA   #!5
                              STA   P1,X
```

(c)
```
          LDX   J           or      LDX   J
          LDA   N,X                 LDY   N,X
          TAX                       LDA   N,Y
          LDA   N,X                 STA   J
          STA   J
```

18-2. (b) $W = V+1+U$

18-3. (a)
```
          LDA   C           or      LDY   C
          TAY                       TYA
          STA   U,Y                 STA   U,Y
```

(c) `INC V`

19-1. (b) This should not be used (and *cannot* be, under LISA 2.5); it contains 11 characters, which is too many.

(d) This can be used.

19-2. (a)
```
LDA   T1     ;   NOTE THAT THE FIRST BCS ERROR IS
CLC          ;   STRICTLY NECESSARY. ONE MIGHT THINK
ADC   T2     ;   OTHERWISE, BECAUSE IF T1+T2 IS TOO
BCS   ERROR  ;   LARGE, THEN CERTAINLY T1+T2+T3 IS ALSO.
ADC   T3     ;   HOWEVER, IF ADDING T2 PRODUCES CARRY,
BCS   ERROR  ;   ADDING T3 MIGHT NOT (FOR EXAMPLE,
STA   M      ;   200+100+100) AND ANSWER IS STILL WRONG.
```

(c)
```
LDA   K
CLC
ADC   L
BCS   ERROR
TAX
LDA   R
CLC          (this instruction is not strictly necessary)
ADC   #!4
BCS   ERROR
STA   T,X
```

20-1. (a)
```
                              LDA   B
                              CLC
                              ADC   C
                              CMP   D
                              BEQ   TWENTY
```

(c)

```
         LDA   C
         SEC
         SBC   T+!6
         CMP   #!3
         BEQ   TWENTY
```

20-2. (b) IF R−1=S THEN 20

20-3. CPX T,Y is not a 6502 instruction; we can compare only the A register, not X or Y, to a subscripted variable, using an index.

21-1. (b)

```
         FOR J = 1 TO 100
         IF W = V(J)  THEN 80
         NEXT J
```

21-2. (a)

```
         LDX   #!0
LOOP     INX
         TXA
         STA   T,X
         CPX   M ;  (or CMP M)
         BNE   LOOP
```

(c)

```
         LDX   K
         INX
         STX   KP1
         LDX   #!0
LOOP     INX
         DEC   T,X
         CPX   KP1
         BNE   LOOP
```

22-1.

```
         LDY   #!0
         LDX   N
LOOP     LDA   T,X
         BNE   NON
         INY
NON      DEX
         BNE   LOOP
         STY   K
```

22-3. The CPY can be eliminated, because DEY sets and clears the zero status flag under exactly the same conditions that CPY does here.

23-1.

```
         LDY   #!0
         LDX   N
LOOP     LDA   T−!1,X
         BNE   NON
         INY
NON      DEX
         BNE   LOOP
         STY   K
```

23-2.   (b) $S = T(I - J - 2)$

23-3.   (a)

```
            LDX    D
            LDA    T+!1,X
```

        (c)

```
            LDX    N
            LDA    T+!10,X
```

24-1.   (b)   VELMA DYES HER HAIR

24-2.   (a)   CE D5 CD C2 C5 D2 A0 D4 CF CF A0 C2 C9 C7

        (c)   C9 CC CC C5 C7 C1 CC A0 C3 CF C4 C5

25-1.   (a)   The sequence reads ten characters and places them in the array
              REV in *reverse* order (REV contains the *last* character, and REV
              +!9 the first).

        (c)   The sequence reads one character, displays it (from RDKEY), and
              also displays the next higher character (''B'' for ''A'', and so on)
              unless the given character was Z, in which case A is displayed.

25-3.   The LDA #$8D could be done *before* the start of the loop (right after
        the JSR), since $8D is now in the A register at all times in this loop.

26-1.   (b)   KPRIME BYT "+"   (or KPRIME BYT $AB)

26-2.   FA (C3 plus 22 plus 15, since ''C'' = $C3—see Table 9 in the
        Appendix—and %10101 = $15.)

27-1.

```
            0840 A2 FF
            0842 BD 00 02
            0845 D0 19
            0847 CA
            0848 D0 F8
            084A 8D 88 08
```

27-3.

```
            FZERO    EQU    $08F0
            INBUF    EQU    $0200
                     ORG    $08E0
                     LDX    #$FF        (or   LDX  #!255)
            LOOP     INX
                     CMP    INBUF,X
                     BEQ    LOOP
                     BNE    FZERO
```

28-1.   (b)   IF U(J) >= U(K) THEN 50

28-2.   (a)

```
            LDA    A2
            LDX    K
            CMP    T+!1,X
            BCS    FIFTY
```

(c)

```
    LDX   J              LDX   J
    LDA   U-!1,X    or   LDY   U-!1,X
    TAX                  LDA   #!2
    LDA   #!2            CMP   U-!1,Y
    CMP   U-!1,X         BCC   FIFTY
    BCC   FIFTY
```

29-1.

```
        LDA   P
        CLC
        ADC   Q
        TAX
        LDA   P+!1
        ADC   Q+!1
        CMP   R+!1
        BNE   DECIDE
        CPX   R
DECIDE  BCC   LESS
```

29-3.

```
        LDX   N
LOOP    LDA   P-!1,X
        CMP   Q-!1,X
        BNE   DECIDE
        DEX
        BNE   LOOP
DECIDE  BCC   LESS
```

Note that, if X becomes zero, we do not want to go to LESS, since P = Q; but then the BNE LOOP will not branch, and neither will the BCC.

30-2.

```
        INC   P
        BNE   NEXT
        INC   P+!1
        BNE   NEXT
        INC   P+!2
NEXT    (next  instruction)
```

31-1. (a) P = 4 * Q + R
      (c) B2 = 8 * B1

31-3. The instruction ASL X would refer to a variable called X, not to the X register.

32-1. (a)

```
        LDA   T+!10
        STA   B
        LDA   T+!11
        STA   B+!1
```

(c)
```
        LDA    K        ; NOTE THAT THE CLC IN
        ASL             ; THIS PROGRAM IS NOT
        TAX             ; STRICTLY NECESSARY,
        LDA    B        ; SINCE THE CARRY
        CLC             ; FLAG IS CLEARED
        ADC    T-!6,X   ; BY THE ASL (SEE
        STA    B        ; THE END OF SECTION
        LDA    B+!1     ; 31) AND IS NOT
        ADC    T-!5,X   ; CHANGED BY TAX
        STA    B+!1     ; OR LDA.
```

32-3.   We have to multiply J and K by 3, not by 2, since there are three bytes in a 24-bit quantity. A program for this is:

```
                LDA    J
                ASL
                ADC    J
                TAX
                LDA    K
                ASL
                ADC    K
                TAY
                LDA    T,X
                CMP    T,Y
                BNE    DECIDE
                LDA    T+!1,X
                CMP    T+!1,Y
                BNE    DECIDE
                LDA    T+!2,X
                CMP    T+!2,Y
        DECIDE  BCC    LESS
```

33-1.   (a) T = 6*T
        (c) F = 13*G

33-3.   There is not a corresponding sequence of five instructions. If the SBC comes first, it must be preceded by SEC. Note that SEC is not needed in the given program because the carry flag setting is known after the BCS.

34-1.   (b)
```
                ASL    P
                ROL    P+!1
                ROL    P+!2
```

34-2.   Because the carry flag is only *one* bit long. In a long sequence (such as the one given), the total carry might be greater than 1 (in this case, it is 2) and you cannot keep such a number in a one-bit flag.

35-1. The bug is that the last bit to be shifted out is not counted. Note that
       ASL sets the zero status flag to the result in the A register; whether the
       carry flag is set or not does not matter. We cannot fix this bug by
       changing the initialization to LDY #!1 (because, for example, there
       might be *no* one-bits in the A register). The following program works,
       however:

```
              LDY    #$FF    ;   INITIALIZE COUNT TO −1
       CB1    INY            ;   INCREASE THE COUNT
       CB2    ASL            ;   LOOK AT THE NEXT BIT
              BCS    CB1     ;   IF 1, INCREASE THE COUNT
              BNE    CB2     ;   IF MORE BITS, LOOK AT NEXT
```

35-3.
```
                     LDX    #!8
              LOOP   LDA    BITS−!1,X
                     LSR
                     ROR    Q
                     DEX
                     BNE    LOOP
```

       The last time through the loop, X is 1 (not zero; the BNE applies to the
       value of X *after* being decreased by 1). Thus LDA BITS,X would be
       wrong because this would load BITS+!1 the last time through the
       loop, and the first byte of BITS would be skipped. The fundamental
       change is that the bits must be rotated into Q from left to right (using
       ROR), rather than right to left, because we are going through the BITS
       array from the end rather than from the beginning.

36-2. The instructions in the loop are INX (2 cycles); STA T,X (5 cycles);
       CPX N (4 cycles); and BNE LOOP (3 cycles, if it branches). The total
       of this is 14 cycles, and N times through the loop give 14N−1 cycles
       (since the BNE does not branch the last time through the loop). To this
       we add the LDX #!0 (2 cycles) and the TXA (2 cycles), giving a total
       of 14N+3 cycles. The number of bytes is 2 (LDX #!0) + 1 (TXA) +
       1 (INX) + 3 (STA T,X) + 3 (CPX N) + 2 (BNE LOOP—remember
       that this contains an 8-bit relative address), for a total of 12.

37-1. Yes. For example, computer time on the first computer might be *over*
       one hundred times more expensive than it is on the second. (The stu-
       dent may be able to think of other such conditions.)

37-3. No; the first of these programs is *both* faster and shorter than the sec-
       ond. Note that the data takes up the same number of bytes, no matter
       whether serial or parallel arrays are used. The last six instructions of
       the first program use the same amount of both space and time as the
       last six instructions of the second program. The above conclusion now
       follows from looking at the rest of the two programs.

38-1. (b)   11
               × 1010
               ———
                  00
                  11
                  00
                  11
               ———
               11110

38-2. (a)   1010   (b)   110   (c)   1111
               111│1000110   1010│1000000   1101│11001000
                   111   1010   1101
                   ———   ————   —————
                   111   1100   11000
                   111   1010   1101
                   ———   ————   —————
                    00   100   10110
                   000   1101
                   ———   —————
                     0   10010
                                                                  1101
                                                                  —————
                                                                    101

39-1. (a) S = (P + Q) * (R − 1)
       (c) K = J*J*J*J

39-2. (b)   LDA   J
                                            SEC
                                            SBC   # ! 5
                                            LDX   K
                                            JSR   MULT
                                            TXA
                                            LDX   J
                                            STA   T−! 1, X

39-3. (b) The first BCC takes 3 cycles if it branches, and 2 cycles (plus 2
            for the CLC and 4 for the ADC, or a total of 8) otherwise. The first
            ROR takes 2 cycles; the second ROR takes 6 cycles; the DEX
            takes 2 cycles; and the BNE, if it branches, takes 3 cycles. This
            makes a total of from 16 to 21 cycles. Thus the loop takes from
            16*8 − 1 to 21*8 − 1 or from 127 to 167 cycles.
       (c) The five instructions at the start of the program take a total of
            4+2+4+2+2 = 14 cycles. The two instructions at the end of the
            program take 4+6 = 10 cycles. Adding 24 cycles to the range of
            part (b) above gives 151 cycles minimum, 191 cycles maximum.

40-1. (a) S = (Q − 1) / (R + 1)
       (c) L = 10*(I − J)/K

40-2. (a)

```
LDA   J
CLC
ADC   K
TAX
LDA   #!0
LDY   L
JSR   DIV
STX   I
```

(c)

```
LDA   #!0
LDX   L
LDY   M
JSR   DIV
LDA   #!0
LDY   N
JSR   DIV
STX   W
```

41-1. (a) 51; 101; 201.
(c) 5; 10; 20.

41-2. (b)

```
LDA   J       ;  (OR LDA #!200
LDX   #!200   ;  AND LDX J)
JSR   MULT
JSR   DECOZ
```

41-3. The A register is not loaded. (It should contain zero before the call to DECOZ.)

42-2. There are two ENDs (the first one must be omitted); there is no RTS after the INX (a subroutine ends with RTS); and I DFS !1 is missing (or, equivalently, there is no data section).

43-1. The LDA is assigned three bytes; it should be assigned two because it loads a constant. The BNE is assigned three bytes; it should be assigned two because relative addresses are only one byte long. The DFS is assigned a byte; it should not be, because we do not know what is in N.

43-3. The machine language at START should be AD 08 09 instead of AD 09 08 (the bytes must be reversed; note that the machine language at LOOP *does* have bytes reversed). The BEQ DONE has machine language form F0 03 (not F0 05). The problem here is forgetting to add 2; it is true that $0911+5 = 0916$, but $0911+2+z = 0916$ where $z = 3$.

44-2. The bug is that the label LOOP should be on the LDA $T - !1,X$ rather than the LDX. Without the change, the loop is endless because you are always jumping back to load X with its *starting* value. The bug becomes apparent, in the walkthrough, the second time that LOOP is executed, and the table at this point (you could also have a column for the carry flag) is

A	SUM	X
~~0~~	~~0~~	~~4~~
~~15~~	15	~~3~~
15		4

Note that 15 occurs twice under A because loading A with T(4), the second time, produces a "new value"—even though this is the same as its old value at this point.

45-1. LDA I runs into the data I; BNE MIX2 can run into the data J (if I = 0). Note that JMP MIX3 does *not* run into the data at K, since it always jumps around K; and, likewise, RTS does not run into the data at L. Also, LDA J does not run into any data because COUT EQU $FDED does not define any data. (Look at the machine language form, and you will see that the next instruction after 0B07, or LDA J, is 0B0A, or JMP MIX3.)

45-3. The first time that START is called, the first time that STA is executed, X will be 100, or 64 in hexadecimal. Since the array T starts at the address 0870, the computer adds 0870 and 64, producing 08D4. However, this is the address of the operation code of LDX #!100. This does not affect the run the first time START is called, since LDX #!100 has already been executed. It will affect the run only the *second* time that START is called. At this point, LDX #!100 is not executed, because cells 08D4 and 08D5 no longer contain A2 64. They contain E9 64, instead (because the first of these cells has been overwritten); and E9 64 is the machine language code for SBC #!100 (see Table 4 in the Appendix). The result is that the computer will do SBC #!100 (which affects only the A register) and then LDA #!233 (which destroys whatever SBC #!100 did). Therefore, the only effective change is that X has not been loaded; the subroutine START will set T + !1 through T + !n to 233 where n is whatever was in X before START was called. If this is greater than 100, the program will overwrite itself with 233's, and proceed to do BNE with a relative address of 233 (which branches 21 bytes backward). This will cause the computer to go back into the array T, and interpret whatever it finds there as instruction code bytes.

46-1. (b)   1 LDA P

46-2. (a)

```
                            I  1
                                    LDA    M
                                    STA    N
```

(c)

```
                            M  4
                                    STA    T
```

47-1.

```
                    083A-      C8                  INY
                    A = 8D  X = 32  Y = 65  P = 30  S = F8
```

(The most important point above is $Y = 65$; here 65 is the hexadecimal value of Y after it has been incremented, with INY.)

47-3. The bug is that the label LOOP1 should be on the ASL, not the DEX. The steps show that the A register is not changing, as it should (or, alternatively, that there is no ASL) between the first BCC and the second.

48-1. (b) 0A03: C8 (C8 is the operation code for INY)

48-2. The problem is that of where to continue after the breakpoint at address *xxxx*. If you continue at *yyyy*, the instruction at *xxxx* is never executed. If you continue at *xxxx*, this is simply a BRK instruction, and you get another break, without executing any more of your program. If you remove the breakpoint at *xxxx* and continue from *xxxx*, your program will continue correctly, but it will not give a break, the next time around the loop.

49-1. If the answer is n, then we clearly have $x/2^n = y$, so that $2^n = x/y$. The definition given in the exercise now shows us that $n = \log_2(x/y)$, or, equivalently, $\log_2 x - \log_2 y$.

49-3. (a) The number of steps taken to reduce a table of size n to a table of size 2 is k, where $n/2^k = 2$, so that $k = \log_2(n/2)$, just as in exercise 1. This is $(\log_2 n) - 1$, and then we must add the two final steps, so that the formula becomes $1 + \log_2 n$. If n is not a power of 2, then $\log_2 n$ is not an integer, and must be interpreted as the next *larger* integer (because a fraction of a step cannot be taken).

(b) Because the loop in this program is executed a *small* number of times. (Even for a table of size 1000, there are only 11 steps, since $2^{10} = 1024$; and 11 is small enough so that ordinary breakpoint debugging may be used.)

50-2.   The modified sequence is

```
              LDA    P
              CLC
              ADC    Q
              BCC    BETA
              JMP    PATCH1
      BETA    STA    Q
```

Note that the three bytes of INC Q+!1 have been replaced by the three bytes of JMP PATCH1. The patch is

```
      PATCH1    INC    Q+!1
                BNE    PATCH2
                INC    Q+!2
      PATCH2    JMP    BETA
```

We use BNE PATCH2 instead of BNE BETA because the patch may well be more than 126 bytes away from the original sequence of instructions (see section 27).

50-3.   The modified sequence is

```
                LDX    #!0
                LDY    #!0
      GAMMA     JMP    PATCH1
                BYT    !0
                BYT    !0
      GAMMA1    BCC    DELTA
                CLC
                ADC    #!1
      DELTA     NOP
                TAY
                INX
                CPX    #!8
                BNE    GAMMA
                STY    BIN
```

Note that the one-byte instruction NOP replaces the one-byte instruction ASL (with the label DELTA). The patch is

```
      PATCH1    LDA    BITS−!1,X
                LSR
                TYA
                ASL
                JMP    GAMMA1
```

The instruction JMP PATCH1 takes three bytes. We cannot use this in place of TYA (one byte) or LSR and TYA (two bytes, total); we must use it in place of LDA, LSR, and TYA (five bytes, total). The two BYT !0 pseudo-operations are there so that five bytes will be replaced by five bytes (the three of JMP PATCH1, and two more).

51-1. (b)

```
POKE 32771,I
POKE 32772,J
CALL 32768
M = PEEK(32772)
```

51-2. (a)

```
FOR J = 1 TO 100
POKE 32999+J,T(J)
NEXT J
```

(c)

```
FOR J = 0 TO 100        or        FOR J = 1 TO 101
POKE 33000+J,T(J)                 POKE 32999+J,T(J)
NEXT J                            NEXT J
```

52-1. (a)

```
20   →   00100000
35   →   00110101
(AND) 00100000  →  20        The answer is 20.
```

(c)

```
55   →   01010101
AA   →   10101010
(AND) 00000000  →  00        The answer is 00.
```

52-2. (b) 70.

52-3.

```
LDA   L5              or       LDA   L5
ROL                           AND   #%11100000
ROL                           ASL
ROL                           ROL
ROL                           ROL
AND   #%00000111              ROL
```

The trick is that we have to do ROL *four* times, not three, because ROL rotates *through* the carry flag.

53-1. (b)

```
F6   →   11110110
C7   →   11000111
(ORA) 11110111  →  F7        The answer is F7.
```

53-2. (a) 3F.
(c) 95.

54-1. (a)

```
20   →   00100000
35   →   00110101
(EOR) 00010101  →  15        The answer is 15.
```

(c)

```
55   →   01010101
AA   →   10101010
(EOR) 11111111  →  FF        The answer is FF.
```

54-2. (b) 82.

54-3.
```
LDA   P
EOR   #%10000000
STA   TEMP
LDA   Q
EOR   #%10000000
CMP   TEMP
BCS   LEQ
```

55-2. The instruction BIT T−!1,X does not exist. (Remember that BIT cannot be used with indexing.)

56-1. (a) Three bytes. The program of section 54 takes 18 bytes, as follows:

INSTRUCTION	LDA	EOR	STA	LDA	EOR	CMP	BCC	TOTAL
BYTES	3	2	3	3	2	3	2	18

while the program of this section takes 15 bytes, as follows:

INSTRUCTION	LDA	SEC	SBC	BVS	BPL	BMI	BPL	TOTAL
BYTES	3	1	3	2	2	2	2	15

(c) Six cycles (minimum) or seven cycles (maximum). The program of section 54 takes 23 cycles if it goes to LESS, as follows:

INSTRUCTION	LDA	EOR	STA	LDA	EOR	CMP	BCC	TOTAL
CYCLES	4	2	4	4	2	4	3	23

(Note that the BCC branches, in this case, so that it takes 3 cycles.) The first three instructions of the program of this section take 10 cycles (LDA, 4 cycles; SEC, 2 cycles; SBC, 4 cycles). There are now two ways to get to LESS. If the BVS *branches* (3 cycles) to OVSET, where the BPL also branches (3 cycles), this takes 6 cycles. If the BVS *does not* branch (2 cycles), and neither does the following BPL (2 cycles), so that the BMI always branches (3 cycles), this takes 7 cycles. The total is either 16 or 17 cycles.

56-2. (a)
```
          LDA   P        ; THE FIFTH AND SIXTH
          SEC            ;   INSTRUCTIONS
          SBC   Q        ;   COULD ALSO BE:
          BVC   OVCLR    ; (1) BPL LESS, BMI GEQ
          BMI   GEQ      ; (2) BMI GEQ, BVS LESS
          BPL   LESS     ; (3) BPL LESS, BVS GEQ
OVCLR     BMI   LESS
GEQ       (next instruction)
```

(b) Space requirements are not affected.

57-2.   Because each RTS would have to be preceded by instructions to restore A, X, and Y; and it saves space, in this case, to have only one such sequence of instructions (followed by RTS) and to jump to this sequence wherever it is desired to do a return from the subroutine. Thus we could replace subroutine (a) below by subroutine (b) below:

(a)   (b)

```
SUBR    STA    SAVEA        SUBR    STA    SAVEA
        STX    SAVEX                STX    SAVEX
        STY    SAVEY                STY    SAVEY
        .  .  .  .  .                .  .  .  .  .
(further  statements)         (further  statements)
        .  .  .  .  .                .  .  .  .  .
;  FIRST RETURN               ;  FIRST RETURN
        LDA    SAVEA                JMP    SUBREX
        LDX    SAVEX        ;  NOTE THAT WE SAVE
        LDY    SAVEY        ;  3 INSTRUCTIONS
        RTS                  ;  (7 BYTES)
        .  .  .  .  .                .  .  .  .  .
;  SECOND RETURN              ;  SECOND RETURN
        LDA    SAVEA                JMP    SUBREX
        LDX    SAVEX        ;  HERE WE SAVE 3
        LDY    SAVEY        ;  MORE INSTRUCTIONS
        RTS                  ;  (7 MORE BYTES)
        .  .  .  .  .                .  .  .  .  .
;  FINAL RETURN               ;  FINAL RETURN
        LDA    SAVEA        SUBREX  LDA    SAVEA
        LDX    SAVEX                LDX    SAVEX
        LDY    SAVEY                LDY    SAVEY
        RTS                          RTS
```

57-3.   (a)   f(Q) is the absolute value of Q.

58-2.

```
        ASL
        TAX
        LDA    JTABLE-!2,X
        STA    IA
        LDA    JTABLE-!1,X
        STA    IA+!1
        JMP    (IA)
```

59-1.

```
        IF  X  =  0  THEN  799
        X  = X-1
        A  = H(X)
```

The test must be made before the other two instructions. Otherwise, the statement A = H(X) makes reference to H(−1), which does not exist, if X is initially equal to 0.

59-3. $X = X + 1$ $A = H(X)$
       $H(X) = A$ $X = X - 1$

       Pushing A   *Pulling A*

60-1. (b) The stack pointer now contains F6. (RTS pulls two bytes; and, each time a byte is pulled, the stack pointer is increased by 1. If it was F4, it will become F4+2, or F6.)

60-2. (a) 2.
       (c) 2.

61-1. $K = T(I - J) + I$

61-3. Replacing JSR KOUT and RTS by JMP KOUT.

62-2. (a) Two bytes (one return address) must be pulled from the stack before the RTS is performed.

62-3. (a) Because the carry must be clear at this point, or we would have branched to DECIB, three instructions earlier.
       (c) Because we must have done the BCC, three instructions earlier; and we did *not* branch, so the carry is in fact set.

63-1. (b) The carry must be clear; otherwise we take the branch on carry set, two instructions earlier.

63-2. (a) True.
       (c) False; CPY #N2 does this (CPY N2 compares the Y register with the contents of the cell whose address is 2).

64-2. (a) 129 (because 128*2—two bytes for the return address—is 256, and the lowest level plus 128 levels gives 129).
       (b) 52 (because 51*5—five bytes including two for the return address and one each for A, X, and Y—is 255. Note that the *lowest* level does not store a return address on the stack, while the *highest* level does not save A, X, or Y.)

64-3. Because a subroutine P at level *n* can call only subroutines at levels less than *n*. If P calls itself, this restriction is clearly violated, since it calls a subroutine (namely P itself) whose level is *not* less than *n* (since it is equal to *n*).

65-1. (b) 53, carry set; ED, carry clear.

65-2. (a) 12, carry set; 18, carry set.
       (c) 33, carry clear; 93, carry clear.

66-1.
```
          LDX    K      ; LENGTH OF STRING TO X
          TXA           ; DIVIDE THIS BY 2, PRODUCING
          LSR           ;   LENGTH OF PACKED STRING
          TAY           ;   AND PUT THIS IN Y
```

```
CONVP    LDA    B-!2,X    ; GET A CHARACTER OF THE STRING
         ASL              ; SHIFT IT FOUR BITS TO THE
         ASL              ;   LEFT, PUTTING ITS RIGHTMOST
         ASL              ;   FOUR BITS INTO THE LEFTMOST
         ASL              ;   FOUR BITS OF THE PACKED STRING
         EOR    B-!1,X    ; NEXT CHARACTER TO RIGHT 4 BITS
         EOR    #$B0      ;   (WITHOUT B IN UPPER HALF)
         STA    N-!1,Y    ; STORE IN ONE CHARACTER OF
         DEX              ;   PACKED STRING, THEN DECREASE
         DEX              ;   STRING INDEX BY 2 AND
         DEY              ;   PACKED STRING INDEX BY 1
         BNE    CONVP     ; IF NONZERO, GET THE NEXT ONE
```

66-3.

```
         LDX    J         ; MUST ADD FROM RIGHT TO LEFT
         CLC              ;   WITH CARRY INITIALLY CLEAR
ADDP     LDA    N1-!1,X   ; LOAD A BYTE OF ONE STRING
         ADC    N2-!1,X   ;   AND ADD WITH PREVIOUS CARRY
         STA    N3-!1,X   ;   TO GET A BYTE OF THE RESULT
         DEX              ; MOVE FROM RIGHT TO LEFT
         BNE    ADDP      ; IF NOT DONE, DO ANOTHER ONE
```

67-1. (b) BNE ALPHA (the Z flag is *zero* if the result was *not* zero)

67-2. (a) CLV

       (c) CLC

68-1. The return address is 0834, so this is pushed (the 08 into location 01F3, since the stack pointer contains F3, and the 34 into location 01F2); then the P register is pushed, so 31 goes into location 01F1. Thus the new contents of the stack are as follows:

ADDRESS	CONTENTS
01F0	A7
01F1	31
01F2	34
01F3	08
01F4	B1
01F5	3C
01F6	08
01F7	9E

The S register now contains F0 (= F3−3). The P register formerly contained $31, or binary 00110001; but the I flag (third bit from the right) is now 1, since the interrupt subroutine call turns the interrupt system off (I flag = 1). Hence P now contains binary 00110101, or hexadecimal 35.

68-3.   Because the three-byte instruction might be a jump (or JSR) to some other address, in which case that address would become the interrupt return address.

69-1.

```
GETLN   LDX   #!0
IWAIT   LDA   INSTAT
        AND   #%00000001
        BEQ   IWAIT
        LDA   INDATA
        STA   $0200,X
        INX
        CMP   #$8D
        BNE   IWAIT
        RTS
```

69-2.

```
IWAIT   LDA   INSTAT
        LSR              (or ROR)
        BCC   IWAIT
        LDA   INDATA
```

70-2.   135,204,616 cycles, or slightly over two minutes. The trick is that zero, when decremented by one, produces an answer that is not zero (255, in fact); so a loop count of zero acts as if it were a loop count of 256. The above number is obtained by substituting 256 for each of L, M, and N.

71-1.   ICHAR must check if the input queue is empty. If so, it calls POLL and loops back to check again if the queue is empty. Eventually, the queue will contain one character (put there by QIN, which is called by POLL), at which point ICHAR can proceed. QOUT, in turn, must check if the *output* queue is empty. If so, it cannot put a character out, and simply returns.

71-3.   After you have just put an element in Q(REAR), you have to increment REAR and check whether REAR = m. In an upside-down queue, you have to *decrement* REAR and check whether REAR = 0, which is a little faster.

72-2.   We have 1,023,000/512 = 1998 (approximately). Subtracting 7 from this, as before, gives 1991; and dividing this by 10, as before, gives 199, with remainder 1. Subtracting 2 for the LDX, and adding 1 for the last BNE, as before, leaves the remainder 0. Therefore we eliminate all the instructions at the end of the loop (the BEQ and the two NOPs), and LDX #!251 becomes LDX #!215.

73-1.   (a) BLK "K9"

73-2.   (b) STR "YES"

73-3.   HEX 0A5634

74-1. (a) Five bytes, one each for lines 1, 3, 8, 10, and 13. Note that line 10 is *always* done eight times, once for each time through the loop; while line 8 may be done any number of times from zero through eight, because line 6 might or might not branch. This makes a total of from 8 to 16 cycles saved. Lines 1, 3, and 13 save one cycle each, so we have from 11 (minimum) to 19 (maximum) cycles saved.

(b) Nine bytes, one each for lines 1, 2, 4, 6, 9, 12, 14, 17, and 18. Note that line 6 is *always* done eight times, once for each time through the loop. If line 8 branches, then we do line 12, and maybe 14, but not 9; if line 8 does not branch, we do line 9, but not 12 or 14. In either case we save from 8 to 16 cycles, plus the eight cycles from line 6; and lines 1, 2, 4, 17, and 18 save one cycle each. The total is thus from 21 (minimum) to 29 (maximum) cycles saved.

75-2.

```
EXCH    LDA    (0, X)
        PHA
        LDA    (2, X)
        STA    (0, X)
        PLA
        STA    (2, X)
        RTS
```

76-1. FF. (Since the address at Z and Z+!1, *with bytes reversed*, is 0809, we must add FF to this to get 0908.)

76-3. Because the final LDA (PTR),Y makes use of the *original* value of PTR; but this has been changed by the preceding STA.

77-1. (b) T(J + 1) = T(J)

77-2. The LDY #!0 which was eliminated takes two bytes and two cycles. The TAY, which takes one byte and two cycles, replaces STA ZP, which takes *two* bytes and *three* cycles (since ZP is in page zero). Thus a total of three bytes and three cycles is saved.

78-1.

```
            LDA  #T          or              LDA  #T
            CLC                              CLC
            ADC  J                           ADC  J
            STA  ALPHA+!1                     TAY
            LDA  /T                          LDA  /T
            ADC  J+!1                        ADC  J+!1
            STA  ALPHA+!2                     STA  ALPHA+!2
    ALPHA   LDA  MODIFY              ALPHA   LDA  MODIFY, Y
            STA  W                           STA  W
```

(In the second of these programs, MODIFY must have lower half zero.)

78-3. It is clearly both faster and shorter than the scheme it replaces; but it also uses the Y register, which the original scheme does not.

79-2.
```
         ARRAY0    STA    ALPHA+!2
                   STX    ALPHA+!1
                   LDA    #!0
         ALPHA     STA    MODIFY,Y
                   DEY
                   BNE    ALPHA
                   RTS
```

80-1. (a) Change CMP J to L1 CMP #!0; change CMP J+!1 to L2 CMP #!0; define JUPPER by JUPPER EQU L2+!1 and change STA J+!1 to STA JUPPER; define JLOWER by JLOWER EQU L1+!1 and change STX J to STX JLOWER.

(b) Four bytes are saved, two for J and one each for CMP J and CMP J+!1. Each time the loop is executed, two cycles are saved for CMP J, and two more for CMP J+!1 if the BNE does not branch. This makes a total of from 200 to 400 cycles.

80-2. (a) Change DIV2 to DIV2 CMP #!0
Change LDX DDATA2 to DIV5 LDX #!0
Define DDATA1 by DDATA1 EQU DIV2+!1
Define DDATA2 by DDATA2 EQU DIV5+!1

80-3. It is DECO9, in the output conversion routine DECO. The only instructions in DECO which refer to DECO9 are STA, INC, and DEC, none of which has an immediate addressing option.

81-1. We have assumed that the five values of K, from 1 to 5, appear with equal frequency. If this is not the case—if $K = 1$ more often than $K \neq 1$, for example, when this program section is executed—then the alternative is considerably faster. One would expect this to happen quite often in practice; indeed, it is extremely rare that the various possible values of *any* variable occur with equal frequency.

81-3. (a) It shifts Q right by $7-X$ places.

(c) 28, 27, 25, 23, 21, 19, 17, or 15 cycles. This includes 12 cycles for STX, LDA, and STA; 3 cycles for BNE; and 2 cycles for each LSR. If the BNE does not branch, it takes one cycle less.

82-2. Change /SPACE to /SPACE−!1
Change #SPACE to #SPACE−!1
Eliminate ADC #!1
Replace the five instructions starting with LDY #!0 by the following:

```
         LDY    LB,X    ;  GET THE LENGTH OF THIS STRING
         CPY    NAME    ;  IF UNEQUAL TO THE LENGTH OF
         BNE    PROC    ;  NAME, STRINGS CANNOT BE =
```

83-1.   Change INY to

```
INC    HST2+!1
INC    HST3+!1
INC    HST4+!1
BNE    HST2
INC    HST2+!2
INC    HST3+!2
INC    HST4+!2
```

where HST2 is a label on the ORA instruction; HST3 is a label on the first STA; and HST4 is a label on the second STA.

83-3.

```
PRNTAX    JSR    PRBYT
          TXA
          JMP    PRBYT
```

The instruction JMP PRBYT is equivalent to JSR PRBYT followed by RTS (as suggested near the end of section 61).

84-2.   Suppose that the test were made for $T(J) < T(J+1)$. Then, if $T(J) = T(J+1)$, we would interchange them *and set the flag*. This would mean that we would do another pass. But the next time through the loop we would do the same thing, and set the flag again, giving us an endless loop.

85-3.   (a)   Yes. The minimum value of the two lengths L1 and L2 is the same as the minimum of L2 and L1.

(b)   The problem is that the saved carry flag status tells us whether $L2 < L1$ or $L2 \geq L1$. Making the suggested change would cause the carry flag status to record whether $L2 \leq L1$ or $L2 > L1$, and this is not the same as before. Note that all three decisions are important here; if $L2 < L1$, we *must* go to EXCH, and otherwise we *must* go to GAMMA.

86-1.   No. It is true that the instruction STX FIRST stores X at FIRST, so that loading A with FIRST, after this is executed, is equivalent to TXA. However, we can also reach L3 by the BCS instruction; and, before this instruction, X is stored in LAST, not in FIRST.

86-3.   Yes, it can. When LDX FIRST is executed, FIRST and LAST must be equal; and just before LDX FIRST we have stored X in either FIRST (STX FIRST) or LAST (STX LAST) without making any subsequent changes to X.

87-1.   (a) $U = T(8,4)$

87-2.   (a)

```
LDX    J
LDA    TENS-!1,X
CLC
ADC    I
TAX
DEC    T-!11,X
```

87-3. (b) We should add 10 to the X register.

88-2.

```
                              LDA     U+!1
                              SEC
                              SBC     V+!1
                              BEQ     C2
                              BVS     OVSET
                              BPL     GEQ
                              BMI     LESS
                    OVSET     BPL     LESS
                              BMI     GEQ
                    C2        LDA     U
                              CMP     V
                              BCC     LESS
                    GEQ       (next  instruction)
```

89-1. (a)

```
           LDY  #!50                              LDY  #!51
    LOOP   LDA  T+!1,Y              LOOP          LDA  T,Y
           STA  T,Y          or                  STA  T-!1,Y
           INY                                    INY
           CPY  #!200                             CPY  #!201
           BNE  LOOP                              BNE  LOOP
```

(c) Two bytes (for the CPY #!200) and 300 cycles (since the CPY #!200 is executed 150 times, at 2 cycles each, in the loop of part (a), and these are all eliminated from the loop).

89-3. No. The loop count N is *variable*, which implies that negative indexing is not applicable.

90-1. (a) 13 bytes (3 for STA, 2 for LDX, 1 for LSR, 3 for EOR, 1 for DEX, 2 for BNE, and 1 for the data byte B) and 82 cycles (4 for STA, 2 for LDX, and 76 for the loop, consisting of 11 cycles—2 for LSR, 4 for EOR, 2 for DEX, and 3 for BNE—done 7 times, with one fewer cycle the last time, since the BNE does not branch).

(b) In the $(k+1)$st bit from the left in the A register, the kth time through the loop. Thus, the first time through, the partial result is kept in the second bit from the left; the second time through, it is kept in the third bit from the left; and so on.

91-1.

```
    DOSCOM   STA   ZP+!1      ; ADDRESS OF MESSAGE IN A AND
             STX   ZP         ;  X - - STORE IN ZP AND ZP+!1
             LDY   #$FF       ; STARTING VALUE OF Y IS -1
    LOOP     INY              ; MOVE TO NEXT CHAR. OF MESSAGE
             LDA   (ZP),Y     ; GET THIS CHARACTER
             CMP   #CRET      ; IF THIS IS A CARRIAGE RETURN,
             BEQ   DONE       ;  OUTPUT IT AND QUIT
             JSR   COUT       ; OTHERWISE, OUTPUT IT AND GET
             JMP   LOOP       ;  NEXT CHARACTER OF MESSAGE
    DONE     JMP   COUT       ; (SAME AS -JSR COUT- AND -RTS-)
```

91-2.

```
DOSCOM  STA   LOOP1+!2 ; ADDRESS OF MESSAGE IN A AND
        STX   LOOP1+!1 ; X -- MODIFY ADDRESS OF LOOP1
        LDX   #$FF     ; STARTING VALUE OF X IS -1
LOOP    INX            ; MOVE TO NEXT CHAR. OF MESSAGE
LOOP1   LDA   MODIFY,X ; GET THIS CHARACTER
        CMP   #CRET    ; IF THIS IS A CARRIAGE RETURN,
        BEQ   DONE     ;   OUTPUT IT AND QUIT
        JSR   COUT     ; OTHERWISE, OUTPUT IT AND GET
        JMP   LOOP     ;   NEXT CHARACTER OF MESSAGE
DONE    JMP   COUT     ; (SAME AS -JSR COUT- AND -RTS-)
```

92-1. Because LOAD *f* loads *binary* files, rather than text files. (This is clear because SAVE *f* saves a binary file, as we have noted.)

92-3.

```
        LDA   P1
        STA   P2
        NLS
        LDA   P5
        STA   P6
        BRK
        END
```

93-1. $p = \alpha + 5*(N - \beta)$.

93-3. (a) It should add 5.

94-2. No, because the statement might be A = B*C1 (for example).

95-1. Yes. As noted in section 86, searching this table (a very common operation in an assembler, as we have noted) is much faster if the table is sorted.

95-3. Yes, if you also have an assembler to translate the resulting assembly language programs into machine language. You will then have a system which does the job of a compiler (which, as noted in the text, is in fact an alternative to the use of an interpreter) in a two-step process.

96-1. (a)

```
              IF C THEN GO TO m;
              S; GO TO n;
        m:    Q1;
              IF NOT D THEN GO TO m;
        n:
```

96-2. (a) IF C1 THEN S1 ELSE WHILE C2 DO S2

96-3. (a)

```
              JMP   L4
        L3    LDA   K        (this instruction may be omitted)
              CLC
              ADC   #!5
              STA   K
        L4    LDA   K
              CMP   L
              BCC   L3
```

97-1. (b) $\frac{3}{5}$

97-2. (a) 00.110011
       (c) 11.001001

98-1. (a) 40600000
       (c) 5D200000

98-2. (b) 101

98-3. 1F000400; the normalized form is 1C400000.

99-2. The product of the hexadecimal fractions .2 and .3 is .06; the *sum* of the unbiased exponents, 1 and 1, is 2, corresponding to the biased exponent 42. The unnormalized result is thus 42060000, which becomes 41600000 when normalized. This may be checked by noting that (41200000)*(41300000) = (41600000) corresponds to the decimal (or hexadecimal) multiplication 2*3 = 6.

100-1. No, because the type of every variable is fixed for a particular run of a program (since there is clearly no way for a variable to change its name while a program is running).

100-3. If TJ = TK = 0, then add J and K as 8-bit quantities and store the result in J. If TJ = TK = 1, then add J and K as 16-bit quantities and store the result in J and J+!1. If TJ = 1 but TK = 0, add the 16-bit quantity J to the 8-bit quantity K (see section 19) and store the result in J and J+!1. The most difficult case is that in which TJ = 0 but TK = 1. Again an 8-bit and a 16-bit quantity must be added, but, this time, the result must go back in the 8-bit quantity J. There are two acceptable ways to treat this problem. One can go to an error exit if the result does not fit into 8 bits (as we did with division); or we can store only the rightmost 8 bits of the result (as the 6502 does with addition and subtraction). What is *not* acceptable is to treat the result as a 16-bit quantity, because then we would have to have TJ = 1 (denoting a 16-bit quantity J); but the conditions of the problem state that the operation of addition does not change the type of J.

BIBLIOGRAPHY

If you are interested in learning more about the assembly languages of various computers, you might read the following:

Birnbaum, I., *Assembly Language Programming for the BBC Microcomputer,* Macmillan, London, 1982.

Camp, R. C., Smay, T. A., and Triska, C. J., *Microcomputer Systems Principles Featuring the 6502/KIM,* Matrix Publishers, Portland, Ore., 1978.

Cohn, D. L., and Melsa, J. L., *A Step By Step Introduction To 8080 Microprocessor Systems,* Dilithium Press, Portland, Ore., 1977.

Daley, H. O., *Fundamentals of Microprocessors,* Holt, Rinehart, and Winston, New York, 1983.

Dow, J. T., and Dow, D. B., *TI Home Computer Assembly Language Primer,* John T. Dow, Pittsburgh, Pa. 15217, 1984.

Findley, R., *6502 Software Gourmet Guide and Cookbook,* Scelbi Publications, Elmwood, Conn., 1979.

French, D., *Inside the Commodore 64,* French Silk, P.O. Box 207, Cannon Falls, Minn. 55009, 1983.

Inman, D., and Inman, K., *The ATARI Assembler,* Reston Publishing Co., Reston, Va, 1981.

Kane, G., Hawkins, D., and Leventhal, L., *68000 Assembly Language Programming,* Osborne/McGraw-Hill, Berkeley, Calif., 1981.

Kudlick, M. D., *Assembly Language Programming for the IBM Systems 360 and 370,* Wm. C. Brown Co., Dubuque, Iowa, 1980.

Lemone, K. A., and Kaliski, M. E., *Assembly Language Programming For The VAX-11,* Little, Brown & Co., Boston, 1983.

Leventhal, L., *6502 Assembly Language Programming,* Osborne/McGraw-Hill, Berkeley, Calif., 1979.

Leventhal, L., *6809 Assembly Language Programming,* Osborne/McGraw-Hill, Berkeley, Calif., 1981.

Leventhal, L., *8080A/8085 Assembly Language Programming,* Osborne, Berkeley, Calif., 1978.

Leventhal, L., and Saville, W., *6502 Assembly Language Subroutines,* Osborne/McGraw-Hill, Berkeley, Calif., 1982.

Mansfield, R., *Machine Language for Beginners,* Compute! Publications, Inc., Greensboro, N.C., 1983.

Mateosian, R., *Programming the Z8000,* Sybex, Berkeley, Calif., 1980.

Morse, S. P., *The 8086 Primer*, Hayden Book Co., Rochelle Park, New Jersey, 1978.

Mottola, R., *Assembly Language Programming for the APPLE II*, Osborne/ McGraw-Hill, Berkeley, Calif., 1982.

Osborne, A., *An Introduction To Microcomputers*, Osborne, Berkeley, Calif., 1976.

Rector, R., and Alexy, G., *The 8086 Book*, Osborne/McGraw-Hill, Berkeley, Calif., 1980.

Rooney, V. M., and Ismail, A. R., *Microprocessors and Microcomputers*, Macmillan, New York, 1984.

Santore, R., *8080 Machine Language Programming for Beginners*, Dilithium Press, Portland, Ore., 1978.

Scanlon, L., *IBM PC Assembly Language*, Robert J. Brady Co., Bowie, Md., 1983.

Spracklen, K., *Z-80 and 8080 Assembly Language Programming*, Hayden Book Co., Rochelle Park, New Jersey, 1979.

Struble, G. W., *Assembler Language Programming: The IBM System/360 and 370*, Addison/Wesley, Reading, Mass., 1975.

Titus, C. A., Rony, P., Larsen, D. G., and Titus, J. A., *8080/8085 Software Design*, Howard W. Sams & Co., Indianapolis, 1978.

Wakerly, J. F., *Microcomputer Architecture and Programming*, John Wiley & Sons, New York, 1981.

Wagner, T. J., and Lipovski, G. J., *Fundamentals of Microcomputer Programming*, Macmillan, New York, 1984.

Weller, W. J., Shatzel, A. V., and Nice, H. Y., *Practical Microcomputer Programming: The Intel 8080*, Northern Technology Books, 1976.

Zaks, R., *Programming the 6502*, Sybex, Berkeley, Calif., 1978.

Zaks, R., *6502 Applications Book*, Sybex, Berkeley, Calif., 1979.

Zaks, R., *6502 Games*, Sybex, Berkeley, Calif., 1980.

INDEX

APPLE ASSEMBLY LANGUAGE DISKETTE

All of the programs and fragments of programs in this book are included in the diskette. They are in several files, each one of which is entitled "Sections **m** to **n**, " abbreviated, for proper interface with the APPLE Disk Operating System, as Sm**T**n. Thus, for example, the file whose name is S41T42 contains programs from sections 41 and 42.

These is also, on the diskette, a program called STEP. This is to be used on any APPLE which does **not** have the step and trace functions described in section 47. Directions for using STEP are given as comments with STEP; you can see these comments by loading STEP and listing it.

To order, please return the order form below with check or credit card information.

*To utilize the diskette, you must order the LISA Assembler.**
For further information contact Computer Science Press.

"Apple" is a registered trademark of Apple Computer, Inc.

----

*Ordering Information

Call (301) 251-9050 or write to Computer Science Press, Inc., 1803 Research Boulevard, Rockville, Maryland 20850, to order our publications. Ask for our complete catalog of quality books at all levels from introductory to the advanced levels.

	QUAN.	PRICE
APPLE ASSEMBLY LANGUAGE DISKETTE @ $17.00		
W. Douglas Maurer		
ISBN 0-914894-85-4		
LISA Assembler (manual and software) @ $79.95		
by LAZERWARE		

Subtotal	
Postage and Handling $2.00	
Total	

☐ Payment enclosed   ☐ VISA No. _____   ☐ MasterCard No. _____

Signature _____   Expiration date _____

Name _____

Address _____

City _____ State _____ Zip _____

ALL ORDERS FROM INDIVIDUALS MUST BE PREPAID .

☐ Add my name to your mailing list.   ☐ Send me your current catalog.

COMPUTER SCIENCE PRESS, INC.,   1803 Research Boulevard   Rockville, MD 20850,

USA - (301) 251-9050

Appropriate state and local taxes apply. All prices shown are subject to change without notice.